A Handbook Series on Electromagnetic Interference and Compatibility

Volume 8

EMI Control Methodology and Procedures

Donald R.J. White
and
Michel Mardiguian

Interference Control Technologies, Inc.
Gainesville, Virginia

Interference Control Technologies, Inc.
Route 625, Gainesville, VA 22065
TEL: (703) 347-0030   FAX: (703) 347-5813

Library of Congress Catalog Card Number: 88-81458
ISBN: 0-944916-08-2

Acknowledgement

I wish to thank the many people who encouraged us to write earlier editions and later to update this handbook on *EMI Control Methodology and Procedures*. Special thanks are expressed to our students all over the world who developed the need and encouragement for this book and its continuing refinement.

I also express my appreciation to Gil Fitzpatrick and his production department personnel for assistance in typing, editing and the many other logistics aspects involved in the preparation of the manuscript.

Finally, my last but not least gratitude goes to George Dickel who, in those frantic days where the printing deadline was getting close, provided timely and unrivalled support.

Michel Mardiguian

Other Books in the 12-Volume Series

Contents

ix

Common Terms
and Abbreviations
in EMC Literature

Prefixes for Decimal Multiples

10^{12}	tera	T
10^{9}	giga	G
10^{6}	mega	M
10^{3}	kilo	k
10^{2}	hecto	h
10	deka	da
10^{-1}	deci	d
10^{-2}	centi	c
10^{-3}	milli	m
10^{-6}	micro	μ
10^{-9}	nano	n
10^{-12}	pico	p

Technical Terms

absolute	abs
alternating current.............	ac
American wire gage	AWG
ampere..............................	A
ampere per meter.............	A/m
ampere-hour......................	Ah
amplitude modulation	AM
amplitude probability distribution.....................	APD
analog to digital	A/D
analog-to-digital converter .	ADC or A/D converter
anti-jamming	AJ
arithmetic logic unit	ALU
audio frequency.................	AF
automatic data processing.	ADP
automatic frequency control	AFC
automatic gain control	AGC

average	avg
bandwidth	BW
binary coded decimal........	BCD
bit.....................................	b
bit-error rate	BER
bits per second..................	bps
British thermal unit..........	Btu
broadband	BB
byte	B
bytes per second...............	Bps
centimeter-gram-second	cgs
central processing unit......	CPU
characters per second	cps
common-mode coupling	CMC
common-mode rejection ratio.............................	CMRR
complementary metal-oxide semiconductor	CMOS
continuous wave	CW
coulomb	C
cubic centimeter..............	cm^3
decibel	dB
decibel above 1 milliwatt ..	dBm
decibel above 1 volt..........	dBV
decibel above 1 watt.........	dBW
degree Celsius...................	°C
degree Fahrenheit	°F
degree Kelvin....................	°K
diameter............................	dia
differential-mode coupling.	DMC
digital multimeter.............	DMM
digital to analog	D/A
digital voltmeter	DVM
digital-to-analog converter .	DAC or D/A conv.

diode-transistor logic	DTL	instantaneous automatic	
direct current	dc	gain control	IAGC
double pole double throw	DPDT	insulated-gate field-effect	
double sideband	DSB	transistor	IGFET
double sideband suppressed		integrated circuit	IC
carrier	DSB-SC	interference-to-noise ratio	I/N
dual in-line package	DIP	intermediate frequency	IF
electric field	E-field	joule	J
electromagnetic		junction field-effect	
compatibility	EMC	transistor	JFET
electromagnetic		kilogram	kg
interference	EMI	kilohertz	kH
electromagnetic pulse	EMP	kilovolt	kV
electromotive force	EMF	kilowatt	kW
electron volt	eV	kilowatt-hour	kWh
electronic countermeasures	ECM	lambert	L
electrostatic discharge	ESD	large-scale integration	LSI
emitter-coupled logic	ECL	least significant bit	LSB
extremely high frequency	EHF	length	l
extremely low frequency	ELF	length (of cable)	l_c
farad	F	line impedance stabilization	
fast Fourier transform	FFT	network	LISN
field intensity	FI	line of sight	LOS
field intensity meter	FIM	liter	l
field-effect transistor	FET	local oscillator	LO
foot	ft or '	low frequency	LF
frequency	freq	lower sideband	LSB
frequency division multiplex	FDM	lumen	lm
frequency modulation	FM	lux	lx
frequency shift keying	FSK	magnetic field	H-field
gauss	G	master oscillator power	
gram	g	amplifier	MOPA
ground	gnd	maximum	max
ground loop coupling	GLC	maxwell	Mx
ground support equipment	GSE	mean time between failure	MTBF
hazards of electromagnetic		mean time to failure	MTTF
radiation to ordnance	HERO	mean time to repair	MTTR
henry	H	medium frequency	
hertz (cycles per second)	Hz	(300 kHz to 3 MHz)	MF
high frequency	HF	metal-oxide semiconductor	MOS
high-power transistor-		metal-oxide semiconductor	
to-transistor logic	HTTL	field-effect transistor	MOSFET
high-speed complementary		metal-oxide varistor	MOV
metal-oxide		meter	m
semiconductor	HCMOS	microfarad	μF
high-threshold logic	HTL	microhenry	μH
hour	hr	micron (10^{-6} meter)	μ
inch	in or "	micro-ohm	$\mu\Omega$
inch per second	ips	microwave	MW
industrial, scientific and		mile	mi
medical	ISM	military specification	MIL-SPEC
infrared	IR		
input/output	I/O	military standard	MIL-STD
inside dimension	ID	milliamp	mA

million instructions per second	MIPS
millisecond	ms
millivolt	mV
milliwatt	mW
minimum	min
minimum discernable signal	MDS
minute	min
modulator-demodulator	modem
most significant bit	MSB
multilayer board	MLB
multiplex, multiplexer	mux
nanofarad	nF
nanohenry	nH
nanosecond	ns
narrowband	NB
negative	neg
negative-positive-negative (transistor)	npn
negative-to-positive (junction)	n-p
newton	N
noise equivalent power	NEP or P_n
non-return to zero	NRZ
N-type metal-oxide semiconductor	NMOS
nuclear electromagnetic pulse	NEMP
oersted	Oe
ohm	Ω
ohm-centimeter	Ωcm
ohms per square	Ω/sq
ounce	oz
outside dimension	OD
peak	pk
peak-to-peak	p-p
phase lock loop	PLL
phase modulation	PM
positive	pos
positive-negative-positive (transistor)	pnp
positive-to-negative (junction)	p-n
pound (sterling)	£
pound per square centimeter	p/cm^2
pound per square inch	psi
power factor	PF
printed circuit board	PCB
private branch exchange	PBX
P-type metal-oxide semiconductor	PMOS
pulse per second	pps

pulse position modulation	PPM
pulse repetition frequency	PRF
pulse-amplitude modulation	PAM
pulse-code modulation	PCM
pulse-duration modulation	PDM
pulse-width modulation	PWM
quasipeak	QP
radiation hazard	RADHAZ
radio frequency	RF
radio interference and field intensity	RI-FI
radio-frequency interference	RFI
random access memory	RAM
receiver	RX
reference	ref
relative humidity	RH
resistance-inductance-capacitance	RLC
return to zero	RTZ
revolutions per minute	rpm
roentgen	R
root-mean-square	rms
second	s
sensitivity time control	STC
shielding effectiveness	SE
sideband	SB
siemens	S
signal-to-interference (ratio)	S/I
signal-to-noise (ratio)	S/N
silicon controlled rectifier	SCR
single sideband	SSB
square meter	m^2
standing-wave ratio	SWR
super high frequency	SHF
super low frequency	SLF
surface acoustic wave	SAW
surface-mount technology	SMT
surface-mounted component	SMC
surface-mounted device	SMD
television	TV
temperature coefficient	TC
tesla	T
time division multiplex	TDM
transistor-to-transistor logic	TTL
ultra high frequency (360 MHz to 3 GHz)	UHF
ultraviolet	UV
very high frequency (30 MHz to 300 MHz)	VHF
very high-speed integrated circuit	VHSIC
very large-scale integration	VLSI
very low frequency (3 kHz to 30 kHz)	VLF

volt	V	length (coil turn, ground loop, etc.)	l
volt meter	VM	length in millimeters	l_{mm}
voltage standing wave ratio	VSWR	magnetic susceptibility	χ
voltage-to-frequency converter	VFC	magnetizing force	H
voltampere	VA	parasitic capacitance	C_p
volt-ohm meter	VOM	permeability of free space	μ_0
watt	W	permeability of medium relative to μ_0	μ_r
waveguide beyond cuttoff	WGBCO	phase constant	β
weber	Wb	radius	r
words per minute	wpm	relative permittivity	ϵ_r
yard	yd	resistance (in ohms)	R

rise time .... τ_r
shield thickness .... d

Mathematical Functions and Operators

time .... t
time constant, transmission factor .... τ

absolute value	abs
approximately equal	$\approx$
argument	arg
cosine	cos
cosine (hyperbolic)	cosh
cotangent	cot
cotangent (hyperbolic)	coth
determinant	det
dimension	dim
exponential	exp
imaginary	im
inferior	inf
limit	lim
logarithm, common (base$_{10}$)	log
logarithm, Napierian (base$_e$)	ln
sine	sin
tangent	tan
tangent (hyperbolic)	tanh

velocity, volume V
wavelength .... λ

Common Variables in EMC Equations

attenuation constant, absorption factor	α
Boltzmann's constant	K
capacitance (in farads)	C
charge	Q
coefficient of self-inductance	L
conductance in mho	G
conductivity, propagation constant, leakage coefficient, deviation	σ
current	I
dielectric constant, permittivity	ϵ
frequency (in Hz)	f
impedance	Z
induced voltage	E
inductance (in henrys)	L
infinity	∞

Preface to the Fifth Edition

In 1979, as a preamble to the very first edition of this book, Don White wrote, "Pioneers always get arrows in the back," referring to the first American settlers of the Wild West who were venturing into unknown, hostile ground. Arrows; we got many of them through the subsequent editions of this manual. But they were "good" arrows, that kind which prod us to questioning and improving our own models, to revisit some widely accepted rules of thumb and to attack analytically some obscure domains like common-mode conversion, differential transfer impedance of shielded pairs, radiated emission of I/O cables, etc.

This fifth edition benefits from what we have learned collectively at ICT/Don White Consulting, teaching EMI/EMC to more than 40,000 engineers throughout the world and solving "hot" problems for more than 100 companies. It also takes into account the many validations that we have been able to carry out, by ourselves or through our colleagues.

Besides a myriad of corrections and clarifications to improve the accuracy of our equations and graphs, the main highlights of this new edition are:

1. A more realistic treatment of the common-to-differential mode conversion (GLC) at and above cable self-resonance
2. A method for using cable shield transfer impedance with electrically long wires
3. A model for entering connectors or shield termination variables into the whole susceptibility prediction

4. A complete treatment for the susceptibility of a cable link exposed to a broadband field like NEMP
5. A precise treatment of crosstalk prediction for high-speed digital printed circuits or flat cables
6. A complete method for predicting rapidly the radiated emissions from I/O cables versus MIL Std., FCC, VDE/CISPR or other limits

Of course, our Prediction Software #5220, which is a companion of this book, has been updated accordingly.

Michel Mardiguian
October, 1988

Introduction

Of the numerous electromagnetic compatibility (EMC) and related handbooks we have enjoyed authoring over the years, we have found this one to be the most difficult, challenging and exciting of all. Perhaps the reason for this is that most of the material contained herein is new and does not appear in other published literature. More importantly, the need has grown out of an urgent requirement by the EMC community to get a quantitative handle on the methodology for the solution of electromagnetic interference (EMI) problems.

We have enjoyed teaching EMC disciplines to thousands of students during recent years, and their concern has also been a motivation for this book. In the past, after a training course, we received comments to the effect that, while we explained the many facets, mathematical models, rationale, hardware and applications of the EMC-related disciplines, one area was missing. This involved the lack of an overall methodology ranging from how to diagnose a significant EMI problem to the effective solution of the problem. In other words, since EMC is a function of so many variables, no methodology existed that permitted the user to quantitatively solve the problem with sufficient rationale and facility.

This handbook emphasizes protecting the victim receptor or system from a hostile electromagnetic ambient. The reverse problem occurs when the victim becomes the noise source and may pollute the electromagnetic environment. This particular problem is presented at the end of the book but with less coverage since, by reciprocity, most EMC practices which reduce susceptibility will likewise reduce emission. The principal exceptions are when reciprocity does not apply; viz., the device is not linear (e.g., saturation in a magnetic shield) or it is not bilateral (e.g., an active device such as an amplifier or logic chip).

This handbook provides the user with an organized approach to diagnose and solve EMI problems. Applications range from the **fire-prevention** stage of systems and equipment design to the **fire-fighting** stage existing in field installations and operations.

Our methodology and technique can be applied to a wide variety of vehicles, systems, sites and equipments. These range from aerospace equipment, ships, surface vehicles, commercial installations and industrial control complexes to consumer products. The technique further provides for internal technical accounting so that the user knows at all times where he has been and where he is now. This permits a step-by-step, orderly process in applying EMI control in either design or field use, and it is presented in the language of the user.

As the reader will see in Chapter 1, the methodology includes EMI prediction and analysis as one part. Here, a wide variety of mathematical models are used to describe different phenomena involving noise sources, coupling paths and victim responses. Several of these models have been validated in varying degrees, and some are reported in the technical literature. Many of the mathematical models are recent, which raises questions concerning accuracy of results. However, it does not reduce the power of the methodology developed and reported herein. Rather, as time goes on, certain individual math models will be updated, replaced or augmented as the technology continues to unfold, and as further validation is done.

Perhaps one of the most exciting parts of the methodology is what is called the **sequencing program** for EMI control. Based on a number of user input constraints involving options in either the original design or solving field problems, there exists a one-by-one selection and application of the EMI fixes to reduce or eliminate an EMI problem. The initial sequence is predicated on what is regarded as the flow of the thought process of a disciplined EMC engineer. As such, one might debate the ranking order in the first sequencing process. However, the system is sufficiently flexible. When a user with a particularly tailored application does not reorder the sequencing himself, the methodology, accounting process and reporting of results lend themselves to sequencing readjustment. In a sense, an adaptive technique unfolds.

This is the fifth edition of this handbook. It is updated and overhauled approximately every two years. Better math models are used, and other refinements are added as each subsequent edition is developed. Accordingly, the authors invite a dialog from all readers, including those who use this material in our "Grounding and Shielding" and other short courses.

If you profit by using this handbook, you may find it even more efficient to use our computer-aided engineering Program #5220. It makes life a lot easier and speeds up application of the methodology.

October, 1988   Donald R.J. White
Gainesville, Virginia   Michel Mardiguian

Chapter 1

EMI: A System Problem

Chapter 1 is a qualitative summary of EMI control methodology and procedures. It provides an introduction to some of the basic EMI control techniques, but the quantitative mathematical models appear in later chapters. As the introduction to this handbook on EMI control methodology and procedures, Chapter 1 provides an overview and offers an advanced picture of these techniques as well as setting the stage for the remaining chapters.

First, this chapter gives a broad view of EMI problems ranging from the chip level to system ensembles. Nine identifiable levels of EMI complexity are identified, with a middle level being at the subsystem or collection of equipment. In general, this handbook concentrates on this intermediate level. If we can get a handle on the EMI problem here, then the user can either go into more complex levels at higher echelons or work down to lower levels at the printed circuit board (PCB) and chip levels. Thus, one of the introductory problems shows a simple two-box problem with interconnecting cables. It depicts the situation in which more than 500,000,000 configuration combinations are possible. If no EMI-control solution is achievable at this middle level, then one may expect little help at any higher level.

Next, the chapter illustrates many different EMI coupling paths. These include antenna-to-cable, field-to-cable, cable-to-cable, common ground impedance coupling and conducted emissions on power mains. Collectively, these five predominate over other coupling paths and account for perhaps 95 percent of EMI situations. Because a single handbook cannot include all possible EMI situations, it is these principal coupling paths that are examined in detail.

Continuing with why effective EMI control is difficult, it is shown that because a great number of combinations of EMI fixes and coupling paths exist, upwards of 100 variables may be involved. The human mind can follow, perhaps, only three to five variables simultaneously. Thus, an organized approach, i.e., a methodology and procedure, is paramount for technical advancement of the EMC disciplines.

The chapter concludes with a discussion of how to use this handbook. Different techniques and flow diagrams are employed to help the user rapidly find the desired material. Both this approach and the more traditional ones involving the table of contents and the index are discussed. Finally, the chapter ends with a number of references.

1.1 EMI: From Chip to System Ensembles

In this section, nine levels of EMI manifestations from, chip to super system are identified. The middle level, interconnected box-to-box, is discussed throughout this handbook, and examples are provided.

Figure 1.1 illustrates these progressive levels of EMI manifestations. Admittedly, the various EMI manifestations could be categorized in as few as 5 levels or, using finer standards of discrimination, as many as 15 levels. However, even though the choice of nine levels was somewhat arbitrary, it was predicated on functional identification. For each of the levels, one or two examples are identified in the right-hand portion of the figure.

The top EMI level is titled "Deployment of Vehicles and Plant Sites." On this level, the EMI susceptible systems are deployed over large geographical areas. The deployed area could be as small as a square kilometer or as expansive as thousands of square kilometers. For example, a Navy task force might be composed of 5 to 10 ships deployed over 1,000 km^2 to minimize its vulnerability to a thermonuclear engagement. Many of the ships would be communicating with each other and with helicopters, aircraft and spacecraft. In addition, an enemy engagement would increase the

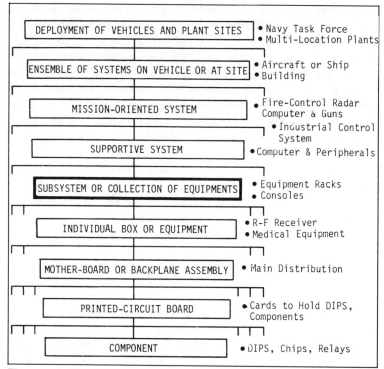

Figure 1.1—The Many Levels of EMI Manifestations

electromagnetic radiation environment. Thus, at this level, the EMI problem is of the greatest magnitude and complexity.

A second example at the highest level is a situation where a number of industrial sites or plants are interconnected by radio or wire telecommunications. This often involves a substantial flow of measurement and control data. A third example might be where a number of unattended power substations are commanded via a microwave relay link from a single control center in a large city.

At the highest level, serious EMI problems are usually characterized by undesired emissions entering or exiting from one or many antenna systems. The problems rarely involve **back-door interference**, i.e., interference between the sites which results from improper grounding, bonding, shielding, cabling, etc.

The second level of EMI manifestations shown in Fig. 1.1 is captioned "Ensemble of Systems on Vehicle or at a Site." In this classification, geographical coverage has been substantially reduced to the size of a single structure. It typically involves an aircraft, ship, land vehicle or one or more buildings at the same site. These vehicles or sites may still contain a number of transmitting and receiving antennas. But the EMI problem now includes equipment racks, consoles and collections of boxes or equipments with interconnecting cables. They may be radiators or victims of EMI emissions, or both. Thus, unlike the top EMI level previously discussed, not all noise sources and victims at the second level involve formal antennas.

The third level of EMI manifestations shown in Fig. 1.1 is captioned "Mission-Oriented System." Examples of this level are restricted to systems which perform an independent mission relative to other systems. They are usually located at a single site or on a vehicle. One example is a fire-control system which includes a radar, computer and associated guns or launchers and missiles. Here, the mission is to detect and destroy enemy targets. The equipment itself constitutes a complete, self-sufficient, vehicle-mounted system.

A second example of the third level is an industrial process control system in which information is sent from remote sensors to a computer. The computer responds with corrective commands which keep the system in balance according to predetermined operational criteria.

The fourth EMI level shown in Fig. 1.1 is called a "Supportive System." At this level, the equipment is not a self-contained, mission-oriented system. Rather, it is a major building block which supports a more complex system. The example cited is a computer and its peripherals. They do not encompass an entire mission but are supportive of other operations.

The fifth level shown in Fig. 1.1 is the center level of EMI complexity. It is captioned "Subsystem or Collections of Equipments." Typical examples at this level are equipment racks, cabinets and consoles which contain a number of individual equipments. These equipments often are interconnected by power and signal cables. As already mentioned, much of this handbook is directed to this level.

The next lower level of EMI complexity is captioned "Individual Box or Equipment Level." In this category one finds great number of individual hardware building blocks. Examples include RF receivers and transmitters, medical and biophysical instruments, individual computer peripherals, computer central processing units and individual equipments and measuring instruments.

The third level from the bottom (seventh level) of EMI manifestations in Fig. 1.1 is called the "Motherboard or Backplane Assembly" level. This usually is the highest classification level of any portion of an individual box or equipment. Thus, the motherboard or PCB assembly level constitutes a main distribution center to many plug-in PCBs. The configuration of the interconnecting wiring, deployment and layout to and from the motherboard relative to the PCBs constitutes latent emission and susceptibility to EMI.

The second from the bottom level in Fig. 1.1 is one of the most fundamental hardware working levels, and it is known as the "Printed Circuit Board" level. This is the most common of all basic electronic packages. The PCB, of course, may vary in size from a few square centimeters to a half square meter. It typically contains many individual dual inline packages (DIPs) and other integrated circuits as well as discrete electronic components which are mounted directly on it. This is particularly the case with digital circuitry containing integrated circuits, RAMs, ROMs, PROMs and other logic circuit configurations as well as analog devices.

Finally, the bottom level of EMI manifestations in Fig. 1.1 contains the individual electronic components. These include the above DIP packages containing chips and relays, inductors and transistors. At this level, susceptibility involves the noise-immunity logic level of digital circuitry and the sensitivity of operational amplifiers (op amps) and other analog devices.

In retrospect, we can see that over the nine levels of EMI manifestation there is an enormous spread, in orders of magnitude, in complexity, size, geographical locations, design and cost factors. Consequently, it can be generally concluded that the higher the level of EMI manifestation, the more lead time is required to implement an EMC solution (design or retrofit) due to the increased complexity of the problem. Higher cost will also be a factor.

1.2   500,000,000 EMI Configuration Combinations

At the middle level of EMI manifestations (i.e., interconnected box-to-box level) more than 500,000,000 EMI configuration combinations exist. Thus, EMI containment requires an effective methodology.

Having identified the nine levels of EMI manifestations in Fig. 1.1, it becomes necessary to choose one level for the purpose of developing an ongoing discussion in this handbook. Occasional examples will be given for other levels, but this book concentrates on one level only. One approach would be to go from the one extreme to the other; from chip level to the vehicle-deployment or plant-site level. However, this approach would make it difficult for the reader to assimilate the methodology and would also lack continuity throughout the handbook.

The approach of this handbook is to begin approximately midway between the extremes. The rationale is that if a methodology for a sound engineering approach to EMI control can be grasped at a middle level, then one can apply the principles to higher or lower EMI manifestation levels as illustrated in Fig. 1.1. Conversely, if one fails to establish a methodology and procedure for EMI prediction, analysis, design implementation and retrofit at this level, there is little hope that he can do so at other levels.

The middle (fifth) level was chosen as the focus of this handbook. Thus, the "Subsystem or Collection of Equipments" level is addressed hereafter, with a number of illustrations covering one or two levels on either side. This suggests that a two-box level model (i.e., two boxes, pieces of equipments, consoles or dual-bay racks with interconnecting cables) will be appropriate for illustrative purposes. An effective EMI-control methodology should be developed at this level first via demonstrative problems and solutions.

Consistent with that approach, the situation shown in Fig. 1.2 corresponds to a two-box, equipment-level EMI situation. In viewing the illustration, it is seen that the box case at the left (Box 1) is "talking to" (i.e., is interconnected) through both power, data and control leads to Box 2 on the right.

In examining Fig. 1.2 more thoroughly, one can locate a total of 29 question marks. A question mark at a toggle switch asks if a connection is made here. (Note that these switches are conceptual — this is not meant to imply that real switches exist in these circuits.) Where an additional question mark appears beside the local ground, this asks, "Is it grounded?" Where grounding of cable shields is shown, in addition to asking the question, "Is it grounded?" the next question mark at the local grounds means, "Where is it to be grounded?"

Beside a component, the question mark asks whether the particular device is to be used. For the purposes of identification in

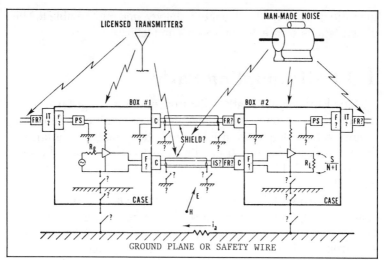

Figure 1.2—A Two-Box/Equipment EMI Situation—500,000,000 Combinations!—Many with an Infinite Range of Variables

the figure, FR stands for ferrites, IT for isolation transformers, IS for isolators (optical or transformers), F for filters, C for connectors and PS for power supplies.

Thus, each question requires one of two choices, and there are 29 questions to yield 2^{29} or 536,870,912 combinations. This illustrates why EMI control is so difficult. A relatively simple situation such as shown in Fig. 1.2 results in over half a billion possible combinations of fixes!

In pursuing the topic still further in Fig. 1.2, it is recognized that the number of true combinations far exceeds 500,000,000. For example, one does not simply ask the question, "Is a filter to be used or not?" Rather, it is recognized that a filter can assume an arbitrarily large number of values corresponding to different cutoff frequencies. For any cutoff frequency, different dB/decade slopes in the stop band exist. Consequently, in Fig. 1.2 represents not simply 500,000,000 combinations but an infinite number.

As a result of the preceding, if one cannot establish an adequate disciplined methodology and technique to solve the EMI problem suggested by Fig. 1.2, then there is little hope that one could get a quantitative handle on EMI problems at all. Accordingly, one organized approach to the situation suggested in Fig. 1.2 is the **EMC design synthesis methodology**. Equipped with this and the rationale to support this methodology, one may be able to handle situations of greater or lesser complexity.

1.3 EMI Coupling Paths

Many EMI coupling paths exist from emitters (culprits) to receptors (victims). Usually only a few paths are significant enough to require special emphasis in EMI prediction, analysis, design and retrofit. Considering the susceptibility aspect first, Figure 1.3 summarizes the EMI situation for both radiated and conducted coupling paths.

For radiated coupling paths, three different classifications of emission and reception paths are shown in the figure. One source is an antenna used for radiation, reception or both. The second is emission from a box (enclosure) containing noise-generating parts or circuits to a victim box. The third is wire-to-wire or cable-to-cable coupling. Thus, the combinations correspond to nine different paths:

1. Antenna-to-antenna
2. Antenna-to-box
3. Antenna-to-wire
4. Box-to-antenna
5. Box-to-box
6. Box-to-wire
7. Wire-to-antenna
8. Wire-to-box
9. Wire-to-wire (cable-to-cable)

Not all nine of these paths contribute equally to electromagnetic interference; three paths tend to dominate. Where equipments are at different sites and where baseband information modulates a carrier, the antenna-to-antenna path usually predominates. Where a transmitting antenna is involved and the victim does not have an antenna, the antenna-to-wire (field-to-wire) path usually predominates. Finally, in situations where cables are routed relatively close to each other, the wire-to-wire path predominates.

Except for low-frequency magnetic fields, it is rare that the box-to-box coupling path predominates. Other situations involving the box as either an emission source or a victim result in relatively less frequent EMI problems. A hierarchy of the coupling paths from the most common (or likely to occur) to the less common ones can be established as follows:

More Frequent:

1. Antenna-to-antenna: frequent between radio communication systems
2. Antenna-to-victim's external wiring: frequent between radio transmitters and non-radio equipment
3. Wiring to wiring: frequent between non-radio equipments
4. Wiring (external) to Antenna: frequent between non-radio equipment and radio receivers

Less Frequent:

5. Box-to-Antenna: if at all, generally appears after the predominant paths 1 through 4 have been fixed
6. Antenna-to-box
7. Box-to-wire
8. Wire-to-box
9. Box-to-box

The last five coupling paths are rated as infrequent because at least one box is involved which (exceptions acknowledged) provides some degree of more or less intentional shielding. Also, since coupling through radiation involve some fortuitous aerials, the physical length of the external cables is usually larger than the dimensions of the inner wiring or printed circuit, making them more efficient radiators or more efficient collectors.

Nevertheless, the last five coupling paths should not be neglected or overlooked. Especially if a great amount of hardening (like with lightning or EMP threats) is desired, the first step which will address external cables as a primary coupling path may not be sufficient. Let's assume that only 10^{-12} of the available EMI power should be let into the ultimate victim circuit (a 120 dB goal in reduction). If the existing situation is such that 10^{-4} fraction of the power is picked up through the cables and 10^{-8} through the box, the coupling to attack first is the cable mode. But once this one will have been reduced by eight orders of magnitude, reaching the desired 10^{-12} objective, the coupling through the box still exists, causing only an 80 dB decrease in EMI power while 120 dB was desired. So the box coupling should be reduced by at least four orders of magnitude to achieve the objective. Determining the amount of shielding and designing the box to achieve this amount is the subject of Volume 3, *Electromagnetic Shielding*, of this EMC handbook series. For the reasons explained above, Volume 8 concentrates on the most frequent and offending mechanisms, i.e., coupling via the cables.

In conclusion, with few exceptions, the nine radiated coupling paths shown in Fig. 1.3 reduce to the above four principal paths, which cover the largest part of the radiated EMI situations found in widespread samplings.

Where conducted emissions over hard wire are involved, the lower part of Fig. 1.3 summarizes the existing situations. One path involves a situation where direct interference is propagated over a wire line and is coupled via the cable to the victim receptor. Often, the EMI problem involves the power mains in which an interfering

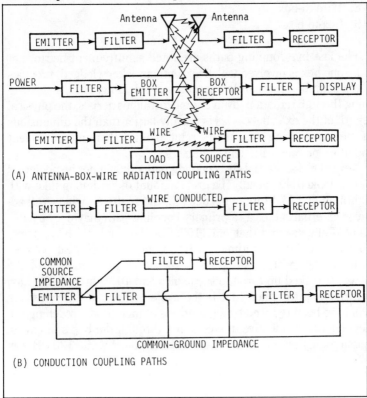

Figure 1.3—Principal EMI Coupling Paths

source is coupled. For example, switching regulator power supplies or transients are developed on power buses and coupled to the victim via the power lines.

Occasionally, common-impedance coupling exists whereby two circuits, networks or equipments share a common section of a ground plane or safety wire bus due to multipoint grounding. On the other hand, the common impedance may be that of the power supply and its feed cables. Either can result in EMI. This problem becomes quite prevalent in complex installations or situations in which many equipments are interconnected.

Figure 1.4 shows a typical susceptibility situation (A) where noise-

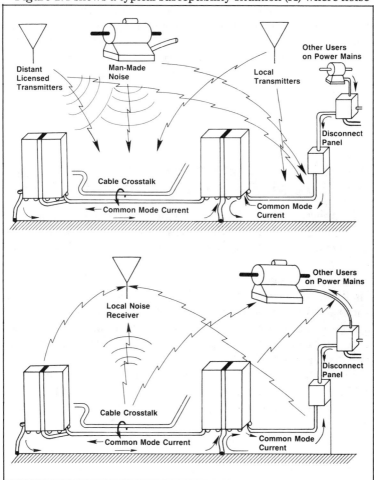

Figure 1.4—Principal EMI Coupling Paths, Susceptibility and Emission

1.11

making sources couple into the victim cabinets and racks by both radiation and conduction. The former involves direct radiation into cables and loop areas formed by cables, cabinets and ground planes. The latter includes the power mains servicing the victim equipments. Thus, Fig. 1.4 is simply another way of looking at the coupling paths which appear more often in practice, with exceptions acknowledged.

The second part (B) of Fig. 1.4 shows the reciprocal situation, i.e., the emission problem. While emission is not a minor aspect, most designers will tend to worry about susceptibility first because they simply want their system to work trouble-free. This is why the first nine chapters of this book deal with susceptibility, i.e., hardening the "victim." Then Chapter 10, using the reciprocity principle, addresses emission control, which is rather easy to understand once its image mechanism has been unscrambled.

The antenna-to-antenna coupling path is excluded here because it is an intersystem EMI problem and is covered in other volumes of this handbook series. The antenna-to-antenna situation, nevertheless, can be included in the design synthesis methodology.

1.4 EMC Design Synthesis: The Methodology and Procedures

This section presents an introduction to and an overview of the EMI control methodology called **design synthesis**. Details of this technique appear throughout the remaining chapters of this handbook.

Figure 1.5 is a general flow diagram used for predicting and solving EMI problems, either manually or via a computer program. This summary diagram presents a qualitative picture of the EMC design synthesis methodology. Each of the individual boxes is discussed in detail in subsequent chapters. This includes the mathematical models, the rationale and illustrative examples.

The methodology begins (see the "START" circle at center left in Fig. 1.5) with the user entering his EMI problem data and EMI application fix constraints (block 1). The problem data pertains to identifying intentional signal levels, receptor or victim characteristics and one or more expected coupling paths. Examples of intentional signals include voltage or power amplitude, frequency or pulse duration, rise times and other data which characterizes

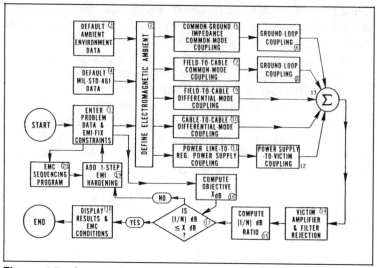

Figure 1.5—General Flow Diagram for Predicting and Solving EMI Problems

the signal. Examples of the potential EMI victim are in-band sensitivities, corner or cutoff frequencies of pass band, slope in the rejection band and minimum out-of-band rejections across the spectrum. The user may employ available default parameters when empirical data are unknown.

In anticipation of an interference problem, the user also supplies a list of different EMI fix constraints which should be employed (block 1); i.e., whether particular EMC components or techniques can be used. The constraints are required since some applications of the EMC design synthesis method emphasize conditions in a laboratory design stage, whereas others apply only for field installation or EMC retrofit conditions. Furthermore, some applications may involve weight or size limitations, whereas others will not. Thus, only the user, in his particular applications, knows what constraints exist. Here again, default parameters are suggested in the absence of actual data.

The next step in the user EMI problem entry is to define his electromagnetic ambient environment (block 2). This involves the electric field strength or magnetic flux density, voltage or current, or other ambient parameters corresponding to a conducted and radiated environment.

If the user's electromagnetic environment is not determined, default conditions can be supplied (block 3). To derive a meaningful default condition, the user must answer questions posed by the methodology process. This helps define some typical industrial and commercial environments. Another of the family of default data, but involving government or military applications, corresponds to MIL-STD-461 specification limits (block 4).

After the input data, EMI fix constraints and electromagnetic ambient have been defined, the next step in the methodology involves processing one or more applicable coupling paths. The flow diagram shown in Fig. 1.5 indicates five major EMI coupling paths (see blocks 5 through 12) which cover most intrasystem EMI problems found in government, industrial and commercial situations. The first coupling path involves computing the **common-mode coupling*** by a common-ground impedance shared between an undesired emission source and the victim (block 5). (Common-mode in a cable or harness corresponds to currents flowing in phase on all wires.)

With the common-impedance coupling voltage computed, the coupling path is completed by determining how much of this voltage manifests itself at the victim input terminals. This is called **ground-loop coupling** (block 6). Thus, the common-impedance coupling path is divided into two parts to facilitate computations and understanding. Another term for the ground-loop coupling is **common-mode rejection** as applied to a system containing a ground loop.

When the potentially interfering source contains a radiating antenna, or when an electromagnetic ambient exists as a field strength at the location of the victim, a second path is **field-to-cable coupling** (block 7). Here the cable defines the wires between the pieces of equipment or boxes as previously shown in Figs. 1.2 and 1.4. Thus, the field strength is converted to an open-circuited, available voltage. This common-mode voltage then is partially coupled to the victim amplifier via the ground-loop coupling path (block 8). This coupling is the same mechanism as that mentioned in the preceding paragraph (block 6).

A third coupling path, also involving field-to-cable, is called **differential-mode** coupling, also sometimes called **normal mode** coupling (see block 9). (Thus, the normal mode for signals flowing in a two-wire line is for their currents to be out of phase; see Section 2.4.2). This third coupling path involves direct radia-

1.14

tion from the electromagnetic ambient field into a cable or harness. This develops a potentially interfering signal directly at the input terminals of the victim amplifier.

A fourth coupling mode, which also develops a differential-mode interference across the victim amplifier input terminals, is **cable-to- cable coupling** (block 10). This coupling involves only near-field conditions and corresponds to one cable or harness coupling undesired source emissions and the other cable or harness feeding the victim amplifier. Actually, both source and victim wires may be located in the same harness but are still separated by a definable distance. The cables may also be located in a common tray or cable hanger.

The fifth and final coupling path shown in Fig. 1.5 corresponds to conducted EMI coupling on ac or dc power mains (block 11). Any form of undesired emission may be coupled onto the power lines by other users who are connected to the same power lines. In this case, either undesired steady-state or transient emissions will appear as a differential mode. However, should the power line be exposed to a radiated electromagnetic ambient at another location, then the undesired emissions thereon would be common-mode as previously illustrated in block 7. Thus, the power line regulated supply coupling will account for filters, the built-in isolation offered by power transformers and a switching regulator or other power supplies.

The second part of the last coupling path involves processing the conducted emissions on the regulated power supply into the sensitive amplifiers (block 12) of the victim. If more than one coupling path is involved, then the voltages produced at the input to the victim amplifier are summed over all applicable paths (circle 13). Usually it is sufficient to choose the larger of two paths, or the largest of three or more paths, since their amplitudes are, in general, substantially different.

Having combined the outputs from all coupling paths at the input terminals of the victim, the sum is next processed through the victim amplifier or logic (block 14). The victim is defined in terms of its passband sensitivity, the corner or cutoff frequency, the rolloff slope in the rejection band and the far region out-of-band known as **audio rectification**. The victim response usually serves to delimit conducted interference unless the EMI exists totally in the passband.

The interference level, I, has now been calculated, the intentional signal, S, and victim sensitivity, N, are identified.* Then both the interference-to-noise ratio, I/N, (block 15) and signal-to-noise-plus interference ratio, S/(N+I), are computed. The I/N ratio is a quantitative measure of the potential EMI situation and constitutes a direct measure of the amount of EMI hardening which may be required.

To determine how much EMI hardening is needed, an objective (X_{dB}) for the controlled I/N ratio must be determined (block 16). This objective is directly calculated from the user design goal and constraints (block 1) about the probability that EMC will exist.

The computed I/N ratio is compared with the design objectives (diamond 17) to determine if EMI or EMC exists. If the I/N is equal to or less than X_{dB} (yes decision, diamond 17), then EMC is construed to exist. For this, all results including the historical record are displayed (block 18) and the program objective has been achieved.

If the I/N ratio is not equal to or less than X_{dB} (no decision, diamond 17), then additional EMI hardening is required. One EMC component or technique is added at a time (block 19), and the entire program is iterated, i.e., run again. While the user can select his own EMI fix (block 1), the selection of usable fixes is prompted by the EMC sequencing program (block 20).† This sequences and iterates the program until an EMC solution has been obtained.

After each EMC component or technique is added (block 19), the iterated prediction of the new I/N ratio is made (block 15). It is again compared with the objective (block 16). The process is continued until I/N $\leqslant X_{dB}$, whereupon the program ends. This avoids EMC overdesign and accomplishes the desired EMC level. Overdesign means that too much EMI hardening has been done.

1.5 How to Use This Handbook

To fully benefit from a handbook, the reader must be armed with an understanding of its makeup and the ability to locate desired information. The table of contents presents a broad overview of the

---

*Sensitivity in analog systems is assumed to be equal to internal noise, N. For digital systems, N = noise immunity voltage level.

†This program is described in greater detail later in this handbook.

topic material, and a comprehensive index is provided at the end. The reader is advised to make extensive use of both. The remainder of this section bridges the gap with a synopsis of the remaining chapters.

Chapter 1 has provided a classical overview of the handbook by outlining the basic EMI control methodology and procedures. Chapter 2 explains how to input and present the victim equipment or system. Of special interest in Chapter 2 is a means of defining the electromagnetic ambient, either conducted or radiated, in which the potentially susceptible victim equipment or system must operate.

The implementation of EMI control methodology and procedures is explained in Chapter 3. Although it may seem premature, this information is presented before Chapters 4 through 9 to familiarize the reader with the technique and the resulting performance display. Both end results and intermediate coupling paths receive high visibility in the output display. Thus, it becomes implementable in increasing stages as the subsequent chapters unravel.

Chapter 4 presents the EMI susceptibility aspects of a victim amplifier or logic, as applicable, contained inside an equipment housing. This applies for both performance in the passband as well as in the out-of-band conditions.

The next five chapters, Chaps. 5 through 9, deal with each of the five principal coupling paths illustrated in Fig. 1.5 (blocks 5 through 12). Throughout each chapter, a number of illustrative examples are given to help the reader understand and exercise the associated design data.

Chapter 10, "EMI Emission and Control," covers the reverse situation from the preceding chapters which involve EMI susceptibility and its control. Applications of radiation from small wires and loops cover DIPs, PCBs, backplanes, switching regulator power supplies, ribbon cables and I/O lines.

1.6 Bibliography

Birken, J.A., "Naval Electromagnetic System Design and Synthesis," *IEEE EMC Symposium Record*, Session IV-A, Atlanta, Georgia, June 20-22, 1978 (New York: IEEE, 1978).

Clark, D.E., "Factors in an EM Methodology," *IEEE EMC Symposium Record*, Session I-C, Atlanta, Georgia, June 20-22, 1978 (New York: IEEE, 1978).

LaMontagne, R., "The Air Force Intrasystem Analysis Program (IAP)," *IEEE EMC Symposium Record*, Session 4B-1, Washington, DC, July 13-15, 1976 (New York: IEEE, 1976).

Showers, R.M.; Johnson, P.J.; and Rees, G.D., "The Application of EMC Prediction Methodology," *IEEE EMC Symposium Record*, San Antonio, Texas, October 7-9, 1975 (New York: IEEE, 1975).

White, D.R.J., "Recent Advances in EMC Design Synthesis," *Second Symposium and Technical Exhibition in Electromagnetic Compatibility Record*, Montreux, Switzerland, June, 1977 (Berne, Switzerland: Swiss PTT, 1977).

White, D.R.J. and Zorn, J., "EMC Design Synthesis Using Programmable Calculators and Minicomputers," *IEEE EMC Symposium Record*, Session 4B-1, Washington, DC, July 13-15, 1976 (New York: IEEE, 1976).

Chapter 2

Victim Definition, Ambient and Input Data

This chapter is devoted to defining the victim equipment or system and its electromagnetic environment in units and terms that facilitate EMI prediction, diagnosis and solution as presented in later chapters. The heavily outlined blocks of Fig. 2.1 correspond to the stages of this process. Problem identification may take place before the fact (equipment yet to be designed or an installation yet

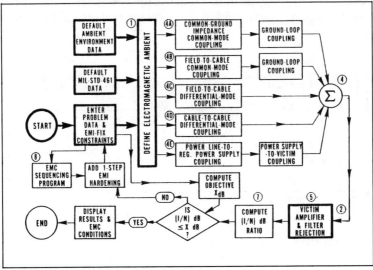

Figure 2.1—EMI Problem Definition and Input Data (Heavy-Lined Blocks)

2.1

to be made), or it can be based on an existing situation. While the two-box level of complexity is stressed, EMC methodology is useful at other application levels (as previously discussed in Section 1.1).

The first step shown in Fig. 2.1 involves defining the victim or potential EMI receptor(s). Following this, the electromagnetic ambient is to be defined. Finally, in preparation for applying EMC design or retrofit techniques, the user must select a number of constraints which apply to his particular problem. This also tailors the process to applications in laboratory design, field installation, aerospace technology, land vehicles, building installation, etc.

2.1 The Two-Box Situation and Multiple Victims

Certain rules must be followed in interpreting and using the two-box EMI situation. This is especially important when the EMI examination will be extended to levels of higher or lower complexity. When multiple victims exist, the most sensitive one is selected first.

2.1.1 Two Interconnected Boxes

A simplified version of the two-box situation depicted in Fig. 2.2 was previously discussed in Section 1.1 in connection with the nine levels of EMI manifestations. Each of the two boxes could correspond to an equipment. For this, the local internal ground to the case

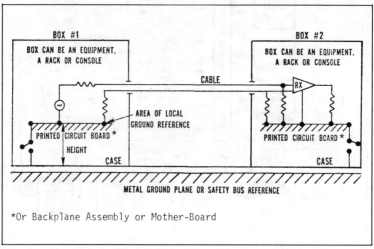

Figure 2.2—The Two-Box Situation Showing Interconnecting Cable

is associated with either a backplane assembly, motherboard or a PCB, as applicable. The outer case is the equipment metal housing. Should each box represent a 19" rack or console, then the outer metal housing could be either floating* or grounded, and the internal grounds correspond to that of individual equipments.

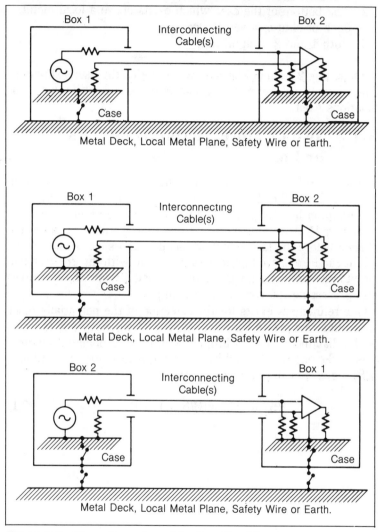

Figure 2.3—Three Examples of the Two-Box Situation

---

*Here, the word **floating** does not mean that one is advised to violate national safety codes. Methods for complying with such codes are discussed later.

To extend the two-box situation up or down in complexity requires following certain ground rules. For example, the local ground plane in both boxes of Fig. 2.2 corresponds in area and height to:

1. A backplane assembly, mother or printed-circuit board mounted above the case ground
2. The bottom of the case which exists above a local metal deck or skin of a vehicle, or
3. Both 1 and 2, if applicable

Thus, Fig. 2.2 should be redrawn to define the user's situation. The above three examples are shown in Fig. 2.3. Still other combinations exist.

2.1.2 Two or More Victim Amplifiers or Logic

Another rule dictates that when the victim amplifier shown in Box 2 of Fig. 2.2 or 2.3 is in reality two or more amplifiers, then the amplifier having the greatest potential susceptibility is deemed to be Box 2.* Determining which is most susceptible calls for a conclusion before the fact, which is usually impossible. However, the intent can be achieved by selecting the unit with the greatest sensitivity (the victim having the lowest in-band dBm or dBμV number) and processing the corresponding amplifier.

One refinement exists for the selection of the potentially most susceptible victim (see Volume 5, *EMC in Components and Devices*, of this handbook series.) From the number of potential victims, choose the one which exhibits the greatest receptor susceptibility (RS) index. For digital victims, RS is:

$$RS_d = 20 \log(B/N_{NIL}) \text{ dBR} \qquad (2.1)$$

---

*As an alternative, the user can define each victim separately and repeat the process for each one.

where,

RS_d = digital receptor susceptibility index

B = bandwidth of logic in Hz

   = $1/\pi\tau_r$, where τ_r = rise time of logic   (2.2)

N_{NIL} = noise immunity level in volts

dBR = decibels above reference index

For analog victims, including amplifiers and receivers, RS is defined as:

$$RS_a = 198 + 10 \log(B/RF) \text{ dBR*} \tag{2.3}$$

$$= 188 + 10 \log(B/R) \text{ dBR for default conditions} \tag{2.4}$$

where,

RS_a = analog receptor susceptibility index

B = bandwidth of analog receptor in Hz

R = receptor input resistance in ohms

F = noise factor or antilogarithm of noise figure
   (noise figure = 10 dB for default conditions)

When the sensitivity of the analog victim is given in units of dBm, Eq. (2.3) becomes:

$$RS_a = 24 + 20 \log(\sqrt{B/R}) - N_{dBM} \tag{2.5}$$

where,

N_{dBM} = sensitivity (S = N) of victim in dBm

Thus, one of the above applicable equations is selected for each victim. All victims are rated with an RS, and the largest RS is selected as having the greatest latent susceptibility.

---

*The 198 in Eq. (2.3) comes from the KT term in FKTB as defined elsewhere.

Illustrative Example 2.1

Given all kinds of electromagnetic ambients, select the greatest latent susceptibility of four different victims: electrocardiograph, FET amplifier, TTL logic and AM broadcast receiver. The applicable data and computed receptor susceptibilities are:

Victim Type	Equation No.	Bandwidth	NIL or dBm	Resistance	RS in dBR
Electrocardiogram	2.4	100 Hz	—	10 kΩ	168
FET Amplifier	2.4	1 MHz	—	10 MΩ	178
TTL Logic	2.1	30 MHz	0.4 V	n/a	158
AM Receiver	2.5	10 kHz	−124.0 dBm	50 Ω	211

From the above RS computations, it is determined that the AM receiver exhibits the greatest latent susceptibility, and the TTL logic exhibits the least. Generally, the first-choice victim would be the AM receiver. Depending upon the time available to the user, he may then proceed to the next most sensitive victim. This process is facilitated when modeled on a computer.

2.2 Applications at Multi-Box Levels

EMI problems at more complex levels than the two-box situation can be accommodated. Complexity rises quickly with an increase in the number of boxes and interconnecting cables. At the two-box level, the previous section indicated that many victims could be housed in a single box. Furthermore, two or more interconnecting cables may exist between the two boxes (control and signal connections, power supply leads, etc.). Therefore, to avoid difficulties of varying complexities, a delimiting process is necessary.

When the two-box level is extended to an N-box level, the complexity can rise exponentially. For the two-box level and one interconnecting cable shown in Fig. 2.2, one ground loop exists. For three boxes, each having only one interconnecting cable per box pair and one ground (see Fig. 2.4), five loops exist. With 4 similarly interconnected boxes, 13 loops exist. The number of such loops, L, is related to the number of boxes, N, by:

$$L = (N - 1)^2 + (N - 2)^2 \qquad (2.6)$$

When each box contains more than one interconnecting cable to every other box, the problem expands further.

The above considerations do not reduce the effectiveness of the EMC design methodology approach, but they require that a supporting technique be used to delimit the problem. This level is commensurate with (1) what the user can invest in lead time to solve the problem and (2) the available data on both victim equipment and electromagnetic ambient information. These factors are described later in this handbook.

Alternatively, computer aids can be used to facilitate a more complex problem as discussed in the last chapter. For present purposes, the problem will be illustrated at the two-box level.

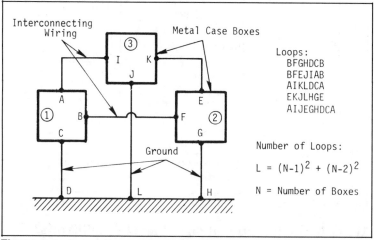

Figure 2.4—Loops Formed by Three Interconnected Boxes

2.3 Defining the Victim Receptor

This section presents the first part of the user input data, including victim definition. It also identifies the intentional signal source, signal box, victim receptor properties, victim box, box-to-box interconnecting cables, local/nearby ground planes and barriers between boxes and electromagnetic ambients.

2.3.1 The Intentional Signal Source

Each of the two boxes shown in Fig. 2.5 may represent an equipment case, console, 19 in. rack or other metal housing which encloses electronic circuits or equipments. The left box in the figure, Box 1, is the enclosure containing the intentional signal source. Both the internals and externals of this box will be examined.

The victim susceptibility to EMI is also a function of the intentional signal level, S. It is defined in two terms as applicable: (1) designed signal level (transition range or swing) for digital circuits or logic or (2) the least useful meaningful signal to be expected for analog circuits. Thus, the first question is:

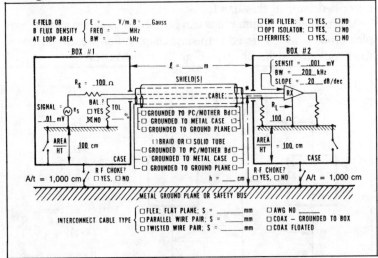

Figure 2.5—Input Data Identification for Two-Box EMI Problem

What is the intentional signal level in millivolts?

If the user does not know the signal level expressed in millivolts or decibels above one millivolt (dBmV), the level may be identified by one or more of the following relationships:

$$dBmV = 10 \log(mV) \tag{2.7}$$

$$= -60 + dB\mu V \tag{2.8}$$

$$= -60 + dB\mu A + 20 \log(R_g) \tag{2.9}$$

$$= 60 + dBA + 20 \log(R_g) \tag{2.10}$$

$$= 47 - 10 \log(50/R_g) + dBm \tag{2.11}$$

$$= -13 - 10 \log(50/R_g) + dBpW \tag{2.12}$$

or, $dBmV = 20 + NdBmV$ for default* conditions   (2.13)

where,

$$dBV = dB \text{ above } 1 \text{ V}$$

$$dB\mu V = dB \text{ above } 1 \ \mu V$$

$$dBA = dB \text{ above } 1 \text{ A}$$

$$dB\mu A = dB \text{ above } 1 \ \mu A$$

R_g = signal source resistance in ohms (see Fig. 2.5)

$$dBm = dB \text{ above } 1 \text{ mW}$$

$$dBpW = dB \text{ above } 1 \text{ pW}$$

NdBmV = sensitivity (noise level) in dBmV for an analog system

= noise immunity level in dBmV for a digital system

In Fig. 2.5 an analog system is illustrated with the lowest useful or significant voltage source level of 10 μV. Here, 10 μV = 20 dBμV = 0.01 mV = −40 dBmV. The 0.01 mV level is shown inside Box 1 in the figure.

The next question asked regarding the intentional signal source is:

What is the signal source impedance in ohms?

This question refers to R_g in Box 1, Fig. 2.5. For the ongoing example, a source impedance of 100 Ω is selected as shown in the figure. A similar question will be asked later about the victim input (load) impedance.

The next question involves balanced and unbalanced signal sources. The question now is:

Is a balanced or unbalanced signal source used?

For unbalanced sources, the resistance is located only on the high

---

*The word **default** means that if the value is unknown, use the suggested number, at least for the time being.

2.9

side of the signal generator. Thus, the resistance on the low side or local ground side is 0 Ω. For balanced sources, the resistance is divided into two approximately equal parts. To determine just how close to equal they may be, a second question is required for balanced sources* only:

What is the balance tolerance in percent?

The percent tolerance is a direct measure of the residual unbalance. As discussed in Chapters 5 and 6, this is important relative to common-mode rejection. The answer to this will also affect a similar situation with respect to Box 2 as discussed later. If the balance tolerance is unknown, a default value of 5 percent may be used.

For the ongoing illustrative problem, an unbalanced signal source is used as shown by checking the "Bal?" question (checked "no" inside Box 1) in Fig. 2.5.

2.3.2 The Signal Box

Grounding plays a significant role in the performance of equipments and systems. The next question is:

Is the local ground inside Box 1 grounded or floated to case?

The local ground could be a backplane assembly, motherboard or printed circuit board. The question will determine if it is bonded or connected to the Box 1 metal case. Since most if not all boards use single-point grounding,† this condition is used as default. Grounding then is assumed in the ongoing example (close the toggle switch between local ground and case in Box 1 of Fig. 2.5).

The next question regarding the signal box is:

What is the Box 1 board area-to-height ratio in centimeters?

For those situations in which the board is not grounded, i.e., is floated, the zero signal reference **local ground plane** acts as one plate of a capacitor, and the metal case acts as the other plate.

---

*Note that for balanced line drivers, the e_s signal generator source in Box 1 of Fig. 2.5 should actually be divided with 0.5 e_s in the high side and 0.5 e_s in the low side. This does not affect the present discussion or performance, however.

†The limitations of this practice are discussed in later chapters.

The separation or height between the board and case shown in Fig. 2.5 completes the capacitor definition. The capacitor is proportional to this area-to-height ratio, which explains the need to ask the above question. Since the area-to-height ratio is unknown, a default value of 100 to 1,000 cm may be used. This default value corresponds within a half order of magnitude to most real-life situations. It is used in the ongoing problem as shown in the figure in Box 1.

The remaining two questions involve the **external** aspects of Box 1:

Is the Box 1 case grounded or floated to the ground plane?
What is the case area-to-height ratio in centimeters?

These two questions for **external** grounding and area-to-height ratio closely follow the similar, previous questions for conditions **inside** the box. The ground plane may actually be the skin of a vehicle, the deck of a ship, a safety wire or concrete wire mesh. For the ongoing problem, the answers are **grounded** and **100 cm or 1,000 cm (10 to 100 pF)**, respectively.

2.3.3 Victim Receptor Properties

Certain questions are pertinent in defining the characteristics of the victim as located in Box 2 of Fig. 2.5:

What is the amplifier sensitivity in millivolts?   This corresponds to the bandwidth-limited, white noise level* for analog victims and NIL for digital logic. For the latter, a default value of 400 mV may be used if a better or more representative value is unknown for the particular logic selected.

In Fig. 2.5, an analog sensitivity of $1\mu V$ or 0.001 mV is illustrated in the ongoing example. This value appears in Box 2.

The next question involves the frequency of the victim amplifier or logic.

---

*Noise (N) $= \sqrt{4RFKTB}$

Is the victim a baseband amplifier or a receiver?

Baseband operation corresponds to the signal information with no modulated carrier, whereas a receiver operates with a modulated carrier. If the answer to the previous question is that the victim is a receiver, then three questions are asked. The first is:

What is the carrier frequency in megahertz of the victim receiver?

This corresponds to the center tuned frequency of the receiver. The second question for receivers only is:

What is the selectivity shape factor?

As detailed in Section 4.2, the shape factor is the ratio of the 60 dB to 6 dB bandwidth. If the shape factor is unknown, a default value of 4 may be used.

The third question for receivers only is:

What is the out-of-band spurious response?

For superheterodyne receivers, this corresponds to mixer modulation products developed between 0.1 and 10 times the fundamental frequency. These products exist at harmonics and subharmonics of the local oscillator, plus or minus the intermediate frequency. As described in detail in Section 4.2, a default value of 80 dB may be used.

For either baseband amplifier, logic or receiver victim, the next question asked is:

What is the victim bandwidth in kHz?

Whether dc, ac, video or RF operated, the bandwidth corresponds to the 3 dB down points in the victim selectivity curve. For logic, this was defined in Eq. (2.2). For the ongoing example in Fig. 2.5, a baseband bandwidth of 200 kHz is used.

The next question involves the stop band, rolloff or slope of selectivity of the victim:

What is the victim stop band slope in decibels per decade?

If given or known in dB/octave, the dB/decade slope is related to the former by:

$$dB/decade = 3.32 \times dB/octave \qquad (2.14)$$

If the slope in the stopband of a baseband amplifier or logic is unknown, a typical default value of 20 dB/decade is used. This corresponds to parasitic shunt capacitance of circuit wiring and components. If the victim is a receiver, the slope is usually unknown, but the selectivity is indirectly defined by the above shape factor questions.

A default value of 20 dB/decade is used in the ongoing illustrative example shown in Box 2 of Fig. 2.5 for the 200 kHz victim baseband amplifier.

Two additional victim questions in Box 2 are similar to those of the signal source in Box 1 previously discussed:

What is the victim input impedance in ohms?
Is a balanced or unbalanced load used?

While the impedance of both signal source (Box 1) and the victim (Box 2) may not be the same (they typically are equal), they both are operated either balanced or unbalanced. Thus, the second question above was previously answered when the companion question was answered for the signal source. When balanced conditions are used, a third question is appropriate:

What is the circuit balance tolerance in percent?

Again, the tolerance of both the signal source and victim impedances are usually the same.

Figure 2.5 shows in Box 2 that a 100 Ω victim input impedance is also used in the ongoing example.

2.3.4 The Victim Box

The four questions asked of the victim (Box 2) are nearly identical to the four asked in Section 2.3.2 of the signal source (Box 1) in Fig. 2.5:

Is the local ground inside Box 2 grounded or floated to case?

What is the Box 2 ratio of board area to height, in centimeters?

Is the Box 2 case grounded or floated to ground plane?

What is the case area-to-height ratio in centimeters?

Similarly, discussions and explanations in Section 2.3.2 also apply here. However, it does not follow that any or all answers are the same. For example, Box 1 could be grounded and Box 2 floated, or vice versa. Since grounding is generally practiced, the answers to the first and third questions above are that both are grounded in the ongoing illustrative example. Also, it is assumed that the default area-to-height value of 100 to 1,000 cm is used for both boxes, as shown in Fig. 2.5.

2.3.5 Box-to-Box Communications

Figure 2.5 has been reproduced in Fig. 2.6 for convenience. The interconnecting cable(s) between Box 1 and Box 2 will now be examined. For the present problem, only the control and signal leads between the two boxes are considered. If there are any power leads involving raw (primary) or regulated (secondary) power, they also must be examined.

The first question, involving the box-to-box communication cable(s) is:

What is the cable length between boxes in meters?

This corresponds to the inside distance between the two boxes unless the cable exits from the back (or front) of Box 1 or enters

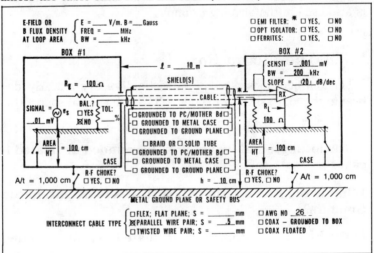

Figure 2.6—Figure 2.5 with Additional Input Data

the back (or front) of Box 2. For this latter condition, the equivalent cable length corresponds to the distance between the connector at one box to the connector of the other, measured in a straight line (disregard any wandering effect of the cable).

For the ongoing example, a cable length of 10 m is used as shown in Fig. 2.6.

The next question involves the average cable height above a reference ground plane. This height, with the above cable length, forms a loop area which acts as an unintentional pickup antenna:

What is the cable height above ground in centimeters?

The height is the **average** height of the cable above local ground over its entire length between boxes or cabinets. Even though its height from point to point may vary substantially along the cable length, its average height is calculable as suggested in Fig. 2.7. In the top frame, the height is well defined and corresponds to the average value of heights sampled at equal increments along its length.

For a poorly defined situation such as shown in the bottom frame of Fig. 2.7, the average height is more complicated to compute. The reference ground plane must be identified first. It could correspond to the safety wire or conduit for the two boxes or cabinets. It might be the deck of a ship or vehicle or the metal skin of an aircraft or spacecraft. If the floor is concrete, the reference plane may be the reinforcing bars or mesh. Whatever the **ground plane,** the bot-

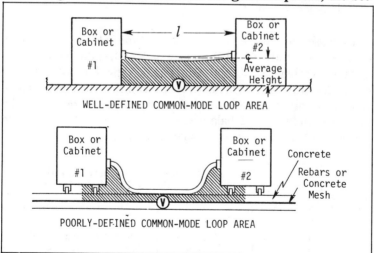

Figure 2.7—Common-Mode Coupling of Field-to-Loop Area

tom frame in Fig. 2.7 suggests how it may be estimated: the average value corresponding to a number of heights sampled at equal increments along the entire cable length.

For the ongoing example, an average height above the ground plane of 10 cm is used as shown in Fig. 2.6. The next question asked is:

What type of cable or wires is used between the two boxes in Fig. 2.6?

Select the applicable cable between boxes:

1. Balanced line (unknown parallel-wire type)*
2. Untwisted wire pair
3. Twisted wire pair
4. Shielded untwisted pair
5. Shielded twisted pair
6. Double-shielded (no insulation between braids) twisted pair
7. Double-shielded (insulated = quadrax) twisted pair
8. Triple-shielded (insulated = quintrex) twisted pair
9. Flat-plane or flex (printed) wiring
10. Unbalanced line (unknown coax type)
11. Coaxial line (braided outer conductor)
12. Coax, double uninsulated braid
13. Coax, double insulated braid (triax)
14. Coax double insulated with inner foil-wrap
15. Semi-rigid coaxial line
16. Unknown

If the user does not know which cable type is to be used (design stage) or is already installed (field stage), he has three options for default: numbers 1, 10 and 16. Default type 1 is for balanced **transmission** lines. This does **not** mean that the signal source and victim are operated in a balanced mode, but only that the transmission line is of a balanced type. For type 1, the worst case is selected,† i.e., type 2, untwisted wire pair.

---

*The term "balanced line" here is applied to a line formed of two **identical** wires, one carrying the outgoing current and the other carrying the return current. See Section 6.5.2 for the influence of the cable balance and the overall system balance. Notice also that a balanced line does not automatically imply that the driver and receiver are balanced.

†The worst case is selected at the beginning since it is usually the least expensive type of transmission line. When the design synthesis methodology is used in later chapters, the EMI-hardening techniques and components will become evident. The correct transmission line will be suggested by the process.

Default type 10 is for an unbalanced transmission line. This does not mean that the signal source and victim are necessarily operated in an unbalanced mode, but only that the transmission line is of an unbalanced type. For type 10, the worst case is selected, i.e., type 11, braided coaxial line.

If the user has no idea whatsoever about the transmission line connecting Boxes 1 and 2, he selects default type 16, unknown. This corresponds to type 2, untwisted, parallel-wire line as a starting condition, provided the victim amplifier bandwidth is below 20 MHz. Above 20 MHz, type 11 is selected to start.

Should the user select from cable types 1 through 9 (balanced line), then the following question is asked (see Fig. 2.6):

What is the inside dimension of cable in millimeters?
If he does not know, a default number of 0.5 mm may be used for types 1 through 8, and 1 mm for type 9. If types 1 through 8 are involved, a second question is asked:

What is the AWG gauge number for wire line?
If the user does not know, a default number of American Wire Gauge (AWG) = 26 is used for signal and control cables.

To continue the ongoing illustrative example, a two-wire untwisted parallel transmission line is assumed in which S = 0.5 mm and AWG #26. These input data are shown in Fig. 2.6.

Should the user select 4 through 8 or 10 through 14 in the above box-to-box cable question (involving either a balanced line shield, a coaxial braid or a shield over a coaxial line), the following selection is made:

Select the applicable grounding for the inner braided shield:

1. Shield not connected to either case (or box)
2. Shield connected only to Box 1 case at connector
3. Shield connected only to Box 2 case at connector
4. Shield connected to both cases at both connectors
5. Unknown

The word **grounding** means where the shield is connected. The word **inner** is used in the event that there are two or more braided shields; for this situation the only innermost shield is considered at the moment. If the user selects **Unknown**, the default conditions correspond to choice 2 for shielded balanced line and choice 4 for coax. Choice 1 is appropriate in the event that a coaxial line is floated relative to the case.

Should the user select type 7, 8 or 13 in the above box-to-box **cable** choice, the next selection becomes:

Select the applicable grounding for the outer braided shield:

1. Shield connected only to Box 1 case at connector
2. Shield connected only to Box 2 case at connector
3. Shield connected to both cases at both connectors
4. Unknown

If the user selects **Unknown**, the default condition corresponds to choice 2.

With a coax, since the shield is also an active signal return, it is assumed that it will be **at least** connected to signal ground at both ends, regardless of whether it is floated from the box chassis (see Section 6.4.2).

For the ongoing example, choice 2 of the 16 cable options is used. Since no shield is involved in this choice, no further input to Fig. 2.6 is required at this time.

2.3.6 Cable-to-Cable Coupling and Crosstalk

The fourth coupling mode shown in Fig. 2.1 does not lend itself readily to the input data identification diagram shown in Fig. 2.6, where emphasis is on field-to-cable coupling. Thus, for cable-to-cable coupling, a different diagram is used as shown in Fig. 2.8. Note that here emphasis is on the cable type, geometry and dimensions. The upper cable line is the culprit source, and the lower cable line is the victim.

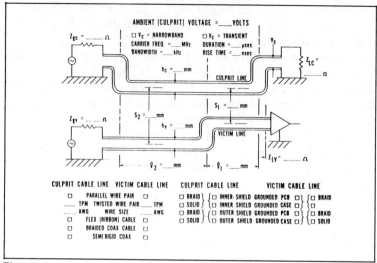

Figure 2.8—Input Data for Cable-to-Cable Coupling

At the left extreme of Fig. 2.8, the culprit source of impedance (Z_{gc} and victim signal source impedance (Z_{gv}) are to be identified. Correspondingly, at the extreme right of the figure the culprit load impedance (Z_{1c} and the victim load impedance (Z_{1v}) also are to be identified.

Regarding the cable geometry, the common culprit-victim, parallel-run length is to be identified next. This common length comes from routing both cables in a harness, cable raceway, tray, hanger or simply from applications where they come in proximity. In Fig. 2.8, this length is identified as l, in units of millimeters and is matched with an average cable-to-cable separation distance over its length of S_1, also in units of millimeters. The left and right bounds of l correspond to those situations in which S_1 takes a sudden increase such as suggested in the figure.

For cases in which the common culprit-victim cable length may be divided into two sublengths having different average separation distances, S, Fig. 2.8 also applies. As before, l, and S, correspond to the closest approach. Now S_2 corresponds to the larger of the two separation distances.

Should three or more discrete l-S combinations exist, Fig. 2.8 may still be used. The procedure is to form the ratios: $l_1/S_1{}^2$, $l_2/S_2{}^2$,

...l_n/S_n^2 and to select the largest two l-S combinations for insertion into Fig. 2.8. Eliminate the remaining l-S combinations because they will not significantly add to the cable-to-cable coupling.

If either or both cables are of the parallel-wire type, their inside wire dimension, h, should be identified. In Fig. 2.8, h_c corresponds to the culprit source wire dimension in millimeters, while h_v is that of the victim wire. Whatever the wire type, the bottom part of Fig. 2.8 is used to identify both culprit and victim cables.

If a twisted wire pair is used in either the culprit or victim cable (or both), the number of twists per meter (TPM) is inserted in the indicated place in Fig. 2.8. Similarly, the AWG number is inserted. Figure 2.8 also provides for identifying one or more shields on the cables and the associated grounding conditions.

2.3.7 Ambient-to-Box Barriers

As previously discussed in Sections 1.3 and 1.4, the electromagnetic ambient may couple to the victim by undesired conducted emissions on the power bus, ground plane or via radiated emissions. The ambient description is presented in Section 2.4. The following identifies any ambient barriers which may exist on the power bus (e.g., filters, isolation transformers, motor generator sets, uninterruptible power supplies) or in the radiated path such as a shielded room enclosure or building. If none of these ambient-to-box barriers exists, or if its performance is unknown, the following questions may be skipped. In this case, the reader may proceed to Section 2.4 where the ambient is defined directly at the victim boxes.

The first selection pertains to EMI barriers or the power mains:

Identify the conducted emission barriers between power service and victim (select one or more, as applicable):

1. Common-mode filter(s) only
2. Differential-mode filter(s) only
3. Both common-mode and differential-mode filter(s)
4. Isolation transformer (no Faraday shield)
5. Single Faraday-shielded isolation transformer, ground for common mode
6. Single Faraday-shielded isolation transformer, ground for differential mode
7. Double-shielded isolation transformer, ground for each mode

8. Triple-shielded isolation transformer, ground outside shields for input-output differential mode and inside shield for common mode
9. Motor generator set (no EMI hardening)
10. Motor generator set (EMI hardening)
11. Uninterruptible power supply
12. Unknown

If **Unknown** is selected, then the above is skipped and the reader proceeds to either the interposed radiated barrier below or directly to Section 2.4, as applicable.

If other than item no. 12 above is selected, the next selection is:

Identify the following (answer one of the three):

1. Detailed performance (enter minimums in table below)
2. General performance:
   Cutoff frequency in kHz
   Stop-band slope in dB/decade
   Minimum attenuation three decades above cutoff
3. Unknown

Frequency	Common-Mode Atten. in dB	Differential-Mode Atten. in dB
0 to 1 kHz		
1 to 30 kHz		
30 kHz to 1 MHz		
1 to 100 MHz		
0.1 to 1 GHz		
Above 1 GHz		

If 3, **Unknown**, is selected concerning barrier performance, default data are used as explained in Chapter 4.

The following decisions involve the use of a shielded room enclosure or building for radiated electromagnetic ambient environments:

Identify the Shielded Barriers Between Outside Area Ambients and Victim:

1. Formal (manufactured) shielded enclosure (screen room)
2. Shielded hut, tank, ship or aerospace vehicular skin
3. Homemade shielded enclosure
4. Building: girder type
5. Building: steel shell type (Quonset™, Butler or hangar)
6. Building: nonmetallic type
7. Unknown

If **Unknown**, no shielded barrier is assumed, and the user should proceed directly to Section 2.4. If other than item no. 7 is selected, the next procedure is:

Give minimum shielding performances to magnetic fields for near fields and to plane waves for far fields (enter in table below) and **reference distance between EMI sources and victim in meters.***

Frequency	Shielding Effectiveness in dB
0 to 400 Hz	
0.4 to 30 kHz	
30 kHz to 1 MHz	
1 to 100 MHz	
0.1 to 1 GHZ	
Above 1 GHz	

Reference distance choice:

1. 0.3 m per MIL-STD-285 or 1 m per MIL-Std 461 susceptibility tests
2. _____ m
3. Unknown

---

*The near-field to far-field interface exists at distance R, of $\lambda/2\pi$ (λ = wavelength) meters or at R = $48/f_{MHz}$ (where f_{MHz} = frequency in MHz).

2.22

If **Unknown** or variable, default data are selected as explained in the next section.

For the purpose of the ongoing illustrative example in Fig. 2.6, no conducted or radiated ambient barrier is assumed to be used at this time.

2.4 Defining the Electromagnetic Ambient

EMI malfunctions, crashes or degradation can take place if a potentially hostile electromagnetic ambient environment influences the victim.* The ambient may contain conducted and radiated emissions which penetrate the victim by one or more coupling modes (see Sections 1.3 and 1.4). This section presents questions necessary to define the electromagnetic ambient. Figure 2.9 serves to remind the reader about the overall flow diagram and wherein the electromagnetic ambient fits.

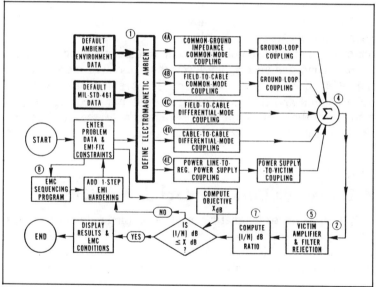

Figure 2.9—Defining the Electromagnetic Ambient

---

*It is assumed that the victim works properly in an electromagnetically quiet ambient, i.e., does not self-jam.

2.4.1 One or Many Emission Sources

This handbook describes the methodology for treating one emission source and a number of different coupling modes simultaneously. The user can, of course, resolve the EMI problem (if one exists) each time for a different emission source. Because the EMC design or EMI fix is likely to be different for each emission source, how does one select a design or fix to accommodate all simultaneous emission sources?

Using that combination which includes OR-gating, the results for each individual design or fix will result in an overdesign condition. By AND-gating the results corresponding to each emission source, an underdesign condition will develop. Between these two extremes, the best design will unfold. While the answer lies in optimization techniques which are beyond the scope of this handbook, a few clues are here summarized.

One procedure for selecting a single design or fix for multiple emission sources is to begin by OR-gating all results corresponding to each source. After this is done, select the fix which was used the least number of times; remove it and check to see if EMI-free operation still exists for all emission sources. If so, then select and remove the next least-employed fix and continue the procedure until an EMI condition once again develops from one or more sources. If an EMI condition developed after the first removal, the fix should be reinstated and the second fix removed and checked. The remainder of the presentation in this section addresses itself to any single emission source acting at one time.

2.4.2 Power Line Conducted Ambients

Undesired electromagnetic energy is coupled onto power mains either by differential-mode or common-mode means, or both. This is shown in Fig. 2.10. At this point it may be helpful to define both classifications and describe some common examples of power line noise.

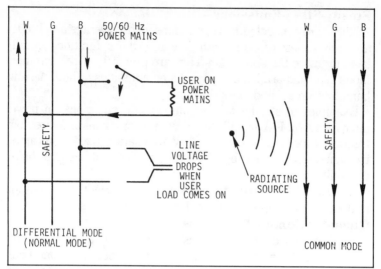

Figure 2.10—Differential-Mode and Common-Mode Currents on Power Mains

Differential-Mode Currents

In a two-wire* line, the **intentional** current is (or should be) of equal amplitude and opposite in phase. This applies to all power mains and signal transmission cables. The **unintentional** EMI current is also differential-mode when the current in each wire is equal and opposite. Sometimes the differential mode is referred to as the **normal mode**.

Common-Mode Currents

In a two-wire line, the **unintentional** EMI current in each wire is more or less of equal amplitude and is in phase. The degree of line amplitude balance usually increases with frequency. Sometimes the common mode is referred to as the **longitudinal mode**.

The undesired conducted emissions† on the power lines may be defined as steady state, quasi-stationary or transient. Their definitions are somewhat arbitrary and involve mostly amplitude and time duration as the distinguishing factors.

---

*In a four-wire, three/phase system, the individual phase currents are usually not equal but should total zero when added as vectors with the unbalance current in the neutral wire.

†These same categories apply for radiated emissions also.

Steady-State Emissions

These are conducted EMI emissions whose average amplitudes are more or less constant with time and whose duration typically lasts for more than one hour. They are primarily of the common-mode type and originate from radiated emissions of both narrow-band and broadband classification.

Examples of steady-state, common-mode emissions on power mains are AM, FM and TV broadcast transmissions and most low-frequency navigation signals. They are characterized by a carrier frequency modulated by the type of licensed service being transmitted.

An example of a **broadband** steady-state, conducted emission is fluorescent lamp noise picked up by power lines.

Quasi-Stationary Emissions

These are conducted emissions whose average amplitudes vary with time over an interval ranging from one second to one hour. They are both of the common-mode and differential-mode types.

The **common-mode** type originates from some of the licensed transmitters such as land mobile radio, air-to-ground communications, citizen's band and amateur radio, walkie-talkies and the like. Their time durations generally last from a few seconds to a few minutes or the time necessary for people to communicate. Some common-mode conducted emissions having these time durations also originate from fluorescent lamps, RF stabilized arc welders and diathermy equipment radiations whose operational cycles may be a few minutes.

The **differential-mode** type of conducted emissions originate primarily from other users on the same power mains. They are usually preceded or terminated by a transient (see below). Examples include any source operated for a short period of time such as motor-operated machine shop equipment, ultrasonic cleaners and electric shavers.

Some of the above quasi-stationary emission sources develop both common-mode and differential-mode noise as a result of both radiated and conducted emissions, respectively. As the frequency increases, the common-mode component tends to predominate because of cable pickup efficiency from radiations and because of both inductive and capacitive coupling between the wires of a cable.

Transient Emissions

These are conducted emissions whose amplitudes vary substantially with time. Their durations, measured at the 50 percent height, are less than 1 s. In the case of a turn-on or turn-off transient associated with the above quasi-stationary emissions, the rise or fall time intervals are defined to be less than 1 s.

Transient durations range from about 1 ns to 1 s and more generally occupy durations of the order of 1 μs (default value). While power line transient statistics are scarce in EMC literature, it is believed that those having rise or fall times of less than 10 ns exist for less than one percent of the samples. (The International Special Committee on Radio Interference, CISPR, defines a **click** as a transient or burst of transients whose total duration does not exceed 200 ms.)

Transients are produced by both poor voltage regulation on a power bus as well as by capacitive inrush currents during line loading, and inductive voltage back EMF during load disconnects. As indicated above, they produce predominately differential-mode emissions.

At higher frequencies, however, the common-mode component increases due to both capacitive coupling to the line and radiation from the power cord from other sources.

2.4.2.1 Emission Source Identification

The first procedure for electromagnetic ambient identification is:

Identify the emission source (select one or more, as applicable):

1. Radiated from licensed transmitters
2. Radiated from broadband, man-made source
3. Conducted emissions on power mains
4. Unknown

Since the present topic involves conducted emissions only, no. 3 and no. 4 apply. Radiated emission sources (responses of 1 and 2) will be discussed in a later section.

When no. 3 is selected, the next choice is:

Select the applicable conducted emission type:

1. Steady-state (duration $\geqslant$ 1 hr), common-mode narrowband
2. Steady-state, common-mode broadband
3. Steady-state, unknown
4. Quasi-stationary (duration < 1 hr and $\geqslant$ 1 s), common-mode narrowband
5. Quasi-stationary, common-mode broadband
6. Quasi-stationary, differential-mode narrowband
7. Quasi-stationary, differential-mode broadband
8. Quasi-stationary, unknown
9. Transient (duration < 1 s), common-mode
10. Transient, differential-mode
11. Transient, unknown
12. Unknown

The following questions involve defining the amplitudes of the conducted emission and either its frequency and bandwidth or pulse duration and rise time, as applicable. Since any or all of these may be unknown, it is necessary to supply default values.

For narrowband emissions (selections 1, 4 and 6), the next three questions are:

What is amplitude in volts?

What is carrier frequency in megahertz?

What is bandwidth in kilohertz?

For broadband (non-transient, choices 2, 5 and 7), the next item of business is:

Identify the maximum spectrum density in the indicated portions of the frequency band.

In the following table, enter the actual spectrum density in the appropriate blank, or use the suggested default.

Frequency	Spectrum Density	Suggested Default
1 to 30 kHz	_____ dBμV/kHz	70 dBμV/kHz
30 kHz to 1 MHz	_____ dBμV/kHz	50 dBμV/kHz
1 to 30 MHz	_____ dBμV/MHz	100 dBμV/MHz
30 MHz to 1 GHZ	_____ dBμV/MHz	100 dBμV/MHz

For transients (selections 9 and 10), the next three questions are:

What is peak amplitude in volts?

What is transient duration (50 percent height) in microseconds?

What is transient rise time in microseconds?

When the conducted emission ambient data are unknown (choices 3, 8, 11 and 12), a default option exists:

Select the desired default option:

1. MIL-STD-461, conducted susceptibility narrowband
2. MIL-STD-461, conducted transient susceptibility
3. IEEE-STD-472 or IEEE-STD-587, conducted transient susceptibility
4. IEC-801/4, conducted transient susceptibility

2.4.3 Safety and Ground Plane Ambients

For shock safety hazard protection, nearly all metal box cases, cabinets, racks and housings are to be grounded to a ground plane (a ship's metal deck, aircraft skin or other vehicular enclosure). Most industrial, commercial and consumer applications do not have a metal ground plane and therefore use a safety wire. This wire is sometimes called the "green wire." The conducted electromagnetic ambients on either the ground plane or safety wire, as applicable, are to be identified in this section because they develop common-mode voltage differences between two or more equipments or systems connected thereto.

Statements from the preceding section defining the electro-magnetic ambient on power mains also apply here. One exception is that the distinction between the differential and common modes is not applicable because only one ground plane or one safety wire is involved. A second possible exception applies when the potential difference between two ground points is not measured. For this case, the safety ground current flow, I_g, is measured with an RF current probe.

The potential difference, V_i, between two boxes which are connected to the safety wire is simply:

$$V_i = ZI_g \tag{2.14}$$

where,

Z = RF impedance of safety wire as defined in Chapter 5

When a safety ground plane is used, the potential difference may also be indirectly obtained with the use of a surface current probe. If the surface probe is used to measure the entire surface current, I_s, by totaling individual currents across the ground plane, (orthogonal to a line connecting the two ground boxes), the result is:

$$V_i = \int_0^l E \times ds = El \text{ for } l \ll \lambda \tag{2.15}$$

$$= lJ/\sigma \tag{2.16}$$

$$= lI_s/A\sigma \tag{2.17}$$

where,

E = tangential ambient electric field strength in volts per meter

l = distance between the two ground boxes in meters

J = current-density vector I_s = total surface current in amps

2.30

A = cross sectional area of ground plane in meters squared orthogonal to l, = tw

t = ground plane thickness or skin depth in m, whichever is less

w = width of ground plane in m

σ = ground plane conductivity in mhos per meter

= 5.8 x 10^7 mhos/m for copper

= 3.6 x 10^7 mhos/m for aluminum

= 10^7 mhos/m for steel

Note that V_i can be directly estimated from Eq. (2.15) if E is known (see Section 2.4.5). Alternatively, V_i can be computed from Eq. (2.17), which is listed in Table 2.1.

Table 2.1 - Potential Difference between Two-Box Ground Points in an Aluminum Ground Plane

A/l Ratio	V_i in dBμV*	A/l Ratio	V_i in dBμV*
10^{-6} cm	9 + I_sdBμA	0.001	−51 + I_sdBμA
3 × 10^{-6} cm	−1 + I_sdBμA	0.003	−61 + I_sdBμA
10^{-5} cm	−11 + I_sdBμA	0.01	−71 + I_sdBμA
3 × 10^{-5} cm	−21 + I_sdBμA	0.03	−81 + I_sdBμA
10^{-4} cm	−31 + I_sdBμA	0.1	−91 + I_sdBμA
3 × 10^{-4} cm	−41 + I_sdBμA	0.3	−101 + I_sdBμA
*The number is computed from 20 log(l/Aσ)			

2.4.4 Radiated Ambients

All electronic equipments exist in electromagnetic ambient radiated fields, and the interaction with such fields determines equipment or circuit susceptibility. Thus, knowledge of a local radiated electromagnetic ambient environment, in both amplitude and frequency, is mandatory for evaluating the possibility of susceptibility for a given equipment.

Radiated electromagnetic ambients originate from three principal sources:

1. Natural sources such as lightning, atmospherics and electrostatics
2. Licensed and other transmitters
3. Broadband, man-made sources such as from gasoline engines, electric ignition systems, overhead power lines and motor-operated equipment

2.4.4.1 Lightning

A lightning stroke has highly variable characteristics which range in current values from 10,000 to over 200,000 A. In an attempt to quantify one of the more severe strokes, the upper decile (10 percent probability of being exceeded) is selected:

> Path length: 3 km
> Stroke duration: 20 μs
> Potential difference: 300 MV
> Stroke rise time: 0.5 μs
> Current: 100,000 A
> Flux density: see below

The resultant magnetic field strength or magnetic flux density is of importance because of the high current levels of a lightning stroke.

The magnetic flux density, B, from a lightning stroke is computed as follows:

$$B = \mu H = 4\pi \times 10^{-7} \times (I/2\pi R) \quad \text{tesla} \qquad (2.18)$$

$$= 2 \times 10^{-3} \, I/R \quad \text{gauss} \qquad (2.19)$$

where,

μ = permeability of air in henries per meter

I = stroke current in amperes

R = distance from stroke in meters

Table 2.2 lists the magnetic flux density from the above 100 kA lightning stroke as a function of distance and frequency. The first row entry (**Peak Stroke dBG***) is a listing of B in units of dBG (decibels above one gauss) as obtained from Eq. (2.19). The second row entry (**Peak Stroke dBG****) is to be used for those coupling mechanisms which increase at 20 dB per decade. The remaining entries in Table 2.2 (beginning with **dc to 17 kHz**) are the spectral densities at the indicated frequency in units of dBG/kHz (decibels above 1 gauss per kilohertz). Primarily, this is of value in computing EMI to receivers having a center tuned frequency at the indicated spectral frequency range.

Table 2.2—Magnetic-Flux Density from 100 kA Lightning Stroke

Strike Distance	Magnetic-Flux Density in dBG/kHz										
	3m	5m	10m	20m	30m	50m	100m	200m	300m	500m	1km
Peak Stroke* dB Gauss	36	22	26	20	16	12	6	0	−4	−8	−14
Stroke** dB G	32	28	22	16	12	8	2	−4	−8	−12	−18
Spectrum Frequency											
dc-17 kHz	8	4	−2	−8	−12	−16	−22	−28	−32	−36	−42
20 kHz	6	2	−4	−10	−14	−18	−24	−30	−34	−38	−44
30 kHz	3	−1	−7	−13	−17	−21	−27	−33	−37	−41	−47
50 kHz	−2	−6	−12	−18	−22	−26	−32	−38	−42	−46	−52
70 kHz	−5	−9	−15	−21	−25	−29	−35	−41	−45	−49	−55
100 kHz	−8	−12	−18	−24	−28	−32	−38	−44	−48	−52	−58
150 kHz	−11	−15	−21	−27	−31	−35	−41	−47	−51	−55	−61
200 kHz	−14	−18	−24	−30	−34	−38	−44	−50	−54	−58	−64
300 kHz	−17	−21	−27	−33	−37	−41	−47	−53	−57	−61	−67
500 kHz	−22	−26	−32	−38	−42	−46	−52	−58	−62	−66	−72
700 kHz	−26	−30	−36	−42	−46	−50	−56	−62	−66	−70	−76
1 MHz	−32	−36	−42	−48	−52	−56	−62	−68	−72	−76	−82
1.5 MHz	−39	−43	−49	−55	−59	−63	−69	−75	−79	−83	−89
2 MHz	−44	−47	−54	−60	−64	−67	−74	−80	−84	−87	−94
3 MHz	−51	−55	−61	−67	−71	−75	−81	−87	−91	−95	−101
5 MHz	−60	−64	−70	−76	−80	−84	−90	−96	−100	−104	−110
7 MHz	−66	−70	−76	−82	−86	−90	−96	−102	−106	−110	−116
10 MHz	−72	−76	−82	−88	−92	−96	−102	−108	−112	−116	−122
15 MHz	−79	−83	−89	−95	−99	−103	−109	−115	−119	−123	−129
20 MHz	−84	−87	−94	−100	−104	−107	−114	−120	−124	−127	−134
30 MHz	−91	−95	−101	−107	−111	−115	−121	−127	−131	−135	−141
50 MHz	−100	−104	−110	−116	−120	−124	−130	−136	−140	−144	−150
70 MHz	−106	−110	−116	−122	−126	−130	−136	−142	−146	−150	−156
100 MHz	−112	−116	−122	−128	−132	−136	−142	−148	−152	−156	−162

Since the best known parameter with lightning is current, the associated field is generally expressed by its magnetic term in A/m,

Gauss or Tesla. This reflects the fact that within the most threatening radius of a stroke (100 m) most of the spectrum is in near-field conditions, where the H-field is most prejudiciable. The lightning radiation can nevertheless be expressed by its equivalent (fictitious) E-field, using the free-space impedance of 120π ohms:

$$E_{equiv} = \frac{I}{2\pi R} \times 120\ \pi = \frac{I}{R} \times 60$$

Illustrative Example 2.2

What is the electromagnetic ambient from a 100 kA lightning stroke 100 m away? From Table 2.2, the stroke produces a magnetic flux density of 6 dBG or 2 gauss.

Illustrative Example 2.3

For each of two victims, determine the electromagnetic ambient from a 100 kA lightning stroke 100 m away when it is known that the coupling mechanism is a cable. The victims are:

1. A high-speed logic device
2. An analog amplifier having a 100 Hz bandwidth

Since logic has a bandwidth much greater than 640 kHz (the second corner frequency of the stroke), Table 2.2 indicates that the stroke produces a magnetic flux density electromagnetic ambient of 6 dBG. Be sure to use 640 kHz when computing the coupling into cables and ground loops.

For the 100 Hz bandwidth analog amplifier, the electromagnetic ambient B is now 2 dBG, but be sure to use 100 Hz when computing the coupling into ground loops and cables.

Illustrative Example 2.4

What is the electromagnetic ambient from a 100 kA lightning stroke 100 m away when the victim is an AM broadcast receiver tuned to 1 MHz? From Table 2.2, the stroke produces a magnetic flux spectral density of −62 dBG/kHz around 1 MHz.

2.4.4.2 Radiated Ambients from Licensed Transmitters

The power density, P_D, from a transmitter producing an effective radiated power, ERP, in watts is:

$$P_D = ERP/4\pi R^2 \qquad (2.20)$$

where,

ERP = transmitter power, P_T, if the antenna is isotropic

ERP = $P_T \times$ antenna gain, if antenna is other than isotropic

R = transmitter-to-victim distance in meters

The electric field strength in the far-field for line-of-sight conditions is:

$$E = \sqrt{P_D Z_W} \qquad (2.21)$$

where,

$$z = \text{wave impedance} = 120\pi = 377 \; \Omega$$

When Eq. (2.21) is substituted into Eq. (2.20), there results:

$$E(V/m) = 1/R\sqrt{30 \; ERP} \qquad (2.22)$$

Figure 2.11 depicts the maximum allowable ERP (the sum of peak power in dBm and antenna gain in dB) for licensed transmitters in North America. (These values can also be considered typical for other countries. In some countries maximum values are 10 to 30 times higher for some services, representing a +10 to +15 dB deviation compared to the typical average case.) When these values are substituted into Eq. (2.22) and plotted, Fig. 2.12 results. This figure is a convenient graph to determine maximum electric field strength given the type of service and the distance away.

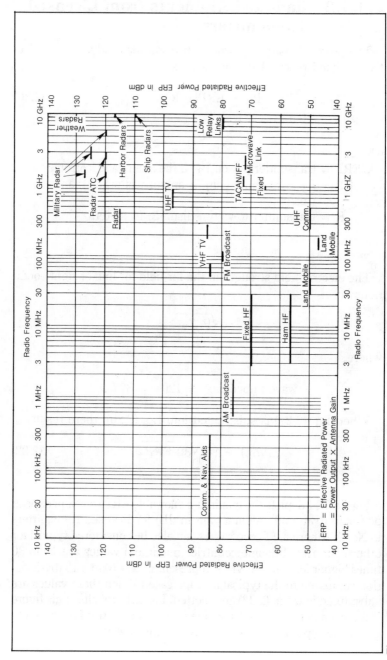

Figure 2.11—North American Frequency Allocation and Maximum ERPs for Some Licensed Transmitters (must be regarded as average values in some other countries)

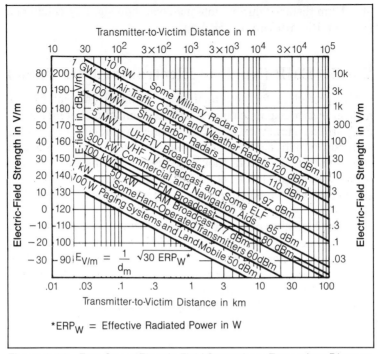

Figure 2.12—Free-Space Electric Field Strength vs. Transmitter Distance and ERP

2.4.4.3 Composite Ambient Environments

Single applications of Figs. 2.11 and 2.12 will provide information regarding approximate field strength value of any signal at any location providing the location of the transmitter is known, or at least its distance from the point at which the ambient is being evaluated. Successive applications are required to provide a total amplitude versus frequency plot for all signals that may exist at the site where evaluation is required.

Illustrative Example 2.5

Determine the electric field strength in the open from an FM transmitter 50 m away and from an ATC radar 1 km away.

From Fig. 2.2, for a 100 kW ERP FM broadcast transmitter 50 m away, the electric field strength in the main beam is 30 V/m. For an ATC radar having a 120 dBm ERP output, the field strength at a 1 km distance during antenna-beam boresighting conditions is about 164 dBμV/m = 158 V/m.

2.4.5   EMP (Nuclear Electromagnetic Pulse)

The procedure for determining the radiated ambient from a nuclear electromagnetic pulse is basically similar to that for a lightning stroke. However EMP is generally regarded as a twofold scenario: low altitude burst and exo-atmospheric burst. For the first case, the generated field should decrease with distance, but the primary effects of the weapon (blast, heat, ionizing radiations) are so intense that the electromagnetic threat is often considered as secondary.

For the high-altitude or exo-atmospheric burst, distance does not enter into the problem since the E- and H-fields are quasi-constant over a huge territory. Key parameters are rise time and pulse duration, which are much shorter than for lightning. Table 2.3 gives the spectrum densities corresponding to a "standard" EMP with q rise time of 5 ns and a 50 percent height duration of 250 ns.

2.4.6 Radiated Ambients Inside Buildings

The electric field strength computed from Eq. (2.22) and depicted in Fig. 2.12 corresponds to radiated ambients out in the open. What would be the field strength if a building existed at the measurement site instead of open spaces? What attenuation is offered by a building? If the radiated emission originates from within the building, the attenuation offered by the building skin or facade is not relevant. However, if the electromagnetic radiation originates from outside the building, such as from a licensed transmitter, the attenuations offered by both the skin facade and girders are pertinent.

Figure 2.13 illustrates the natural shielding attenuation offered by girdered buildings with facades of brick, concrete, stone and glass. Only the girders significantly contribute to reflection loss. From the figure, note that the attenuation is relatively low in the 30 MHz to 300 MHz portion of the spectrum where the center-to-center separation of the girders is of the order of $\lambda/2$. Also note that the attenuation at lower frequencies is significant for the E-

Table 2.3—EMP Spectrum Densities

Topic	Units	Value	10 kHz	100 kHz	1 MHz	10 MHz	100 MHz	1 GHz	10 GHz
Coverage dBHz	Hz	20 log (Hz)	3-30 kHz 88	30-300 kHz 108	0.3-3 MHz 128	3-30 MHz 148	30-300 MHz 168	0.3-3 GHz 188	3-30 GHz 208
EMP	dBV/m/Hz	$2A_r$ + Slope	-32	-32	-34	-50	-80	-120	-160
EMP	dBV/m	Above value + dBHz	56	76	94	98	88	68	48

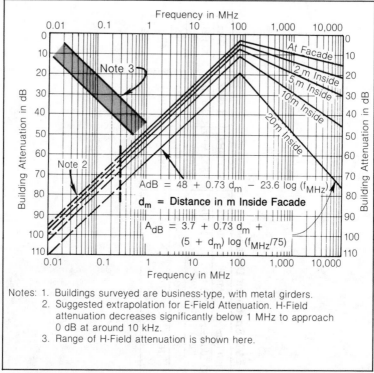

Figure 2.13—Building Attenuation to Outside Radiated Emissions vs. Frequency and Distance inside Facade

field and corresponds to a frequency dependent slope of about 20 dB/decade.

Unfortunately, for long wavelengths, some of the ambient transmitters become near-field sources (see Volume 3 of this series), and the H-field attenuation becomes rather mediocre.

If the building has no metal framework, the attenuation below VHF is virtually nil.

2.4.7 Radiated Ambients Underground

Earth and water offer natural attenuation to electromagnetic radiation and ambients. This attenuation may be calculated directly from the skin depth of various lands and waters:

$$A_{dB} = 8.686 \ t/\delta \tag{2.23}$$

$$= 8.686 \ t\sqrt{\pi f \mu \sigma} \tag{2.24}$$

$$= 131.43 \ t_{mm}\sqrt{f_{MHz}\mu_r\sigma_r} \tag{2.25}$$

where,

t = thickness or depth of earth below surface

t_{mm} = thickness in millimeters

f = frequency in hertz

f_{MHz} = frequency in megahertz

μ = permeability of earth in henries per meter

μ_r = permeability of earth or water relative to copper

σ = conductivity of earth or water in mhos per meter

σ_r = conductivity of earth relative to copper

δ = skin depth in mm

Table 2.4 presents the depth of earth below surface corresponding to an attenuation of one skin depth (8.7 dB) and 11.5 skin depths (100 dB). These depths are rated for four different earth crusts:

1. Desert land
2. Average land
3. Marsh land
4. Sea water at 50/60 Hz, 400 Hz, 1 kHz, 100 kHz, 10 MHz and 1 GHz

Table 2.4—Natural Absorption Loss of Water & Land

	Desert $\sigma=0.011$ mho/m		Average Land $\sigma = 0.03$ mho/m		Marsh Land $\sigma=0.111$ mho/m		Sea Water $\sigma =$ mho/m	
	8.7 dB	100 dB	8.7 dB	100 dB	8.7 dB	100 dB	8.7 dB	100 dB
FREQUENCY								
50 to 60 Hz	647 m	7.5 km	392 m	4.5 km	205 m	2.4 km	30 m	349 m
400 Hz	239 m	2.7 km	145 m	1. 7 km	76 m	874 m	11 m	130 m
1 kHz	152 m	1.7 km	92 m	1.1 km	48 m	552 m	7.1 m	82 m
100 kHz	15 m	175 m	9 m	106 m	4.8 m	55 m	71 cm	8.2 m
10 MHz	1.5 m	17.5 m	92 cm	11 m	48 cm	5.5 m	7.1 cm	82 cm
1 GHZ	15 cm	1.75 m	9 cm	1.1 m	5 cm	55 cm	7.1 mm	8 cm

Illustrative Example 2.6

Calculate the electric field strength at a distance of 1 km from a 10 kW, 100 kHz Loran D transmitter having an antenna gain of 1.6. Also determine the field strength 10 m underground for marsh land.

From Fig. 2.12, the field strength above ground at 1 km corresponding to an ERP of 16 kW is −3 dBV/m (0.7 V/m). By interpolation from Table 2.4, the attenuation 10 m underground is 10 m/4.8 m = 2.08 skin depths × 8.7 dB = 18 dB. Thus, the field strength 10 m underground is −3 dBV/m − 18 dB = −21 dBV/m = 89 mV/m.

2.4.8 Broadband Radiated Ambients from Man-Made Noise

Broadband electromagnetic ambients can also originate from many man-made devices. Some examples include electrical appliances, power tools, fluorescent lamps, motor vehicle ignition systems, overhead power transmission and distribution lines, electrified railways, industrial scientific and medical devices. More details are available from a paper by J.R. Herman, "The Radio Noise Environment in Near Space: A Review" (see bibliography).

If no discrete broadband data are available, default data may be used. Figure 2.14 illustrates one form of such default data corresponding to the media incidental, man-made noise located near the earth's surface. The amplitude is in units of broadband electric field strength, viz., dBμV/m/kHz. The data are divided into three concrete areas centered about large metropolitan areas:

1. A 16 km radius of the inner urban zone
2. An annular ring from 16 to 50 km, corresponding to the suburban zone
3. A rural zone extending beyond 50 km

Some measure of the standard deviation about the median is indicated for each of the three zones. The lack of continuity of data above 10 MHz with corresponding zones below 20 MHz is due to different measurement equipments in which vertical polarization is used below VHF and horizontal polarization is used at and above VHF. Thus, the dash lines should be used from 1 MHz to 100 MHz

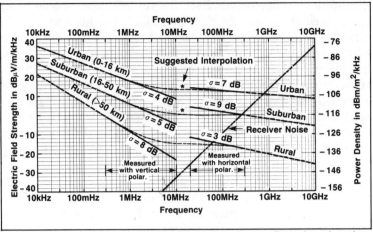

Figure 2.14—Median Incidental Man-Made Noise Based on Lossless Omnidirectional Antenna near the Earth's Surface

for interpolation. For reference, typical receiver sensitivity (sensitivity = noise) is also shown, corresponding to an isotropic pickup antenna (antenna gain G = 0 dB). This allows converting receiver sensitivity into an equivalent field intensity.

Illustrative Example 2.7

Identify the default electromagnetic ambient in urban areas at 30 MHz which exceeds 5 percent of the locations.

From Fig. 2.14, the median ambient at 30 MHz is 14 dBμV/m/kHz and the standard deviation is 7 dB. For a log-normal distribution, 5 percent of the locations corresponds to 1.65 σ (see Fig. 3.7 in Chapter 3) or 11.6 dB. Thus, the urban ambient default situation is about 14 dBμV/m/kHz + 12 dB or 26 dBμV/m/kHz.

2.5 Identifying the EMC Design and Retrofit Constraints

EMI hardening can be practiced at any time during the life cycle of a product, equipment or system. This span ranges from the conceptual stage to the retrofit of an older operating equipment in an existing installation. Generally, cost and performance considerations favor EMI hardening as early in the cycle as possible. Thus, the identification of appropriate EMC fixes or techniques should be accomplished at the earliest possible stage in the life cycle.

Some examples will serve to clarify the above. First, what viable options exist in EMI hardening during the design stages of an equipment or system versus the operating installation stage? In the design stage, attention tends to be focused more on the **internals** of an equipment or system in contrast to its **externals**, which are considered after installation. For example, during design, EMI hardening using balanced circuits, floating PCB or PCB assembly **grounds**, optical isolation, audio-rectification filters or by isolating a shield box within a shield box can be economically achieved. However, this usually cannot be done after installation, when it is more common to apply external options such as shielded rooms, isolating motor-generator sets, Faraday-shielded isolation transformers and filters in the power mains, and cable harness location and routing.

Other considerations on EMI hardening constraints covered in this section include the platform type and location (e.g., space vehicle or office building), duration of life cycle and subjective management constraints.

2.5.1 Design vs. Field Installation Stage

Table 2.5 summarizes general constraints which may typify allowable EMI fixes in the two principal stages of the life cycle of an equipment or system. In reviewing the list, it is acknowledged that some readers may disagree with the constraints on the life cycle stage because of their peculiar or special situations. This notwithstanding, it is important to identify and determine the options available in EMI hardening, whatever the stage. This does not imply that any or all options will be either needed or used; however, high visibility of the available options is paramount to sound EMC engineering.

Table 2.5—General Applicability of EMI-Hardening Fix

EMI Hardening Fix	Design Stage	Installation Stage	Relative Cost
External EM Ambient (Culprit) Sources			
Use Formal Shielded Enclosure	No	Yes	Very High
Apply Limited Wall/Floor/Ceiling Shielding	No	Yes	High
Victim Box Housings & Internals:			
Filter Inside Amplifier or Logic	Yes	No	Very Low
Filter Input to Amplifier or Logic	Yes	Sometimes	Low
Float PCB or Assembly Grounds	Yes	Rare	Very Low
Use Balanced Circuits	Yes	No	Low
Use Optical Isolators	Yes	No	Low
Use Isolation Transformers (Control/Data Lines)	Yes	Rare	Medium
Use Power-Line Isolation Transformers	Yes	Sometimes	Medium
Filter Input to Power Mains	Yes	Usually	Medium
Float Internal Shielded Box within a Box	Yes	Rare	Medium
Shield Box Housing	Yes	Sometimes	Medium
Connections to Box Housings:			
Control Routing of Interconnecting Cables	No	Usually	Low
Float Metal Box Housings	No	Sometimes	Very Low
Float Housings via R-F Inductor	Rare	Yes	Low
Float with Inductor and Board Cabinets	Rare	Yes	Low
Use Twisted-Wire Interconnecting Cables	Yes	Sometimes	Very Low
Use Grounded Braided Cable Shields	Yes	Sometimes	Medium
Control Grounding/Ungrounding of Shields	No	Yes	Low
Use Fiber-Optic Interconnecting Cables	Yes	No	Medium
Use DC-to-DC Converters (Isolators)	Sometimes	Sometimes	Medium

2.5.2 Relative EMI Hardening Costs

The range of costs of the different EMI hardening components or techniques is broad. This fact alone may act as a constraint in identifying which to use for many applications, e.g., inexpensive consumer products. Some techniques not only cost nothing but may even reduce costs, e.g., floating PCB assembly-to-box grounds versus grounding them. Other EMI hardening costs may become very high, relatively speaking. For example, a shielded enclosure to house a medical operating room may exceed $100,000.

The last column entry in Table 2.5 attempts to suggest a relative cost quantification which can act as a constraint in identifying viable EMI hardening components and techniques. The list is by no means complete but indicates the considerations with which the design or field service engineer may be confronted.

2.5.3 Platform Type and Location

The use of the word **platform** here is obtained from the military sector, but it aptly describes the external housings and locations of the overall equipment or system, whether military or industrial, commercial or consumer. To a degree, it defines the maximum electromagnetic ambient environment to which an equipment or system is likely to be exposed. Recognizing that there are many exceptions, Table 2.6 attempts to crudely quantify this maximum radiated ambient.

Some platforms are weight critical, while weight is of little consequence for others. This factor may affect the applicability of shielded enclosures, power line filters, isolation transformers, harness shields and the like in a given situation. Table 2.4 also lists a rather crude quantification of the weight penalties versus platform type or location.

**Table 2.6—Some Principal Platforms Where Equipment
and/or Systems May Be Located**

Platform Identification	Maximum Ambient	Weight Penalties
Orbiting Spacecraft	Low	Very High
Spacecraft Outside Earth's Orbit	Very Low	Very High
Launch Vehicle	High	High
Military Aircraft in Flight	High	High
Military Aircraft, Penetration Run	Very High	High
Helicopter in Flight	High	High
Helicopter Landing on Frigate	Very High	High
Commercial Aircraft	Medium	High
Truck and Automobiles, Commercial	High	Medium
Truck and Automobiles, Military	Very High	Medium
Tanks and Half Treads	Very High	Medium
Military Ship or Frigate Above Deck	Very High	Low
Military Ship or Frigate Below Deck	Medium	Low
Submarine	Low	Low
Heavy Industry	High	Very Low
Light Industry	Medium	Very Low
Shopping Centers and Malls	Medium	Very Low
Schools	Medium	Very Low
Airports	High	Very Low
Commercial Office Building, Upper Floors	High	Very Low
Commercial Office Building, Lower Floors	Medium	Very Low
Residential, High Rise	Medium	Very Low
Residential, Detached Houses	Low	Very Low
Receiving Antenna Farm	Very Low	Very Low

2.6 Bibliography

Adams, J.W.; Kanda, M.; Shafer, J.; and Wu, Y., "Near-Field Electric Field Strength Levels of EM Environments Applicable to Automotive Systems," *IEEE EMC Symposium Record* (New York: IEEE), Session 5B, Seattle, Washington, August 2-4, 1977.

Baran, D.E., "Prediction of Relative Available Noise Power for Vehicular Ignition Noise," *IEEE EMC Symposium Record* (New York: IEEE), Session V-C, Atlanta, Georgia. June 20-22, 1978.

Baum, C.E., "The Use of Topology as a Means of Subdividing Complex Electromagnetic Scatterers and Controlling the Entry of Electromagnetic Energy," *IEEE EMC Symposium Record* (New York: IEEE), Session IV-A, Atlanta, Georgia. June 20-22, 1978.

Bensema, W.D., "Amplitude, Time and Frequency Statistics of Quasi-Impulsive Noise," Second Symposium and Technical Exhibition, Session 2, Montreux, Switzerland, June 28-30, 1977.

Bolton, E.C., "Comparative Statistics of Atmospheric Radio Noise and Man-Made Radio Noise Below HF Band," Second Symposium and Technical Exhibition, Session L, Montreux, Switzerland, June 28-30, 1977.

Bolton, E.C., "Man-Made Noise Study at 76 and 200 kHz," *IEEE Transactions on EMC*, Volume EMC-18, Number 3. August, 1976.

Bridges, J.E., "Biological Influences of Power Line Fields and Switchyard Environments," *IEEE EMC Symposium Record* (New York: IEEE), Session 4-A, Washington, DC, July 13-15, 1976.

Bridges, J.E.; Frazier, M.J.; and Houser, R.G., "Internal Body Potentials and Currents from ELF Electric Fields and Household Appliances," *IEEE Electromagnetic Symposium Record* (New York: IEEE), Session IV-B, Atlanta, Georgia, June 20-22, 1978.

Bronaugh, E.L.; Kerns, D.R.; and McGinnis, W.M., "Electromagnetic Emission From Typical Citizen's Band Mobile Radio Installations in Three Size Vehicles," *IEEE EMC Symposium Record* (New York: IEEE), Session II-C, Atlanta, Georgia, June 20-22, 1978.

Chapman, J.C., "Transient Radiation From Digital Signals on Transmission Lines," *IEEE EMC Symposium Record* (New York: IEEE), Session 4B-2, Washington, DC, July 13-15, 1976.

Chowdhuri, P., "Study of Transient Voltages in Transit Systems," *IEEE Transactions on EMC*, Volume EMC-17, Number 3. August, 1975.

Das Gupta, P.C. and Schulz, J., "Interference in Telephone Circuits Due to Thyristor-Controlled DC Traction," Electromagnetic Compatibility 1977, Second Symposium and Technical Exhibition, Session F, Montreux, Switzerland, June 28-30, 1977.

Duff, W.G.; Polisky, L.E.; and Whitehouse, R.E., "Airborne Electromagnetic Environment Survey," *IEEE EMC Symposium Record* (New York: IEEE), Session 2B-1, Washington, DC, July 13-15, 1976.

Egidi, C.; Galliano, P.G.; and Nano, E., "Ignition Noise Interference on Short Waves," Second Symposium and Technical Exhibition, Session E, Montreux, Switzerland, June 28-30, 1977.

Engstrom, J.R. and Malack, J.A., "Stimulation of EDP/OM Equipment Emanations in AM Broadcast Receiver Studies," *IEEE Electromagnetic Symposium Record* (New York: IEEE), Session 2A. Washington, DC July 13-15, 1976.

Erikson, S.A., "Spacecraft Electromagnetic Environment Prediction," *IEEE EMC Symposium Record* (New York: IEEE), Session II-C, Atlanta, Georgia, June 20-22, 1978.

Ferraris, P.; Lazzari, M.; and Villata, F., "Noise Problems on DC Lines Supplying Static Frequency Converters," Second Symposium and Technical Exhibition, Montreux, Switzerland, June 28-30, 1978.

Fontaine, J.; Faure, J.L.; and Gary, C., "Electromagnetic Field in a High Frequency Range of High-Voltage Transmission Lines and Its Effects on the Response of a Terminated One-Wire Transmission Line Set Near the Ground," *IEEE EMC Symposium Record* (New York: IEEE), Session 2B-2, Washington, DC, July 13-15, 1976.

Galliano, P.G., "Impulsive Disturbances on Car Electric Circuitry," Second Symposium and Technical Exhibition, Session E, Montreux, Switzerland, June 28-30, 1977.

Haber, F., "The Magnetic Field in the Vicinity of Parallel and Twisted Three-Wire Cable Carrying Balanced Three-Phased Current," *IEEE Transactions on EMC, Volume EMC-16, Number 2*, May, 1974.

Haber F.; Kocker, C.P.; and Forest, L.A., "Space Shuttle Electromagnetic Environment Measurement," *IEEE EMC Symposium Record* (New York: IEEE), Session 2B-1, Washington, DC, July 13-15, 1976.

Hagn, G.H.; Shepard, R.A.; and Gaddie, J.C., "Measured Degradation Effects of Powerline Noise and Ignition Noise on an Non-Coherent FSK Digital Communications Systems," Second Symposium and Technical Exhibition, Session Z, Montreux, Switzerland, June 28-30, 1977.

Herman, J.R., "The Radio Noise Environment in Near Space: A Review," *IEEE EMC Symposium Record* (New York: IEEE), Session V-C, Atlanta, Georgia, June 20-22, 1978.

Hoff, R.J., "EMC Measurements in Hospitals," *IEEE EMC Symposium Record* (New York: IEEE), Session II, San Antonio, Texas, October 7-9, 1975.

Hsu, H.P.; Storwick, R.M.; Schlick, D.C.; and Maxam, G.L., "Measured Amplitude Distribution of Automotive Ignition Noise," *IEEE Transactions on EMC*, Volume EMC-16, Number 2, May 1974.

Kanda, M., "Time and Amplitude Statistics for Electromagnetic Noise Mines," *IEEE Transactions on EMC*, Volume EMC-17, Number 3, August 1975.

Lauber, W.R., "Radio Noise Surveys at Canadian HF Communication Sites," *IEEE Transactions on EMC*, Volume EMC-19, Number 2, May 1977.

Lauber, W.R. and Betrand, J.M., "Preliminary Urban VHF/UHF Radio Noise Intensity Measurements in Ottawa, Canada," Second Symposium and Technical Exhibition, Session L, Montreux, Switzerland, June 28-30, 1977.

Lynn, J.F., "Man-Made Electromagnetic Noise in Southern California and Southern Nevada," *IEEE Transactions on EMC*, Volume EMC-14, Number 3, May 1972.

Malack, J.A., "Power Line Conducted Interference Measurement Differences Using U.S. and CISPR Line Impedance Stabilization Networks," *IEEE Transactions on EMC*, Volume EMC-17, Number 2, May 1975.

Malack, J.A., "Statistical Correlation Between Conducted Voltages on the Powerline and Those Measured with a Line Impedance Stabilization Network," *IEEE Transactions on EMC*, Volume EMC-20, Number 2, May 1978.

March, D.N., "Electromagnetic Communications Quality Measurements at Residences Before and After Construction of Nearby Powerlines," *IEEE EMC Symposium Record* (New York: IEEE), Session 4B, Seattle, Washington, August 2-4, 1977.

Martin, H., "A Generalized Model of Man-Made Electrical Noise," *IEEE EMC Symposium Record* (New York: IEEE), Session V-C, Atlanta, Georgia, June 20-22, 1978.

Middleton, D., "Statistical-Physical Models of Electromagnetic Interference," Second Symposium and Technical Exhibition, Session L, Montreux, Switzerland, June 28-30, 1977.

Middleton, D., "Statistical-Physical Models of Urban Radio-Noise Environments—Part I: Foundations," *IEEE Transactions on EMC*, Volume EMC-14, Number 2, May 1972.

Mondin, P.L., "Experimental Measurement of Man-Made Electromagnetic Noise at Orbital Altitudes," *IEEE EMC Symposium*

Record (New York: IEEE), Session 2B, San Antonio, Texas. October 7-9, 1975.

Mussino, F., "EMC Measurement on the Electrical Equipment of Cars," Second Symposium and Technical Exhibition, Session E, Montreux, Switzerland, June 28-30, 1977.

Pearlston, C.B., "EMC Utility Corridors," *IEEE EMC Symposium Record* (New York: IEEE), Session 2B-2, Washington, DC, July 13-15, 1976.

Pellegrini, G.; Raimo, A.; and Reynaud, C., "EMC Problems in HV Substations," *IEEE EMC Symposium Record* (New York: IEEE), Session 2B-2, Washington, DC July 13-15, 1976.

Pike, C.J. and Lauber, W.R., "Measurements of the HF Radio Noise Environment in Arctic Canada," *IEEE EMC Symposium Record* (New York: IEEE), Session V-C, Atlanta, Georgia, June 20-22, 1978.

Pullen, F.D., "Comments on 'The Radio Interference Field of an Overhead Transmission Line'," *IEEE Transactions on EMC*, Volume EMC-14, Number 4, November 1972.

Ruggera, Paul S, "Radiofrequency E-Field Measurements within a Hospital Environment," *IEEE EMC Symposium Record* (New York: IEEE), Session II, San Antonio, Texas, October 7-9, 1975.

Rusakiewicz, W., "Measurements of Interference from RF Heating Equipment with Rapidly Changing Field Strength and Operating Frequency," Second Symposium and Technical Exhibition, Session N, Montreux, Switzerland, June 28-30, 1977.

Sato, R., "Recent Studies of Man-Made Noise in Japan," Second Symposium Land Technical Exhibition, Session R, Montreux, Switzerland, June 28-30, 1977.

Showers, R.M. and Kocher, C.P., "Modeling of Harmonics on Power Systems," *IEEE EMC Symposium Record* (New York: IEEE), Session 6B, Seattle, Washington, August 2-4, 1977.

Skomal, E.N. "Analysis of Airborne VHF Incidental Noise over Metropolitan Areas—Part II: Horizontal Dipole Antenna," *IEEE Transactions on EMC*, Volume EMC-17, Number 2, May, 1975.

Smith, S.W. and Brown, D.G., "Nonionizing Radiation Levels in the Washington, DC Area," *IEEE Transactions on EMC*, Volume EMC-15, Number 1, February, 1973.

Smith, A.A. Jr., "Power Line Noise Survey," *IEEE Transactions EMC*, Volume EMC-14, Number 1, February, 1972.

Stewart, J.R. and Wilson, D.D., "Electromagnetic Environmental

Aspects of New High Voltage Electric Power Transmission Technologies," *IEEE EMC Symposium Record* (New York: IEEE), Session 4B, Washington, DC, July 13-15, 1976.

Stuart, G.F. and Dites, M.J., "Man-Made Radio Noise Levels at 150 kHz to 32 MHz Near a Large Antarctic Base," *IEEE Transactions on EMC*, Volume EMC-15, Number 3, August, 1973.

Taylor, R.E. and Hill, J.S., "Airborne Urban/Suburban Noise Measured at 121.5/243 MHz," *IEEE EMC Symposium Record* (New York: IEEE), Session 4B, Seattle, Washington, August 2-4, 1977.

Taylor, R.E. and Hill, J.S., "0.4 to 10 GHz Airborne Electromagnetic Environment Survey Over U.S.A. Urban Areas," *IEEE EMC Symposium Record* (New York: IEEE), Session 2B-1, Washington, DC, July 13-15, 1976.

Taylor, R.E. and Hill, J.S., "Aircraft Measurement of Radio Frequency Noise at 121.5 MHz, 243 MHz and 406 MHz," Second Symposium and Technical Exhibition on EMC, Montreux, Switzerland, June 28-30, 1977.

Tell, R.A.; Lambdin, D.L.; and Mantiply, E.D., "Hospital Proximities to Nearby Broadcast Stations," *IEEE EMC Symposium Record* (New York: IEEE), Session II-C, Atlanta, Georgia, June 20-22, 1978.

Toler, J.C., "Electromagnetic Interference Levels in Hospitals," *IEEE EMC Symposium Record* (New York: IEEE), Session II, San Antonio, Texas, October 7-9, 1975.

Yamamoto, S. and Furuhashi, M., "Electrical Environmental Characteristics for Automotive Electronic Systems," *IEEE EMC Symposium Record* (New York: IEEE), Session 5B, Seattle, Washington, August 2-4, 1977.

Zamites, C.J. Jr. and Hurburt, K.H., "Measurements of Interference Levels in the UHF Band From Aircraft Altitudes," *IEEE Transactions EMC*, Volume E, C-12, Number 3, August, 1970.

Chapter 3

EMI Prediction and Performance

Chapter 2 defined the two-box geometry and conditions, victim characteristics and the electromagnetic ambient environment. This chapter presents the executive program for using and controlling the input from Chap. 2 and processing it on a summary basis to determine the EMI/EMC performances as shown in Fig. 3.1 (see heavy-lined boxes). The resulting output will determine if more EMI

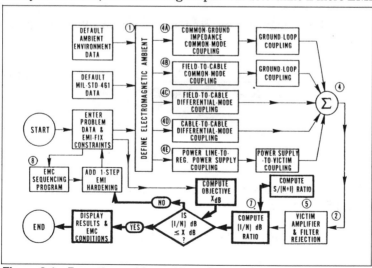

Figure 3.1—Executive and Control Parts (Heavy-Lined Boxes) of a General Flow Diagram for Predicting and Solving EMI Problems

3.1

hardening is required or if the objective has been achieved. In both cases, the accounting of performance is reported. Subsequent chapters detail individual mathematical models of coupling and EMI hardening fixes and the EMC sequencing process.

3.1 Signal to Noise Plus Interference— Overall System Performance

This section overviews signal-to-noise (S/N), interference-to-noise (I/N) and signal-to-noise-plus-interference [S/(N + I)] ratios. More exactly, since N always exists, S/N should be expressed as S + N/N. For S > 10 N however, it is easy to demonstrate that S + N/N = S/N. All three are important in design and real-life situations because:

1. Signal-to-noise ratio* corresponds to a design engineer's functional objective if the world were free of EMI.
2. Interference-to-noise ratio corresponds to the EMC engineer's emphasis because interference is supposed to be suppressed below internal noise (often it is not).
3. Signal-to-noise-plus-interference ratio corresponds to the overall measure of a design when immersed in the real world containing EMI emissions from many sources.

The S/(N + I) may be expressed in an operationally more useful form:

$$\frac{S}{N + I} = \frac{S/N}{1 + I/N} \tag{3.1}$$

$$\approx S/N \text{ for } I/N \ll 1 \tag{3.2}$$

$$\approx S/I \text{ for } I/N \gg 1 \tag{3.3}$$

The approximation in Eq. (3.2) is adequate (i.e., the error is less than 0.5 dB) when:

$$I/N < 0.122, \text{ i.e., } < -9 \text{ dB} \tag{3.4}$$

---

*(antilogarithm of x/20)^2 → antilogarithm of x/10

Similarly, Eq. (3.3) applies when I/N > 9 dB, i.e., I > 8 N.

Equation (3.1) is especially useful since it breaks into two parts which correspond to the way a designer usually thinks (S/N) versus the way an EMC engineer thinks (I/N). The S/(N+I) and I/N ratios are also separately used and displayed in performance summaries as described in Section 3.3.

Equation (3.1) applies only if the entries are each in units of power, P. Since most programs involve voltages (V), the terms of Eq. (3.1) must be root-sum-squared (RSS) since they are derived from incoherent sources:

$$\left[\frac{S}{N + I} \right]_P = \frac{S/N}{1 \sqrt{I + (I/N)_v^2}} \tag{3.5}$$

Since,

$$(I/N)_{dB} = 20 \log (I/N) \tag{3.6}$$

$$I/N = \log^{-1} [(I/N)_{dB}/20] \tag{3.7}$$

Thus,

$$\left[\frac{S}{N + I} \right] = (S/N)_{dB} - 20 \log \{1 + [\log^{-1} (I/N)_{dB}/20]^2\}^{1/2} \tag{3.8}$$

$$= (S/N)_{dB} - 10 \log \{1 + \log^{-1}[(I/N)_{dB}/10]\} \tag{3.9}$$

Note: (antilog of x/20)^2 → antilog of x/10

Equation (3.9) is the equation used to compute all [S/(N+I)] dB situations in this handbook.

3.2 Signal and Interference Performance

In this section, detailed relations are given for both S/N and I/N ratios. The latter is defined in terms of the principal coupling paths and associated EMC fixes, when applicable.

3.2.1 Signal-to-Noise Ratios

The signal, S, is usually defined by the user design input (see Section 2.3.1) at the source in Box 1 as manifested at the potential victim amplifier input in Box 2. Figure 3.2 shows the illustrative example of S = 0.01 mV (or 10 μV) which appeared in Fig. 2.6.

The intentional signal may be defined in units other than millivolts as discussed in Section 2.3.1. When defined in units of millivolts, Eq. (2.7) showed that:

$$S_{dBmV} = 20 \log(S_{mv}) \tag{3.10}$$

For the ongoing illustrative example, Eqs. (3.10) and (2.8) yield:

$$S_{dBmV} = 20 \log(0.01) = -40 \text{ dBmV} \tag{3.11}$$

$$= 20 \text{ dB}\mu V$$

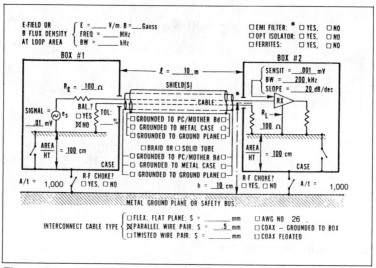

Figure 3.2—Ongoing Illustrative Example

Noise, N, is usually defined by the user design input (see Section 2.3.3) at the potential victim amplifier or logic input in Box 2, Fig. 3.2. As previously explained in Section 2.3.3, N corresponds to the sensitivity of analog circuits and the noise-immunity level of digital circuits. For the illustrative example of N = 0.001 mV (or 1 μV) shown in Fig. 3.2:

$$N_{dBmV} = 20 \log (N_{mV}) \qquad (3.12)$$

$$= 20 \log (0.001) = -60 \text{ dBmV} \qquad (3.13)$$
$$= 0 \text{ dB}\mu\text{V}$$

The signal-to-noise ratio is often of interest. As discussed in Eqs. (3.1) and (3.2), it is defined as:

$$(S_{mV}/N_{mV})_{dB} = (S_{\mu V}/N_{\mu V})_{dB} \qquad (3.14)$$

$$= 20 \log (S_{mV}/N_{mV}) \qquad (3.15)$$

$$= S_{dBmV} - N_{dBmV} \qquad (3.16)$$

For the above illustrative example, the S/N ratio becomes:

$$(S/N)_{dB} = 20 \log (0.01/0.001) = 20 \text{ dB}$$

$$= 20 \text{ dB}\mu\text{V} - 0 \text{ dB}\mu\text{V} = 20 \text{ dB}$$

3.2.2 Interference-to-Noise Ratios

The development of the $(I/N)_{dB}$ models follows directly from the discussion in the previous Section 3.2.1. Generally, however, $(I/N)_{dB}$, as shown in Fig. 3.1 for the combined effect of all five coupling paths, is computed as follows:

$$(I/N)_{dB} = \sum \begin{array}{l} 20 \log I_A + CMCG_{dB} + GLC_{dB} \\ 20 \log (E_{V/m}) + CMCF_{dB} + GLC_{dB} \\ 20 \log (E_{V/m}) + DMC_{dB} \qquad\qquad + AR_{dB} - N_{dBV} \\ 20 \log V_c + CCC_{dB} \\ 20 \log V_p + LPS_{dB} + PSV_{dB} \end{array} \qquad (3.17)$$

where, for the potential EMI sources,

I_A = ground plane EMI current in amperes (see Section 2.4)

$E_{V/m}$ = potential interference field strength in volts per meter (see Section 2.4)

V_c = EMI voltage on nearby cable in volts (see Section 2.3.6)

V_p = EMI voltage on power bus in volts (see Section 2.4.2)

and where, for the coupling paths:

$CMCG_{dB}$ = common-mode coupling from ground impedance
GLC_{dB} = ground-loop coupling
$CMCF_{dB}$ = common-mode coupling from field to cable
DMC_{dB} = differential-mode coupling from field to cable
CCC_{dB} = cable-to-cable, differential-mode coupling
LPS_{dB} = power line to regulated power supply coupling
PSV_{dB} = power supply to victim coupling

and,

AR_{dB} = combined effect of coupling through the victim amplifier and any EMI filter, if used

With one exception, the summation process indicated in Eq. (3.17) and shown in Fig. 3.3 is an incoherent addition, namely an RSS addition. This develops because the various potential EMI components are derived from different (incoherent) sources. The exception corresponds to the two field-to-cable coupling modes which require coherent addition.

For the case of the two field-to-cable coupling situations only, Eq. (3.17) becomes (see Fig. 3.4):

$$(I/N)_{dB} = 20 \log (E_{V/m}) + \sum \left\{ \begin{matrix} CMCF_{dB} + GLC_{dB} \\ DMC_{dB} \end{matrix} \right\}$$

$$+ AR_{dB} - N_{dBV} \qquad (3.18)$$

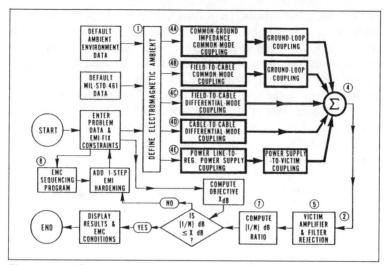

Figure 3.3—Summation of Five EMI Coupling Paths

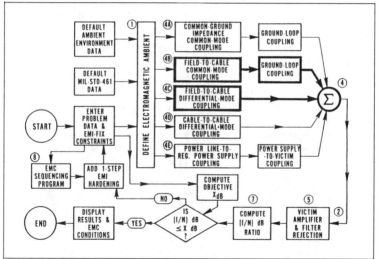

Figure 3.4—Coherent Summation of Two Field-to-Cable Coupling Paths

Where the summation in Eq. (3.18) is formed coherently:

$$
\begin{aligned}
(I/N)\ dB = {}& 20\ \log\ (E_{V/m}) \\
& + 20\ \log\ \{\log^{-1}\ [(CMCF_{dB} + GLC_{dB})/20] \\
& + \log^{-1}\ (DMC_{dB}/20)\} + AR_{dB} - N_{dBV}
\end{aligned} \tag{3.19}
$$

3.7

The bracketed expression in Eq. (3.18) is used in Fig. 3.5 for the addition of two coherent sources. The expression also corresponds to selecting the larger of the two coupling paths and adding a correction (which is a function of the difference between the two paths in dB). For example, when the EMI levels from each of the two paths are equal, the combination level is 6 dB higher than either. For a different level of 20 dB, the resultant level is less than 1 dB (0.83) more than the larger of the two alone. In general, for manual computations, it is sufficient to simply select the larger of the two coupling paths in Eq. (3.18).

Should the field strength in Eq. (3.18) be expressed in units of dbV/m or dBμV/m, the corresponding units of victim amplifier sensitivity would be dBV and dBμV, respectively.

More generally:

$$(E/N)_{dB} = 20 \log (E_{V/m}/N_V) = E_{dBV/m} - N_{dBV} \qquad (3.20)$$

The units do not agree in Eq. (3.20) since E is field strength and N is voltage. Therefore, the units of E/N are meter^{-1}. This is accommodated, however, by the definition of CMC_{dB} and DMC_{dB} which act like transducers to convert electric field strength to

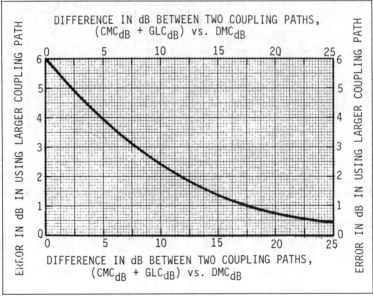

Figure 3.5—Coherent Addition of Two EMI Coupling Paths

voltage. This is explained more fully in the next chapter, especially when magnetic flux density is used to describe the radiated ambient rather than electric field strength.

3.2.3 Objective I/N Ratios

Figure 3.6 shows that the computed $(I/N)_{dB}$ must be compared with some design or field-installation objective, X_{dB}. From a consideration of Eqs. (3.1) and (3.2) alone, it appears that if X_{dB} is selected equal to about -10 dB [see Eq. (3.4)], an error of less than 0.5 dB in effective S/N results. Such a statement assumes that the computation of I/N is precise and subject to no error, i.e., is deterministic. Unfortunately, this is not the case in real life since EMI prediction is subject to many errors.

As explained below, EMI prediction is a probabilistic situation because of the uncertainties or errors involved. For some math-model building blocks, the errors are not known since little validation exists to support them.* However, the mechanics for processing the errors can be discussed together with estimates of the bulk-error effect. From this, the objective I/N ratio X_{dB} can be computed.

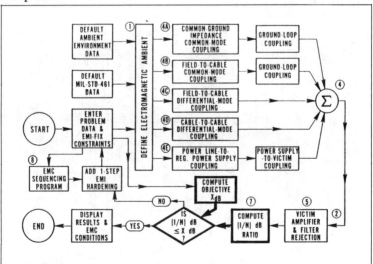

Figure 3.6—Objective and Comparison of I/N Ratios

---

*In time, the math models will be updated and improved in accuracy. The EMC field is a young science, moving slowly out of the art status.

Observe that many of the contributing errors in EMI prediction are either log normally distributed or can be approximated by a log normal distribution up to about two standard deviations. A log normal probability distribution is shown in Fig. 3.7. A best estimate at this time is that the bulk average of the probable errors in the prediction process is about 8 dB. The probable error corresponds to the 50 percent probability that the error is greater or less than the amount indicated.

Figure 3.7 shows that the probable error, ϵ_r, is related to the standard deviation, σ, by:

$$\sigma_{dB} = \epsilon_r/0.6745 \tag{3.21}$$

For $\epsilon_r \approx 8$ dB, the standard deviation is, $\sigma \approx 12$ dB. It remains to determine the additive requirement to $(I/N)_{dB}$ in units of standard deviation to define the objective X_{dB} in Fig. 3.6.

Figure 3.8 is obtained by placing Fig. 3.7 on an $(I/N)_{dB}$ axis. For this situation, the mean value, μ, corresponds to the 50 percent point on the $(I/N)_{dB}$ axis at -10 dB: the objective if I/N were a deterministic situation. Since it is probabilistic rather than deterministic, Fig. 3.7 is scaled to yield a standard deviation of 12 dB about the -10 dB I/N ratio point.

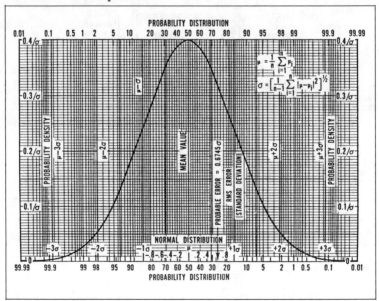

Figure 3.7—Log-Normal Probability Distribution

To determine the objective $(I/N)_{dB}$, X_{dB}, it remains only to select the desired probability of no EMI, i.e., that EMC exists:

$$X_{dB} = (I/N)_{dB} - k\sigma_{dB} \qquad (3.22)$$

where,

$(I/N)_{dB}$ = -10 dB deterministic objective

σ = -12 dB standard deviation of error

k = multiplier based on the log normal distribution of Fig. 3.7 to give desired probability of no EMI

Illustrative Example 3.1

For a prediction process having a 12 dB standard deviation and a 90 percent probability of no EMI, compute the design objective for $(I/N)_{dB}$.

Figure 3.7 shows that k corresponds to 1.28 standard deviation for a 90 percent probability that the value is less than the indicated amount. Thus, Eq. (3.22) becomes:

$$X_{dB} = -10 \text{ dB} - 1.28 \times 12 \text{ dB} \qquad (3.23)$$
$$= -10 \text{ dB} - 16 \text{ dB} = -26 \text{ dB}$$

The $(I/N)_{dB}$ on a deterministic basis is shifted in Fig. 3.8 from

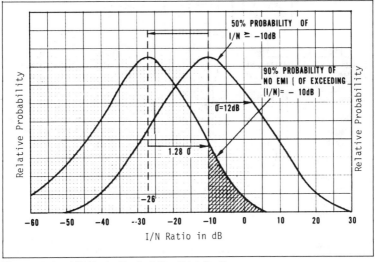

Figure 3.8—I/N Ratio Probability Distribution

3.11

−10 dB by 16 dB to the left to yield a new mean value of −26 dB. For this situation then, 10 percent of the area under the probability curve (10 percent chance of EMI) exceeds the $(I/N)_{dB}$ value of −10 dB.

3.3 Performance Reporting and Display

This section describes a novel method of organizing the results of the EMI control methodology and procedures. A good bookkeeping system is a must if the technique is to be a success. Of still greater importance is the visibility of performance status at any time. Many methods fail because the user does not know what is going on, i.e., where he has been, where he is now and what factors contribute to method success or failure.

One display which offers high visibility is an organization chart as shown in Fig. 3.9. Imagine that this is either a CRT display or an LED display board showing the EMI/EMC performance. At the top center is I/N ratio displayed in dB. This is where the attention is focused. Off to either side is supporting information: the overall S/(N+I) ratio and the objective I/N ratio.

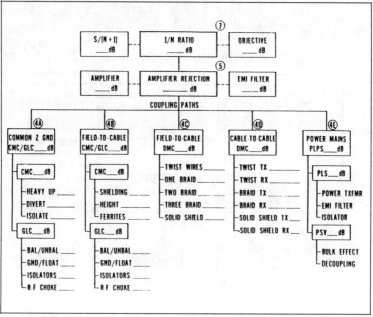

Figure 3.9—I/N Ratio and System Performance Organization Chart

Since all potentially susceptible emissions must be processed through the victim amplifier or logic, it is shown next in line on the organization chart. The total amplifier or logic rejection is shown in the center box. It is composed of in-band/out-of-band and audio rectification (left center box) and that due to a supporting EMI filter (right center box), if applicable.

The third tier in the I/N organization chart is composed of the five principal EMI coupling paths, previously shown in several flow diagrams such as Fig. 3.3 (see paths 4A through 4E). The dB performance contribution is shown in Fig. 3.9 for each of the five paths (provided each is involved in any one problem). Since some of the paths contain two-step parts, each is also depicted separately. For example, the coupling path second from the left is field-to-cable coupling and includes both common-mode coupling (CMC) and ground-loop coupling (GLC).

Finally, Fig. 3.9 illustrates a contribution from each of the potential EMI fixes, as applicable. These entries are at the lowest level on the organization chart. This is not intended to imply lesser importance.

The display shown in Fig. 3.9 is intended to portray the entire EMI/EMC performance resulting from a user-selected problem and its corresponding input data. The eye can quickly glance at the chart and get a panoramic view of what is happening. Thus, this high-visibility display corresponds to any single user-selected situation and the resulting performance. But the display suffers from one major drawback: there is no record of what previous displays look like, i.e., how did this design affect the previous trial EMC design?

While one can record and compare two or more displays of the type shown in Fig. 3.9, the combined displays begin to lose their mutual visibility. Historical comparison of trial and performance is the essence of EMC design or retrofit. Thus, a search was made to find a three-dimensional display to give the **best of all worlds**. Such a display, in part, has been found and is the topic of the next section.

3.3.1 The EMC/EMI Performance Display

Figure 3.10 shows that the captions and columnar headings for the EMI/EMC performance display were selected in accordance with the considerations presented in the previous discussion. The operating conditions correspond to all major blocks shown in the first three tiers of the organization chart previously shown in Fig. 3.9. The numerical headings in circles correspond to the same numerical headings in both Fig. 3.9 and the flow diagram of Fig. 3.3.

Column 1 corresponds to the electromagnetic ambient in units of dBμV/m, dBμV or other unit, as applicable. Column 2 is the sensitivity (N) of the victim amplifier or digital logic device (NIL) as discussed in Section 2.3.3. While columns 1 and 2 are not necessarily the same units, column 3 is their difference in dB and is one measure of the potential severity of the latent EMI problem, if indeed one exists.

Columns 4A through 4E correspond to the five principal EMI coupling paths, as applicable. Column 4 is their sum in the sense discussed in Section 3.2.2. The amplifier or logic rejection appears in column 5. The objective (later the actual) I/N ratio is listed under column 7, and the difference in I/N ratios (improvement or @20 I/N) in column 6 corresponds to each succeeding historical design/retrofit trial run. The −26 dB under column 7 uses the illustrative example discussed in Section 3.2.3 and Fig. 3.8.

3.3.2 The Initial Performance Trial Run

To lend action to Fig. 3.10, the ongoing illustrative example previously shown in Fig. 3.2 is repeated in Fig. 3.11. Added to this figure is a potential interfering radiated emission from an AM broadcast transmitter at 1,000 kHz, i.e., 1 MHz. The field strength is 10 V/m.

Figure 3.12 shows the result of the first trial EMC design run (Chapter 7 will cover how this was obtained). Column 3 is obtained by subtracting the 0.001 mV amplifier sensitivity (IμV = 0 dBμV) from the electric field strength of 10 V/m (140 dBμV/m). Since this

	①	②	③	④A	④B	④C	④D	④E	④	⑤	⑥	⑦
OPERATING CONDITIONS	AMB dBμV	N dBμV	A/N dB	GCM GLC	FCM GLC	DMC	C-C	P1·PS PS·V	SUM 4A·4E	AMP REJ	Δ I/N	I/N
OBJECTIVE												-26

Figure 3.10—Columnar Headings Used for the Selected EMI/EMC Performance Display

3.14

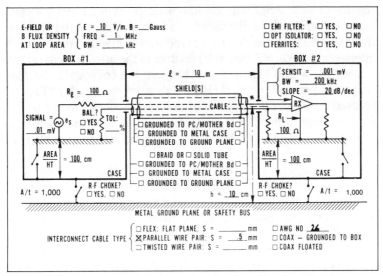

Figure 3.11—Input Data Identification for Two-Box EMI Problem

	①	②	③	④A	④B	④C	④D	④E	④	⑤	⑥	⑦
OPERATING CONDITIONS	AMB dBμV	N dBμV	A/N dB	GCM GLC	FCM GLC	DMC	C-C	P1·PS PS·V	SUM 4A·4E	AMP REJ	Δ I/N	I/N
OBJECTIVE												-26
START: FIRST RUN	140	0	140	NA	-47	-86	NA	NA	-47	-14		+79

Figure 3.12—First Trial Run Corresponding to Fig. 3.11 Conditions

is a field-to-cable coupling problem, only columns 4B and 4C are used. The larger of the two coupling paths (4B = CMC and GLC together yield −47 dB) also appears in column 4. The amplifier rejection (column 5) to the out-of-band AM broadcast station corresponds to −14 dB. Finally, the resultant EMI problem corresponds to an I/N ratio of +79 dB — a formidable situation.

3.3.3 Performance of Subsequent EMI Fixes

Observe that 105 dB of EMI hardening (EMI fixes), i.e., 79 dB − (−26 dB), is required. Figure 3.13 shows the historical performance record of what the user tried and the corresponding results. (The attempt may be automatically synthesized if a computer is employed, as discussed in a later chapter.) After the first trial run, the user decided that to reduce the effect of the near I/N interference (f_{EMI} = 1,000 kHz) relative to the amplifier cut-off frequency (f_{co} = 200 kHz in Fig. 3.11), that the equivalent of a five-stage, low-pass filter rolloff (100 dB/decade) was needed. This increased the amplifier rejection from -14 dB (column 5) to -60 dB, for a net improvement of 46 dB (column 6). Thus, the new I/N ratio is now 33 dB — still a bad situation, although less formidable than before.

Figure 3.13 shows that the next user trial EMC fix involves converting to a balanced transmission/reception system from the previous unbalanced system shown in Fig. 3.11. This improves (reduces) the ground-loop coupling from -47 dB to -106 dB (column 4B), but it has no effect on the differential-mode coupling (column 4C). For this reason, the full 59 dB improvement (106 dB $-$ 47 dB) cannot be realized since the -86 dB DMC coupling path is now the larger. Therefore, the net improvement is 39 dB (column 6) which corresponds to going from the -47 dB of FCM/GLC (column 4B) to -86 dB of DMC (column 4C). The net resultant I/N ratio of -6 dB represents lowering the previous 33 dB I/N ratio by 39 dB (column 6).

The final user-selected EMC fix is twisting the wires of the cable pair in Fig. 3.11 with 40 twists per meter. Figure 3.13 shows that only 20 dB improvement resulted in column 6, although the DMC improved by 56 dB (142 dB $-$ 86 dB, column 4C). This improve-

	(1)	(2)	(3)	(4A)	(4B)	(4C)	(4D)	(4E)	(4)	(5)	(6)	(7)
OPERATING CONDITIONS	AMB dBμV	N dBμV	A/N dB	GCM GLC	FCM GLC	DMC	C-C	P1·PS PS·V	SUM 4A·4E	AMP REJ	Δ I/N	I/N
OBJECTIVE												-26
START: FIRST RUN	140	0	140	NA	-47	-86	NA	NA	-47	-14		+79
AMPL SLOPE = 100 dBD	140	0	140	NA	-47	-86	NA	NA	-47	-60	46	+33
BAL GEN/ AMPL = 5%	140	0	140	NA	-106	-86	NA	NA	-86	-60	39	-6
TWIST WIRES 40TPM	140	0	140	NA	-106	-142	NA	NA	-106	-60	20	-26

$$(I/N)dB: \text{⑦} = \text{③} + \text{④} + \text{⑤}$$

Figure 3.13—Subsequent Runs until EMC ($-$26 dB) is Achieved

ment truncation resulted in switching from the DMC coupling path as the larger (−86 dB, column 4C) to the FCM/GLC path as the larger (−106 dB, column 4B). Since the −26 dB objective has been achieved (new I/N performance −26 dB, column 7), no further EMC design is necessary.

The next six chapters present the mathematical models and details for EMI prediction and analysis.

3.4 Bibliography

Freeman, E.R. and Sachs, H.M., "HF AM Signal-to-Interference Ratio (SIR) Study," *IEEE International Symposium Record* (New York: IEEE), Session 2A, Washington, DC, July 13-15, 1976.

Kubina, S.J.; Vuille, M.; and Widmer, H., "Interactive Graphics for EMC Analysis," *IEEE EMC International Symposium Record* (New York: IEEE), Session V-A, Atlanta, GA, June 20-22, 1978.

Chapter 4

Victim Receptor Performance

Victim receptor response and performance are detailed in this chapter. To avoid distracting the user from the design data presented herein, derivations and detailed math models are presented in Appendix A. For the most part, this chapter presents application-oriented graphics together with illustrative examples.

This chapter covers the performance of the victim receptor corresponding to receivers, amplifiers and digital logic to both in-band and out-of-band and undesired EMI emissions. Figure 4.1 shows

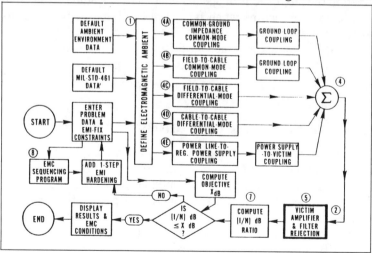

Figure 4.1—EMI Prediction and Analysis Flow Diagram Showing Location of the Victim Receptor

4.1

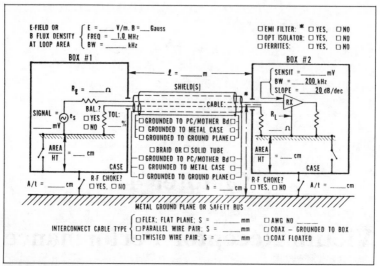

Figure 4.2—The Two-Box EMI Problem Showing Location of the Victim Receptor

the victim in the lower right-hand corner of the flow diagram, and Fig. 4.2 shows the victim location in Box 2. The performance in the passband is rated in terms of sensitivity (noise) for receivers and analog amplifiers, and in terms of noise immunity levels for digital logic. The cutoff frequency and skirt slope (selectivity) defined in the stopband is of special importance. Audio rectification can happen to victims when far out-of-band and EMI emissions are present on their cable leads. This problem accounts for many existing EMI situations such as citizen's band transmitters interfering with other consumer electronic products.

4.1 In-Band Performance

The sensitivity (N = noise) of receivers and amplifiers and the noise immunity level (NIL) of digital logic circuits were defined in Section 2.3 and will not be repeated here (see Fig. 4.2, Box 2). It is presumed that the transfer function or gain in the passband of the victim is relatively flat. Therefore, it is necessary to define that frequency for which the performance (gain) falls off, viz., where the 3 dB cutoff frequency, f_{co}, exists.

4.2 Out-of-Band Performance of Victim and Filters

Out-of-band performance of analog and digital devices is defined in terms of the slope or reduction in sensitivity versus frequency. Above cutoff frequency, an amplifier gain degenerates and exhibits a slope in the stopband of X dB per decade. This slope is related to the slope in units of decibels per octave (dB/octave) by:

$$X_{dB/decade} = [\log_2(10)] \, X_{dB/octave} \qquad (4.1)$$

$$= 3.32 \times X_{db/octave} \qquad (4.2)$$

Parasitic shunt capacitance often accounts for performance degradation to produce the stopband. It corresponds to a one-stage (N = 1) lowpass filter[1] which exhibits a rolloff of 6 dB/octave or 20 dB/decade. Hereafter, the term **dB/decade** will be used to describe the stopband performance of all transfer functions of circuits, cables, equipments, filters, isolators, shields, etc.

Many EMI problems exist out of band to the victim rather than in band. Therefore, the out-of-band performance of receivers, analog and digital circuits is very important. As stated above, unless the designer makes a special effort, the out-of-band rolloff due to parasitic capacitance corresponds to 20 dB/decade or behaves like an N = 1, one-stage filter. This raises the question regarding amplifier out-of-band performance if the designer intentionally forces a faster rolloff.

4.2.1 Baseband Victims

Victims may be divided into baseband and radio receiver types. The former involves no carrier modulation of the information content or intelligence. It includes the family of dc and ac coupled amplifiers, digital logic and low-pass filters (passive or active). Radio receivers involve the intentional reception of radiated, carrier-modulated, baseband information. While they include baseband victims after final detection, they also include antennas, predetector RF and IF amplifiers and converters. Radio receivers are also defined here to include passive bandpass filters and predetectors.

The word **radio receivers** is used here instead of **receivers** to avoid confusion with certain other word usages (such as in the term **differential line drivers and receivers**). Additionally, frequency-division multiplexed (FDM) signals can be sent over hardwire or fiber optics. For this condition, the victim is a baseband. If the FDM signals are using subcarriers, the entire baseband may be carrier modulated for radiated transmission and reception by radio receiver victims.

In summary, the dichotomy between baseband and radio receiver victims is intended to distinguish between the different resulting performance of low-pass and bandpass victims, respectively.

In many respects, the performance of an amplifier in the stopband is similar to that of a passive filter, especially when faster rolloff is designed into the amplifier. Figure 4.3 shows the most common response or that of a maximally flat or Butterworth filter for N = 1 to five stages. Beyond the cutoff region, i.e., in the stopband, the slope equals 20 N dB/decade. The X-axis corresponds to the EMI frequency, f_{EMI}, in normalized units of amplifier cutoff frequency, f_{co}. Thus, the ratio of f_{EMI}/f_{co} is formed to determine the X-axis value. For any number of stages, N, the Y-axis gives the performance relative to passband sensitivity or NIL, in units of dB.

Figure 4.3 shows that all rejection responses are truncated at a default value of -60 dB. This is to remind the user that active amplifiers, logic and passive filters are not perfect devices. If the user knows that the out-of-band susceptibility response is greater or less than the -60 dB truncated value, then he should use the known measured data. Otherwise, -60 dB is used as a default value for non-ideal, real-world situations (-60 dB is used in many other EMI models for similar reasons; sometimes other default values are used).

Sometimes a faster rolloff for $1 < f_{EMI}/f_{co} < 2$ is desired than that offered by the Butterworth response of Fig. 4.3. One such response is the Chebychev shown in Fig. 4.4. This response corresponds to a passband ripple of 0.5 dB. For N > 2, for the same number of stages and near-in region of $1 < f_{EMI}/f_{co}$, a comparison of Figs. 4.3 and 4.4 indicates that the Chebychev response gives more attenuation than the corresponding Butterworth response. Appendix A gives responses of other equal-ripple Chebychev functions available to the designer.

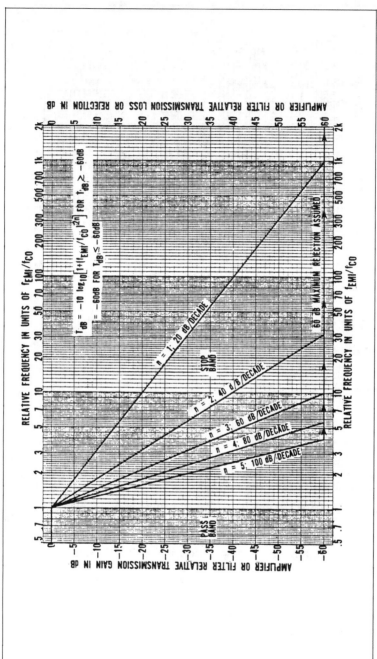

Figure 4.3—Butterworth or Maximally-Flat Response of Amplifiers and Filters

4.5

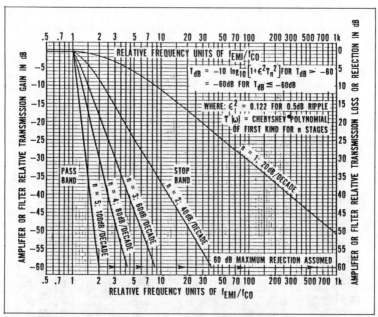

Figure 4.4—Chebychev Response of a 0.5 dB Passband Ripple

Illustrative Example 4.1

In the ongoing two-box EMI problem shown in Fig. 4.2, f_{EMI} = 1 MHz and f_{co} = 0.2 MHz (200 kHz shown in Box 2). Therefore, the X-axis entry point in Fig. 4.3 is f_{EMI}/f_{co} = 1/0.2 = 5. The victim amplifier slope shown in Fig. 4.2 is 20 dB/decade, which corresponds to an N = 1 stage. Thus, for a Butterworth response shown in Fig. 4.3, the out-of-band rejection, AR_{dB}, is – 14 dB.

To get a 60 dB rejection, the slope must be somewhere between N = 4 and N = 5. Since only integers may be used, N = 5 is selected in Fig. 4.3 to assure at least a 60 dB rejection at 1 MHz.

A potentially interfering source may exhibit a significant 3 dB bandwidth relative to the 3 dB bandwidth (i.e., passband) of the victim. If the bandwidth, BW_c, of the potential EMI source falls in the victim passband, BW_v, no bandwidth correction is necessary. However, if $BW_c > BW_v$, then a bandwidth limiting action will result:

$$AR_{dB} = k \log(BW_c/BW_v), \text{ for } BW_c/BW_v \geqslant 1 \text{ and } N = 1 \quad (4.3)$$

where,

  k = 10 for incoherent EMI sources (e.g., bandwidth-limited white noise, corona, gas lamps, noise diodes, etc.)

or

  k = 20 for coherent EMI sources (e.g., transients, impulses, pulses, step functions, etc.)

Equation (4.3) may also be expressed in terms of the transient or pulse duration, τ, at the 50 percent height if such is the EMI source:

$$AR_{dB} = 20 \log(1/\pi\tau BW_v), \text{ for } \pi\tau BW_v \leqslant 1 \text{ and } N = 1 \qquad (4.4)$$

Illustrative Example 4.2

A 1 μs transient is coupled into the input leads of an EKG amplifier having a 100 Hz bandwidth and a stopband slope of 20 dB/decade (N = 1). Determine the rejection offered by the amplifier to the transient amplitude. From Eq. (4.4):

$$AR_{dB} = 20 \log(1/\pi \times 10^{-6} \times 100) = 70 \text{ dB}$$

Figure 4.5 is a generalization of Eq. (4.4) for an amplifier having

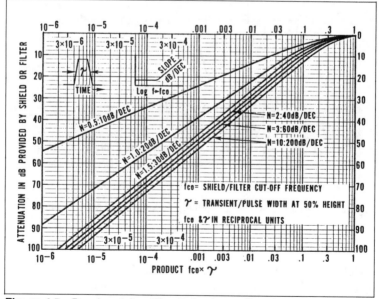

Figure 4.5—Baseband Amplifier Rejection to Transients

4.7

any slope in the stopband. In contrast to narrowband emissions in the stopband, note that for broadband EMI sources there is little advantage to increasing the amplifier stopband slope beyond 60 dB/decade ($N = 3$).

4.2.2 Radio Receiver Victims

The susceptibility of radio receivers to out-of-band emissions is a very complex subject and is beyond the scope of this handbook. The present discussion is limited to the RF selectivity curve in the adjacent-channel frequency region as shown in Fig. 4.6.

Figures 4.3 and 4.4 may be adapted for bandpass applications by a transfer of variables in which the X-axis is transferred from low-pass to bandpass terms. This is accomplished by substituting $f_{EMI} - f_c$ for f_{EMI} (f_c = center frequency of bandpass filter) and 0.5 BW for f_{co} (BW = 3 dB filter bandwidth). Thus, the frequency ratio f_{EMI}/f_{co} in the previous section becomes $(f_{EMI} - f_c)/0.5$ BW.

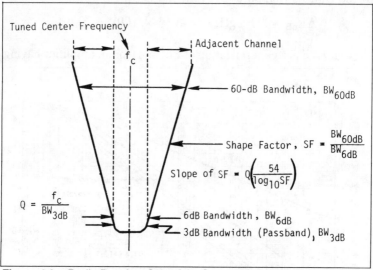

Figure 4.6.—Radio Receiver Selectivity Curve in Adjacent-Channel Region

Illustrative Example 4.3

Determine the rejection offered by an AM radio receiver tuned to a 1,000 kHz station when a 1,040 kHz out-of-band station is being picked up by the same antenna. The IF amplifier of the receiver has three stagger-tuned stages. The transmission and reception bandwidths are both 10 kHz.

The X-axis in Figs. 4.3 and 4.4 becomes:

$$\frac{|\, f_{EMI} - f_c \,|}{0.5 \; BW} = \frac{1,040 - 1,000 \; kHz}{0.5 \times 10 \; kHz} = 8$$

For maximally flat, N = 3 tuned stages, Fig. 4.3 indicates that AR_{dB} = 55 dB.

The normalized X-axis frequency may also be defined in terms of the Q-factor of a bandpass filter as shown in Fig. 4.6:

$$\frac{|\, f_{EMI} - f_c \,|}{0.5 \; BW} = 2 \left| \frac{f_{EMI}}{BW} - Q \right| \tag{4.5}$$

where,

$$Q = f_c/BW \tag{4.6}$$

Unless otherwise stated, it is assumed that the passive filter is a single-tuned stage (N = 1).

Illustrative Example 4.4

What benefit is obtained (additional rejection) by adding a passive bandpass filter in front of the receiver in Illustrative Example 4.3 in which the filter loaded Q-factor is 100?

From Eq. (4.5):

$$2 \left| \frac{1,040 \; kHz}{10 \; kHz} - 100 \right| = 8$$

From Fig. 4.3, for N = 1:

$$AR_{dB} = 18 \; dB$$

Sometimes it is more operationally useful to define the radio receiver selectivity curve in terms of the shape factor, SF (see Fig. 4.6), of the IF amplifier (and, hence, RF for superhets):

$$SF = BW_{60\text{ dB}}/BW_{6\text{ dB}} \qquad (4.7)$$

where,

$BW_{60\text{ dB}}$ = RF bandwidth at the 60 dB rejection level
$BW_{6\text{ dB}}$ = RF bandwidth at the 6 dB rejection level

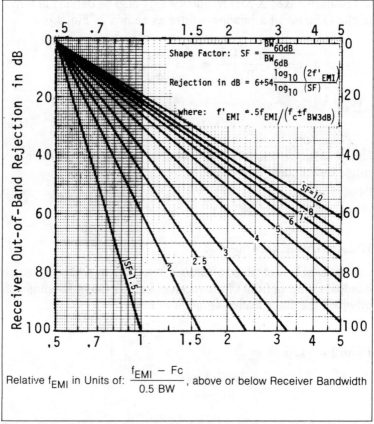

Figure 4.7—Response of Radio Receivers in Terms of Shape Factor

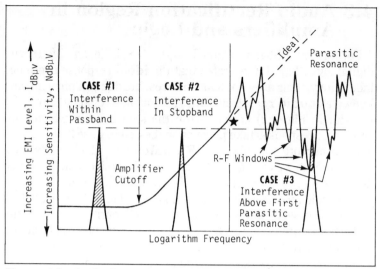

Figure 4.8—Audio Rectification Phenomena in Amplifiers and Logic Circuits

Shape factors of radio receivers may vary from less than 2 (a highly selective receiver) to somewhat greater than 10 (a cheap or poorly designed receiver). If the shape factor is unknown, a default value of SF = 4 may be used. Figure 4.7 gives the receiver rejection (selectivity curve) for radio receivers in terms of different shape factors. The X-axis is presented in normalized frequency units as discussed in Example 4.3. If it is known that the minimum out-of-band rejection in the adjacent-channel region is less than 100 dB, then the known figure should be used. For receivers, an 80 dB default is suggested, while 60 dB can be used for lumped-element, bandpass filters.

Illustrative Example 4.5

Using the same example as Example 4.3, assume it is not known that three tuned stages are used in the IF amplifier. Unless otherwise specified, a default shape factor of four will be used. For an X-axis of 8 and an SF = 4, the out-of-band rejection from Fig. 4.7 is more than 80 dB.

4.3 Audio Rectification Region in Amplifiers and Logic

For the out-of-band region ($f_{EMI}/f_{co} \gg 1$) in amplifiers and digital logic, Fig. 4.8 indicates that the **ideal** response continues indefinitely. This does not happen in real life due to a phenomenon known as **audio rectification**. A frequency region (denoted by the star in Fig. 4.8) is reached in the stop band in which anti-resonance responses take place as suggested in Case 3 of Fig. 4.8. They constitute a number of RF **windows** in which the far out-of-band responses are much less than both the ideal and a 60 dB-down frequency previously suggested in Figs. 4.3 and 4.4.

The audio rectification phenomenon is explained by the fact that any active device exhibits a degree of nonlinearity. For example, when the victim is overdriven by an out-of-band emission, the RF carrier is rectified at an emitter base junction, and the carrier sees a low capacitive reactance to ground as in a superheterodyne second detector. The modulation envelope is stripped off or recovered and processed through the amplifier. Audio rectification explains why a radar can jam a computer, or a CB (citizens band) transmitter can cause EMI to a consumer's stereo amplifier. It is a recurring EMI problem in all active electronic devices.

The only way to know the audio rectification response in an amplifier is to measure its out-of-band susceptibility performance. However, if this is not done or is otherwise unknown, a default model may be used. Figure 4.9 shows the default model* for audio rectification in an amplifier. For the near-in response corresponding to $f_{EMI}/f_{co} > 1$, Figs. 4.9 and 4.3 are identical. For $f_{EMI}/f_{co} \gg 1$, however, the figures depart in a major way.

The lowest frequency for which audio rectification exists is:

$$\text{In } \textbf{relative} \text{ terms:} \quad f_{ar} = 100/\sqrt{f_{co}}, \text{ in MHz} \quad (4.8)$$

$$\text{In } \textbf{absolute} \text{ terms:} \quad f_{ar} = 100\sqrt{f_{co}}, \text{ in MHz} \quad (4.9)$$

For values of $f_{EMI}/f_{co} > f_{ar}$, the response becomes equal to the horizontal line corresponding to $N = 1$, $N = 2$ or $N \geqslant 3$, as applicable.

---

*This default math model has been derived from engineering estimates since very little published data are available. It is subject to substantial error since it is also a function of emission level and modulation type.

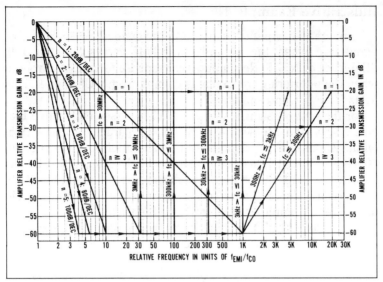

Figure 4.9—Default Model for Audio Rectification

The discontinuities in Fig. 4.9 range from 0 dB (e.g., at f_{EMI}/f_{co} = 10 and N = 1) to 40 dB (e.g., from the -60 dB minimum default line to -20 dB corresponding to N = 1). Since jump discontinuities do not exist in physics, a quantization of the discontinuity is suggested to reflect the effect of emission level at the input terminals. Three differential-mode voltage levels V_d, are used:

a. For $V_d \geqslant 500$ mV, use Fig. 4.9 directly.

b. For 10 mV $\leqslant V_d \leqslant 500$ mV:

$$AR_{dB} = A_{dB} - \Delta AR_{dB} \log [1 + 0.018 \, (V_d - 10)], \quad (4.10)$$
$$\text{for } V_d \text{ in mV}$$

where,

A_{dB} = attenuation due to filtering action only
ΔAR_{dB} = difference in dB between the filter curve portion and applicable AR levels in Fig. 4.9

c. For $V_d \leqslant 10$ mV, use attenuation due to filtering action only.

4.13

Illustrative Example 4.6

Compute the amplifier response to the ongoing problem in Example 4.1 when the out-of-band rolloff corresponds to 100 dB/decade or $N = 5$. Recompute the response for an $N = 5$ rolloff when the interfering frequency is coming from a Channel 9, 200 MHz VHF TV transmitter.

For the first problem, $f_{EMI}/f_{co} = 1/0.2 = 5$ (see Illustrative Example 4.1). The intersection of the $N = 5$ parameter line with 5 on the X-axis of Fig. 4.9 indicates that an out-of-band rejection of 60 dB is achieved. This also explains why the $AR_{dB} - 60$ dB was used in Fig. 3.13 (Chapter 3). This display is repeated in Fig. 4.10 for the convenience of the reader, where $- 60$ dB is shown in Column 5 for an amplifier slope of 100 dB/decade.

For the 200 MHz TV problem mentioned in Illustrative Example 4.2, Eq. (4.8) is used as the first step to test for audio rectification:

$$\text{In relative terms, } f_{ar} = 100/\sqrt{f_{co}} = 100/\sqrt{0.2} = 224$$

For channel 9, $f_{EMI} = 200$ MHz. Thus, $f_{EMI}/f_{co} = 200/0.2 = 1,000$. Since $f_{EMI} = f_{co} > f_{ar}$ an audio rectification susceptibility may exist. Thus, the response corresponding to the horizontal line $N \geqslant 3$ (for $N = 5$) in Fig. 4.9 is selected; viz., $- 40$ dB.

OPERATING CONDITIONS	AMB dBµV ①	N dBµV ②	A/N dB ③	GCM GLC ④A	FCM GLC ④B	DMC ④C	C-C ④D	P1·PS PS·V ④E	SUM 4A·4E ④	AMP REJ ⑤	Δ I/N ⑥	I/N ⑦
OBJECTIVE												-26
START: FIRST RUN	140	0	140	NA	-47	-86	NA	NA	-47	-14		+79
AMPL SLOPE = 100 dBD	140	0	140	NA	-47	-86	NA	NA	-47	-60	46	+33
BAL GEN/ AMPL = 5%	140	0	140	NA	-106	-86	NA	NA	-86	-60	39	-6
TWIST WIRES 40TPM	140	0	140	NA	-106	-142	NA	NA	-106	-60	20	-26

$(I/N)dB: \; ⑦ = ③ + ④ + ⑤$

Figure 4.10—Typical EMI Prediction and Analysis Showing Amplifier Rejection of 60 dB

4.4 EMI Filter Response

The victim receptor shown in the lower right corner of Fig. 4.1 may also include an EMI filter. If such a low-pass filter is used, it should be indicated in the **yes** selection box in the upper right corner of Fig. 4.2.

Filters will exhibit the same response function as those shown in Figs. 4.3 and 4.4. Since EMI filters do not have nonlinear components over their **intended** operating conditions, the audio rectification problem discussed in connection with Figs. 4.8 and 4.9 does not apply. However, if the filter is not of an EMI type,* it too will exhibit parasitic resonances and anti-resonances. Therefore, spurious responses may result.

To apply Figs. 4.3 and 4.4, three considerations are important:

1. To prevent the filter from interacting with the intentional amplifier or logic bandwidth, the filter cutoff frequency should be chosen somewhat above that of the amplifier or logic. Thus, the filter will have a somewhat lower f_{EMI}/f_{co} ratio used in the X-axis of Figs. 4.3 and 4.4.
2. The filter should be mounted in the essence of an infinite baffle. This means that the degrading effects of the filter input-output capacitance, especially at higher frequencies, are removed by a shield completely surrounding either the input or output. For example, a **feedthrough** type of filter mounting uses the natural shielding effect of the bulkhead or box panel walls.
3. The undesired emission to be filtered is differential mode (see Section 2.4.2). The filter may be transparent to common-mode emissions unless special measures (e.g., the common-mode choke) are taken to filter them.

Illustrative Example 4.7

Compute the attenuation offered by a pi-filter (low-pass, N = 3 stage) having passband, input-output impedances matched to the source and load impedances. The EMI filter is inserted in each line in a shielded area behind the bulkhead feedthrough connector in Box 2 from the interconnecting cable with Box 1. The same con-

---

*For non-EMI filters, inductors have winding capacitances, and capacitors have series lead inductances of such magnitudes to significantly limit performance well into the stop band.

ditions apply as those in the ongoing problem used in Illustrative Examples 4.1 and 4.2.

The victim amplifier cutoff frequency in Examples 4.1 and Fig. 4.2 was stated as 200 kHz. The filter cutoff frequency will be selected somewhat higher, say 250 kHz. For the 1 MHz interference broadcast radiation, $f_{EMI}/f_{co} = 1.0/0.25 = 4$. The N = 3 parameter line and the X-axis relative frequency of 4 intersect at -36 dB in Fig. 4.3. Thus, the pi-filter will give 36 dB rejection to the 1 MHz emission.

4.5 Total Victim Response

The total victim response, VR_{dB}, shown in Fig. 4.1 is that due to both the amplifier or logic circuit, AR_{dB}, and the EMI filter, FR_{dB}, if both are used simultaneously:

$$VR_{dB} = AR_{dB} + FR_{dB} \qquad (4.11)$$

Here it is presumed that the EMI filter is mounted in an infinite baffle or a shielded box. This prevents any crosstalk between input and output ports due to parasitic capacitance coupling.

Illustrative Example 4.8

Compute the combination of the amplifier rejection (-14 dB) in Example 4.1 and the EMI filter response (-36 dB) in Example 4.3. From Eq. (4.11), the total victim response is $VR_{dB} = -14$ dB -36 dB $= -50$ dB.

4.6 References

1. White, D.R.J., *A Handbook on Electrical Filters, Synthesis, Design and Applications* (Gainesville, VA: Interference Control Technologies, Inc., 1963).

4.7 Bibliography

Clark, O.M., "Capabilities and Limitations of Low Voltage Transient Suppressors," Second Symposium and Technical Exhibition on Electromagnetic Compatibility, Montreux, Switzerland, June 28-30, 1977.

Cohen, T.J., "The Susceptibility of Home Entertainment Devices to Strong RF Fields," *IEEE Electromagnetic Compatibility Symposium Record* (New York: IEEE) Session 4A, San Antonio, TX, October 7-9, 1975.

Converse, M.E., "Time Domain Filters — Principles and Applications," *IEEE Electromagnetic Compatibility Symposium Record* (New York: IEEE), Session 5A, San Antonio, TX, October 7-9, 1975.

Cowdell, Robert B., "Susceptibility on the Freeways," IEEE *Electromagnetic Compatibility Symposium Record* (New York: IEEE), Session 1B, Washington, DC, July 13-15, 1976.

deBruyne, P. and Bachman, W., "Performance of a Receiver During the Recovery Period from Strong Bursts of Broadband Interference," Second Symposium and Technical Exhibition on Electromagnetic Compatibility, Montreux, Switzerland, June 28-30, 1977.

Dorbuck, Anthony, "RF Susceptibility Tests on Home-Entertainment Devices," *IEEE Electromagnetic Compatibility Symposium Record* (New York: IEEE), Session 1B, Washington, DC, July 13-15, 1976.

Dvorak, T., "Electromagnetic Field Immunity — A New Parameter in Receiver Design," *IEEE Transactions on EMC*, Volume EMC-16, Number 3, August, 1974.

Dvorak, T., "Measurement of Electromagnetic Field Immunity," *IEEE Transactions on EMC*, Volume EMC-16, Number 3, August, 1974.

Engstrom, J., "Susceptibility of Household AM Radio Receivers to Powerline Conducted RF Noise," *IEEE EMC Symposium Record* (New York: IEEE), Sessions 4B, Seattle, WA, August 2-4, 1977.

Engstrom, J., Malack, J.A., and Rosenbarker, I.E., "Broadband EMI Control for Data Processing and Office Equipment," Second Symposium and Technical Exhibition on Electromagnetic Compatibility, Montreux, Switzerland, June 28-30, 1977.

Favors, H.A., "Trade Off Considerations in the Design Wave Filters for TEMPEST, EMP and Communications Applications," *IEEE EMC Symposium Record* (New York: IEEE), Session 5A, San Antonio, TX, October 7-9, 1975.

Ha, I.W. and Yarbrough, R.B., "A Lossy Element for EMC Filters," *IEEE Transactions on EMC*, Volume EMC-18, Number 4, November, 1976.

Hagedorn, R., "Influences of Electromagnetic Fields on Audiofrequency Equipment," Second Symposium and Technical Exhibition on Electromagnetic Compatibility, Montreux, Switzerland, June 28-30, 1977.

Jenkins, Sqd. Ldr. T.J., "Techniques for Assessing RF Susceptibility of Electro-Explosive Devices in Aircraft System," *IEEE EMC Symposium Record* (New York: IEEE), Session 5B, Washington, DC, July 13-15, 1976.

Kendall, C.M. and Hebson, B., "Microfiltering of Input/Output Cables: A New Solution to High Frequency I/O Cable Radiation and Susceptibility Fields," *IEEE EMC Symposium Record* (New York: IEEE), Session II-C, Atlanta, GA, June 20-22, 1978.

Ku, W.H.; Erickson, J.E.; Rabe, R.E.; and Seashotz, G.L., "Design Techniques and Intermodulation Analysis of Broadband Solid-State Power Amplifiers," *IEEE Transactions on EMC*, Volume EMC-19, Number 2, May, 1977.

Malack, J., "Television Receiver Susceptibility to Broadband Noise," *IEEE EMC Symposium Record* (New York: IEEE), Session II-C, Atlanta, GA, June 20-22, 1978.

Richardson, R.E.; Pugliella, V.G.; and Amadori, R.A., "Microwave Interference Effect in Bipolar Transients," *IEEE Transactions on EMC*, Volume EMC-17, Number 4, November, 1975.

Richardson, R.E., "Modeling of Microwave Rectification RFI Effects in Low Frequency Circuitry," *IEEE EMC Symposium Record* (New York: IEEE), Session II-C, Atlanta, GA, June 20-22, 1978.

Roe, J.M., "Microwave Interference Effects in Integrated Circuits," *IEEE EMC Symposium Record* (New York: IEEE), Session 4A, San Antonio, TX, October 7-9, 1975.

Rostek, F.M., "Techniques of Shielding and Filtering Digital Computers for EMI Emissions and Susceptibility," *IEEE EMC Symposium Record* (New York: IEEE), Session 4B, San Antonio, TX, October 7-9, 1975.

Schlicke, H.M., "Assuredly Effective Filters," *IEEE Transactions on EMC*, Volume EMC-18, Number 3, August, 1976.

Schulz, R.B., "A Review of Interference Criteria for Various Radio Services," Second Symposium and Technical Exhibition on Electromagnetic Compatibility, Montreux, Switzerland, June 28-30, 1977.

Sripaipan, C. and Holmes, W.H., "Achieving Wide-Band Common-Mode Rejection in Differential Amplifiers," *IEEE Transactions on EMC*, Volume EMC-12, Number 2, May, 1970.

Whalen, J.J., "The RF Pulse Susceptibility of UHF Transistors," *IEEE Transactions on EMC*, Volume EMC-17, Number 4, November, 1975.

Walko, L.C.; Maxwell, K.J.; Schneider, J.G.; and Serrano, A.V., "Susceptibility of Home Entertainment Equipment to High Power Interference," *IEEE EMC Symposium Record* (New York: IEEE), Session II-C, Atlanta, GA, June 20-22, 1978.

Weiner, D.D.; Spina, J.F.; and Fitch, A.W., "Relationship Between the Output Auto-Correlation Functions of Various Nonlinear Devices Subjected to Signal Pulse Noise and Interference," *IEEE Transactions on EMC*, Volume EMC-16, Number 1, February, 1974.

Whalen, J.J., "A Comparison of DC and RF Pulse Susceptibility of UHF Transistors," *IEEE Transactions on EMC*, Volume EMC-19, Number 2, May, 1977.

Whalen, J.J. and Trout, J., "Computer-Aided Analysis of RFI Effects in Integrated Circuits," *IEEE EMC Symposium Record*, Session II-A, Atlanta, GA, June 20-22, 1978.

Chapter 5

Coupling by Common-Ground Impedance

This chapter describes the first of the five principal coupling paths. As shown in Fig. 5.1, this coupling path (path 4A) is divided into two parts: (1) common-ground-impedance coupling and (2) ground-loop coupling. Common-ground-impedance coupling converts ground currents to a common-mode voltage, V_i, as shown in

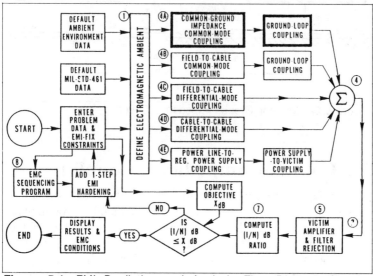

Figure 5.1—EMI Prediction and Analysis Flow Diagram Showing Common-Ground-Impedance and Ground-Loop Coupling

5.1

Fig. 5.2. This voltage then acts as a potential EMI source to push current around the loops ABCDEFGHA and ABCIJFGHA, which includes the victim cable. (Unless floated, the loop would tend to remain external to Boxes 1 and 2 for coaxial cables.) The resulting differential-mode voltage component developed in the victim cable appears across the amplifier or logic input terminals to constitute the potential EMI threat.

It could be argued that common impedances between EMI sources and victim circuits are not just found in ground returns but in any conductor that they share, e.g., typically the power feeders. This is addressed in Chapter 9 under the fifth coupling path, **power line coupling**, since it relates to the power supply's ability (or inability) to regulate varying load demands.

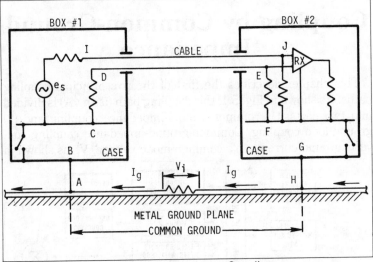

Figure 5.2—Common-Ground-Impedance Coupling

5.1 Common-Impedance Coupling

The ground impedance at both ends of a two-box situation as shown in Fig. 5.2 may correspond to that of a metallic ground plane (e.g., metal deck of a ship or skin of an aerospace vehicle), a safety wire (i.e., the **green** wire), a metal water pipe or the like. The common impedance may also correspond to that of the return paths of two or more amplifiers or logic. The next two sections derive these common impedances. The current(s) flowing through this common impedance may originate from a discrete external source, as shown in Fig. 5.3, or it may come from many other sources.* The former is readily calculated as discussed below. The latter, on the other hand, is either best measured with a surface current probe or estimated from a known data base corresponding to similar electromagnetic ambient environments. Details on grounding network characteristics can be found in Refs. 1 and 2.

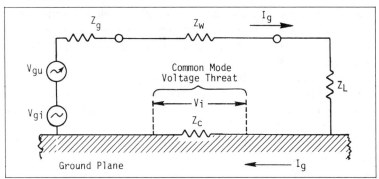

Figure 5.3—Ground Currents in Generator-to-Load Network

The ground plane involves a power mains source in which both the neutral at the generator and its load are grounded (a poor EMC practice). The current, I_g, which flows through this ground plane can be computed as follows:

$$I_g = V_g/(Z_g + Z_L + Z_w + Z_c) \qquad (5.1)$$

where,

$$V_g = \text{generator voltage} \qquad (5.2)$$
$$= V_{gi} + V_{gu}$$

V_{gi} = intentional dc or 50/60/400 Hz available generator voltage

V_{gu} = unintentional generator EMI voltage(s) developed at other frequencies, including harmonics of the generator

Z_g = generator source impedance

Z_L = load impedance

Z_w = generator-to-load wire impedance

Z_c = common-ground-plane impedance

---

*It may also originate from terminating the tangential electric field, E, which goes to zero, whereby $I_g = \sigma E$. Here, σ is the conductivity of the ground plane.

At dc or at 50, 60 or 400 Hz, Eq. (5.1) may be approximated by:

$$I_{gi} \approx V_{gi}/(Z_L + Z_w) \qquad (5.3)$$

since,

$$Z_c \ll Z_g \ll Z_L \text{ and } Z_w \qquad (5.4)$$

Since the generator also unintentionally develops harmonics of the power mains frequencies and high-frequency noise, Eq. (5.3) is not applicable well above the fundamental since Eq. (5.4) may no longer hold. Because of inductances, all impedances will increase with frequency above their corner frequencies.* This results in a corresponding reduction of I_g. This current also reduces with an increase in frequency because of a lowering V_{gu}. However, at some frequency Z_g will resonate, and so will Z_L. Above those first resonant frequencies, Z_c may be more or less than the other impedances. Thus, Eq. (5.1) must then be used, and Z_c should be measured or estimated if not known.

Illustrative Example 5.1

Compute the common-impedance current and common-mode voltage threat when a 60 Hz, 115 Vac generator has both its neutral and load grounded to a 1 mm steel ground plane. The load consumes 1 kW. Among the different undesirable currents is the tenth harmonic from the generator, which is 2 percent of the fundamental.

The load impedance is $Z_L = V^2/P_L = (115)^2/1,000 = 13.2\ \Omega$. From Eq. (5.3), $Z_w \ll Z_L$ (to avoid poor voltage regulation) and $I_{gi} = V_{gi}/Z_L = 115/13.2 = 8.7$ A. As defined in Section 5.2 for a steel ground plane of 1 mm thickness, $Z_c \approx 108\ \mu\Omega$ at 60 Hz and 300 $\mu\Omega$ at 600 Hz (tenth harmonic). Thus, the common-mode voltage threat at 60 Hz is:

$$V_{ii} = I_{gi} \times Z_c = 8.7 \text{ A} \times 108\ \mu\Omega = 940\ \mu V$$

At 600 Hz, the threat is:

$$V_{iu} = I_{gu} \times Z_c = 8.7 \times 0.02 \times 300\ \mu\Omega = 52\ \mu V$$

---

*The corner frequency is defined as that for which the inductive reactance equals the resistance.

5.2 Impedance of Metal Ground Planes

The impedance of metal ground planes is relatively low. This serves to reduce common-impedance coupling from potentially interfering ground currents. However, the impedance may not be low enough, and EMI may exist.

Between two points separated by a distance l, the dc resistance, R_{dc}, of a metal ground plane of cross section A is:

$$R_{dc} = \rho l/A \qquad (5.5)$$

$$= 1{,}000 l/\sigma l t$$

$$R_{dc} = 1{,}000/\sigma t \ \Omega/sq \qquad (5.6)$$

where,

ρ = resistivity of the metal in ohms $\times$ meters

$\sigma = \sigma_c \sigma_r$ conductivity of the metal $= 1/\rho$

$\sigma_c = 5.80 \times 10^7$ mhos/m for copper

σ_r = conductivity relative to copper

$\qquad$ = 0.17 for cold-rolled steel

t = metal thickness in mm

Thus, Eq. (5.6) becomes:

$$R_{dc} = 17.2/\sigma_r t \qquad \mu\Omega/sq \qquad (5.7)$$

The RF reactance[3] of a metal ground plane is:

$$Z_{RF} = \frac{369\sqrt{\mu_r f_{MHZ}/\sigma_r}}{1 - e^{-t/\delta}} \qquad (5.8)$$

where,

μ_r = permeability relative to copper $\qquad (5.9)$

$\qquad$ = 200 for cold-rolled steel

5.5

f_{MHz} = frequency in MHz

δ = skin depth in millimeters

$= 0.066/\sqrt{\mu_r \sigma_r f_{MHz}}$ for any metal

A complete treatment of metal plane impedances is provided in Volume 2, *Grounding and Bonding*, of this EMC handbook series. The impedance of a metal ground plane at any frequency including dc is:

$$Z = (R_{dc} + jZ_{RF}) [1 + \tan | (2\pi d/\lambda) |] \qquad (5.9A)$$

$$\approx R_{dc} + jZ_{RF}, \text{ for } d \leqslant 0.05\lambda \qquad (5.9B)$$

The impedance between two points in a ground plane will approximate the above ohms per square provided the ground plane is at least wide as the distance between the two ground points and this distance, d, is short compared with wavelength, λ.

A somewhat more accurate expression of Eq. (5.9B) (see Appendix G) was used to compute the tabulated data in Table 5.1. The table includes both copper and cold-rolled steel, from 10 Hz to 10 GHz, for six different thicknesses: 0.03 mm (about 1 mil), 0.1 mm, 0.3 mm, 1 mm, 3 mm and 10 mm.

Examine Table 5.1 and note that the dc resistance governs at 10 Hz for the thin metals (t = 0.03 mm). However, the RF impedance already applies at 10 Hz for the thick metals because they are several skin depths thick. For the same frequency above approximately 100 MHz for copper, the RF impedances are the same for different thicknesses. This also applies for steel above about 10 MHz because the skin depth is much less than metal thickness.

The impedance of any other metal may be determined with the use of Table 5.1 provided that its relative conductivity and permeability are known. The dc and RF impedances are:

$$R_{dc} = (\text{Table 5.1 value for copper})/\sigma_r \qquad (5.10)$$

$$Z_{RF} = (\text{Table 5.1 value for copper}) \times \sqrt{\mu_r/\sigma_r} \qquad (5.11)$$

Table 5.1—Metal Ground Plane Impedances in Ohms/Square

Freq.	COPPER, COND-1, PERM-1						STEEL, COND-0.17, PERM-200					
	t = 0.03	t = 0.1	t = 0.3	t = 1	t = 3	t = 10	t = 0.03	t = 0.1	t = 0.3	t = 1	t = 3	t = 10
10 Hz	574 μ	172 μ	57.4 μ	17.2 μ	5.74 μ	1.75 μ	3.38 m	1.01 m	338 μ	101 μ	38.5 μ	40.3 μ
20 Hz	574 μ	172 μ	57.4 μ	17.2 μ	5.75 μ	1.83 μ	3.38 m	1.01 m	338 μ	102 μ	49.5 μ	56.6 μ
30 Hz	574 μ	172 μ	57.4 μ	17.2 μ	5.75 μ	1.95 μ	3.38 m	1.01 m	338 μ	103 μ	62.3 μ	69.3 μ
50 Hz	574 μ	172 μ	57.4 μ	17.2 μ	5.76 μ	2.30 μ	3.38 m	1.01 m	338 μ	106 μ	86.2 μ	89.6 μ
70 Hz	574 μ	172 μ	57.4 μ	17.2 μ	5.78 μ	2.71 μ	3.38 m	1.01 m	338 μ	110 μ	105 μ	106 μ
100 Hz	574 μ	172 μ	57.4 μ	17.2 μ	5.82 μ	3.35 μ	3.38 m	1.01 m	338 μ	118 μ	127 μ	126 μ
200 Hz	574 μ	172 μ	57.4 μ	17.2 μ	6.04 μ	5.16 μ	3.38 m	1.01 m	340 μ	157 μ	179 μ	179 μ
300 Hz	574 μ	172 μ	57.4 μ	17.2 μ	6.38 μ	6.43 μ	3.38 m	1.01 m	342 μ	199 μ	219 μ	219 μ
500 Hz	574 μ	172 μ	57.4 μ	17.3 μ	7.36 μ	8.27 μ	3.38 m	1.01 m	350 μ	275 μ	283 μ	283 μ
700 Hz	574 μ	172 μ	57.4 μ	17.3 μ	8.55 μ	9.77 μ	3.38 m	1.01 m	362 μ	335 μ	335 μ	335 μ
1 kHz	574 μ	172 μ	57.4 μ	17.5 μ	10.4 μ	11.6 μ	3.38 m	1.01 m	385 μ	403 μ	400 μ	400 μ
2 kHz	574 μ	172 μ	57.5 μ	18.3 μ	16.1 μ	16.5 μ	3.38 m	1.02 m	495 μ	566 μ	566 μ	566 μ
3 kHz	574 μ	172 μ	57.5 μ	19.5 μ	20.3 μ	20.2 μ	3.38 m	1.03 m	623 μ	693 μ	694 μ	694 μ
5 kHz	574 μ	172 μ	57.6 μ	23.0 μ	26.2 μ	26.1 μ	3.38 m	1.06 m	862 μ	896 μ	896 μ	896 μ
7 kHz	574 μ	172 μ	57.8 μ	27.1 μ	30.9 μ	30.9 μ	3.38 m	1.10 m	1.05 m	1.06 m	1.06 m	1.06 m
10 kHz	574 μ	172 μ	58.2 μ	33.5 μ	36.9 μ	36.9 μ	3.38 m	1.18 m	1.27 m	1.26 m	1.26 m	1.26 m
20 kHz	574 μ	172 μ	60.4 μ	51.6 μ	52.2 μ	52.2 μ	3.40 m	1.57 m	1.79 m	1.79 m	1.79 m	1.79 m
30 kHz	574 μ	172 μ	63.8 μ	64.3 μ	63.9 μ	63.9 μ	3.42 m	1.99 m	2.19 m	2.19 m	2.19 m	2.19 m
50 kHz	574 μ	173 μ	73.6 μ	82.7 μ	82.6 μ	82.6 μ	3.50 m	2.75 m	2.83 m	2.83 m	2.83 m	2.83 m
70 kHz	574 μ	173 μ	85.5 μ	97.7 μ	97.7 μ	97.7 μ	3.62 m	3.35 m	3.35 m	3.35 m	3.35 m	3.35 m
100 kHz	574 μ	175 μ	104 μ	116 μ	116 μ	116 μ	3.85 m	4.03 m	4.00 m	4.00 m	4.00 m	4.00 m
200 kHz	575 μ	183 μ	161 μ	165 μ	165 μ	165 μ	4.95 m	5.66 m	5.66 m	5.66 m	5.66 m	5.66 m
300 kHz	575 μ	195 μ	203 μ	202 μ	202 μ	202 μ	6.23 m	6.93 m	6.94 m	6.94 m	6.94 m	6.94 m
500 kHz	576 μ	230 μ	262 μ	261 μ	261 μ	261 μ	8.62 m	8.96 m	8.96 m	8.96 m	8.96 m	8.96 m
700 kHz	578 μ	271 μ	309 μ	309 μ	309 μ	309 μ	10.5 m	10.6 m	10.6 m	10.6 m	10.6 m	10.6 m
1 MHz	582 μ	335 μ	369 μ	369 μ	369 μ	369 μ	12.7 m	12.6 m	12.6 m	12.6 m	12.6 m	12.6 m
2 MHz	604 μ	516 μ	522 μ	522 μ	522 μ	522 μ	17.9 m	17.9 m	17.9 m	17.9 m	17.9 m	17.9 m
3 MHz	638 μ	643 μ	639 μ	639 μ	639 μ	639 μ	21.9 m	21.9 m	21.9 m	21.9 m	21.9 m	21.9 m
5 MHz	736 μ	827 μ	826 μ	826 μ	826 μ	826 μ	28.3 m	28.3 m	28.3 m	28.3 m	28.3 m	28.3 m
7 MHz	855 μ	977 μ	977 μ	977 μ	977 μ	977 μ	33.5 m	33.5 m	33.5 m	33.5 m	33.5 m	33.5 m
10 MHz	1.04 m	1.16 m	1.16 m	1.16 m	1.16 m	1.16 m	40.0 m	40.0 m	40.0 m	40.0 m	40.0 m	40.0 m
20 MHz	1.61 m	1.65 m	1.65 m	1.65 m	1.65 m	1.65 m	56.6 m	56.6 m	56.6 m	56.6 m	56.6 m	56.6 m
30 MHz	2.03 m	2.02 m	2.02 m	2.02 m	2.02 m	2.02 m	69.4 m	69.4 m	69.4 m	69.4 m	69.4 m	69.4 m
50 MHz	2.62 m	2.61 m	2.61 m	2.61 m	2.61 m	2.61 m	89.6 m	89.6 m	89.6 m	89.6 m	89.6 m	89.6 m
70 MHz	3.09 m	3.09 m	3.09 m	3.09 m	3.09 m	3.09 m	106 m	106 m	106 m	106 m	106 m	106 m
100 MHz	3.69 m	3.69 m	3.69 m	3.69 m	3.69 m	3.69 m	126 m	126 m	126 m	126 m	126 m	126 m
200 MHz	5.22 m	5.22 m	5.22 m	5.22 m	5.22 m	5.22 m	179 m	179 m	179 m	179 m	179 m	179 m
300 MHz	6.39 m	6.39 m	6.39 m	6.39 m	6.39 m	6.39 m	219 m	219 m	219 m	219 m	219 m	219 m
500 MHz	8.26 m	8.26 m	8.26 m	8.26 m	8.26 m	8.26 m	283 m	283 m	283 m	283 m	283 m	283 m
700 MHz	9.77 m	9.77 m	9.77 m	9.77 m	9.77 m	9.77 m	335 m	335 m	335 m	335 m	335 m	335 m
1 GHz	11.6 m	11.6 m	11.6 m	11.6 m	11.6 m	11.6 m	400 m	400 m	400 m	400 m	400 m	400 m
2 GHz	16.5 m	16.5 m	16.5 m	16.5 m	16.5 m	16.5 m	566 m	566 m	566 m	566 m	566 m	566 m
3 GHz	20.2 m	20.2 m	20.2 m	20.2 m	20.2 m	20.2 m	694 m	694 m	694 m	694 m	694 m	694 m
5 GHz	26.1 m	26.1 m	26.1 m	26.1 m	26.1 m	26.1 m	896 m	896 m	896 m	896 m	896 m	896 m
7 GHz	30.9 m	30.9 m	30.9 m	30.9 m	30.9 m	30.9 m	1.06 Ω	1.06 Ω	1.06 Ω	1.06 Ω	1.06 Ω	1.06 Ω
10 GHz	36.9 m	36.9 m	36.9 m	36.9 m	36.9 m	36.9 m	1.26 Ω	1.26 Ω	1.26 Ω	1.26 Ω	1.26 Ω	1.26 Ω

* t is in units of mm
μ = microhms
m = milliohms
Ω = ohms

NOTE: Do not use table at frequencies in MHz above $5/l_m$ since the separation distance in meters, l_m, of two grounded equipments will exceed 0.05λ where error becomes significant.

Illustrative Example 5.2

Compute the potential difference between two equipment cases, both of which are grounded to a 1 mm aluminum ground plane in which 100 A of 60 Hz power is also flowing.

From Table 5.1, copper has a resistance of 17.2 $\mu\Omega$ for t = 1 mm. For aluminum, σ_r = 0.6 and μ_r = 1. Since the impedance values around 60 Hz show only a small change with frequency, the impedance is mainly resistance, and Eq. (5.10) applies. Thus, the impedance of the aluminum ground plane is:

$$R_{dc}/\sigma_r = 17.2\ \mu\Omega/0.6 = 29\ \mu\Omega$$

The potential drop between the two equipment cases is:

$$I \times R = 100\ A \times 29\ \mu\Omega = 2.9\ mV$$

If the circuits inside the two boxes are grounded to their respective cases and those cases are grounded to the ground plane as shown in Fig. 5.2, a common-mode potential exists across both circuit boards. Except for the reduction by ground-loop coupling as described in Section 5.4, the 2.9 mV potential can interfere with sensitive analog amplifiers.

Illustrative Example 5.3

Compute the potential drop for this same problem (Example 5.2) using a 0.3 mm thick, steel ground plane.

Table 5.1 shows that the ground plane impedance for 0.3 mm steel at 60 Hz is 338 $\mu\Omega$. For 100 A flowing through the ground plane, the potential drop is 34 mV. This is a substantial value for sensitive equipment grounded thereto. The 100 A can be a normal current if the ground is used as an active return, or it can be a temporary fault condition.

With some modification, Eq. (5.9B) can be used to approximate the impedance of configurations other than ground planes. For example, Fig. 5.4 shows a beam having a periphery, p, and a length *l.* The modified RF impedance in ohms between two points located at opposite ends is:

$$Z_1 \approx \frac{Z_{RF} \times l}{p} \qquad (5.12)$$

where,

l = length of beam in millimeters

Z_{RF} = value from Eq. (5.9B)

p = periphery in millimeters

The above equation is applicable provided $l/p \leqslant 10$. This constraint is required to assure that the external self-inductance will not become significantly larger than the surface inductance, at which point the metal piece would start behaving as a wire. The equivalent thickness for calculating Z_{RF} is approximately half the least cross sectional dimension of the beam.

The dc resistance of a bar is:

$$R_1 = \frac{1{,}000\ l}{\sigma A} \qquad (5.13)$$

$$= 17.2\ l/A\ \mu\Omega \text{ for copper} \qquad (5.14)$$

$$= 29\ l/A\ \mu\Omega \text{ for aluminum}$$

$$= 101\ l/A\ \mu\Omega \text{ for steel} \qquad (5.15)$$

where,

A = area of cylinder cross section in square millimeters

l = length of cylinder in millimeters

To compute the impedance of the cylinder, Eqs. (5.12) and (5.13) are added as complex numbers. When one is more than 10 times the other, the larger is selected.

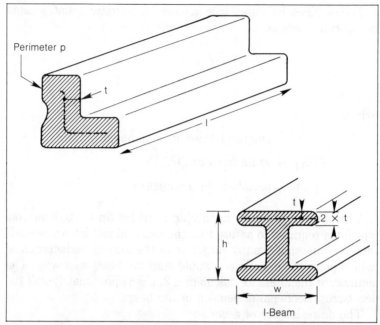

Figure 5.4—A Beam of Arbitrary Cross Section and an I-Beam

Illustrative Example 5.4

In this example, lightning strikes a small building containing four vertical steel girders. Two interconnected pieces of equipment are grounded to one of the girders at a 3 m separation between grounds. The I-beam has a cross sectional area of 25 cm², a periphery of 90 cm and a thickness of 6 mm. Calculate the potential drop between ground points if the stroke current is 30,000 A and has a rise time of 0.5 μs.

From Eq. (5.15), the dc resistance is R_1 = 101 × 3,000/2,500 = 121 $\mu\Omega$. The corner frequency corresponding to the 0.5 μs rise time of the stroke is $1/\pi\tau_r$ = 637 kHz. From Table 5.1, the value of Z_{RF} for t = 6 mm/2 (see Fig. 5.4) is 9.9 mΩ by interpolation. Equation (5.12) can be used since $l/p \leqslant 10$. The adjusted value for Z_1 from Eq. (5.12) is: 9.9 mΩ × 3,000/900 = 33 mΩ. Since $Z_1 \gg R_1$, the Z impedance will govern.

The voltage drop between the two grounded equipment cases corresponding to 30,000 A flowing in the girder is: 30,000 × 0.033

5.10

= 990 V. Unless some EMC measures are taken, the solid-state electronic packages inside the equipments can burn out. As described later, possible EMC approaches include grounding both cases at one point only, using optical isolators in the interconnecting cable path or floating the zero-volt reference within one of the cases and using transient suppressors.

5.3 Impedance of Safety Wires, Straps and Printed Wiring

The preceding sections treated the impedance of conductive planes and large metallic mass configurations such as building girders. This section involves computing impedances of safety wires (the **green wire**), metal straps and printed circuit wiring. Each will be treated separately. The major difference with ground planes is that for long form factors, the external self-inductance governs the HF impedance. A more extensive coverage of wire and strap impedances is given in both Volume 2, *Grounding and Bonding*, and Volume 5, *EMC in Components and Devices*, of this EMC handbook series.

5.3.1 Impedance of Safety Wires and Bonding Conductors

From Eq. (5.13), the dc resistance of a round wire is:

$$R_1 = \frac{1,000\, l}{\sigma A} = \frac{4,000\, l}{\sigma \pi D^2} \tag{5.16}$$

$$= 22\, l/D^2\ \mu\Omega \text{ for copper} \tag{5.17}$$

where,

A = area of cylinder cross section in square millimeters

l = wire length in millimeters

D = wire diameter in millimeters

$$= \frac{11.68}{92[(AWG + 3)/39]}$$

AWG = American Wire Gauge number

The inductance of a round straight wire at RF is:

$$L \approx 0.0002 \, l \left[l_n \left(\frac{4 \, l}{D} \right) + \frac{1}{4} \right] \qquad (5.19)$$

where,

$$l_n = \text{natural log}$$

The natural logarithm is the external self-inductance, and the 1/4 accounts for internal wire inductance. The impedance of a copper wire is obtained by converting Eq. (5.19) to inductive reactance and adding quadratically the resistance of Eq. (5.17). This impedance is tabulated in Table 5.2 for 1 cm, 10 cm, 1 m and 10 m lengths of AWG No. 2, No. 10 and No. 22 copper wire.

In addition, Table 5.2A provides resistance and inductance values of straight wires from AWG No. 0 to No. 34.

Table 5.2—Impedance of Straight Circular Copper Wires**

FREQ.	AWG# = 2, D = 6.54 mm				AWG# = 10, D = 2.59 mm				AWG# = 22, D = 0.64 mm			
	l = 1cm	l = 10cm	l = 1 m	l = 10 m	l = 1cm	l = 10cm	l = 1 m	l = 10 m	l = 1cm	l = 10cm	l = 1 m	l = 10 m
10 Hz	5.13 µ	51.4 µ	517 µ	5.22 m	32.7 µ	327 µ	3.28 m	32.8 m	529 µ	5.29 m	52.9 m	529 m
20 Hz	5.14 µ	52.0 µ	532 µ	5.50 m	32.7 µ	328 µ	3.28 m	32.8 m	529 µ	5.29 m	53.0 m	530 m
30 Hz	5.15 µ	52.8 µ	555 µ	5.94 m	32.8 µ	328 µ	3.28 m	32.9 m	529 µ	5.30 m	53.0 m	530 m
50 Hz	5.20 µ	55.5 µ	624 µ	7.16 m	32.8 µ	329 µ	3.30 m	33.2 m	530 µ	5.30 m	53.0 m	530 m
70 Hz	5.27 µ	59.3 µ	715 µ	8.68 m	32.8 µ	330 µ	3.33 m	33.7 m	530 µ	5.30 m	53.0 m	530 m
100 Hz	5.41 µ	66.7 µ	877 µ	11.2 m	32.9 µ	332 µ	3.38 m	34.6 m	530 µ	5.30 m	53.0 m	530 m
200 Hz	6.20 µ	99.5 µ	1.51 m	20.6 m	33.2 µ	345 µ	3.67 m	39.6 m	530 µ	5.30 m	53.0 m	530 m
300 Hz	7.32 µ	137 µ	2.19 m	30.4 m	33.7 µ	365 µ	4.11 m	46.9 m	530 µ	5.30 m	53.0 m	531 m
500 Hz	10.1 µ	219 µ	3.59 m	50.3 m	35.3 µ	425 µ	5.28 m	64.8 m	530 µ	5.31 m	53.2 m	533 m
700 Hz	13.2 µ	303 µ	5.01 m	70.2 m	37.7 µ	500 µ	6.66 m	84.8 m	530 µ	5.32 m	53.4 m	537 m
1 kHz	18.1 µ	429 µ	7.14 m	100 m	42.2 µ	632 µ	8.91 m	116 m	531 µ	5.34 m	53.9 m	545 m
2 kHz	35.2 µ	855 µ	14.2 m	200 m	62.5 µ	1.13 m	16.8 m	225 m	536 µ	5.48 m	56.6 m	589 m
3 kHz	52.5 µ	1.28 m	21.3 m	300 m	86.3 µ	1.65 m	25.0 m	336 m	545 µ	5.71 m	60.9 m	656 m
5 kHz	87.3 µ	2.13 m	35.6 m	500 m	137 µ	2.72 m	41.5 m	559 m	571 µ	6.39 m	72.9 m	835 m
7 kHz	122 µ	2.98 m	49.8 m	700 m	189 µ	3.79 m	58.1 m	783 m	609 µ	7.28 m	87.9 m	1.04 Ω
10 kHz	174 µ	4.26 m	71.2 m	1.00 Ω	268 µ	5.41 m	82.9 m	1.11 Ω	681 µ	8.89 m	113 m	1.39 Ω
20 kHz	348 µ	8.53 m	142 m	2.00 Ω	533 µ	10.8 m	165 m	2.23 Ω	1.00 m	15.2 m	207 m	2.63 Ω
30 kHz	523 µ	12.8 m	213 m	3.00 Ω	799 µ	16.2 m	248 m	3.35 Ω	1.39 m	22.0 m	305 m	3.91 Ω
50 kHz	871 µ	21.3 m	356 m	5.00 Ω	1.33 m	27.0 m	414 m	5.58 Ω	2.20 m	36.1 m	504 m	'6.48 Ω
70 kHz	1.22 m	29.8 m	498 m	7.00 Ω	1.86 m	37.8 m	580 m	7.82 Ω	3.04 m	50.2 m	704 m	9.06 Ω
100 kHz	1.74 m	42.6 m	712 m	10.0 Ω	2.66 m	54.0 m	828 m	11.1 Ω	4.31 m	71.6 m	1.00 Ω	12.9 Ω
200 kHz	3.48 m	85.3 m	1.42 Ω	20.0 Ω	5.32 m	108 m	1.65 Ω	22.3 Ω	8.59 m	142 m	2.00 Ω	25.8 Ω
300 kHz	5.23 m	·128 m	2.13 Ω	30.0 Ω	7.98 m	162 m	2.48 Ω	33.5 Ω	12.8 m	214 m	3.01 Ω	38.7 Ω
500 kHz	8.71 m	213 m	3.56 Ω	50.0 Ω	13.3 m	270 m	4.14 Ω	55.8 Ω	21.4 m	357 m	5.01 Ω	64.6 Ω
700 kHz	12.2 m	298 m	4.98 Ω	70.0 Ω	18.6 m	378 m	5.80 Ω	78.2 Ω	30.0 m	500 m	7.02 Ω	90.4 Ω

Table 5.2—(continued)

FREQ.	AWG#=2, D=6.54 mm				AWG#=10, D=2.59 mm				AWG#=22, D=0.64 mm			
	l=1cm	l=10cm	l=1 m	l=10 m	l=1cm	l=10cm	l=1 m	l=10 m	l=1cm	l=10cm	l=1 m	l=10 m
1 MHz	17.4 m	426 m	7.12 Ω	100 Ω	26.6 m	540 m	8.28 Ω	111 Ω	42.8 m	714 m	10.0 Ω	129 Ω
2 MHz	34.8 m	853 m	14.2 Ω	200 Ω	53.2 m	1.08 Ω	16.5 Ω	223 Ω	85.7 m	1.42 Ω	20.0 Ω	258 Ω
3 MHz	52.3 m	1.28 Ω	21.3 Ω	300 Ω	79.8 m	1.62 Ω	24.8 Ω	335 Ω	128 m	2.14 Ω	30.1 Ω	387 Ω
5 MHz	87.1 m	2.13 Ω	35.6 Ω	500 Ω	133 m	2.70 Ω	41.4 Ω	558 Ω	214 m	3.57 Ω	50.1 Ω	646 Ω
7 MHz	122 m	2.98 Ω	49.8 Ω	700 Ω	186 m	3.78 Ω	58.0 Ω	782 Ω	300 m	5.00 Ω	70.2 Ω	904 Ω
10 MHz	174 m	4.26 Ω	71.2 Ω	1.00 kΩ	266 m	5.40 Ω	82.8 Ω	1.11 kΩ	428 m	7.14 Ω	100 Ω	1.29 kΩ
20 MHz	348 m	8.53 Ω	142 Ω	2.00 kΩ	532 m	10.8 Ω	165 Ω	2.23 kΩ	857 m	14.2 Ω	200 Ω	2.58 kΩ
30 MHz	523 m	12.8 Ω	213 Ω	3.00 kΩ	798 m	16.2 Ω	248 Ω	3.35 kΩ	1.28 Ω	21.4 Ω	301 Ω	3.87 kΩ
50 MHz	871 m	21.3 Ω	356 Ω	5.00 kΩ	1.33 Ω	27.0 Ω	414 Ω	5.58 kΩ	2.14 Ω	35.7 Ω	501 Ω	6.46 kΩ
70 MHz	1.22 Ω	29.8 Ω	498 Ω	7.00 kΩ	1.86 Ω	37.8 Ω	580 Ω	7.82 kΩ	3.00 Ω	50.0 Ω	702 Ω	9.04 kΩ
100 MHz	1.74 Ω	42.6 Ω	712 Ω	10.0 kΩ	2.66 Ω	54.0 Ω	828 Ω	11.1 kΩ	4.28 Ω	71.4 Ω	1.00 kΩ	12.9 kΩ
200 MHz	3.48 Ω	85.3 Ω	1.42 kΩ	20.0 kΩ	5.32 Ω	108 Ω	1.65 kΩ	22.3 kΩ	8.57 Ω	142 Ω	2.00 kΩ	25.8 kΩ
300 MHz	5.23 Ω	128 Ω	2.13 kΩ	30.0 kΩ	7.98 Ω	162 Ω	2.48 kΩ	33.5 kΩ	12.8 Ω	214 Ω	3.01 kΩ	38.7 kΩ
500 MHz	8.71 Ω	213 Ω	3.56 kΩ	50.0 kΩ	13.3 Ω	270 Ω	4.14 kΩ	55.8 kΩ	21.4 Ω	357 Ω	5.01 kΩ	64.6 kΩ
700 MHz	12.2 Ω	298 Ω	4.98 kΩ	70.0 kΩ	18.6 Ω	378 Ω	5.80 kΩ	78.2 kΩ	30.0 Ω	500 Ω	7.02 kΩ	90.4 kΩ
1 GHz	17.4 Ω	426 Ω	7.12 kΩ		26.6 Ω	540 Ω	6.28 kΩ		42.8 Ω	714 Ω	10.0 kΩ	

* AWG = American Wire Gage
D = wire diameter in mm
l = wire length in cm or m
μ = microhms
m = milliohms
Ω = ohms

 Non-Valid Region for which $l \geq \lambda/4$

* * Values derived from free-space inductance, when the conductor is far from its return circuit or plane

Table 5.2A—Resistance and Inductance of a Straight Wire from AWG No. 0 to 34

Diam	AWG	R/L	10 cm	20 cm	30 cm	50 cm	70 cm	1 m	2 m	3 m	5 m	7 m	10 m	20 m	30 m
8.2	0	Res/μ	32	64	96	160	225	322	645	967	1,613	2,259	3,227	6,455	9,683
		Ind/n	62	153	254	474	710	1,086	2,450	3,918	7,042	10,329	15,470	33,712	53,001
6.5	2	Res/μ	51	102	153	56	358	512	1,026	1,539	2,565	3,592	5,132	10,265	15,398
		Ind/n	67	162	267	497	743	1,132	2,543	4,057	7,273	10,654	15,933	34,639	54,392
5.2	4	Res/μ	81	162	244	408	570	816	1,631	2,447	4,080	5,712	8,161	16,322	24,484
		Ind/n	71	171	281	520	775	1,179	2,635	4,196	7,505	10,978	16,397	35,567	55,783
4.1	6	Res/μ	129	259	389	648	907	1,297	2,594	3,892	6,488	9,083	12,976	25,954	38,931
		Ind/n	76	180	295	543	807	1,225	2,728	4,335	7,737	11,303	16,860	36,494	57,174
3.2	8	Res/μ	206	412	618	1,031	1,443	2,062	4,126	6,189	10,316	14,443	20,634	41,269	61,904
		Ind/n	80	189	309	566	840	1,271	2,821	4,474	7,969	11,627	17,324	37,422	58,566
2.6	10	Res/μ	328	655	983	1,640	2,296	3,280	6,561	9,842	16,404	22,967	32,810	65,621	98,432
		Ind/n	85	199	323	589	872	1,318	2,913	4,613	8,200	11,952	17,788	38,349	59,957
2	12	Res/m	0.5	0.1	1.5	2.5	3.5	5	10	15	25	36	51	103	156
		Ind/n	90	208	336	612	905	1,364	3,006	4,753	8,432	12,277	18,252	39,277	61,348
1.6	14	Res/m	.08	1.6	2.4	4	5.6	8	16	24	40	57	82	165	248
		Ind/n	94	217	350	635	937	1,410	3,099	4,892	8,664	12,601	18,715	40,204	62,739
1.3	16	Res/m	1	2	3	6	8	12	25	39	65	91	131	263	395
		Ind/n	99	226	364	659	969	1,457	3,191	5,031	8,896	12,926	19,179	41,132	64,131
1	18	Res/m	2	4	6	10	14	20	41	62	104	146	209	418	628
		Ind/n	103	235	378	682	1,002	1,503	3,284	5,170	9,128	13,250	19,643	42,059	65,522
0.8	20	Res/m	3	6	9	16	22	32	66	99	166	232	332	666	999
		Ind/n	108	245	392	705	1,034	1,549	3,377	5,309	9,360	13,575	20,107	42,987	66,913
0.6	22	Res/m	5	10	15	26	36	52	105	158	264	370	529	1,060	1,590
		Ind/n	113	254	406	728	1,067	1,596	3,470	5,448	9,592	13,900	20,570	43,914	68,305
0.5	24	Res/m	8	16	24	42	58	83	168	252	421	589	842	1,685	2,529
		Ind/n	117	263	420	751	1,099	1,642	3,562	5,587	9,823	14,224	21,034	44,842	69,696
0.4	26	Res/m	13	26	39	66	93	133	267	401	669	937	1,340	2,680	4,021
		Ind/n	122	273	434	774	1,132	1,688	3,655	5,726	10,055	14,549	21,498	45,769	71,087
0.3	28	Res/m	21	42	63	106	148	213	425	639	1,065	1,491	2,131	4,263	6,394
		Ind/n	127	282	448	798	1,164	1,735	3,748	5,865	10,287	14,873	21,962	46,697	72,478
0.25	30	Res/m	34	67	101	168	236	338	677	1,016	1,694	2,372	3,389	6,776	10,168
		Ind/n	131	291	461	821	1,197	1,781	3,841	6,005	10,519	15,198	22,425	47,624	73,870
0.2	32	Res/m	54	107	161	268	376	538	1,077	1,616	2,694	3,772	5,389	10,779	16,168
		Ind/n	136	300	475	844	1,229	1,828	3,933	6,144	10,751	15,523	22,889	48,552	75,261
0.16	34	Res/m	85	170	256	428	599	856	1,713	2,570	4,284	5,998	8,569	17,139	25,709
		Ind/n	140	310	489	867	1,261	1,874	4,026	6,283	10,983	15,847	23,353	49,479	76,652

μ = microhm, m = milliohm
n = nanohenry

The table shows that the impedances at low frequencies are inversely proportional to the wire areas (diameters squared). For example, going from AWG No. 22 to No. 2, the cross sectional area of the latter is about 100 times larger, and the resistance is about 1 percent. At high frequencies, however, the added benefit of a larger wire diameter becomes considerably less pronounced. In fact, going from a No. 22 to No. 2 wire decreases the high-frequency impedance by only 30 percent. The impedance also increases somewhat more rapidly than a corresponding increase in wire length. It should be noted also that ohmic resistance increases with frequency due to skin effect. However, when this happens, the inductive part of the impedance already predominates.

5.3.2 Impedance of Conductor Straps

For the same cross sectional area, Section 5.2 showed that one way to reduce the RF impedance of a conductor is to increase its periphery. (Another way is to use Litz wire instead of solid wire. However, this is used for signal lines, not ground safety wires.) Again, the dc resistance is obtained from Eq. (5.13):

$$R = \frac{1,000 \, l}{\sigma A} = \frac{1,000 \, l}{\sigma wt} \qquad (5.20)$$

$$= 17.2 \, l/wt \, \mu\Omega \text{ for copper} \qquad (5.21)$$

where,

l = strap length in millimeters

w = strap width in millimeters

t = strap thickness in millimeters

σ = conductivity

The inductance in microhenries of the same strap is:

$$L = 0.002 \, l \left[l_n \left(\frac{2 \, l}{w + t} \right) \right.$$

$$\left. + 0.5 + 0.2235 \left(\frac{w + t}{2 \, l} \right) \right] \qquad (5.22)$$

5.14

The impedance of a copper strap is obtained by converting Eq. (5.22) to inductive reactances and adding quadratically the resistance of Eq. (5.20). This impedance is tabulated in Table 5.3 for 10 cm, 1 m and 10 m lengths of three straps of copper: 0.3 mm thick ×

Table 5.3—Impedance of Copper Straps

FREQ.	0.3 mm × 10 mm Strap				1 mm × 10 mm Strap				2 mm × 50 mm Strap			
	l=3 cm	l=10 cm	l=1 m	l=10 m	l=3 cm	l=10 cm	l=1 m	l=10 m	l=15 cm	l=50 cm	l=1 m	l=10 m
10 Hz	173 μ	574 μ	5.74 m	57.4 m	52.4 μ	172 μ	1.72 m	17.2 m	30.1 μ	108 μ	180 μ	1.90 m
20 Hz	174 μ	574 μ	5.74 m	57.5 m	53.3 μ	172 μ	1.73 m	17.3 m	34.4 μ	130 μ	201 μ	2.36 m
30 Hz	175 μ	574 μ	5.75 m	57.5 m	54.1 μ	172 μ	1.73 m	17.5 m	38.8 μ	151 μ	232 μ	2.98 m
50 Hz	176 μ	575 μ	5.75 m	57.6 m	55.8 μ	173 μ	1.76 m	17.9 m	47.4 μ	195 μ	312 μ	4.40 m
70 Hz	178 μ	575 μ	5.76 m	57.9 m	57.5 μ	175 μ	1.79 m	18.6 m	56.0 μ	238 μ	404 μ	5.93 m
100 Hz	181 μ	576 μ	5.79 m	58.3 m	60.0 μ	177 μ	1.86 m	19.9 m	69.0 μ	304 μ	549 μ	8.29 m
200 Hz	189 μ	581 μ	5.92 m	60.9 m	68.5 μ	192 μ	2.24 m	26.4 m	112 μ	522 μ	1.05 m	16.3 m
300 Hz	198 μ	589 μ	6.14 m	65.0 m	76.9 μ	215 μ	2.75 m	34.7 m	155 μ	739 μ	1.57 m	24.3 m
500 Hz	215 μ	614 μ	6.79 m	76.6 m	93.8 μ	275 μ	3.97 m	53.1 m	242 μ	1.17 m	2.61 m	40.5 m
700 Hz	233 μ	615 μ	7.66 m	91.3 m	111 μ	346 μ	5.30 m	72.5 m	328 μ	1.61 m	3.65 m	56.7 m
1 kHz	259 μ	721 μ	9.25 m	116 m	136 μ	462 μ	7.37 m	102 m	457 μ	2.26 m	5.22 m	81.1 m
2 kHz	345 μ	1.04 m	15.5 m	210 m	220 μ	874 μ	14.4 m	201 m	889 μ	4.44 m	10.4 m	162 m
3 kHz	432 μ	1.43 m	22.4 m	309 m	304 μ	1.29 m	21.5 m	302 m	1.32 m	6.62 m	15.6 m	243 m
5 kHz	605 μ	2.25 m	36.7 m	510 m	473 μ	2.15 m	35.8 m	503 m	2.84 m	11.0 m	26.1 m	405 m
7 kHz	779 μ	3.11 m	51.0 m	712 m	642 μ	3.00 m	50.2 m	704 m	3.05 m	15.3 m	36.5 m	567 m
10 kHz	1.04 m	4.40 m	72.7 m	1.01 Ω	895 μ	4.29 m	71.7 m	1.00 Ω	4.34 m	21.9 m	52.2 m	810 m
20 kHz	1.91 m	8.75 m	145 m	2.02 Ω	1.74 m	8.57 m	143 m	2.01 Ω	8.66 m	43.6 m	104 m	1.62 Ω
30 kHz	2.77 m	13.1 m	217 m	3.04 Ω	2.58 m	12.8 m	215 m	3.01 Ω	13.0 m	65.4 m	156 m	2.43 Ω
50 kHz	4.51 m	21.8 m	362 m	5.07 Ω	4.27 m	21.4 m	358 m	5.03 Ω	21.6 m	109 m	261 m	4.05 Ω
70 kHz	6.24 m	30.5 m	507 m	7.10 Ω	5.95 m	30.0 m	501 m	7.04 Ω	30.2 m	152 m	365 m	5.67 Ω
100 kHz	8.84 m	43.7 m	725 m	10.1 Ω	8.42 m	42.8 m	716 m	10.0 Ω	43.2 m	218 m	522 m	8.10 Ω
200 kHz	17.5 m	87.4 m	1.45 Ω	20.2 Ω	16.9 m	85.7 m	1.43 Ω	20.1 Ω	86.4 m	436 m	1.04 Ω	16.2 Ω
300 kHz	26.2 m	131 m	2.17 Ω	30.4 Ω	25.3 m	128 m	2.15 Ω	30.1 Ω	129 m	653 m	1.56 Ω	24.3 Ω
500 kHz	43.5 m	218 m	3.62 Ω	50.7 Ω	42.2 m	214 m	3.58 Ω	50.3 Ω	216 m	1.09 Ω	2.61 Ω	40.5 Ω
700 kHz	60.8 m	305 m	5.07 Ω	71.0 Ω	59.1 m	300 m	5.01 Ω	70.4 Ω	302 m	1.52 Ω	3.65 Ω	56.7 Ω
1 MHz	86.9 m	437 m	7.25 Ω	101 Ω	84.4 m	428 m	7.16 Ω	100 Ω	432 m	2.18 Ω	5.22 Ω	81.0 Ω
2 MHz	173 m	874 m	14.5 Ω	202 Ω	169 m	857 m	14.3 Ω	201 Ω	863 m	4.36 Ω	10.4 Ω	162 Ω
3 MHz	260 m	1.31 Ω	21.7 Ω	304 Ω	253 m	1.28 Ω	21.5 Ω	301 Ω	1.29 Ω	6.53 Ω	15.6 Ω	243 Ω
5 MHz	434 m	2.18 Ω	36.2 Ω	507 Ω	422 m	2.14 Ω	35.8 Ω	503 Ω	2.16 Ω	10.9 Ω	26.1 Ω	405 Ω
7 MHz	607 m	3.05 Ω	50.7 Ω	710 Ω	590 m	3.00 Ω	50.1 Ω	704 Ω	3.02 Ω	15.2 Ω	36.5 Ω	567 Ω
10 MHz	867 m	4.37 Ω	72.5 Ω	1.01 kΩ	843 m	4.28 Ω	71.6 Ω	1.00 kΩ	4.32 Ω	21.8 Ω	52.2 Ω	810 Ω
20 MHz	1.73 Ω	8.74 Ω	145 Ω	2.02 kΩ	1.69 Ω	8.57 Ω	143 Ω	2.01 kΩ	8.63 Ω	43.6 Ω	104 Ω	1.62 kΩ
30 MHz	2.60 Ω	13.1 Ω	217 Ω	3.04 kΩ	2.53 Ω	12.8 Ω	215 Ω	3.01 kΩ	13.0 Ω	65.3 Ω	156 Ω	2.43 kΩ
50 MHz	4.33 Ω	21.8 Ω	362 Ω	5.07 kΩ	4.21 Ω	21.4 Ω	358 Ω	5.03 kΩ	21.6 Ω	109 Ω	261 Ω	4.05 kΩ
70 MHz	6.07 Ω	30.5 Ω	507 Ω	7.10 kΩ	5.90 Ω	30.0 Ω	501 Ω	7.04 kΩ	30.2 Ω	152 Ω	365 Ω	5.67 kΩ
100 MHz	8.67 Ω	43.7 Ω	725 Ω	10.1 kΩ	8.43 Ω	42.8 Ω	716 Ω	10.0 kΩ	43.2 Ω	218 Ω	522 Ω	8.10 kΩ
200 MHz	17.3 Ω	87.4 Ω	1.45 kΩ	20.2 kΩ	16.9 Ω	85.7 Ω	1.43 kΩ	20.1 kΩ	86.3 Ω	436 Ω	1.04 kΩ	16.2 kΩ
300 MHz	26.0 Ω	131 Ω	2.17 kΩ	30.4 kΩ	25.3 Ω	128 Ω	2.15 kΩ	30.1 kΩ	130 Ω	653 Ω	1.56 kΩ	24.3 kΩ
500 MHz	43.3 Ω	218 Ω	3.62 kΩ	50.7 kΩ	42.1 Ω	214 Ω	3.58 kΩ	50.3 kΩ	216 Ω	1.09 kΩ	2.61 kΩ	40.5 kΩ
700 MHz	60.7 Ω	305 Ω	5.07 kΩ	71.0 kΩ	59.0 Ω	300 Ω	5.01 kΩ	70.4 kΩ	302 Ω	1.52 kΩ	3.65 kΩ	56.7 kΩ
1 GHz	86.7 Ω	437 Ω	7.25 kΩ		84.3 Ω	428 Ω	7.16 kΩ		432 Ω	2.18 kΩ	5.22 kΩ	81.0 kΩ

* Strap dimensions are thickness × width in mm

l = strap length in cm or m
μ = microhms
m = milliohms
Ω = ohms

Value Subject To Error Where l ⩾ λ/20

**Worst-case values derived from free-space inductance, when the conductor is far from its return circuit or plane.

10 mm wide, 1 mm × 10 mm, and 2 mm × 50 mm. The table shows that the impedance at low frequencies is inversely proportional to the cross sectional strap area (width × thickness). At high frequencies, however, the added benefit of a much wider strap (compare 10 mm and 50 mm width) becomes considerably less pronounced. The impedance also increases somewhat more rapidly than a corresponding increase in strap length.

Illustrative Example 5.5

Two equipment boxes interconnected by a harness are also grounded to a AWG No. 10 **green** copper safety wire. Ten milliamps of 60 Hz reactive power is also flowing through the safety wire from the inputs of power line filters of other equipments connected to the same 60 Hz power mains. The ground points of the two boxes are separated by 1 m. Compute the potential difference between the boxes. Repeat the example and compare the results for a 1 mm × 10 mm copper strap and an aluminum metal ground plane of 1 mm thickness. Repeat all for 1 mA of a 27 MHz citizen's band (CB) transmission pickup in the ground wire/strap/plane column:

Ground	Applicable Table	Impedance for $l = 1$ m	CM Current	Potential Difference
For 60 Hz Power				
AWG #10 Wire	5.2	3.32 mΩ	10 mA	33.2 μV
1 × 10 mm Strap	5.3	1.78 mΩ	10 mA	17.8 μV
Al Plane	5.1	29 μΩ*	10 mA	0.29 μV
For 27 MHz CB Transmitter				
AWG #10 Wire	5.2	225 Ω	1 mA	225 mV
1 × 10 mm Strap	5.3	193 Ω	1 mA	193 mV
Al Plane	5.1	2.8 mΩ*	1 mA	2.8 μV

*Copper ground plane is corrected for Al in which $\sigma_r = 0.6$.

The above results indicate that while ground planes are generally **noisy**, wire conductors and straps are likely to be much worse. For example, the ground plane is about 1 percent at low frequencies and 0.003 percent at high frequencies of either the wire conductor or strap potential difference.

Table 5.4—Impedance of Printed Circuit Board Traces

FREQ.	w=1mm, t=0.03mm				w=3mm, t=0.03mm			w=10mm, t=0.03mm		
	ℓ=10mm	ℓ=30mm	ℓ=100mm	ℓ=300mm	ℓ=30mm	ℓ=100mm	ℓ=300mm	ℓ=30mm	ℓ=100mm	ℓ=300mm
10Hz	5.74m	17.2m	57.4m	172m	5.74m	19.1m	57.4m	1.72m	5.74m	17.2m
20Hz	5.74m	17.2m	57.4m	172m	5.74m	19.1m	57.4m	1.72m	5.74m	17.2m
30Hz	5.74m	17.2m	57.4m	172m	5.74m	19.1m	57.4m	1.72m	5.74m	17.2m
50Hz	5.74m	17.2m	57.4m	172m	5.74m	19.1m	57.4m	1.72m	5.74m	17.2m
70Hz	5.74m	17.2m	57.4m	172m	5.74m	19.1m	57.4m	1.72m	5.74m	17.2m
100Hz	5.74m	17.2m	57.4m	172m	5.74m	19.1m	57.4m	1.72m	5.74m	17.2m
200Hz	5.74m	17.2m	57.4m	172m	5.74m	19.1m	57.4m	1.72m	5.74m	17.2m
300Hz	5.74m	17.2m	57.4m	172m	5.74m	19.1m	57.4m	1.72m	5.74m	17.2m
500Hz	5.74m	17.2m	57.4m	172m	5.74m	19.1m	57.4m	1.72m	5.75m	17.2m
700Hz	5.74m	17.2m	57.4m	172m	5.74m	19.1m	57.4m	1.72m	5.75m	17.2m
1kHz	5.74m	17.2m	57.4m	172m	5.74m	19.1m	57.5m	1.72m	5.76m	17.3m
2kHz	5.74m	17.2m	57.4m	172m	5.75m	19.1m	57.6m	1.73m	5.81m	17.5m
3kHz	5.74m	17.2m	57.5m	172m	5.76m	19.2m	57.8m	1.74m	5.89m	18.0m
5kHz	5.75m	17.2m	57.5m	172m	5.78m	19.3m	58.4m	1.77m	6.15m	19.2m
7kHz	5.75m	17.2m	57.6m	173m	5.82m	19.5m	59.4m	1.83m	6.52m	21.0m
10kHz	5.76m	17.3m	57.9m	174m	5.89m	20.0m	61.4m	1.93m	7.23m	24.4m
20kHz	5.81m	17.5m	59.2m	180m	6.32m	22.4m	72.1m	2.45m	10.5m	38.6m
30kHz	5.89m	17.9m	61.4m	189m	6.97m	26.0m	87.1m	3.14m	14.4m	54.7m
50kHz	6.14m	19.2m	67.9m	215m	8.74m	35.1m	123m	4.71m	22.7m	88.3m
70kHz	6.51m	21.0m	76.6m	250m	10.8m	45.5m	163m	6.37m	31.3m	122m
100kHz	7.21m	24.3m	92.5m	311m	14.3m	62.0m	225m	8.93m	44.4m	174m
200kHz	10.4m	38.5m	155m	545m	26.9m	119m	440m	17.6m	88.2m	346m
300kHz	14.3m	54.4m	224m	795m	39.9m	177m	657m	26.3m	132m	519m
500kHz	22.5m	87.8m	367m	1.30Ω	66.1m	295m	1.09Ω	43.8m	220m	866m
700kHz	31.1m	121m	510m	1.82Ω	92.4m	413m	1.52Ω	61.4m	308m	1.21Ω
1MHz	44.0m	173m	727m	2.59Ω	131m	590m	2.18Ω	87.7m	440m	1.73Ω
2MHz	87.5m	344m	1.45Ω	5.18Ω	263m	1.17Ω	4.36Ω	175m	880m	3.46Ω
3MHz	131m	516m	2.17Ω	7.76Ω	395m	1.76Ω	6.54Ω	263m	1.32Ω	5.19Ω
5MHz	218m	861m	3.62Ω	12.9Ω	659m	2.94Ω	10.9Ω	438m	2.20Ω	8.66Ω
7MHz	305m	1.20Ω	5.07Ω	18.1Ω	922m	4.12Ω	15.2Ω	613m	3.08Ω	12.1Ω
10MHz	437m	1.72Ω	7.25Ω	25.8Ω	1.31Ω	5.89Ω	21.8Ω	876m	4.40Ω	17.3Ω
20MHz	874m	3.44Ω	14.5Ω	51.7Ω	2.63Ω	11.7Ω	43.6Ω	1.75Ω	8.80Ω	34.6Ω
30MHz	1.31Ω	5.16Ω	21.7Ω	77.6Ω	3.95Ω	17.6Ω	65.4Ω	2.63Ω	13.2Ω	51.9Ω
50MHz	2.18Ω	8.61Ω	36.2Ω	129Ω	6.59Ω	29.4Ω	109Ω	4.38Ω	22.0Ω	86.6Ω
70MHz	3.05Ω	12.0Ω	50.7Ω	181Ω	9.22Ω	41.2Ω	152Ω	6.13Ω	30.8Ω	121Ω
100MHz	4.37Ω	17.2Ω	72.5Ω	258Ω	13.1Ω	58.9Ω	218Ω	8.76Ω	44.0Ω	173Ω
200MHz	8.74Ω	34.4Ω	145Ω	517Ω	26.3Ω	117Ω	436Ω	17.5Ω	88.0Ω	346Ω
300MHz	13.1Ω	51.6Ω	217Ω	776Ω	39.5Ω	176Ω	654Ω	26.3Ω	132Ω	519Ω
500MHz	21.8Ω	86.1Ω	362Ω	1.29kΩ	65.9Ω	294Ω	1.09kΩ	43.8Ω	220Ω	866Ω
700MHz	30.5Ω	120Ω	507Ω	1.81kΩ	92.2Ω	412Ω	1.52kΩ	61.3Ω	308Ω	1.21kΩ
1GHz	43.7Ω	172Ω	725Ω	2.58kΩ	131Ω	589Ω	2.18kΩ	87.6Ω	440Ω	1.73kΩ
2GHz	87.4Ω	344Ω	1.45kΩ	5.17kΩ	263Ω	1.17kΩ	4.36kΩ	175Ω	880Ω	3.46kΩ
3GHz	131Ω	516Ω	2.17kΩ	7.76kΩ	395Ω	1.76kΩ	6.54kΩ	263Ω	1.32kΩ	5.19kΩ
5GHz	218Ω	861Ω	3.62kΩ	12.9kΩ	659Ω	2.94kΩ	10.9kΩ	438Ω	2.20kΩ	8.66kΩ
7GHz	305Ω	1.20kΩ	5.07kΩ	18.1kΩ	922Ω	4.12kΩ	15.2kΩ	613Ω	3.08kΩ	12.1kΩ
10GHz	437Ω	1.72kΩ	7.25kΩ	25.8kΩ	1.31kΩ	5.89kΩ	21.8kΩ	876Ω	4.40kΩ	17.3kΩ

* Wiring dimensions are width x thickness in mm

ℓ = wiring length in mm
m = milliohms
μ = microhms
Ω = ohms

Values subject to error where ℓ ≥ λ/20

NOTE: Computations appearing in this table are based on the assumption that: (1) ℓ >> W. Any interpolation should consider this assumption. (2) Conductor is far (several times W) from its return circuit or plane.

5.3.3 Impedance of Printed Circuit Board Wiring

The impedance of V_{EE} supply lines, circuit lines and zero-signal reference return lines in printed circuit board (PCB) wiring is of substantial concern. This especially applies for fast logic such as Schottky TTL and ECL-10k logic, having lead edge rise times of 2 or 3 ns. Significant effort is required to keep line inductance small to avoid common-impedance coupling.

Equations (5.21) and (5.22) are used to compute printed wiring impedance from dc to 10 GHz. The results are shown in Table 5.4 for copper wiring having a thickness of 0.03 mm (1.2 mils, or about 1 oz foil). Three different PCB wiring widths are listed (1, 3 and 10 mm) with four different given wire lengths for each (1, 3, 10 and 30 cm).

Examine Table 5.4 and see that the impedance at low frequencies is inversely proportional to the PCB wire width. At high frequencies, however, the added benefit of wider printed wiring becomes considerably less pronounced. For example, by increasing the width 10 times (from 1 to 10 mm), the impedance is reduced by less than 50 percent. Due to self-inductance, the impedance also increases somewhat more rapidly than a corresponding increase in wire length.

Illustrative Example 5.6

Dual in-line package (DIP) chips containing Schottky TTL logic share a common return path in the PCB wiring. The length of the common printed wiring to the connector pin, where V_{EE} is decoupled, is 10 cm. The switching current is 20 mA with 3 ns transition time. Determine if common-impedance coupling is an EMI problem.

The significant, upper transition frequency associated with the rise time, τ_r, is $1/\pi\tau_r = 1/(\pi \times 3 \times 10^{-9}) = 106$ MHz. From Table 5.4, the common impedance is about 73 Ω. For a 20 mA switching current, the voltage drop is $V_i = 0.02$ A $\times$ 73 Ω = 1.46 V. This is well above the noise immunity level of about 300 mV, and EMI will be a problem if other logic devices share the same return path.

If a wider wiring were used, such as 3 mm, Table 5.4 shows that the dc resistance is effectively reduced 3 times, which will improve dc regulation, but the HF impedance is only reduced from about

73 to 59 Ω. Thus, this is not a viable solution. A two-step solution is (1) do not share the same printed zero-signal return wire; use a dedicated line for each DIP back to the connector pins, and (2) decouple the V_{EE} line impedance at the DIPs with a 1 nF ceramic disk capacitor.

Decoupling capacitors placed close to the DIP do not need to be above about 1 nF for fast logic. Larger capacitors would exhibit lower Z at low frequencies but, above resonance, they will not perform better than short-lead ceramic capacitors. The inductance of a 2 mm pigtail lead soldered into position on a PCB is about 2 nH. For instance, with a 100 nF capacitor, self-resonance is $1/2\pi\sqrt{LC}$ = 11 MHz, and the impedance at 106 MHz = 1.3 Ω inductive reactance. To more accurately compute the optimal size of the decoupling capacitor use the following formula:

$$C = \frac{I}{dV/dt} \qquad (5.23)$$

where,

I = logic switching current

dV = allowable voltage drop = noise immunity voltage level = 0.4 V for TTL digital technology

dt = switching speed of logic

For the above problem,

C = 0.02/(0.4 V/3 × 10⁻⁹)

    = 150 pF

Notice the enormous difference in results when using the much slower, lower power CMOS logic. Here, the switching current is about 200 μA, and the rise time is about 35 ns. Thus, $1/\pi\tau_r = 1/(\pi \times 35 \times 10^{-9})$ = 9.1 MHz. From Table 5.4, the impedance of 1 mm wide, 10 cm long printed wiring is about 7 Ω. The voltage drop V_i = 200 × 10⁻⁶ × 7 = 1.4 mV. This is about three orders of magnitude below the noise immunity level for CMOS. The V_{EE} supply line drop is correspondingly less than for Schottky TTL and ECL-10k and DIP decoupling capacitors are not as often required. Cost is less and reliability is higher. In short, do not use high-speed logic unless the speed is really needed.

It is common practice to land fill all PCB wiring with a copper ground plane to (1) reduce the impedances of the zero-signal reference areas and (2) provide some natural shielding from neighboring PCBs. For double-sided wire wrap boards in which one side is the ground plane, the other is a V_{EE} plane which serves to reduce the V_{EE} source impedance as seen from DIPs to board connectors. This substantially lowers the number of required decoupling capacitors.

5.3.4 Methods of Power and Signal Bus Impedance Control

As shown in the previous section, minimization of power and signal bus impedances leads to reduction of the possibility of common-impedance coupling. As shown in Tables 5.1 through 5.4 for single conductors, impedance values, composed of series resistance and inductance, increase with frequency. If another approach is chosen, that of treating conductors as transmission lines, control of impedance values with increasing frequency is possible. Table 5.5 shows the values of characteristic impedance of five types of conductor pairs for multiple geometries. For the first two cases (parallel wires or a single wire over a ground plane) as a function of geometry, the impedance values are high (>100 Ω) and increase with distance from the reference conductor. For the remaining three cases (parallel strips, a strip over a ground plane or strips side by side) for similar progressions, the characteristic impedance tends to decrease. In a realistic sense, the strip over a ground plane closely represents the condition of a signal or power distribution conductor on one side of a double-sided printed circuit board with a ground plane on the other. This configuration suggests the use of power distribution planes and conductors on thin dielectrics. In the case of power distribution planes, Z_{03} shows that as ratios W/h become arbitrarily large, such as in the case of a multilayer printed circuit board, the characteristic impedance drops to the point of being negligible. The behavior of these PCB impedances strongly suggest that, from a point of view of controlling common-impedance coupling, a very strong case can be made for multilayer boards.

Table 5.5—Characteristic Impedance of Different Conductor Pairs

D/d, h/d, W/h or D/W	Parallel Wires	Wire Over Ground Plane	Parallel Strips	Strip Over Ground Plane	Strips Side by side	Strip Line
0.5	NA	0	140	104	NA	52
0.6	NA	37	124	100	NA	50
0.7	NA	52	114	98	NA	49
0.8	NA	63	110	95	NA	47
0.9	NA	72	106	92	NA	46
1.0	0	79	104	90	0	45
1.1	53	86	98	84	25	42
1.2	75	91	92	80	34	40
1.5	118	106	86	70	53	35
1.7	135	114	80	66	62	33
2.0	158	124	72	60	73	30
2.5	188	138	60	54	87	27
3.0	212	149	54	48	98	24
3.5	231	158	48	43	107	21
4.0	248	166	42	40	114	20
5.0	275	180	34	34	127	17
6.0	297	191	28	28	137	14
7.0	316	200	24	24	146	12
8.0	332	208	21	21	153	11
9.0	346	215	19	19	160	9
10.0	359	221	17	17	166	8
12.0	381	232	14	14	176	
15.0	408	246	11.2	11.2	188	
20.0	443	263	8.4	8.4	204	
25.0	469	276	6.7	6.7	217	
30.0	491	287	5.6	5.6	227	
40.0	526	305	4.2	4.2	243	
50.0	553	318	3.4	3.4	255	
100.0	636	359	1.7	1.7	293	

- For Z_{01} and Z_{02},
  Air Dielectric Assumed; $\epsilon_r = 1.0$

  $Z_{01} = (120/\sqrt{\epsilon_r})\, \ln_e (D/d + \sqrt{(D/d^2 - 1)})$

  $Z_{02} = (60/\sqrt{\epsilon_r})\, \ln_e (2h/d) + \sqrt{(2h/d)^2 - 1})$

- For Z_{03},
  Mylar Dielectric Assumed;
  $\epsilon_r = 5.0$

  $Z_{03} = (377/\sqrt{\epsilon_r}\, (h/W)$, for $W > 3h$ and $h > 3t$

  $= \dfrac{754}{\sqrt{\epsilon_r}} [2\,W/h + 1.39 + 0.67\,\ln_e (2W/h + 1.44)]$, for $W < h$

- For Z_{04}, Z_{05} and Z_{06}

  Paper Base Phenolic or Glass Epoxy Assumed; $\epsilon_r \cong 4.7$

  $Z_{04} = (377/\sqrt{\epsilon_r})\, (h/W)$, for $W > 3h$, $= \dfrac{138}{\sqrt{\epsilon}\ \text{eq.}}\, \ln_e \dfrac{6h}{0.8\,w + t}$ for $W < 3h$

  $Z_{05} = (120/\sqrt{\epsilon_r})\, \ln_e (D/W + \sqrt{(D/W^2 - 1)})$,

  for $W \gg t$, $D \gg$ Nearby Ground Plane

- For Geometries Corresponding to Shaded Areas, Impedance Values Shown Can Be Higher than Actual Results Due to Fringing Capacitance

  $Z_{06} \cong \dfrac{Z_{04}}{2}$, for $t \ll 2h$

5.4 Ground-Loop Coupling

Ground-loop coupling (GLC) is the process (sometimes called **mode conversion**) by which a common-mode voltage, like the one created across a common-ground impedance, appears differentially at the victim input terminals. The several ways to reduce GLC involve floating, isolating and decoupling.

Ground-loop coupling is the second step in the first coupling path, shown in Fig. 5.1. GLC is also the second step in the second coupling path, as shown in that same figure. Since GLC is discussed in substantial detail in Section 6.4 and Appendix D, it will not be duplicated here. To avoid possible difficulty, however, the reader is encouraged to review Section 6.4 before continuing.

The term **ground-loop coupling**, which is related to common-mode rejection,* is defined as:

$$GLC_{dB} = 20 \log(V_o/V_i) \qquad (5.24)$$

where,

V_o = the voltage produced at the input terminals to the victim amplifier or logic in Box 2 (see Figs. 5.2 and 5.5)

V_i = open-circuit, common-mode voltage (shown in Fig. 5.2)

The complete expression of GLC contains the signal source impedances, the cable impedances and the load impedances. Therefore the victim's CMRR is a contributor to the overall GLC. If the source and cabling impedances were perfectly (100 percent) symmetrical to ground, the GLC would be equal to the CMRR of the load.

Figure 5.5 shows that the induced common-mode (CM) voltage, V_i, pushes common-mode current around the loops ABCDEFGHA and ABCIJFGHA for a single wire pair (cf. Fig. 5.2). Since the impedance of the two paths are not the same, even for a balanced system, the result is a differential voltage, V_o, available at the input terminals of the victim amplifier or logic. It is this voltage that produces EMI if it is above the sensitivity of the amplifier or the noise-immunity level of the logic. Therefore, the ratio of V_i/V_o is the common-mode rejection, and its inverse is the ground-loop coupling.

Equation (5.24) is plotted in Fig. 5.6 for the condition of an unbalanced circuit corresponding to a box-to-box interconnecting cable length of 1 m. Equation (5.24) is also plotted in Fig. 5.7 for bal-

---

*The common-mode rejection ratio (CMRR) is the ratio of the common-mode sensitivity to the differential-mode sensitivity in an operational amplifier or complementary-driven logic. It is usually measured at 60 Hz, under rather idealized conditions, and does not define performance at higher frequencies where the CMRR further degrades.

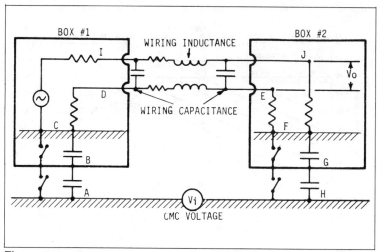

Figure 5.5.—Ground-Loop Coupling and Undesired Emissions Appearing at Victim Amplifier/Logic Input Terminals

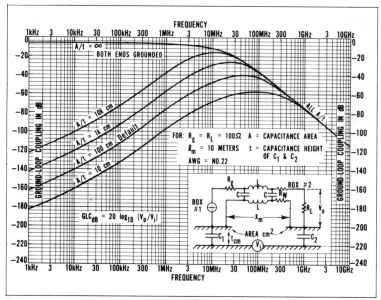

Figure 5.6—Ground-Loop Coupling for 10 m Interconnecting Cable on Unbalanced System

5.23

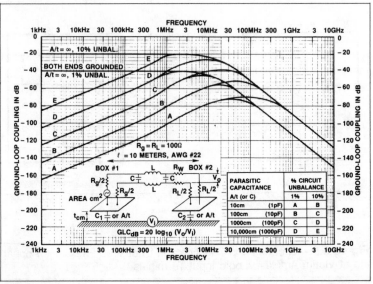

Figure 5.7—Ground-Loop Coupling for 10 m Interconnecting Cable on Balanced System

anced circuits having a 1 m interconnecting cable length. Both figures are plots of GLC versus frequency from 1 kHz to 10 GHz. The parameter is A/t, which corresponds to the ratio of the area to height of either the printed circuit boards or the bottom of the box/equipment case above the ground plane. This forms the capacitance, C, illustrated in Fig. 5.5 when any of the units are not grounded (conceptual toggle switch is open). If the A/t ratio of the designer's situation is unknown or can't be measured, a default value of 10 pF (or 100 cm) for small devices to 100 pF for large units may be used. Section 6.4 and Appendix D present further explanation and details.

Except when both boxes are grounded, Figs. 5.6 and 5.7 show the GLC becoming worse (more coupling or less negative values) as frequency rises from 1 kHz to higher frequencies. They achieve their worst case (least values) at resonance of the interconnect cable inductance with the parasitic capacitance. Above this frequency the GLC begins to fall off due to line losses. As explained in Section 6.4 and Appendix D, the reference cable is AWG No. 22 (see insert drawing in figures). Its AWG rating has little effect upon the GLC. Similarly, the reference 100 Ω signal source impedance in Box 1 and the 100 Ω victim input impedance in Box 2 have a relatively small effect on GLC, provided the impedances are above about 30 Ω.

Figure 5.6 corresponds to unbalanced systems in which the full signal source and victim load impedance appear in the high side of the wiring. Conversely, Fig. 5.7 corresponds to balanced systems in which the source and load impedances are approximately split between their high and low sides. Examine Fig. 5.7 and observe that a second parameter exists in addition to the A/t parameter. This parameter corresponds to the tolerance of balance relative to the split of the high-side and low-side impedances. Therefore, this tolerance parameter is referenced in percent in Fig. 5.7 as "1% Unbal" and "10% Unbal."

Figure 5.6 shows that the ground-loop coupling at lower frequencies is only −6 dB* (worst condition) when both PCBs or backplane wiring are grounded to their cases and the cases are grounded to the ground plane, as shown in Fig. 5.5, when all toggle switches are closed. The corresponding GLC values for balanced systems in Fig. 5.7 is −20 dB for a 10 percent tolerance and −40 dB for a 1 percent tolerance.

This clearly demonstrates the unfavorable condition which develops from the resulting low-impedance ground loop. In order to achieve a substantial improvement in ground-loop decoupling below a few tens of megahertz, the figures show the need to float (unground) one or both PCBs relative to their case grounds. For a 1 m link, the benefit of floated versus grounded ends vanishes around a few tens of megahertz and above, and other solutions to reduce the GLC are necessary (see Chapter 6).

Illustrative Example 5.7

Using the ongoing illustrative example of the victim described in Fig. 3.2 and the current flowing in the ground plane described in Example 5.3, calculate the resultant I/N ratio. For convenience, Fig. 3.2 is reproduced as Fig. 5.8 and contains the ground currents from Example 5.3. These data are also summarized here:

---

*When the wires in the pair are extremely close, the all-grounded GLC can be somewhat smaller than −6 dB, reaching −10 to −15 dB due to the mutual inductance between the two wires, which neutralizes part of the CM currents. This benefit has not been considered in our worst-case model.

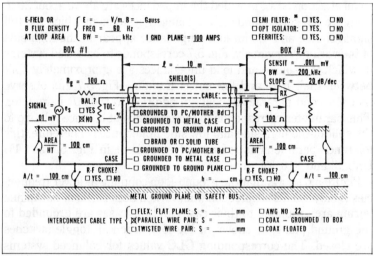

Figure 5.8—Ongoing Illustrative Example from Fig. 3.2

1. Signal Level: 0.01 mV = 20 dBμV
2. Victim Sensitivity: 0.001 mV = 0 dBμV
3. Victim Stopband Slope: 20 dB/decade
4. EMI Source (Example 5.3): 100 A at 60 Hz in ground plane
5. Ground Plane: 0.3 mm steel
6. A/t ratios: 100 cm (or 10 pF)
7. All PCB and Box Cases: Grounded
8. Signal Source Impedance: 100 Ω
9. Victim Input Impedance: 100 Ω
10. Transmission System: Unbalanced
11. Box-to-Box Cable: Parallel Wires
12. AWG No. 22
13. Cable Length: 10 m

Illustrative Example 5.3 indicated that the ground-plane current at 60 Hz is 100 A. Thus, 100 A = 40 dBA = 160 dBμA is entered into heading Column 1 in Fig. 5.9. Column 2 is the amplifier sensitivity (noise) or 0 dBμV. Column 3 is the difference between Columns 1 and 2 or 160 dBμA − 0 dBμV = 160 dB (above 1 mho).

Attention is now directed to Column 4A, the subject of this chapter, viz., common-ground-impedance coupling (GCM) and ground-loop coupling (GLC). The other four columns, 4B to 4E (also

	①	②	③	④A	④B	④C	④D	④E	④	⑤	⑥	⑦
Operating Conditions	AMB dBµA	N dBµV	A/N dB	GCM GLC	FCM GLC	DMC	C-C	PL-PS PS-V	PICK 4A-4E	AMP REJ	Δ I/N	I/N
Objective												-26
Start: First Run	160	0	160	-70 -6	NA	NA	NA	NA	-76	0		84

(I/N)dB: ⑦=③ + ④+⑤

Figure 5.9—EMI Prediction from Ground-Plane Current

see Fig. 5.1) do not apply in this chapter. Thus, NA (not applicable) is entered in each.

Illustrative Example 5.3 indicates that the ground-plane impedance of the 0.3 mm steel is 338 $\mu\Omega$, which equals -70 dBΩ. This is entered into column 4A. Before proceeding, note that adding Columns 1 and 4A yields 160 dBμA + (-70) dBΩ = 90 dBμV = 30 mV of common-mode voltage—the same answer as obtained in Example 5.3.

The ground-loop coupling from Fig. 5.6 at 60 Hz for both ends grounded is -6 dB by extrapolation. This is also entered into Column 4A of Fig. 5.9. Column 4 is the sum of the two entries in Column 4A or -76 dB. Column 5 is 0 dB since the 60 Hz is in the passband of the 200 kHz amplifier. Finally, Column 7 is the sum of Columns 3, 4 and 5. Thus, the I/N ratio is 160 $-$ 76 + 0 = 84 dB.

In order to eliminate the EMI problem, one solution is to float the PCB at the receiver end. Figure 5.6 shows that the GLC would change from -6 dB to about -156 dB at 1 kHz, which becomes about -180 dB at 60 Hz by extrapolation. This EMC solution is shown in Fig. 5.10.

In a situation like this, one could be tempted to run a piece of wire between the grounding points of the two boxes (Points A and H on Fig. 5.5) to shunt the noisy ground and "make them equipotential." Looking more closely at the problem, it is apparent that this would prove disappointing. The metal plane already has a low impedance (338 $\mu\Omega$) and looks like a voltage source to the loop, so the 10 m "shunting wire" would need a diameter greater than 25 mm to have less than 338 $\mu\Omega$ impedance at 60 Hz! However, if one box is floated, a bonding wire braid or strap can reduce GLC as ex-

	(1)	(2)	(3)	(4A)	(4B)	(4C)	(4D)	(4E)	(4)	(5)	(6)	(7)
Operating Conditions	AMB dBµA	N dBµV	A/N dB	GCM GLC	FCM GLC	DMC	C-C	PL to PS PS to V	PICK 4A to 4E	AMP REJ	Δ I/N	I/N
Objective												−26
Start: First Run	160	0	160	−70 −6	NA	NA	NA	NA	−76	0		84
FLOAT PCB AT RX END	160	0	160	−70 −180	NA	NA	NA	NA	−274	0		−90

(I/N) dB: (7) = (3) + (4) + (5)

Figure 5.10—Eliminating EMI by Floating PCB at Receiver End

plained in Section 6.5 and Appendix C. An exception to the above would be the case where the ground is **not** a metal plane but a mediocre conductor like earth, carbon composite etc. Here, a shunting conductor could exhibit a lower 60 Hz impedance, and the EMI would be reduced by reducing Z_{CM} (not the GLC).

Section 6.4 and Appendix D discuss GLC in considerably greater detail, and Section 6.5 covers reducing GLC by different EMI-hardening techniques.

5.5 References

1. Mardiguian, M., Handbook Series on Electromagnetic Interference and Compatibility, Volume 2, *Grounding and Bonding* (Gainesville, VA: Interference Control Technologies, Inc., 1988).
2. Denny, H.W., *Grounding for the Control of EMI* (Gainesville, VA: Interference Control Technologies, Inc., 1980).
3. White, D.R.J., *Electromagnetic Shielding Materials and Performance* (Gainesville, VA: Interference Control Technologies, Inc., 1980), p. 1.12.

5.6 Bibliography

Bannister, P.R., "Image Theory Results of the Mutual Impedance of Crossing Earth Return Circuits," *IEEE Transactions on EMC*, Volume EMC-15, Number 4, November, 1973.

Chen, C.L., "Transient Protection Devices," *IEEE Electromagnetic Compatibility Symposium Record* (New York: IEEE), Session 3A. San Antonio, Texas, October 7-9, 1975.

Cooper, J.A. and Allen, L.J., "The Lightning Arrestor-Connector Concept: Description and Data," *IEEE Transactions on EMC,* Volume EMC-15, Number 3, August, 1973.

McLellan, D.W. and Heirman, D.N., "Mitigation of ELF Interference on Telephone Lines," *IEEE Transactions on EMC,* Volume EMC-15, Number 4, November, 1973.

Miller, D.A. and Valentino, A.B., "ELF Earth Return Coupling into Power Systems," *IEEE Transactions on EMC,* Volume EMC-15, Number 4, November, 1973.

Nordgard, J.D. and Chen, C.L., "Lightning-Induced Transients on Buried Shielded Transmission Lines," *IEEE EMC Symposium Record,* Session 3A, San Antonio, Texas, October 7-9, 1975.

Valentino, A.R. and McLellan, D.W., "ELF Earth Return Current Coupling," *IEEE Transactions on EMC,* Volume EMC-15, Number 4, November, 1973.

White, D.R.J., *EMI Control in the Design of Printed Circuit Boards and Backplanes* (Gainesville, VA: Interference Control Technologies, Inc., 1981).

Chapter 6

Radiated Common-Mode and Ground-Loop Coupling

This section describes the second of the five principal coupling paths: field-to-cable, common-mode coupling. In this case the common-mode voltage is coupled to the victim input terminals via ground loops. They are always present, even if high impedance.

As shown in Fig. 6.1, this coupling path is divided into two parts: (1) common-mode coupling (CMC) and (2) ground-loop coupling

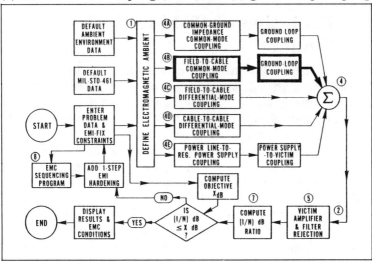

Figure 6.1—EMI Prediction and Analysis Flow Diagram Showing Common-Mode and Ground-Loop Coupling

6.1

(GLC). Common-mode coupling converts an ambient electric or magnetic field to a common-mode voltage into the loop area as shown in Fig. 6.2. This voltage then acts as a potential EMI source to push current around the loop area which includes the victim cable. The resulting differential-mode voltage developed in the victim cable appears across the amplifier or logic input terminals to constitute the potential EMI threat.

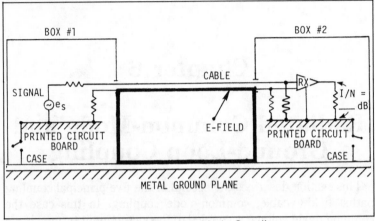

Figure 6.2—Field-to-Cable, Common-Mode Coupling

6.1 Evolution of Field-to-Cable Coupling

Ground loops are formed when two interconnected boxes are located near a ground plane or safety wire, regardless of whether they are directly connected. Thus, ground-loop impedances may be low or high at any frequency, but the induced common-mode voltage is independent of the loop impedance.

Because the term **ground** has various connotations, it is a poor word to use. Here, it is intended to imply a location or place to which any circuits, equipment or system potential may be referenced, and it may or may not mean **earth ground**.

The term **ground loop** is also misused because it may or may not include the earth, a **ground plane**, a safety wire, a cold-water pipe, etc. A ground loop, however, does convey the idea of some form of a closed loop, usually having a low impedance, perhaps at dc. Most engineers agree that a ground loop exists when two or more interconnected circuits, equipments or systems also are connected to a common ground reference. This definition, however, would be overly restrictive because a loop, i.e., a ground loop, might assume any impedance and configuration.

One way of looking at a ground loop or, more generally, a loop area, is to consider the evolution of a loop area shown in Figs. 6.3 through 6.6. First, consider a cable or harness suspended in the air, well removed from the presence of any ground or earth. Figure 6.3 shows such a horizontally deployed cable in the presence of a horizontal electric (E) or orthogonal magnetic (H) field. The cable is acting like an unintentional pickup antenna. For the presence of a matched, horizontally polarized E-field, the open-circuit induced voltage, V, into the cable is defined as:

$$V = \int_0^l E \times ds \qquad (6.1)$$

$$= El \text{ for } l \ll \lambda \qquad (6.2)$$

where,

E = electric-field strength in volts per meter

l = length of cable in meters

λ = wavelength corresponding to frequency of the E-field

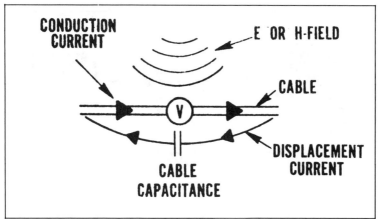

Figure 6.3—Open Circuit Voltage Induced Directly into Cable.

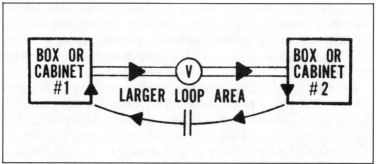

Figure 6.4—Increase in Common-Mode Current Due to Increase in Capacitance.

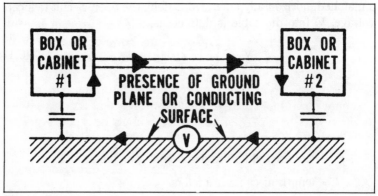

Figure 6.5—Further Increase in Common-Mode Current and Definable Loop Area.

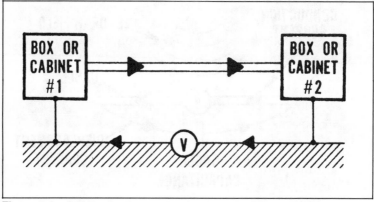

Figure 6.6—Still Further Increase in CM Current and Definable Loop Area.

The common-mode voltage, V, causes a cable conduction current to flow as shown in Fig. 6.3. For a current to flow, there must be a closed loop. The return loop current, called displacement current, flows through an ever-present, end-to-end cable capacitance. While this capacitance is distributed along the cable length, an equivalent bulk capacitance results in a definable loop area shaped like a football. This is generally referred to as the **equivalent area** (loop) of an antenna, even though the **cable antenna** appears to be physically one dimensional. The current will be very low at low frequency when $l \ll \lambda$ since the capacitive reactance is very high.

When boxes, equipments, racks or consoles are connected to both ends of the suspended cable antenna, an increase in both the end-to-end cable capacitance (**top-hat** effect) and loop area results. Consequently, the induced common-mode voltage and current increase. The current increases at a greater rate, however, because of the presence of both a larger voltage (larger loop area) and a lower circuit impedance (higher capacitance).

In Fig. 6.5, the **suspended** configuration of Fig. 6.4 has been brought down to a location near the presence of a ground plane, a safety wire or earth (hereafter, it will simply be called a conducting **ground**). This situation dictates that the capacitance between both ends of the cable substantially increased as a result of the capacitance between both boxes to ground. The direct capacitance between both ends of the cable, *per se* (see Fig. 6.3), is now small relative to that via the box-ground-box route, and the loop area is better defined. Thus, the induced common-mode voltage is more apparent, and the common-mode current further increases due to the lower circuit impedance (increased capacitance).

In Fig. 6.6, both boxes are now directly connected to ground. The loop area may not have changed much (depending on where the boxes are connected to ground). However, the common-mode current can increase substantially provided that (1) the cable circuits inside each box are grounded to the box case (refer to Fig. 2.3) or (2) the cable is a coaxial line or shielded line with both ends of the braid or shield connected to the boxes.

Figure 6.6 is an example of what most engineers would agree is a **ground loop**. However, it is also believed that most engineers would say that Fig. 6.5 is not an example of a ground loop since both boxes are not connected (direct hard wire or strap) to ground. Yet, the only significant difference is in the circuit impedance, not the loop area. Thus, both Figs. 6.5 and 6.6 depict ground loops. At some frequencies, the circuit impedance of Fig. 6.5 will be **lower** than that of Fig. 6.6 because the circuit would have gone through series resonance (box-to-ground capacitance and cable inductance). The reader should now identify with the loop area and loop impedance separately and not limit his thinking to a low-resistance, dc ground loop path.

As suggested above, not all cable ground loop areas are well defined. Figure 6.7 shows a well defined loop area in which both boxes or cabinets are directly bonded to the metal decking or skin of a vehicle. The cable has a small droop forming a modest catenary. The length is simply the inside distance between the boxes. The equivalent cable height is computed by averaging different heights at equal increment samplings along the cable length.

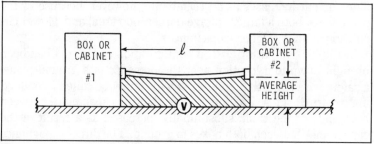

Figure 6.7—Well Defined Common-Mode Loop Area

In Fig. 6.8, the common-mode loop area is relatively poorly defined. If one or both cabinets are floating (this violates electrical safety codes), capacitances are developed between the bottom of the cabinets and any nearby metal, (cf. Fig. 6.5). Here, the proximate metal **ground** may be reinforcing bars or mesh immersed in concrete below the cabinet casters. The shaded area in the figure suggests how the loop area may be calculated. In fact, the cable may enter and exit the bottom wells of the cabinets.

A question may arise as to whether ordinary earth (gravel, stones, sand, etc.) can be thought as the RF ground plane for the system lying above. It has been verified that, even though ordinary earth resistivity (ranging from 10 to 1,000 Ω/m) is many times higher than that of metal planes, it is still a thousand times less than for air. Therefore the air-to-earth interface is still a sufficiently reflective medium to be taken as the reference plane for radio frequencies.

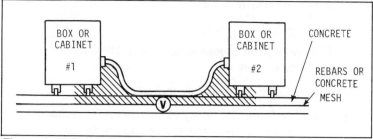

Figure 6.8—Poorly Defined Common-Mode Loop Area

6.2 Field-to-Cable, Common-Mode Coupling

This section discusses the induced open-circuit voltage in a loop area from the presence of either an electric field strength or magnetic flux density. Each field type will be discussed separately.

6.2.1 Electric Field Coupling into Cables and Harnesses

Field common-mode coupling converts an electric field strength into an open-circuit voltage:

$$CMC = 20 \log (V_i/E) \text{ dB above V per V/m} \qquad (6.3)$$

where,

$$V_i/E = 2l \times \cos \theta \times \sin\left(\frac{\pi h}{\lambda} \cos \alpha\right), \qquad (6.4)$$

for both h and $l \ll \lambda$

V_i = induced loop voltage in volts

E = impinging electric field strength in volts per meter

h = average loop height in meters

l = loop length in meters

6.7

λ = wavelength in meters

$= 300/f_{MHz} = C/f_{Hz}$

C = velocity of propagation $= 3 \times 10^8$ meters per second

f_{Hz} = interfering frequency in hertz

f_{MHz} = interfering frequency in megahertz (broadband emissions are discussed in later sections)

α = angle between plane of loop and direction of propagation

θ = angle between direction of l and E-field

sin () = in units of radians

The general case of diagonal polarization is assumed in which $\alpha = \Theta = 45°$ and $\cos \alpha = \cos \Theta = 1/\sqrt{2}$. This assumption is used hereafter because the user generally does not know either α or Θ, which may take on any value. Thus:

$$\frac{V_i}{E} \approx \sqrt{2}\, l \sin \left(\frac{\pi h}{\sqrt{2}\,\lambda} \right) \quad \text{for } l/\lambda \text{ and } h/\lambda \leqslant 0.5 \tag{6.5}$$

$$= \sqrt{2}\, l \sin (2.22 h/\lambda) = \sqrt{2}\, l \sin (0.0074\ h f_{MHz}) \tag{6.6}$$

Should the polarization and propagation axis (Poynting's vector) be worst case, like in a radiated EMI susceptibility test, we would have $\alpha = \theta = 0°$, and $\cos = \cos = 1$, In this extreme case:

$$\frac{V_i}{E} = 2\, l \sin \frac{\pi h}{\lambda} \cong 2\pi\, l\ h/\lambda \text{ (for } h < 0.3\ \lambda) \tag{6.7}$$

The difference between the general case and worst case is $\sqrt{2}$ or 4 dB.

The field-to-cable CMC is shown in Figs. 6.9 and 6.10. For frequencies lower than $\lambda/2$, field-to-cable CMC increases with frequency at a rate of 20 dB/decade, as can be expected from Eq. (6.6). This increase continues until the half-wave length resonance

6.8

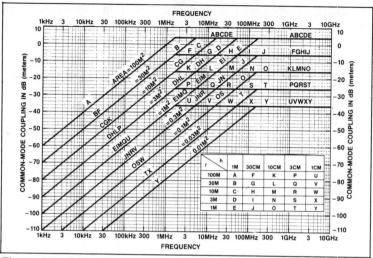

Figure 6.9—E-Field Common-Mode Coupling into Box-Cable-Box Ground Loop Area for Large Loops.

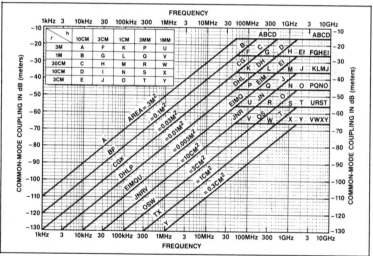

Figure 6.10—E-Field Common-Mode Coupling into Box-Cable-Box Ground Loop Area for Small Loops.

$l = \lambda/2$ is reached. Above this, the length l exhibits multiple resonances. Adjacent half-wave length sections tend to cancel each other and leave only one $\lambda/2$ segment to become the effective pickup

antenna. Therefore, l is replaced by $\lambda/2$ in Eq. (6.6), which becomes:

$$V_i/E = \frac{\sqrt{2}}{2}\, \lambda \sin\left(\frac{\pi h}{\sqrt{2}\lambda} \right) \qquad (6.8)$$

$$\approx \frac{212}{f_{MHz}}\, \sin\,(2.22\ h/\lambda),\ \text{for}\ l \geqslant 0.5\ \lambda\ \text{and}\ h < 0.5\lambda \qquad (6.9)$$

This is represented by the flat portion of the curves. Should the height h eventually be larger than length l, the $\lambda/2$ resonance is reached by the height first, and the CMC becomes:

$$V_i/E \approx \sqrt{2}\ l,\ \text{for}\ l < 0.5\ \lambda\ \text{and}\ h \geqslant 0.5\ \lambda \qquad (6.10)$$

This, too, corresponds to a flat curve, independent of frequency. Appendix H addresses the cases where the cable is not lying over an infinite ground plane but over a finite, thin metallic structure (aircraft, rocket, tower, ship, etc.) which itself can be excited to resonance. A complete study of field-to-cable coupling, using a rigorous transmission line approach, has been provided by Smith.[1,2]

For some very specific angles between the field polarization and the loop orientation, when **both** l and h exceed $\lambda/2$, the effective area of the loop is **becoming shorter**, causing the CMC to decrease at −20 dB/decade. Since this condition does not often exist, it is not assumed here.

To facilitate use of the graphs in Figs. 6.9 and 6.10, determine the proper parameter line by choosing the closest l and h dimensions in the inset box and read the corresponding parameter letter. First locate the parameter letter in the increasing line slope regions. For higher frequencies, follow the parameter letter upward until it forks off horizontally to the right. The intersection of the EMI frequency with the parameter line gives the corresponding CMC.

Illustrative Example 6.1

In the ongoing illustrative example previously shown in Fig. 3.11 and repeated in Fig. 6.11, the cable length is 10 m, and its average

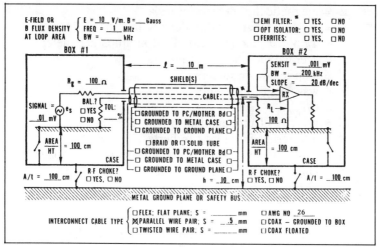

Figure 6.11—The Two-Box EMI Problem

height is 10 cm. The interfering AM broadcast station is 1,000 kHz or 1 MHz and corresponds to an E-field strength of 10 V/m. Using the inset table of Fig. 6.9 for $l = 10$ m and h = 10 cm, **parameter** line M is applicable. This corresponds to a loop area of 1 m^2 (10 m × 0.1 m). Line M intersects the 1 MHz frequency at a CMC value of −40 dB. (The proper value is −40 dB(V/V/m) = −40 dB(m). Hereafter, it will simply be called −40 dB).

Since CMC converts electric field strength in units of V/m (10 V/m in the example) to open-circuit voltage, V, the common-mode voltage is 40 dB below the E-field value. Thus, the voltage is 0.1 V or 100 mV.

6.2.2 Magnetic-Flux Density Coupling into Cable Harnesses

The common-mode coupling also converts a magnetic flux density into open-circuit voltage:

$$CMC_{dB} = 20 \log (V_i/B) \quad \text{dB above V/tesla} \qquad (6.11)$$

where,

$V_i/B = 2\, l\, C \times \sin \theta \times \sin [(\pi h/\lambda) \cos \alpha]$, for h and $l \ll \lambda$ (6.12)

V_i = induced loop voltage in volts

$$B = \text{magnetic-flux density in tesla}$$
$$= 10^{-4} \times \text{magnetic-flux density in gauss}$$
$$= 4\pi \times 10^{-7} \times \text{magnetic field in amps per meter}$$

h = average loop height in meters
l = loop length in meters
λ = wavelength in meters
$= C/f$
C = velocity of propagation = 3×10^8 m/s
f = interfering frequency in hertz
α = angle between plane of loop direction of propagation
θ = angle between direction of l and orthogonal plane to B

$\sin ()$ = in units of radians

In a manner similar to the diagonal polarizations leading to Eq. (6.6), the application of Eqs. (6.11) and (6.12) yields:

$$V_i/B = \sqrt{2} \; lC \sin \left(\frac{\pi h}{\sqrt{2}\lambda} \right) \text{ V/tesla for } l\lambda \text{ and } h/\lambda \leqslant 0.5 \tag{6.14}$$

$$\cong \pi \, l \, h \, f_{MHz} \, 10^6 \text{ V/tesla} \tag{6.15a}$$

$$\cong \pi \, l \, h \, f_{MHz} \, 10^2 \text{ V/gauss} \left.\right\} \text{ for } l \text{ and } h \ll \lambda \tag{6.15b}$$

$$\cong 1.25 \, \pi \, l \, h \, f_{MHz} \text{ V/A/m} \tag{6.15c}$$

$$= \sqrt{2} \; \lambda C/2 \times \sin (\pi h/\sqrt{2} \; \lambda) \text{ for } l/\lambda > 0.5 \text{ and } h/\lambda < 0.5 \tag{6.16}$$

$$= 42{,}426C/f \times \sin (2.22h/\lambda) \text{ V/gauss} \tag{6.17}$$

$$\cong 94 \, h \text{ V/gauss for } L/\lambda > 0.5 \text{ and } h/\lambda < 0.3 \tag{6.17a}$$

Since magnetic fields are usually measured and reported only when in the near field, 10 MHz is an adequate upper frequency (near-far field = $\lambda/2\pi$ = 4.77 m for 10 MHz). This means that $h/\lambda \ll 0.5$ for all magnetic fields, and $h/\lambda > 0.5$ does not need to be included in the above cases.

As already mentioned for E-fields, should the user want to address the absolute worst cases for polarization and orientation, all the above values need to be multiplied by $\sqrt{2}$, i.e., a 4 dB correction must be added to the CMC term. Interestingly, in this case, Eq. (6.12) becomes nothing other than the well-known Lenz law:

$$V_i = - \frac{d\phi}{dt} = \omega B l \times h$$

Equations (6.14) through (6.17) are plotted in Fig. 6.12. The explanation and selection of the parameter values is similar to that previously discussed for E-field coupling (cf. Figs. 6.9 and 6.10).

Illustrative Example 6.2

Using the similar ongoing example of Fig. 6.11, replace the potentially interfering E-field from an AM broadcast station with a field from power lines. A nearby 60 Hz power bus is carrying a current of 200 A and produces an average magnetic flux density in the victim loop area of 100 milligauss (mG). Compute the common-mode coupling and the induced common-mode voltage.

From Fig. 6.12, for $l = 10$ m and h = 10 cm, parameter line M is chosen. This corresponds to a loop area of 1 m². Line M intersects the 60 Hz frequency at a CMC value of −34 dBV/G.

Since CMC here converts magnetic flux density in units of gauss (0.1 gauss in the example = −20 dBG) to induced voltage, V, the common-mode voltage is 34 dB below the B flux density value. Thus, the voltage is −20 dBG − 34 dBV/G = −54 dBV = 2 mV.

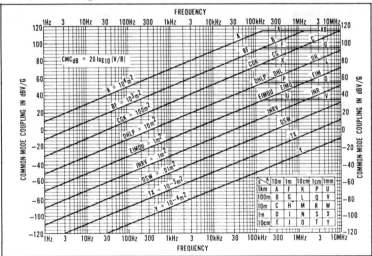

Figure 6.12—Magnetic-Flux Density, Common-Mode Coupling into Box-Cable-Ground Loop Area.

6.13

6.3 Reducing Common-Mode Coupling

Some measures can be taken to reduce the common-mode voltage induced into the inevitable loop area, A = lh, shown in Figs. 6.2 through 6.6. These reduction techniques are:

1. Reduce ground loop area:
   a. Reduce cable length, l
   b. Reduce average cable height, h
   c. Reduce both l and h
2. Shield the entire location containing Boxes 1 and 2, interconnecting cables and ground plane
3. Re-orient the cable layout to reach a minimum polarization or flux intercept. However, this is more a one-of-a-kind field fix than a real engineering improvement.

Each CMC reduction technique will be discussed next.

6.3.1 Ground-Loop Area

Of the above three measures to reduce the ground loop area, it is presumed that only the second will work, viz., reducing the average cable height, h. The reason is that, generally, the cable length used is already the shortest path length consistent with practical considerations such as location of cable trays, raceways, cable hangers and raised flooring. Thus, the first and third measures, both involving reducing the cable length, will not be considered further.

Section 6.2 and Figs. 6.9, 6.10 and 6.12 indicate that the common-mode voltage is proportional to the loop area or average height for h/λ < 0.5. Thus, for this condition, the CMC reduction in dB, CMC_{RdB}, is:

$$CMC_{RdB} = 20 \log (h_b/h_a) \quad \text{for h/}\lambda < 0.5 \qquad (6.18)$$

where,
   h_b = average cable height in centimeters before reducing height
   h_a = average cable height in centimeters after reducing height

6.14

Illustrative Example 6.3

Compute both the common-mode reduction and the net CMC in Example 6.1 when the average height is reduced such that h_b = 10 cm and h_a = 2 cm.

From Eq. (6.18):

$$CMC_{RdB} = 20 \log (10 \text{ cm}/2 \text{ cm}) = 14 \text{ dB}$$

The new common-mode coupling, CMC_{NdB}, is:

$$CMC_{NdB} = CMC_{dBV/E} - CMC_{RdB} \qquad (6.19)$$

$$= -40 \text{ dBV/E} - 14 \text{ dB} = -54 \text{ dBV/E}$$

The common-mode voltage resulting from a field strength of E = 10 V/m is:

$$V_{dBV} = E_{dBV/m} + CMC_{NdB}$$

$$= 20 \text{ dBV/m} - 54 \text{ dBV/E} = -34 \text{ dBV} = 20 \text{ mV}$$

The above new CMC_{NdB} could also be obtained by interpolating between the intersection of the R (corresponding to h = 3 cm) and W (corresponding to h = 1 cm) parameter lines in Fig. 6.9 and the 1 MHz frequency of the AM broadcast station. This also yields CMC_{NdB} = -54 dBV/E.

A variation of this solution is the case when, instead of bringing the cable closer to an inaccessible RF ground, a wide metal tray is erected between the two boxes. Provided this metal tray has a moderate length-to-total-width ratio (less than 10 as explained in Section 5.2) and that the various sections are well bonded together (including to the boxes), it becomes a substitute to the RF ground. **In a sense, if one cannot decrease h by bringing the cable down, this is the ground reference which is brought up**.

6.3.2 Shielded Enclosures

Another approach to reduce the common-mode coupling is to shield the entire area which encloses all the boxes and interconnecting cables. In essence, this amounts to a shielded room. Because of the substantial expense, this approach usually should be considered only as a last resort. Three identifiable types of enclosures are included in this category:

1. Natural building attenuation offered by the skin and girders of various buildings
2. Home-made enclosures of various configurations and types
3. Formal enclosures purchased from and installed by shielded enclosure manufacturers

Among enclosures of the above types, one may expect enormous variations in performance. Some details are given in Section 2.4.6 and Ref. 3.

6.3.2.1 Natural Building Attenuation

If the radiated emission originates from within the building, the attenuation offered by the building skin or facade is not relevant. However, if the electromagnetic radiation originates from outside the building, such as from a licensed transmitter, the attenuations offered by both the skin facade and girders are pertinent. Figure 6.13 illustrates the natural shielding attenuation offered by girdered buildings with facades of brick, concrete, stone and glass. Only the girders significantly contribute to reflection loss. From Fig. 6.13, note that the attenuation is relatively low in the 30 to 300 MHz portion of the spectrum where the center-to-center separation of the girders is of the order of $\lambda/2$. Also note that the E-field attenuation at lower frequencies is significant and corresponds to a frequency dependent slope of about 20 dB/decade. By contrast, low-frequency H-field attenuation is extremely poor.

Illustrative Example 6.4

Calculate the reduction in radiated emission from an AM broadcast station offered by a girdered commercial office building. The victim site is located 3 m inside the building and is situated near a large window. Figure 6.13 shows that the attenuation at 1 MHz is about 51 dB for a 3 m distance.

Had the emission source been an L-band radar at 1,300 MHz,

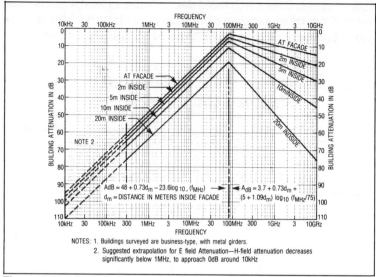

Figure 6.13—Building Attenuation to Outside Radiated Emissions vs. Frequency and Distance inside the Facade

the building would have offered an attenuation of about 17 dB. To an FM broadcast station at 100 MHz, the attenuation would have been only 7 dB. On the other hand, if the victim site were located toward the center of the building, say at a distance of 20 m from the facade, the attenuation would be more significant.

6.3.2.2 Attenuation of Home-Made Enclosures

Home-made shielded enclosures are defined as those not purchased from and installed by a commercial shielded enclosure manufacturer. They may be fabricated from all kinds of materials, and the quality of the job may range from very amateurish to outstanding. Correspondingly, the mid-range attenuation from 10 kHz to 1 GHz may range from 20 dB to over 80 dB. This large range is mostly due to the treatment given to windows, doors and other regions of shielding degradation. Such enclosures may include wire screen, overlapping metal foil or flame spray of metals on insulating bases.

The attenuation to use here should be based on actual measurements. If measurements do not exist and the construction is not known, then a suggested default value of 30 dB can be used for the mid-frequency-range attenuation. This is in addition to the basic attenuation offered by the building described above.

6.3.2.3 Attenuation of Manufactured Shielded Enclosures

In the case of manufactured shielded enclosures, use the manufacturer's attenuation data. However, if the enclosure is old and the attenuation is unknown, it is advisable to perform an actual measurement or to contact the manufacturer for an estimate of the enclosure's attenuation. If all else fails, use a mid-frequency-range default attenuation of 70 dB if the enclosure is in poor condition, or 100 dB if it is in good condition.

Abundant details on the fabrication and availability of both home-made and manufactured shielded rooms can be found in Volume 3, *Electromagnetic Shielding*, of this handbook series.

6.4 Ground-Loop Coupling

Ground-loop coupling is the second step of the second coupling path shown in Fig. 6.1. It is also the second step in the first coupling path. This section presents graphs for predicting ground-loop coupling, and the next section will discuss some EMI control techniques for reducing that coupling.

Ground-loop coupling, which is closely related to common-mode rejection, is defined as:

$$\text{GLC}_{\text{dB}} = 20 \log (V_o/V_1) \tag{6.20}$$

where,

V_o = voltage produced at the input terminals to the victim amplifier or logic in Box 2 (see Fig. 6.14)

V_i = induced common-mode voltage previously used in Eqs. (6.6) and (6.14)

Figure 6.14 shows a balanced **source and load impedance**. Since GLC applies to unbalanced sources and loads as well, Fig. 6.14 could have shown an unbalanced circuit. Furthermore, Fig. 6.14

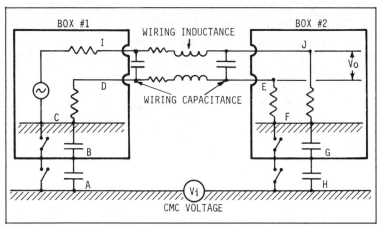

Figure 6.14—Ground-Loop Coupling and Undesired Emissions Appearing at Victim Amplifier/Logic Input Terminals

shows a balanced wire line (parallel wire pair with both wires having the same characteristics). Again, since GLC applies to both balanced and unbalanced **transmission or interconnection lines**, Fig. 6.14 could have shown an unbalanced line such as a coaxial cable. Of course, the performance of all four combinations would be different. Therefore, GLC will be discussed separately for each, with the transmission line type being the major division.

6.4.1 Balanced Transmission Lines

Figure 6.14 shows that the induced CMC voltage, V_i, pushes common-mode current around the loops ABCDFHIJA and ABCEGHIJA for a single wire pair. Since the impedance of the two loop paths is not the same, even for a balanced system, there results a differential voltage, V_o, available at the input terminals of the victim amplifier or logic. It is this voltage which will produce EMI if it is above the sensitivity of the amplifier or the noise immunity level of logic. Thus, the ratio of V_i/V_o is the common-mode rejection ratio, and its inverse is the ground-loop coupling.

---

*This should not be confused with the manufacturer's reported common-mode rejection ratio of amplifiers (CMRR) which corresponds to a very restricted set of conditions including both 60 Hz and the test bench setup, and has very little or no cable contribution.

Appendix D develops the details of Eq. (6.20). The results of this are plotted in Figs. 6.15 and 6.16 for the condition of an unbalanced circuit corresponding to box-to-box interconnecting cable lengths of 1 and 10 m, respectively. Equation (6.20) is also plotted in Figs.

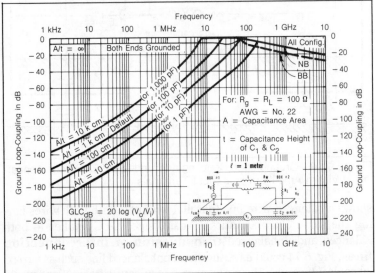

Figure 6.15—Ground-Loop Coupling for 1 m Interconnecting Cable of Unbalanced System.

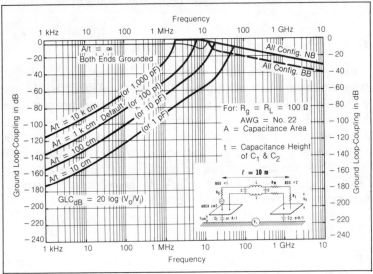

Figure 6.16—Ground-Loop Coupling for 10 m Interconnecting Cable on Unbalanced System.

6.20

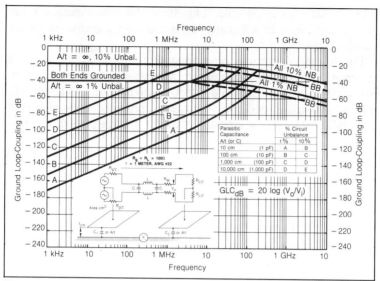

Figure 6.17—Ground-Loop Coupling for 1 m Interconnecting Cable on Balanced System

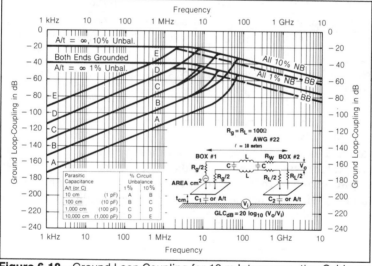

Figure 6.18—Ground-Loop Coupling for 10 m Interconnecting Cable on Balanced System.

6.17 and 6.18 for balanced circuits having cable lengths of 1 and 10 m. All figures are plots of GLC versus frequency from 1 kHz to 10 GHz. The parameter, A/t, corresponds to the ratio of the area to height of either the printed circuit boards above their cases shown in Fig. 6.11, or the bottom of the box/equipment case above the

6.21

ground plane, as applicable. This forms the capacitances, C, illustrated in Fig. 6.14 when any of the units is not grounded (toggle switch is open).

The A/t parameter may be estimated or measured. If measured indirectly with a capacitance bridge, any grounds must first be temporarily removed. If estimated, the A/t ratio may be computed from the parallel-plate capacitor equation, provided the dielectric (generally air) thickness is smaller than the average plate dimension:

$$C = \epsilon \ \frac{A}{t} \ pF \qquad (6.21)$$

where,

ϵ = permittivity of plate dielectric
  = $1/(36\pi \times 10^9)$ F/m = 0.0884 pF/cm
A = parallel plate area in cm^2
t = plate separation in cm

Table 6.1 may be used to determine the A/t ratio from C in pF.

Table 6.1—Capacitance Equivalent of A/t Ratios for $\sqrt{A} \gg$ t

A/t	Capacitance	A/t	Capacitance	A/t	Capacitance
10 cm	0.88 pF	100 cm	8.84 pF	1,000 cm	88.4 pF
15 cm	1.33 pF	150 cm	13.3 pF	1,500 cm	133 pF
20 cm	1.77 pF	200 cm	17.7 pF	2,000 cm	177 pF
30 cm	2.65 pF	300 cm	26.5 pF	3,000 cm	265 pF
50 cm	4.42 pF	500 cm	44.2 pF	5,000 cm	442 pF
70 cm	6.19 pF	700 cm	61.9 pF	7,000 cm	619 pF
				10,000 cm	884 pF

If the PCB-to-ground or chassis-to-floor distance becomes significant and the parallel-plate capacitor cannot be assumed any longer, the value will become asymptotic to what can be called **capacitance to infinity.** For instance, a volume with an average radius of 10 cm, when its distance to the surrounding ground increases to infinity, cannot reach a capacitance less than:

$$C_{min} = 4\pi \times 8.8 \ pF/m \times 0.1 \ m = 11 \ pF$$

If the A/t ratio of the designer's situation is unknown* or cannot be measured, a default value of 100 to 1,000 cm may be used. Ap-

---

*For information, statistics on parasitic capacitance of 45 various electronic devices including small items, racks, consoles etc. has produced the following results: PCB-to-chassis: mean value = 29 pF, Std. deviation = 15 pF chassis-to-surrounding ground: mean value 66 pF, Std. deviation 58 pF.

pendix D presents further explanation and details.

Figures 6.15 and 6.16 show that the ground-loop coupling at lower frequencies is only −6 dB (worst condition) when both printed circuit boards are grounded to their cases and the cases are grounded to the ground plane. Except when both boxes are grounded, Figs. 6.15 through 6.16 show the GLC becoming worse (more coupling or less negative values) as frequency rises above 1 kHz. They achieve their worst case (greatest values) at the $LC\omega^2$ resonance of the interconnecting cable inductance with the floating capacitance. Above this frequency, the GLC begins to fall off because of cable losses. As explained in Appendix D, the reference cable shown in the inserts of the figure is AWG No. 22. Its AWG rating has only secondary effects upon the GLC. Similarly, the reference 100 Ω signal source impedance in Box 1 and 100 Ω victim input impedance in Box 2 has a relatively small effect on GLC provided the impedances are above about 30 Ω.

Figures 6.15 and 6.16 correspond to unbalanced circuits in which the full signal source and victim load impedance appear in the high side of the wiring as shown in Fig. 6.19. Conversely, Figs. 6.17 and 6.18 correspond to balanced circuits in which the source and load impedances are approximately split between their high and low sides as shown in Fig. 6.20. In examining Figs. 6.17 and 6.18, observe that a second parameter exists in addition to the A/t parameter. This second parameter corresponds to "X" in Fig. 6.20, which is the decimal equivalent of the tolerance of balance on the split of the high-side and low-side impedances. Thus, this tolerance

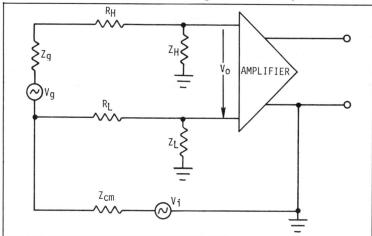

Figure 6.19—Conceptual Circuit of Unbalanced System

6.23

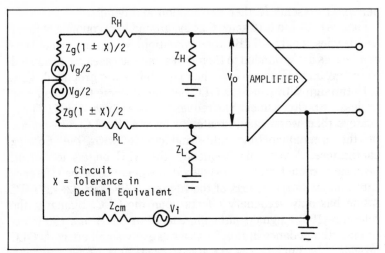

Figure 6.20—Conceptual Circuit of Balanced System

is referenced in percent in Figs. 6.17 and 6.18 as "1% unbal" and "10% unbal" parameters.

For balanced circuits, Figs. 6.17 and 6.18 show the corresponding GLC condition to be −20 dB for a 10 percent tolerance and −40 dB for a 1 percent tolerance. For an all-grounded condition, this is already better than the −6 dB of the balanced case. However, to achieve a substantial improvement in ground-loop decoupling, all figures show a need to float (unground) one or both circuit boards relative to the ground plane.

Figures 6.15 through 6.18 correspond to cable lengths of either 1 or 10 m. What about other cable lengths? The figures also correspond to 100 Ω source and load impedances and to AWG No. 22 interconnecting control and signal loads. What about other conditions? Appendix D develops and presents 15 different graphs which correspond to different quantified conditions of balanced versus unbalanced, cable length, impedance levels and AWG ratings. It is suggested that the reader acquaint himself with the important design data in Appendix D.

Illustrative Example 6.5

In Fig. 6.14, both PCBs are grounded to their cases, and both cases are grounded to the ground plane. Compute the ground-loop coupling of the AM broadcast EMI problem presented earlier.

Figure 6.16 shows that the 1 MHz emission and the A/t = ∞ line (both ends grounded) intersect at a GLC = −7 dB. Thus, if V_i = −20 dBV = 100 mV (see Example 6.1), then $V_o = V_i$ + GLC = −20 dBV − 7 dB = −27 dBV = 45 mV.

The GLC values in Figures 6.15 through 6.18 for A/t from 10 cm to 10,000 cm correspond to a float condition (either mother board to case or case to ground plane) at both Boxes 1 and 2. How is GLC determined when only one float condition prevails? Since the figures are based on two capacitances in series, the impedance decreases when only one applies. Thus, either recalculate the new A/t or add 6 dB to the GLC reading (assumes A/t of Box 1 equals A/t of Box 2).

6.4.2 Unbalanced Transmission Lines

The unbalanced transmission line family includes single-braided coaxial lines, double-braided lines, triaxial lines and semi-rigid coax. When Fig. 6.14 is redrawn for a coaxial line, Fig. 6.21 results. In the typical mode of operation, a coaxial line is grounded to the box cases through the backshell of the coax connector and jack as shown in Fig. 6.21. As discussed later for reducing GLC at low frequencies, this **automatic** grounding to the case can be avoided with the use of a special insulated connector, resulting in the situation shown in Fig. 6.22.

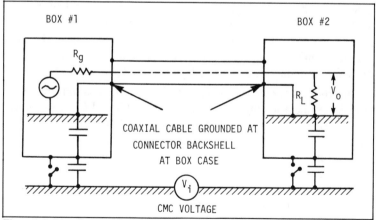

Figure 6.21—Ground-Loop Coupling in Unbalanced Transmission Lines with Cable Grounded at Both Box Cases in Traditional Manner (cf Fig. 6.14).

6.25

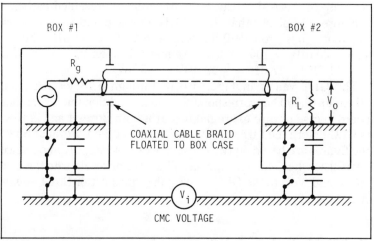

Figure 6.22—Ground-Loop Coupling in Unbalanced Transmission Lines with Cable Floated at Both Ends.

Based on the coaxial transfer impedance (Z_T) concept (see Section 7.1), the GLC in Eq. (6.20) is plotted in Fig. 6.23 for RG-8A/U. For typical grounding at both ends of the coaxial sheath, below about 1 kHz, the GLC is only −6 dB. Half of V_i is dropped across the coax source impedance and half is dropped across the load, V_o. From about 1 kHz to 800 kHz, the GLC falls off at 20 dB/decade since the coax external impedance (inductive reactance) increases while the coax transfer impedance (resistance) is constant. Above 800 kHz, the GLC degrades due to an increase in transfer impedance until the coax line achieves an electrical length of λ/2. Thereafter, the GLC since the characteristic impedance of the coaxial line above the ground plane is constant, while the effective transfer impedance of the braid becomes $Z_T \times$ λ/2.

Figure 6.24 shows the results of floating the coaxial line at the special connector entry to the box cases. The GLC improvement for all A/t ratios compared to grounded conditions is very evident at low and mid frequencies. For high frequencies, however, the GLC improvement vanishes due to the A/t capacitances grounding the configuration.

How can one use the GLC curves of Fig. 6.23 and 6.24 when the coaxial line is not RG-8A/U? One could recalculate the GLC by the equations shown in Fig. 6.23 using specific values for Z_T and Z_{sh}

6.26

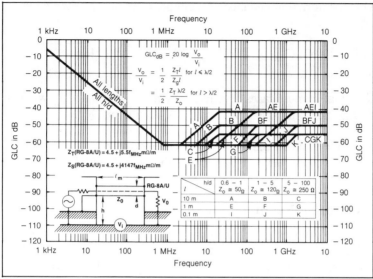

Figure 6.23—Ground-Loop Coupling for RG-8A/U Coaxial Cable for Sheath Grounded at Both Box Connectors, and Several Lengths and Height/Diam. Ratios.

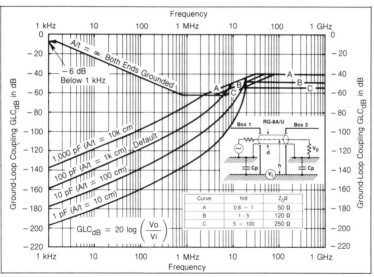

Figure 6.24—General GLC for RG-8A/U Coaxial Cable (Fig. 6.23 Plus Effect of Floating Coaxial Outer Jacket at Bond Ends), Shown for 10 m Cable Length

(shield external impedance). Or simply compute the correction as follows:

$$GLC_{new} = GLC_{(RG-8)} + 20 \log \frac{new\ Z_T}{Z_{T(RG-8)}} - 20 \log \frac{new\ Z_{sh}}{Z_{sh(RG8)}}$$

Note that in most cases, if h and d are about the same, Z_{sh} will not change and only the first correction term is needed.

More details on the transfer impedance are given in Chapter 7, since this concept is used to calculate the cable direct pickup as well.

Illustrative Example 6.6

The two boxes of the ongoing EMI scenario in Example 6.5 (1 MHz, 10 m unbalanced link) are now connected by 10 m of RG8 coax, with ordinary BNC connectors bonded to the chassis. From Fig. 6.23 the GLC is −63 dB, a significant improvement over the −7 dB for the "all-grounded" wire pair case. Since the induced loop voltage V_i has not changed, the victim's input noise is:

$$V_o = V_i + GLC = -20\ dBV - 63 = -83\ dBV, \text{ or } 70\ \mu V$$

Notice that had we used a balanced source and load with an excellent balance of 1 percent and floated both PCBs, the GLC (Fig. 6.18) would have been in the same range of values for A/t in the 100 pF range. This is about the frequency where coaxial line and balanced pair performances cross. At lower frequencies, a balanced pair with floated signal grounds will provide better ground-loop rejection than coax with normally grounded connectors. If the designer uses an **isolated** coaxial connector where the braids connect to the signal ground but not to the chassis, the new GLC (Fig 6.24) would drop into the −90 to −110 dB range.

6.5 Reducing Ground-Loop Coupling

Ground-loop coupling may be reduced by an application of one or more of the following:

1. Float either or both PCBs.
2. Use a balanced circuit or balanced drivers and receivers.

3. Use an isolation transformer or optical isolator.
4. Use RF chokes in the case-to-ground path and bond the cases together.
5. Float box shields inside equipment enclosures.
6. Add ferrites on cable.
7. Use feed-through capacitors.
8. Replace hard wires with fiber optics.

These eight GLC reduction techniques are reviewed in the following subsections.

6.5.1 Floated Printed Circuit Boards

Figure 6.25 shows one way to increase the ground-loop impedance, viz., float either the box or the PCB. Floating both would be largely redundant since two capacitances would be in series with the induced common-mode voltage. If the box case were floated, it would violate National Electrical Codes for safety unless the two boxes were also bonded together by a jumper cable. Thus, floating the PCB would be preferred. Figure 6.26 shows one familiar practical example of breaking the ground loop in a two-equipment situation.

By floating (ungrounding or disconnecting the short) both board-to-case grounds in Fig. 6.27, the A/t parameter line in Figs. 6.15 through 6.18 changes from infinity (grounded) to either the new operational condition or A/t = 100 to 1,000 cm (10 to 100 pF) if the GLC default value is used. When only one of the two grounds (both at Box 1 and Box 2) is broken as in Fig. 6.27, 6 dB is added

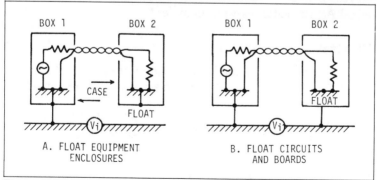

Figure 6.25—Increasing Ground-Loop Impedance by Floating Circuits, Boards, Boxes, Equipments and Enclosures.

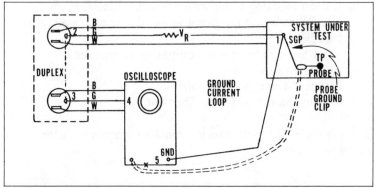

Figure 6.26A—Scope Noise and 60 Hz Pickup Due to Ground Loop of Path 123451.

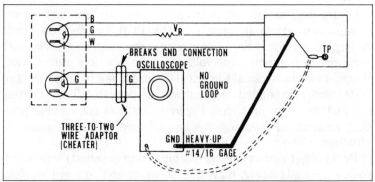

Figure 6.26B—Eliminating Scope Noise and 60 Hz Pickup by Opening Ground Current Loop at Adaptor and Heavy-Up Scope-to-System Ground.

back to the corresponding GLC value. This happens because the corresponding A/t capacitance is double what it would be if two equal A/t capacitances were in series.*

Illustrative Example 6.7

Compute the new ground-loop coupling corresponding to floating the PCB in Box 2 of Fig. 6.27 for the same 1 MHz AM broadcast interfering emission problem.

Figure 6.16 previously showed that the value of GLC was −7 dB for both ends grounded. The figure now shows that the intersec-

---

*Should the corresponding capacitances (or A/t ratios) be unequal, the correction will not be 6 dB. However, the correction may be readily computed from the ratio the two capacitances in series (i.e., $C_1 \times C_2/C_1 + C_2$) over the only capacitance which is floating.

6.30

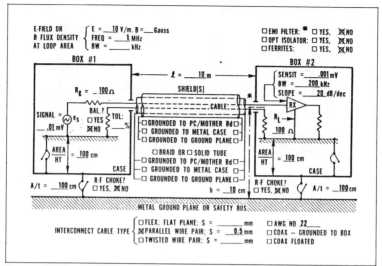

Figure 6.27—Fig. 6.11 with PCB and Cases Grounded

tion of 1 MHz and A/t ≡ 100 pF yields a GLC of −50 dB for both ends (boxes) floated. For only one end floated and one end grounded, however, add back 6 dB. Thus, the new GLC is −44 dB, representing a GLC reduction or improvement of 36 dB.

The example is a significant demonstration of the effect of multi-point grounding versus single-point grounding. As seen from Fig. 6.16, the effectiveness is even greater at lower frequencies, whereas it vanishes at higher frequencies. For example, at 10 kHz the improvement is 108 dB. Above approximately 15 MHz, the improvement reduces to zero since the PCB-to-case capacitance grounds the PCB at VHF/UHF.

6.5.2 Use of a Balanced System

Figures 6.19 and 6.20 showed the conceptual circuits of unbalanced and balanced systems, respectively. Figure 6.28 shows both systems operated in a grounded configuration. For the balanced circuit, one-half of the source and load resistances are nominally allocated between the upper and lower branches of the balanced circuit. The tolerance term X contributes to the residual imbalance (asymmetry) of the circuit as follows:

If both ends are grounded, the worst possible GLC factor (if all tolerances accumulate in the most unfavorable way) becomes (see Fig. 6.28):

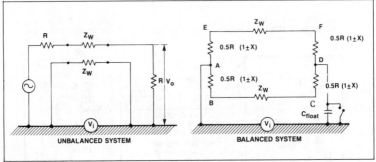

Figure 6.28—Comparison of Grounded Unbalanced and Balanced Systems.

$$GLC = \frac{V_{DM}}{V_{CM}} = \frac{V_{FC}}{V_i}$$

where,

V_{DM} = differential-mode voltage
V_{CM} = common-mode voltage
V_i = induced loop voltage

Since $V_{FC} = V_{FD} - V_{CD}$,

$$V_{FC} = V_i \left[\frac{0.5R(1 + X)}{0.5\,R\,(1 + X) + 0.5\,R\,(1 - X)} - \right.$$

$$\left. \frac{0.5\,R\,(1 - X)}{0.5\,R\,(1 - X) + 0.5\,R\,(1 + X)} \right] \qquad (6.22)$$

Note that V_{FC}, V_{FD} and V_{CD} refer to the voltages between points F and C, points F and D, and points C and D, respectively, in Fig. 6.28. After manipulation,

$$V_{FC} = X \times V_i \qquad (6.23)$$

Therefore,

$$GLC_{dB} = 20 \log (X) \qquad (6.24)$$

6.32

where,

X = resistor tolerance (in decimal percent equivalent)

If **one or both ends are floated** (switch open in Fig. 6.28), the floating capacitance further reduces the ground loop coupling:

$$GLC = \frac{V_{FC}}{V_i} = \frac{X \times V_{AD}}{V_i} = \frac{X_x Z_{AD}}{Z_{AD} + Z_{float}}$$

$$= X \left[\frac{0.5 (2 \times 0.5 R + Z_w)}{0.5 (2 \times 0.5 R + Z_w) + Z_{float}} \right] \tag{6.25}$$

$$GLC_{dB} = 20 \log \left[X \left(\frac{0.5 (R + Z_w)}{0.5 (R + Z_w) + Z_{float}} \right) \right] \tag{6.26}$$

For both grounded and ungrounded operation, Fig. 6.15 may be compared with Fig. 6.17 for a 1 m interconnecting cable length, and Fig. 6.16 may be compared with Fig. 6.18 for a 10 m cable. Using the latter two, for example, it can be seen that the balanced system yields a better performance (more negative GLC) when both ends are floated for mid and high frequencies. However, for a poor balance (e.g., 10 percent tolerance), the unbalanced system actually gives somewhat better performance at low frequencies.

It must be remarked that the wire pair itself may contribute to the total imbalance, especially when frequency increases. The benefit of a 1 percent trimmed driver and receiver set will not be seen if the lack of symmetry of the wire pair introduces a 10 percent imbalance.

Illustrative Example 6.8

Determine the GLC corresponding to a balanced circuit having a 1 percent tolerance (1) for both PCB boards grounded, then (2) for both boards floated. Use the ongoing 1 MHz, AM broadcast station radiation as the example.

The $A/t = \infty$ (grounded) and 1 percent tolerance parameter line in Fig. 6.18 intersects the 1 MHz frequency line at -40 dB. This represents a 33 dB improvement $(-40 - [-7])$ over the original unbalanced conditions determined from Fig. 6.16 (see Example 6.4).

6.33

For ungrounded conditions, the A/t ≡ 100 pF and 1 percent imbalance curve C in Fig. 6.18 intersects the 1 MHz frequency line at − 72 dB. Since only one PCB is ungrounded, adding back 6 dB yields a GLC of − 66 dB. Comparing this to the − 50 dB unbalanced condition in Example 6.9 indicates that 16 dB additional improvement is achieved by balancing.

When both ends are floated, if the radiated emission frequency is 10 kHz and the balance tolerance is 10 percent, Figs. 6.16 and 6.18 indicate that the GLC is − 120 dB and − 92 dB, respectively. This illustrates a previous statement that an unbalanced circuit may give better results at low frequencies than a poorly balanced one (lack of symmetry through the worst-case accumulation of tolerances).

6.5.3 Influence of Shielded Cable

Chapter 7 discusses the third coupling path, direct radiation into a cable (differential-mode coupling) and the effect of adding one or more shields to the cable. Under certain conditions there also may be an interaction between this path and the second coupling path (GLC) discussed in this chapter.

The subject of this section is illustrated in Fig. 6.29. When a shielded cable, having a shield impedance, Z_{sh}, is added, an alternate flow path is developed for a common-mode current, I_s. Since the source impedance, Z_s is small compared with Z_{sh}, it would appear that I_s does not influence the GLC which exists without the cable shield. I_s is simply a **drain current** which is not in the path of either the circuit generator impedance, Z_g, or load impedance, Z_L. Therefore, I_s seems to have no effect upon V_o, the undesired load voltage.

Certainly, the preceding remarks apply when either switch S_1 or S_2 is open, i.e., the left or the right end of the cable is floated (not grounded). Can there be an interaction, however, when S_1 and S_2 are both grounded? By transfer impedance action Z_T, (see Chapter 7), I_s on the sheath will induce a common-mode voltage along the wire pair, which in turn will develop an undesired differential mode voltage, V_o. Thus we can define a differential transfer impedance Z_{Td} such that:

$$Z_{Td} = V_o/I_s \qquad (6.27)$$

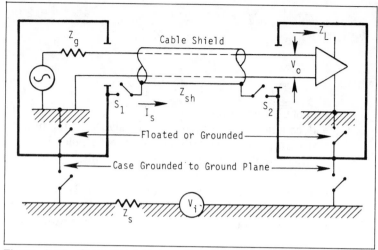

Figure 6.29—Cable Shield Interaction and Grounding Conditions.

While I_s is independent of Z_g and Z_L, V_o is not. Furthermore, V_o is also dependent on whether Z_g and Z_L are balanced. Thus, to remove the dependence of Z_{Td} upon V_o, Eq. (6.27) is redefined, starting from the conventional definition of surface transfer impedance Z_T:

$$Z_T = V_1/I_s \quad \text{ohms/meter} \tag{6.28}$$

where,

> V_1 = induced voltage along the wire pair per meter length. **This equals the longitudinal voltage drop inside the shield due to shield-to-wire mutual inductance above a few kilohertz.**

> Z_T = Shield Transfer Impedance normalized to a 1 m length of cable

To compute V_o, then:

$$V_o = \frac{l V_1 Z_L}{Z_g + Z_L} \times C_b \tag{6.29}$$

6.35

$$= I_s Z_t l \times \frac{Z_L}{Z_g + Z_L} \times C_b \qquad (6.29A)$$

where,

l = cable length in meters
C_b = decoupling due to percent pair balance (if unknown, use 10 percent for ordinary, low-cost shielded twisted pair or 3 percent for good quality twinax)

Finally, since $I_s \approx V_1/Z_{sh}$ (for switches S_1 and S_2 closed and boxes grounded) when substituting Eq. (6.28) into Eq. (6.29), there results an additional coupling which will be called a **shield coupling, SC**:

$$SC = \frac{V_o}{V_i} = \frac{l Z_t Z_L C_b}{l Z_{sh}(Z_g + Z_L)} = \frac{Z_t C_b}{Z_{sh}} \times \frac{Z_L}{(Z_g + Z_L)} \qquad (6.30)$$

with,

Z_{sh} = shield external impedance per meter length

To determine if SC is significant, both the GLC and SC must be separately calculated, and either the larger of the two is selected or they are coherently added. An example will be given below.

Thus, a new **figure of merit**, describing the propensity of a shielded pair to convert common-mode voltages impressed on its shield, can be derived.[4,5] This is called the differential transfer impedance and is defined as follows:

$$Z_{TD} = \frac{Z_L}{Z_g + Z_L} \times Z_T \times C_b \qquad (6.30a)$$

There exists very little data in EMC literature on shield coupling for balanced shielded transmission lines. As modified from one source,* the following approximations (based on RG-22/U with 3

---

*See Ref. 6. The transfer impedance is increased by 6 dB to normalize for source and load impedance and another 20 dB increase for removing the 10 percent balance.

percent imbalance) can be used for default values of good quality, dense braid, shielded pairs:

$$Z_T \approx (5 + j5\ f_{MHz})\ m\Omega/m \text{ above a few kHz} \qquad (6.31)$$

$$Z_{sh} = (5 + j\ 3{,}500\ f_{MHz})\ m\Omega/m \qquad (6.32)$$

When Eqs. (6.26), (6.31) and (6.32) are substituted into Eq. (6.30), Fig. 6.30 results. Since the equation contains Z_t/Z_{sh}, SC curves are valid for any length smaller than $\lambda/2$.

Above $\lambda/2$, the SC behaves like the coaxial GLC model (see Section 6.4.2), i.e.:

1. Z_{sh} must be replaced by Z_0, the characteristic impedance of the cable above the ground plane (typically 250 Ω for a height-to-diameter ratio in the 5 to 100 range).
2. $Z_T \times l$ must be replaced by $(Z_T \times \lambda/2)$ ohms, or $Z_T \times 150/f_{MHz}$.

To better visualize how SC is evolving, it has been overlaid, in Fig. 6.30 on two typical GLC curves for a 10 m cable.

Since GLC (the mode conversion) exists at any frequency regardless of whether a shield is there or not, this is the highest of the two couplings which predominates for converting V_i into V_o. It is visible that below a few megahertz, grounding the shield at both ends compromises the excellent isolation offered by the floating PCBs scheme. Above a few megahertz, the shield contribution is overridden by the GLC, so grounding the shield at both ends does not aggravate the coupling, while it contributes to the overall system shielding integrity.

This model validates *a posteriori* the old precept which recommends grounding a shield at one end only at low frequencies. The "low-frequency" frontier (depending on the tradition) is regarded as $\lambda/4$, $\lambda/10$, $\lambda/20$, etc. Looking at Fig. 6.30, and taking 0.5 to 2 MHz as the crossover region for an average shield and a 10 m length, this corresponds to $\lambda/50$ to $\lambda/15$. This number tracks the most stringent of the empirical rules but reveals that the $\lambda/4$ rule was too lax.

In reality, what is important is to interrupt the current flowing in the shield, because it couples some energy inside. The idea of interrupting the shield current has sometimes degenerated into a precept where this is the shield which is systematically interrupted.

Interrupting the shield current without interrupting the shield implies that the loop be opened somewhere else. The next section will analyze few EMC solutions of this kind.

Illustrative Example 6.9

Compute the SC for the GLC problem defined in Example 6.8 and compare the two. What action should be taken?

For grounded boxes, both internally at the mother board level and externally (see Fig. 6.29), a 1 percent balanced system, and $Z_L = Z_g$, GLC = -40 dB (see Fig. 6.18). From Fig. 6.30, the shielded coupling at 1 MHz, corresponding to both ends of the shield being grounded, is -90 dB for RG 22/U. Thus, since SC $\ll$ GLC (GLC is worse), SC is unimportant for grounded box and PCB conditions.

When the internal PCBs are floated to case, the respective values are GLC ≈ -72 dB (Fig. 6.18) and SC = -90.

Now, the SC coming close starts to degrade the GLC isolation. One could say that, in this case, the circuit balance (1 percent) was better than the combined effect of shield transfer impedance and pair unbalance (3 percent). In this example, below ≈ 1 MHz (or $l < 0.03$ λ) the shield should have been floated, or a better shield like the tight double-braid (RG22 B/U) should have been selected.

The respective values at 1 MHz, if the circuit had been unbalanced and the PCB floated, are (for 10 m) GLC = -50 dB and SC = -90 dB. If the EMI problem were in the audio region at 30 kHz, GLC unbalanced = -100 dB for SC = -65 dB. Note also the value of SC for **low-quality** shielded pairs. Here SC, when both sides of the shield are grounded, is higher than a 10 m unbalanced GLC up to 1 MHz ($l = 0.03$ λ). Thus to avoid compromising good floating isolation when PCB is floating, at **low frequencies** ($l \ll \lambda$) the shield should be grounded at one end only (preferably the receiver end). Exceptions to this would be cables that have a very low transfer impedance relative to Eq. (6.31), such as offered by super screens and thin-walled homogeneous sheaths (100 percent optical coverage). At higher frequencies, it does not matter if the shield is grounded at both ends since **GLC predominates anyway**. Therefore, since a shield is primarily intended for differential-mode field protection (see Chapter 7), this last consideration will dictate the grounding condition.

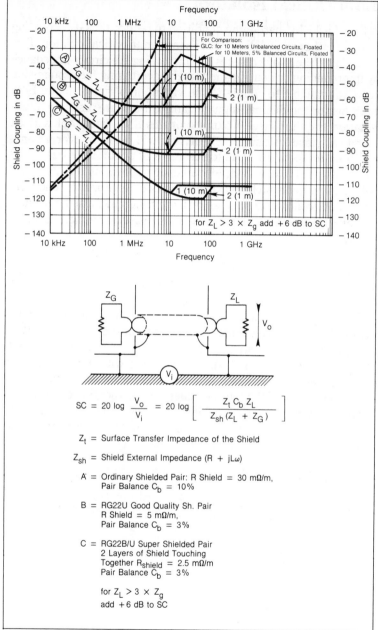

Figure 6.30—GLC Due to Double Grounded Braided Shield (SC)

6.39

6.5.4 Optical Isolators

The third EMI-hardening condition to reduce the GLC coupling is to use either an isolation transformer or an optical isolator. This is similar to the above objective of increasing the circuit impedance by ungrounding or floating and thereby decreasing the ground-loop current available to couple to the victim amplifier or logic. Both optoisolators and small-signal transformers are used in ultra-isolation amplifiers (see Volume 5 of this EMC handbook series).

Optical Isolators using LED drivers will perform over a bandwidth up to about 50 MHz (clock rates of about 10 MHz). They work on both logic and high-level analog above 100 mV, but will not perform easily on low-level analog circuits. For this condition, other EMI-control techniques described herein must be used.

While offering hundreds of megohms resistance at dc, the input-output capacitance of *in situ* optical isolators typically ranges from 0.3 to 10 pF. This limits their high-frequency usefulness since, for example, 3 pF equals 50 Ω at 1 GHz. Optical isolators are available in a number of configurations ranging from TO-5 cans to 6- and 8-pin dual-in-line packages (DIPs).

Figure 6.31 corresponds to Fig. 6.14 with the addition of an optical isolator in the GLC path at the input of the victim amplifier or logic in Box 2. Notice that the optical isolator input/output capacitance is in series in the ground loop with any of the four capacitances (board-to-case or case-to-board for both Box 1 and 2) if, indeed, any of the four switches is open (floating conditions).

Thus, optical isolators normally may be used only for all grounded conditions (all four switches are closed). Otherwise the use of an optical isolator is redundant with the concept of floating a box

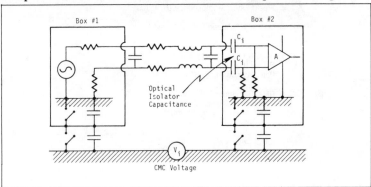

Figure 6.31—Ground-Loop Coupling Improvement (CM Rejection) Offered by Optical Isolator Input/Output Capacitance, C_i

since only one series capacitance is needed. (However, the advantage would be noticeable if, even though floated, the circuit-to-ground parasitic capacitance was very large such as 1,000 pF or more)

To determine the effect of optical isolators on GLC, the graphs in Figs. 6.15 through 6.18 and 6.24 may be used as a gross approximation. Here, instead of the A/t related capacitance being used, it is substituted by C_i in accordance with Table 6.1 to calculate the new GLC. However, a more exact approach is to use the curves of Fig. 6.31A giving the actual GLC for optical isolators. Notice that the GLC slope with an optical isolator is typically 20 dB/dec (instead of 40 dB/dec for the true PCB floating). It can be concluded that if less than 100 pF of PCB-to-ground capacitance can be achieved, a mere floating is more efficient than an opto-isolator below a few megahertz. Above this crossover, opto-isolator is more efficient.

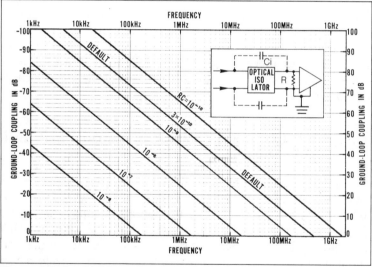

Figure 6.31A—GLC from Optical Isolators, for Several Values of Load Resistance and Isolator Capacitance

Illustrative Example 6.10

For the ongoing EMI problem, compute the GLC by using an optical isolator having a $C_i = 1$ pF when both Boxes 1 and 2 and their corresponding PCBs are grounded, instead of floating one of the PCBs as was done in Example 6.5.

Figure 6.31A shows that the optical isolator results in GLC = −65 dB corresponding to the interception of a 1 MHz, AM. This −65 dB GLC is 15 dB better (lower) than the −50 dB corresponding to an A/t = 1,000 (capacitance = 100 pF) discussed in an earlier example. This EMC fix (optical isolator) would be used instead of and not in addition to floating, to avoid redundant results.

6.5.5 Signal Isolation Transformers

When boxes or PCBs cannot be floated, signal and pulse transformers are widely used for breaking low-frequency ground loops or converting an unbalanced source and driver configuration into a balanced link. The features of these transformers regarding EMI are their parasitic capacitances, their percentage of symmetry and their bandwidth.

The parasitic capacitance ranges from 3 pF for a good quality DIP device to 100 pF for ordinary, audio-type transformers. Therefore, as a rough estimation the resulting GLC can be found from the curves in Fig. 6.15 or 6.15 Q by entering the proper parasitic capacitance value. If only one transformer is used, +6 dB must be added. Otherwise, for two transformers, the curve can be used as is.

6.5.6 RF Chokes in Safety Ground Path and Box Bonds

The fourth EMI-control technique for reducing GLC is the use of RF chokes in the box case-to-ground path (lower path) of Fig. 6.27. Here, the objective is to provide a low impedance to the 50/60/400 Hz power mains frequency for shock hazard control while exhibiting a high impedance at radio frequencies. To get the technique to work best, it is also recommended to provide a low-impedance path between the boxes such as offered by AWG No. 2 wire or large braid bonded to both boxes.

Figure 6.32 shows the conceptual comparison of the GLC path with and without an RF choke and box-to-box bonding cable. The illustration to the left shows the ground-loop path, AB/CDA in which the impedance of the loop is in part determined by the impedance of the printed circuit board (Z of PCB) to ground. It can be low (PCB

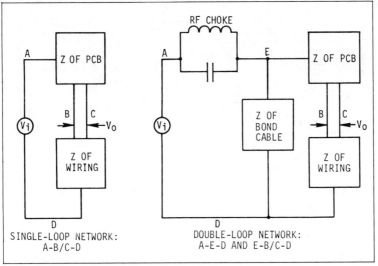

Figure 6.32—Comparison of Box Shield Ground with RF Choke and Box-to-Box Bonding Strap.

grounded) or high (PCB floated). Of course, the loop impedance is also determined by the wiring impedance and whether ferrites or optical isolators are used.

When an RF choke is added in the ground path to one or more metal box cases, the illustration to the right in Fig. 6.32 results. The shunt capacitance across the choke is due to the A/t value of the box-to-ground capacitance. If branch E-D is excluded, a single loop AEB/CDA results. The loop impedance will now be a function of the value of the RF choke and shunt A/t capacitance. At low frequencies, where the inductive reactance is low, the left and right illustrations are nearly identical. However, when branch E-D is added, a second loop and node are added, and further GLC reduction results. Basically, the improvement in GLC in Fig. 6.32 is due to the voltage-dividing action of path impedance ED to path AED.

Table 5.2A (see page 5.11a) may be used to compute the value of the bonding cable impedance. The net improvement (GLC reduction compared to both ends grounded of Fig. 6.15) due to adding this bond is developed in Appendix C and is plotted in Fig. 6.33 for the typical condition of an AWG No. 2 wire. The relatively flat GLC reduction versus frequency at low frequencies is due to the ratio of the AWG No. 2 wire and RF choke resistances. Above about

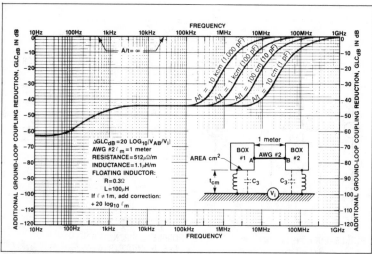

Figure 6.33—Improvement in GLC by Floating Boxes with RF Chokes and Bonding Boxes Together with Heavy AWG #2 Wire (Shown for 100 μH Chokes)

1 MHz for a 1 m wire, and A/t = 1,000, however, the improvement in GLC degrades due to the wire inductance and is nullified when the RF choke becomes totally bypassed by parasitic capacitance.

Figure 6.34 shows the additional GLC reduction offered by adding both a 100 μH RF choke and box-to-box braid. At low frequencies (e.g., 50/60 Hz), the improvement is not large, but over the mid range of 1 kHz to approximately 10 MHz, it is very significant. Even better results are obtainable if, instead of a wire or braid, a wide, homogeneous, flat copper strap is used with a length-to-width ratio less than 10. However, this solution is only practical if the frame separation is in the range of meters or less.

This could be a larger installation, where the safety wire has to be a bigger (AWG) size, and therefore the 100 μH choke has less dc resistance (60 mΩ).

Conversely, the boxes are bonded by a large braid. This braid has less total cross section than the previous AWG No. 2; therefore, its dc resistance is higher (10 mΩ/m). But due to its flat shape, the self-inductance is lower (0.1 μH/m). Although the shield of the signal cable itself could achieve this goal, there is a risk of re-injecting CM noise via the shield transfer impedance (see Section 6.5.3 on shield coupling). Therefore, it is better to make this bond by a distinct, as wide as possible, braided strap. It must be routed close to the interconnect cables to avoid re-creating a pickup loop.

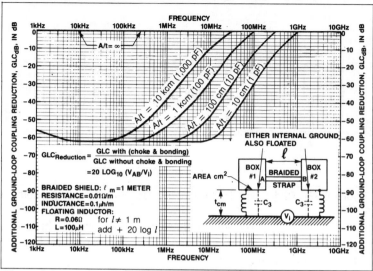

Figure 6.34—Additional GLC Reduction by Floating Boxes with RF Chokes and Bonding them Together with Large Braid

Illustrative Example 6.11

For the same ongoing EMI problem, calculate the additional reduction in GLC by adding both an RF choke in the box-to-ground path and a connecting braid between boxes to bond them.

The 1 MHz and A/t = 1,000 cm lines in Fig. 6.34 intersect at a Δ GLC of –54 dB. Since this corresponds to a 1 m box-to-box bonding cable length, add 20 dB to adjust for a 10 m length for the conditions of Fig. 6.27. Therefore, the –50 dB GLC of our unbalanced link becomes: –50 + (–54 + 20) = –84.

6.5.7 Shield Case within Equipment Enclosure

A final recommended EMI-control technique for reducing GLC is to float a box shield inside an equipment enclosure shield such as that shown in Fig. 6.35. Here, the PCB can be grounded to the inside shield. The outer shield can also be directly grounded to the ground plane without developing a low-impedance ground loop. The shield-to-shield capacitance A/t ratio now replaces that of floating PCB, and Figs. 6.15 through 6.18 can once again be used to determine the GLC reduction. It is imperative to assure that no acciden-

6.45

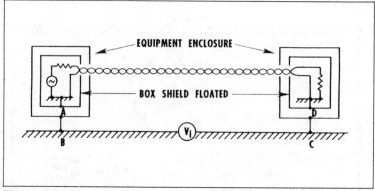

Figure 6.35—Reducing GLC by Floating Box-Shield Inside Equipment Enclosure.

tal inner shield to outer shield short has taken place. This could happen, for example, if a shielded box-to-box cable accidentally touched both shields.

This solution is used to solve the conflict in low-level instrumentation where there must be a guard shield connected to the amplifier common while simultaneously this reference must be floated.

6.5.8 Ferrite Absorbers

Another technique for reducing common-mode coupling is the use of ferrite beads, rods or tubes. They may be slipped over a single wire, wire pair or an entire harness. For harnesses, ferrite tubes also come in half-cylindrical sections with clamps to hold them together. This allows for retrofit after connectors are in place. The ferrite both increases the self-inductance of the wire or cable and acts like a frequency-dependent resistance. The resistance converts undesired common-mode currents into heat which is a good way to eliminate EMI.

6.5.8.1 Ferrites on a Single Wire

Figure 6.36 illustrates typical insertion loss corresponding to small ferrite beads, Stackpole CERAMAG #7D. The parameter lines, Z/B, in the figure correspond to the loop impedance, Z, divided by the number of beads, B. Note that the loop impedance may not be that of the victim circuit impedance, per se, but might include the vic-

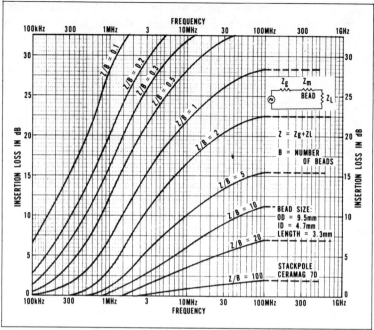

Figure 6.36—Insertion Loss of Ferrite Beads on Wire or Cable to Common-Mode Current, Typical of Small Size Ferrites.

tim input wiring. To use the figure, it is necessary both to compute the loop impedance and select the desired insertion loss. From this the Z/B parameter is determined.

Illustrative Example 6.12

For the ongoing example of a 1 MHz AM broadcast station radiation shown in Fig. 6.11, a common-mode current flows from the voltage induced in the victim loop. Select the number of ferrite beads to be placed on the cable to reduce EMI by at least 10 dB.

To obtain a minimum insertion loss of 10 dB, Fig. 6.36 indicates that the required Z/B ratio is approximately 0.7. For a total loop impedance of the upper leg of 200 Ω ($R_g = R_L = 100\ \Omega$ in Fig. 6.36) this indicates that B = Z/0.7 = 286 beads are required. Thus, for this example, it is concluded that ferrite beads do not work sufficiently well at 1 MHz. If a typical 3 to 10 ferrite beads were to be used, the EMI problem would remain since less than 1 dB of attenuation would result.

6.47

If the example were changed to a frequency of 100 MHz, such as that originating from an FM broadcast station, it is seen in Fig. 6.36 that a Z/B ratio of about 12 now corresponds to a 10 dB insertion loss. This situation requires 16 beads, corresponding to an overall bead length of about 5 cm. If multi-hole beads are used, the wires can be passed two or three times through the ferrite (provided they enter the core in the same direction), making each bead two or three times more efficient. Thus, the beads are very practical at 100 MHz. As a general guideline, it is concluded for circuit impedances of the order of 100 Ω that ferrite beads and rods do not work well below about 10 MHz.

The loop impedance also plays a major role in EMC effectiveness. If Z is high, say about 1 kΩ, then no practical number of ferrite beads would yield 10 dB even above 100 MHz, where loss is high since Z/B >. Conversely, if Z is low, say below 1 Ω, then only a few beads would yield significant attenuation at 100 kHz as seen in Fig. 6.36.

6.5.8.2 Ferrites on a Wire Pair or Cable Harness

The preceding discussion on ferrite beads and rods applies to a single wire, a coax or a shielded cable or harness. For a single wire, their use is limited to reducing EMI at the risk of reducing the desired signal also (if the frequency of the desired emissions extends into that of the interference). How then does one reduce common-mode current in a wire pair or cable harness using ferrites? Here the ferrites must be slipped over both wires or the unshielded cable harness, as applicable.

Since 1980, significant improvements have been made in common-mode ferrite suppressors. While Fig. 6.36 showed small ferrites (3.3 mm long) to slip over individual wires, very large ferrites have been developed which can embrace a whole cable harness or a stack of ribbon cables.

From the schematic Fig. 6.37A, the improvement due to the ferrite can be expressed by:

$$\text{Insertion loss} = 20 \log \left(\frac{V_o/V_i \text{ without ferrite}}{V_o/V_i \text{ with ferrite}} \right) \quad (6.33)$$

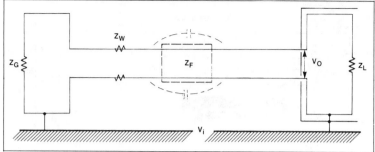

Figure 6.37A—Insertion Loss of Common-Mode Ferrite Sleeves

$$= 20 \log \left(1 + \frac{Z_F}{Z_L + Z_G + Z_W} \right) \quad (6.34)$$

This fix is fairly efficient when:

1. The circuit impedances are not too high (since ferrites work through their added equivalent series resistance); 300 Ω seems to be a maximum to obtain a noticeable improvement.
2. The EMI frequency is below the peaking region of the GLC curve (for instance, about 50 MHz for 1 m cable, in Fig. 6.15) but none of the boxes or PCBs can be floated. Indeed, if they have already been floated and this is not sufficient, it is doubtful that the ferrite will improve anything because the loop impedance is already high).
3. The EMI frequency is at or above the region where floating does not work because the stray capacitance to ground (A/t in the GLC curves) is practically a short.

Figure 6.37B shows the insertion loss [per Eq. (6.33)] of two types of ferrite suppressors for cables. Item 1 is typical RF suppressant tubing. (Sometimes these are available as cables which are coated with a flexible ferrite compound; see Ref. 7). Item 2 is a large ferrite bead designed for flat cables. For example, we see that for RG and RL = 100 Ω, the large ferrite bead provides about 10 dB between 100 and 1,000 MHz. This is not an enormous reduction, but if only 10 dB is needed, the ferrite is an easy fix that avoids redesign and disruption of the installation.

Limitations of ferrites are due to their relative permeability, μ_r, which collapses above a few hundred megahertz, and the parasitic capacitance shown in Fig. 6.37A.

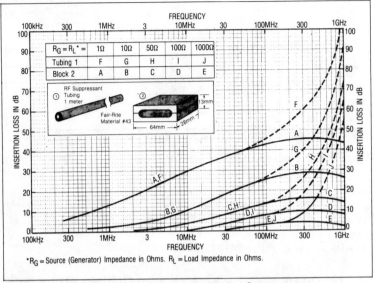

Figure 6.37B—Insertion Loss of Large Ferrite Suppressors

6.5.9 Reduction by Adding Feed-Through Capacitors on Wire Leads

Among the GLC fixes, feed-through capacitors are often favored because of their simplicity of installation and moderate cost. In brief, the feed-through capacitors divert the GLC common-mode current out of the source and receiver asymmetric impedances (see Fig. 6.38). If it is assumed that the major contributor of CM to DM conversion is the I_{CM} drop in R_L, then **the most efficient capacitors are those put on the load impedance side.**

Consider a PC board grounded to box and a box grounded to common ground where:

$$GLC = \frac{R_L}{R_G + R_L} = -6 \text{ dB if } R_G = R_L$$

The GLC for a feed-through capacitor C **on the load side** becomes:

$$V_{diff} \text{ in } R_L = \frac{(R_L \times |X_C|/(R_L + |X_C|)}{R_G + (R_L \times |X_C|)/R_L + |X_C|)} \times V_1 \quad (6.35)$$

6.50

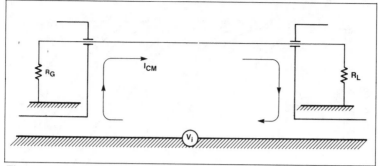

Figure 6.38—CM Loop Current Bypassed by Feed-Through Capacitors.

The benefit of feed-through is largely dependent on R_G and R_L. The benefit decreases if R_L and R_G decrease. For PC boards and floated boxes, the feed-through benefit at low frequencies is swamped in the drastic GLC reduction caused by floating. As frequency increases, floating becomes less efficient and the GLC reduction by feed-through is noticeable. Provided that the capacitors are equal within tight tolerances, they can be regarded, for the floated victim, as a high frequency balancing of the wire pair(s) to ground.

Figure 6.39 shows the additional rejection of common-mode EMI offered by feed-through capacitors having values of 100, 1,000 and 10,000 pF. **It is important that these HF bypasses be placed at the point where the cable penetrates the victim box** so that the CM currents stay outside of the electronics.

For signal lines, decoupling values > 10,000 pF are generally not used because they would affect the useful signal bandwidth above a few kHz. (Remember, the differential signal sees a line loaded by C/2. Therefore, if the line carries a wanted signal with a fundamental frequency F_o, one must make sure that putting C/2 across the line will preserve a minimum bandwidth, BW, $\geqslant 2F_o$.) Values below 30 or 10 pF are not used because they cannot compete with the *in situ* PCB to ground parasitic capacitance of 10 pF or so. **One could remark that this fix does not work by increasing the loop impedance like the others but, rather, by offering the CM current a low impedance path which does not include the victim circuit.**

Feed-through capacitors can be gainfully complemented by ferrite beads placed on the cable side. Especially if R_G or the cable impedance is low, the ferrite impedance would add up to R_G in Eq. (6.35), increasing the efficiency of the decoupling capacitors.

6.51

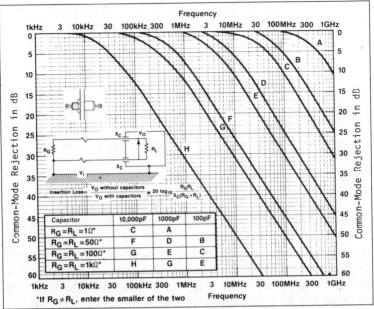

Figure 6.39—Additional Common-Mode Rejection by Feed-Through Capacitors on Wire Leads.

6.5.10 Ground Loop Elimination by Optical Fibers

Optical fibers are the ultimate solution to electrical isolation and minimum path loss over the transmission link. Fibers are immune to ambient EMI fields, do not radiate and are insensitive to ground or earth voltages differences (CM impedance coupling). The ground-loop isolation provided by the fiber alone is beyond what is reasonably measurable, i.e. 140 or 160 dB. What is actually seen during CM rejection measurement is the mode conversion in the light transmitter itself where some fraction of the EMI CM voltage may be processed in the form of light.

Even though optical fibers provide unsurpassed immunity to the link itself, this does not exonerate the designer from taking EMC precautions at the transmitter and receiver ends. If improper shielding, insufficient CM rejection, crosstalk etc. are already resident in the transmitting or receiving equipment, they will corrupt the electrical signal before its conversion into light or after it has been recovered from the light beam.

More details on EMI performance of fiber links are provided in Volume 5, *EMC in Components and Devices*, of this EMC handbook series. The problem of box shield penetration is addressed in Volume 3, *Electromagnetic Shielding*.

6.6 Composite Example

An EMI problem involving both halves of the second coupling path, CMC and GLC, will serve to help assimilate much of the material covered in this chapter. This section summarizes much of the preceding material with a composite example using the ongoing EMI problem. A worst case of poor EMC design is selected as shown in Fig. 6.27, where some of the highlights are:

1. Signal level: 0.01 mV = 20 dBμV
2. Victim sensitivity: 0.001 mV = 0 dBμV
3. Victim bandwidth: 200 kHz
4. Victim stop-band slope: 20 dB/decade
5. EMI source: AM broadcast station
6. A/t ratios: 1,000 cm (default)
7. EMI field strength: 10 V/m = 140 dBμV/m
8. All PCB and box cases: grounded
9. Signal source impedance: 100 Ω
10. Victim input impedance: 100 Ω
11. Transmission system: unbalanced
12. Box-to-box cable: parallel wires
13. Wire separation: 0.5 mm
14. AWG No.: 22
15. Cable length: 10 m
16. Average cable height: 10 cm

The present problem is limited to the second single coupling path of CMC-GLC as shown in Fig. 6.1. For convenience, the previous EMI prediction form shown in Fig. 3.12 is repeated in Fig. 6.40 in modified form. Column 1 corresponds to the ambient EMI source of 140 dBμV/m, whereas Column 2 is that of the victim sensitivity or 0 dBμV. Column 3 is the difference between the ambient and sensitivity levels (A/N ratio), or 140 dB (above 1/m).

Next, of columns 4A, 4B, 4C, 4D and 4E, only column 4B in Fig. 6.40 is used. This corresponds to the CMC-GLC coupling path. The

OPERATING CONDITIONS	AMB dBμV (1)	N dBμV (2)	A/N dB (3)	GCM GLC (4A)	FCM GLC (4B)	DMC (4C)	C-C (4D)	P1·PS PS·V (4E)	SUM 4A·4E (4)	AMP REJ (5)	Δ I/N (6)	I/N (7)
OBJECTIVE												-26
START: FIRST RUN	140	0	140	NA	-47	NA	NA	NA	-47	-14		+79

$$(I/N)dB: \;(7) = (3) + (4) + (5)$$

Figure 6.40—Initial Prediction to Determine I/N Ratio.

former path contributed a -40 value as previously discussed in Example 4.4 for a 10 m cable with an average height of 10 cm above the ground plane. The GLC path contributed a -7 dB value as presented in Example 6.5. Thus, the combined effect of -40 dB CMC and -7 dB of GLC is -47 dB. This value appears in Column 4B. Since it is the only coupling path of 4A–4E, -47 dB also appears in Column 4.

For the amplifier rejection in Column 5, Example 4.1 showed that a 1 MHz emission is rejected by 14 dB. This corresponds to the amplifier having a 200 kHz cutoff frequency and a stop-band slope of 20 dB/decade. Thus, -14 dB is entered under Column 5.

To calculate the resulting I/N ratio of Column 7, Eq. (3.17) is used. This is equivalent to adding Columns 3, 4 and 5. When this is done:

$$(I/N)_{dB} = (A/N)d_B + (CMC/GLC)d_B + AR_{dB} \qquad (6.36)$$

$$= 140 \text{ dB} - 47 \text{ dB} - 14 \text{ dB} = 79 \text{ dB}$$

Therefore, 79 dB appears in Column 7 of Fig. 6.40. This corresponds to a very bad EMI situation in which the amplifier clearly will be jammed and inoperable.

Now the task remains to eliminate the EMI problem by an amount equal to the above $(I/N)_{dB}$ minus the objective (I/N). If the original example of -26 dB objective (as shown in Fig. 6.40) is used, 79 dB $- (-26$ dB$)$ or 105 dB of EMI hardening is required. The technique is to perform one or more iterations of EMI fixes as shown in the lower left-hand region of Fig. 6.1 (see "Add 1-Step EMI Hardening" and "EMC Sequencing Program" boxes).

While all may not work, the different EMC procedures that might be tried are:

1. To improve amplifier rejection:
   a. Increase stopband slope from 20 dB/decade to greater values.
   b. Add an EMI filter.
2. To reduce common-mode coupling:
   a. Lower cable height.
   b. Shield the entire area with an enclosure.
3. To reduce ground-loop coupling:
   a. Float PCB or mother board, as applicable.
   b. Use a balanced system.
   c. Use an optical isolator or isolation transformer.
   d. Use an RF choke and bond the boxes together.
   e. Install ferrites on the cable.
   f. Use feed-through capacitors.
   g. Use a shielded case within the equipment enclosure.

As discussed later, there is a sequencing procedure for selecting specific fixes. In the meantime, a trial-and-error kind of approach will be used.

Example 4.1 showed that the −14 dB amplifier rejection in Column 5 may be increased to −60 dB by increasing the stopband rolloff from 20 dB/decade to 100 dB/decade. It was previously shown that this was achieved by increasing the internal number of low-pass filter stages from $N = 1$ to $N = 5$. Thus, when this is done, Fig. 6.41 shows that the first EMI fix iteration reduces the I/N ratio from 79 dB to 33 dB (Δ improvement in Column 6 is 46 dB).

The second iteration shown in Fig. 6.41 involves ungrounding the system, i.e., floating one PCB. In Example 6.7 it was shown that this changed the GLC from −7 dB to −44 dB for a net improvement of 37 dB. Thus, CMC + GLC in Column 4B is changed from −47 dB (i.e., −40 − 7 dB) to −84 dB (i.e., −40 dB − 44 dB). This 37 dB improvement (Column 6, Fig. 6.41) results in an I/N of −4 dB in Column 7. The I/N is now negative, but we yet have to achieve our −26 dB I/N objective. The RF choke plus braid strap of Fig. 6.34 can be added, providing a Δ GLC = (−54 + 20) = −34 dB (see Examply 6.10). This is shown on a third iteration. Column 4B now reads: −40 −44 −34 = −118 dB, resulting in −38 dB I/N.

	①	②	③	④A	④B	④C	④D	④E	④	⑤	⑥	⑦
Operating Conditions	AMB dBµV	N dBµV	A/N dB	GCM GLC	FCM GLC	DMC	C-C	P1 to PS PS to V	SUM 4A to 4E	AMP REJ	Δ I/N	I/N
Objective												−26
Start: First Run	140	0	140	NA	−47	NA	NA	NA	−47	−14		+79
Ampl Slope = 100 dB/Dec	140	0	140	NA	−47	NA	NA	NA	−47	−60	46	+33
Float PCB at RX	140	0	140	NA	−84	NA	NA	NA	−84	−60	37	−4
RF Choke + Strap	140	0	140	NA	−118	NA	NA	NA	−118	−60	34	−38
Ampl Slope = 60 dB/Dec	140	0	140	NA	−118	NA	NA	NA	−118	−56	−4	−34

(I/N) dB: ⑦ = ③ + ④ + ⑤

Figure 6.41—Three EMI-Fix Iterations to Achieve EMC

In retrospect, if the number of stages in the amplifier were reduced from 5 to 4 stages, Fig. 4.3 shows that the stopband rejection would be reduced from 60 to 56 dB (remember that f_{EMI}/F_{CO} = 1 MHz/0.2 MHz = 5. The entry in Column 5 of Fig. 6.41 would correspondingly change to −56 dB. The net result is that (I/N) dB would increase from −38 dB to −34 dB, which is closer to the −26 dB objective.

The above problem was easily solved by reducing the susceptibility of the victim amplifier in the stopband and by floating one of the two PCBs. EMI problems with high I/N at the start, such as in the example, are usually not so easily solved. It was easy here since only one coupling path was involved. Because two or more paths are usually involved, it will be shown later that an EMC solution is much more difficult. However, except for the need to identify and attack the largest coupling path at any point in time, the methodology and procedures are the same.

6.7 References

1. Smith, A.A., "A More Convenient Form of the Equations for the Response of a Transmission Line Excited by Non-uniform Fields," *IEEE Transactions on EMC*, Vol. EMC-15, no. 3, August 1973.
2. Smith, A.A., *Coupling of External Electromagnetic Fields to Transmission Lines* (Gainesville, VA: Interference Control Technologies, Inc, 1987).
3. White, D.R.J., *Shielding Materials and Performance* (Gainesville, VA: Interference Control Technologies, Inc, 1980, 2nd ed.).
4. DeGauque, P. and Demoulin, B., "Caracterisation des cables blindes," *3eme Colloque EMC 1985*, Clermont-Ferrand, France.
5. Mardiguian, M., "Differential Transfer Impedance of Balanced Cables," ESTEC EMC Symposium, Nordjwik, 1982.
6. Smith, A.A., *Coupling of External Electromagnetic Fields to Transmission Lines*, p. 90.
7. Mayer, F., "Distributed Filters as RFI Suppression Components," *IEEE EMC Symposium Record* (New York: IEEE), Session 5A-II, San Antonio, TX, October 7-9, 1975.

6.8 Bibliography

Andrews, C.L. and Libelo, L.F., "Electric and Magnetic Fields on The Shadow Side of Circular Disks and Rectangular Plates for Normal and Oblique Incidence," *Second Symposium and Technical Exhibition on EMC*, Montreux, Switzerland, June 28-30, 1977.

Aronson, R., "RF Shielded Structures Against: A. EMP (Electromagnetic Pulse), B. Interference to Frequencies Up to 40 GHz," *Second Symposium and Technical Exhibition on EMC*, Montreux, Switzerland, June 28-30, 1977.

Blake, C.L., "Electromagnetic Problem Associated With the Use of Advanced Composites," *IEEE EMC Symposium Record* (New York: IEEE), Session 3B, Washington, DC, July 13-15, 1976.

Bridges, J., "Measurements and Use of Incremental Cable Penetration Parameters," *IEEE EMC Symposium Record* (New York: IEEE), Session 2C, Washington, DC, July 13-15, 1976.

Burns, R.S., "Effects of Shield Impedance Connector Resistance and Coaxial Inductors on Ground Noise Interference in Nuclear Reaction Instrumentation Systems," *IEEE EMC Symposium Record* (New York: IEEE), Session 4A, Washington, DC, July 13-15, 1976.

Butler, C.M., "A Review of Electromagnetic Diffraction by Small Apertures in Conducting Surfaces," *IEEE EMC Symposium Record* (New York: IEEE), Session II-B, Atlanta, GA, June 20-22, 1978.

Casey, K.F., "Advanced Composite Materials and Electromagnetic Shielding," *IEEE EMC Symposium Record* (New York: IEEE), Session IV-A, Atlanta, GA, June 20-22, 1978.

Chang, D.C.; Prehoda, R.J.; and Swink, R.M., "Design Considerations Concerning Electromagnetic Penetration Into Long, Cylindrical Enclosures at High Frequencies," *IEEE EMC Symposium Record* (New York: IEEE), Session 4C, Seattle, WA, August 2-4, 1977.

Chang, D.C.; Harrison, C.W., Jr.; and Taylor, C.D., "Note Regarding the Propagation of Electromagnetic Fields Through Slots in Cylinders," *IEEE Transactions on EMC*, Vol. EMC-15, no. 3, August 1973.

Chow, T.Y. and Adams, A.T., "The Coupling of Electromagnetic Waves Through Long Slots (with Editorial Summary)," *IEEE Transactions on EMC*, Vol. EMC-19, nc 2, May 1977.

Demoulin, B.; DeGauque, P.; Fontaine, J.; Canterman, M.; and Gabillard, R., "Theoretical Investigation and Experiment of Shielding Effectiveness of a Multi-Braided Coaxial Cable, *IEEE EMC Symposium Record* (New York: IEEE), Session 4A-1 Washington, DC, July 13-15, 1976.

Degauque P., Demoulin B. "Effect of Cable Grounding on Shielding," *EMC Technology*, Oct. 1984.

Eppero, W.C., "Electro-Optical Technology: Systems, Components, Trends and Awareness to Compatibility and Safety," *IEEE EMC Symposium Record* (New York: IEEE), Session 2A-II Washington, DC, July 13-15, 1976.

Frankel, S., "Terminal Response of Braided-Shield Cables External Monochromatic Electromagnetic Fields," *IEEE Transactions on Electromagnetic Compatibility*, Vol. EMC-16, no. 1, February 1974.

Graves, B.D.; Crow, T.T.; and Taylor, C.D., "On the Electromagnetic Field Penetration Through Apertures (with Editorial Summary)," *IEEE Transactions on EMC*, Vol. EMC-18, no. 4, November 1976.

Griffith, D.E., "Surface Transfer Impedance of Cable Shields Having a Longitudinal Seam," *IEEE Transactions on EMC*, Vol. EMC-14, no. 1, February 1972.

Harrison, C.W., "Comments on Shielding Performance of Metallic Cylinders," *IEEE Transactions on EMC*, Vol. EMC-15, no. 3, August 1973.

Harrison, C.W., "Generalized Theory of Impedance Loaded Multiconductor Transmission Lines on an Incident Field," *IEEE Transactions on EMC*, Vol. EMC-4, no. 2, May 1972.

Harrison, C.W. and Taylor, C.D., "Response of a Terminated Transmission Line Excited by a Plane Wave Field for Arbitrary Angles of Impedance," *IEEE Transactions on EMC*, Vol. EMC-14, no. 4, November 1972.

Harrison, C.W. and King, R.W.P., "Excitation for a Coaxial Line Through a Transverse Slot," *IEEE Transactions on EMC*, Vol. EMC-14, no. 4, November 1972.

Hess, R.F., "Properties of Induced Transients Associated with EM Fields Produced by Lightning or Other Relatively Slow Rise Time EMP," *IEEE EMC Symposium Record* (New York: IEEE), Session IV-A, Atlanta, GA, June 20-22, 1978.

Holzschuh, T.C. and Gajda, W.J., "DC Electrical Behavior of Graphite Fibers," *IEEE EMC Symposium Record* (New York: IEEE), Session 6A, Seattle, WA, August 2-4, 1977.

Knowles, E.D. and Brossier, J.C., "Measuring Connector Shielding Effectiveness Testing," *IEEE Transactions on EMC*, Vol. EMC-16, no. 1, February 1974.

Knowles, E.D. and Olson, L.W., "Cable Shielding Effectiveness Testing," *IEEE Transactions on EMC*, Vol. EMC-16, no. 1, February 1974.

Kung, J.T. and Amason, M.P., "Electrical Conductive Characteristics of Graphite Composite Structures," *IEEE EMC Symposium Record* (New York: IEEE), Session 6A, Seattle, WA, August 2-4, 1977.

Kung, J.T. and Amason, M.T., "New Lightning Protection Design Concepts For Advanced Composite," *IEEE EMC Symposium Record* (New York: IEEE), Session 3B; Washington, DC, July 13-15, 1976.

Kunkel G.M., "Introduction—An Overview of Problems Associated with the Design of EM Shields," *IEEE EMC Symposium Record* (New York: IEEE), Session 2C, Washington, DC, July 13-15, 1976.

Kunkel, G.M., "Introduction to Shielding of Electromagnetic Fields and the Application to EMI/RFI Gaskets," *IEEE EMC Symposium Record* (New York: IEEE), Session 5A, San Antonio, TX, October 7-9, 1975.

Liao, S.Y., "Light Transmittance an RF Shielding Effectiveness of a Metallic-Film Coating on a Plastic Substrate," *IEEE EMC Symposium Record* (New York: IEEE), Session 2C, Washington, DC, August 2-4, 1977.

Liao S.Y., "Light Transmittance and RF Shielding Effectiveness of Copper, Gold or Silver Film Coating on a Glass Substrate," *Second Symposium and Technical Exhibition on EMC*, Montreux, Switzerland, June 28-30, 1977.

Liao S.Y., "RF Shielding Effectiveness and Light Transmission of Copper or Silver Film Coating on Plastic Substrate," *IEEE Transactions on EMC*, Vol. EMC-18, no. 4, November 1976.

Madle, P., "Panel Assemblies, Honeycomb Air-Vent Assemblies and Thin Metallic Foils," *IEEE EMC Symposium Record* (New York: IEEE), Session 3B, Washington, DC, July 13-15, 1976.

Madle, P., "System Shielding Design—A Pragmatic Approach," *IEEE EMC Symposium Record* (New York: IEEE), Session 2C, Washington, DC, July 13-15, 1976.

Maxam, P., "Field Penetration by Diffusion Into a Conducting Shell," *IEEE EMC Symposium Record* (New York: IEEE), Session 4C; Seattle, WA; August 2-4, 1977.

Mayer, F., "RFI Suppression Components: State of the Art; New Developments," *IEEE Transactions on EMC*, Vol. EMC-18, no. 2, May 1976.

Mendez, H.A., "Shielding Theory of Enclosures with Apertures (with Editorial Summary)," *IEEE Transactions on EMC*, Vol. EMC-20, no. 2, May 1978.

Mullin, A.J., "Penetration of Shielding Barriers Low Frequency Effects," *IEEE EMC Symposium Record* (New York: IEEE), Session II-B, Atlanta, GA, June 20-22, 1978.

Nakauchi, E., "Technique for Controlling Emissions Due to Common Mode," *IEEE EMC Symposium Record* (New York: IEEE), Santa Clara, CA, September 1982.

Neff, Robert, "Trends in Applications of Advanced Composites in Military Hardware," *IEEE EMC Symposium Record* (New York: IEEE), Session 3B, Washington, DC, July 13-15, 1976.

Nichols, Fred, "Aspects of VLF Shielding Design and Fabrication," *IEEE EMC Symposium Record* (New York: IEEE), Session 2C, Washington, DC, July 13-15, 1976.

Paul, Clayton R., "Lumped Circuit Modeling of Transmission Lines," *IEEE EMC Symposium Record* (New York: IEEE) 1985.

Paul, Clayton R, "Frequency Response of Multiconductor Transmission Lines Illuminated by an Electromagnetic Field," *IEEE EMC Symposium Record* (New York: IEEE), Session 3A, San Antonio, TX, October 7-9, 1975, and pub. *IEEE Transactions on EMC*, Vol. EMC-18, no. 4, November 1976.

Rashid, A., "A Mathematical Method of Calculating and Measuring the Shielding Effectiveness of Cylindrical Enclosures," *IEEE EMC Symposium Record* (New York: IEEE), Session 4C, Seattle, WA, August 2-4, 1977.

Rostek, P.M., "Techniques of Shielding and Filtering Digital Computers for EMI Emissions and Susceptibility," *IEEE EMC Symposium Record* (New York: IEEE), Session 4B, San Antonio, TX October 7-9, 1975.

Schieher, D., "Shielding Performance of Metallic Cylinders," *IEEE Transactions on EMC*, Vol. EMC-15, no. 1, February 1973.

Scruggs, L.A. and Gajda, W.J., Jr., "Low Frequency Conductivity of Unidirectional Graphite/Epoxy Composite Samples," *IEEE EMC Symposium Record* (New York: IEEE), Session 6A, Seattle, WA, August 2-4, 1977.

Sellers, G.J., "METGLAS Alloys: An Answer to Low Frequency Magnetic Shielding," *IEEE EMC Symposium Record* (New York: IEEE), Session 2C, Seattle, WA, August 2-4, 1977.

Soltys, J.J., "Maintaining EMI/RFI Shielding Integrity of Equipment Enclosures with Conductive Gasketing," *IEEE EMC Symposium Record* (New York: IEEE), Session V-B, Atlanta, GA, June 20-22, 1978.

Sripaipan, C. and Holmes, W.H., "Achieving Wide-Band Common-Mode Rejection in Differential Amplifiers," *IEEE Transactions on EMC*, Vol. EMC-12, no. 2, May 1970.

Szekers, B., "Building Attenuation, A Factor to Improve EMC Calculations," *Second Symposium and Technical Exhibition*, Montreux, Switzerland, June 28-30, 1977.

Taylor, C.D. and Harrison, C.W., Jr., "On the Excitation of a Coaxial Line by an Incident Field Propagating Through a Small Aperture in the Sheath," *IEEE Transactions on EMC*, Vol. EMC-15, no. 3, August 1973.

Tsai, L.L.; Wu, T.K.; Longvor, Major C.R.; and Brown, G.L. "Currents Induced on Conducting Rods by Near and Far Zone Sources," *IEEE EMC Symposium Record* (New York: IEEE), Session 5A, Washington, DC, July 13-15, 1976.

Vance, E.F., "EMP-Induced Transients in Long Cables," *IEEE EMC Record* (New York: IEEE), Session 3A-II, San Antonio, TX, October 7-9, 1975.

Vance, E.F., "Cable Grounding for the Control of EMI," *EMC Technology*, January 1983.

Van Den Heuval, A., "EMC of the E-O Systems: Optical-to-Optical Interference, RF-to-Optical Interference, Optical-to-RF Interference, Needed or New Concepts of Analysis and Measurements, *IEEE EMC Symposium Record* (New York: IEEE), Session 2A-II, San Antonio, TX, October 7-9, 1975.

Wait, J.R., "Comments on 'Shielding Performance of Metallic Cylinders and Comments by C.W. Harrison, Jr. and Reply by D. Schieber'," *IEEE Transactions on EMC*, Vol. EMC-16, no. 1, February 1974.

Walker, W.F. and Heintz, R.E., "Conductivity Measurements of Graphite/Epoxy Composite Laminates at UHF Frequencies," *IEEE EMC Symposium Record* (New York: IEEE), Session 6A, Seattle, WA, August 2-4, 1977.

Wu, Chang-Yu and Cheng, D.K., "Field Distribution Inside a Box With Aperture," *IEEE EMC Symposium Record* (New York: IEEE), Session 4C, Seattle, WA, August 2-4, 1977.

Wu, T.K. and Tsai, L.L., "Shielding Properties of Thick Conducting Cylindrical Shells," *IEEE Transactions on EMC*, Vol. EMC-16, no. 4, November 1974.

Young, T.T. and Yang, J.J., "The Effect of Cylindrical Ferromagnetic Shells on the Self- and Mutual Inductance of Parallel Wires," *IEEE Transactions on EMC*, Vol. EMC-17, no. 4, November 1975.

Chapter 7

Radiated
Differential-Mode Coupling

This chapter describes the third of the five principal coupling paths shown in Fig. 7.1. This coupling path converts ambient electric and magnetic fields into a differential-mode voltage. The field couples into an area formed by the wire pair separation in a cable and its length as shown in Fig. 7.2. This area should not be confused

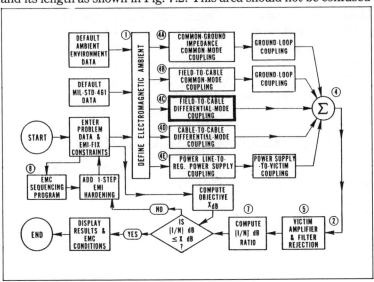

Figure 7.1—EMI Prediction and Analysis Flow Diagram Showing Differential-Mode Coupling

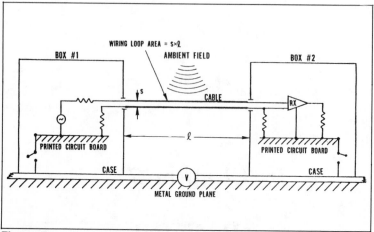

Figure 7.2—Field-to-Cable, Differential-Mode Coupling

with the much larger ground-loop area previously shown in Fig. 6.2. The differential-mode voltage then appears across the input terminals of the victim amplifier or logic circuit to produce the EMI threat.

Field-to-cable differential-mode coupling (DMC) also exists for coaxial cables. A DMC path does exist, although there is no identifiable cable area for coax in the sense shown in Fig. 7.2. As explained later, field-coupled surface currents are produced on the outer surface of the coax. By the transfer impedance of the coaxial line, a differential-mode voltage is then produced. This chapter presents graphs and illustrations for predicting field-to-cable differential-mode coupling and EMI control techniques for reducing this coupling to acceptable values.

7.1 Differential-Mode Coupling

Both E-field and magnetic flux density ambients are coupled directly into box-to-box interconnecting cables. This section presents design graphs on differential-mode coupling versus frequency with cable geometry as a parameter. DMC is discussed in two parts: (1) balanced lines consisting of wire pairs with and without either twists or shields and (2) unbalanced lines of the coaxial and triaxial family.

7.1.1 Balanced Lines

In modified form, Eqs. (6.7), (6.8), (6.15) and (6.17) also apply here for converting an electric field strength or a magnetic flux density into a differential-mode voltage. Repeating (for emphasis): the main difference is that the wiring area shown in heavily lined portion of Fig. 7.2 applies for DMC, whereas the loop area previously shown in Fig. 6.2 applies for the larger CMC loop area. Thus, when "h" is replaced in the above equations with the loop separation distance "s" shown in Fig. 7.2, the DMC relationships exist.

The DMC for electric field coupling is plotted in Fig. 7.3 and in Fig. 7.4 it is shown for magnetic flux density coupling. The parameters in the graphs correspond to the wire pair area dimensions shown in Fig. 7.2 and the inserts of Figs. 7.3 and 7.4. Like the earlier CMC, it is noted that the DMC increases with frequency at the rate of 20 dB/decade until the corner frequency condition corresponding to $l = \lambda/2$ is reached. This was observed earlier in Eqs. (6.7) and 6.15). Above this frequency, the envelope of DMC is independent of frequency as also shown earlier in Eqs. (6.8) and (6.17).

To assist the user, the selection of the parameter line is made by choosing the closest l and s loop dimensions shown in the inserts of both figures and then reading the corresponding parameter letter. The intersection of the EMI frequency on the X-axis with the applicable parameter line gives the corresponding DMC value on the Y-axis of the figures. Small adjustments are made for interpolation when applicable. As for the CMC curves, average field polarization and incidence of 45° have been assumed (3 dB below worst case).

Illustrative Example 7.1

The ongoing illustrative example, previously shown in Fig. 6.27, is repeated here in Fig. 7.5. The cable length between the two boxes is 10 m, and the average inside distance separation between the cable wires is 0.5 mm.* The potentially interfering AM broadcast station is 1 MHz, which produces an E-field strength of 10 V/m at the victim site. For l = 10 m and s = 0.5 mm in the insert of

---

*This is due primarily to twice the insulation thickness for a parallel-wire or twisted-wire pair used in the example. It corresponds to the inside dimension (typically about 1 mm) for flex wiring. It does not apply for coaxial cables (unbalanced lines), which are discussed later.

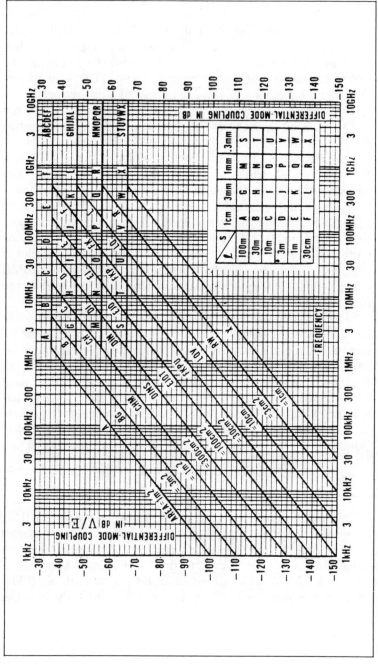

Figure 7.3—E-Field, Differential-Mode Coupling into Box-to-Box Cable-Loop Area

7.4

Differential-Mode Coupling

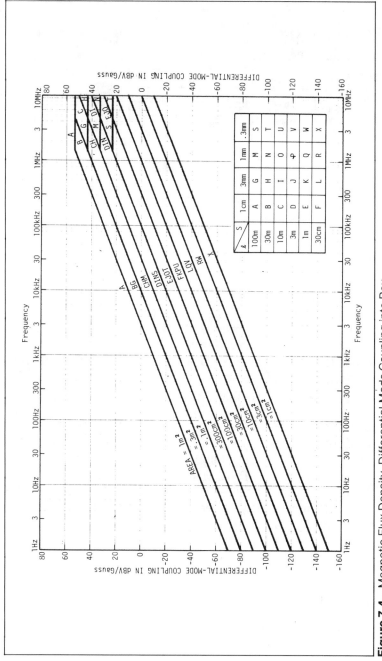

Figure 7.4.—Magnetic Flux Density, Differential-Mode Coupling into Box-to-Box Cable-Loop Area

7.5

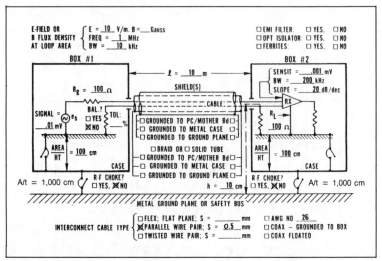

Figure 7.5—Input Data for Defining the Two-Box EMI Problem

Fig. 7.3, the nearest parameter line "O" is selected. This corresponds to a loop area of 100 cm² (1,000 cm long × 0.1 cm separation). Line O intersects the 1 MHz frequency at a DMC value of −80 dB. Because the true value of d is 0.5 mm and not 1 mm, an additional −6 dB must be added for interpolation. Thus the DMC coupling is −86 dB above 1 m or 86 dB/m.

Since DMC converts the electric field strength in units of V/m (10 V/m in the example), the differential-mode voltage, V_o, is 86 dB below the field strength, and DMC allows for a change in units. Thus, the DMC voltage is 20 dBV/m − 86 dB(m) = −66 dBV = −6 dBmV or 0.5 mV or 500 μV.

It is noted that the DMC voltage of −6 dBmV is 54 dB above the amplifier sensitivity of −60 dBmV or 0 dBμV, therefore an EMI problem is immediately evident. Had the victim been TTL logic, for example, with a noise immunity level of 400 mV or 52 dBmV, the DMC voltage would be [52 dBmV − (−6 dBmV)] or 58 dB below logic sensitivity, and no EMI problem would exist.

7.1.2 Unbalanced Lines

Unbalanced lines include the coaxial cable family. For unbalanced lines, the DMC coupling physics is divided into two parts: (1) field-to-cable coupling in the form of coupled cable surface currents, and (2) transfer impedance of the cable. The latter converts surface currents into differential-mode voltages at the input terminals of the victim amplifier or logic network. The combination of the two, then, produces the net DMC relations:

$$DMC_{dc} = 20 \log \left(\frac{I_s}{E} \times \frac{Z_T}{2} \right) \tag{7.1}$$

$$= 20 \log (I_s/E) + Z_{TdB\Omega} - 6 \text{ dB} \tag{7.2}$$

where,

I_s = induced cable shield current from ambient electric field

Z_T = transfer impedance of coaxial cable

7.1.2.1 Surface Current

As shown in Fig. 6.3, an arriving electric field produces a current in the cable which is limited primarily by the return circuit, end-to-end cable capacitance. On the cable the induced, open circuit voltage, V_i, is:

$$V_i = \int E \times ds = E \times h_{eff} \tag{7.3}$$

$$\cong 0.5 \; El \cos \theta \quad \text{for } l < \lambda$$

where,

θ = angle between direction of l and the arriving E-field

h_{eff} = effective antenna height $\cong 0.5 \; l$ (The effective height of a free-space dipole is about half its geometric length.)

Similar to common-mode coupling, the most general situation of diagonal polarization is assumed for DMC in which $\theta = 45°$ and $\cos \theta = 1/\sqrt{2}$. This assumption is used hereafter since the user generally does not know the angle θ, which may take on any value. Thus,

$$V_i/E \approx 0.5\ l/\sqrt{2} \qquad \text{for } l/\lambda < 0.5 \qquad (7.4)$$

$$= 0.64\ \frac{l}{\sqrt{2}} \text{ at resonance}$$

$$\approx \lambda/2^{\sqrt{}} \qquad \text{for } l/\lambda > 0.5 \qquad (7.5)$$

The current, I_s, flowing on the surface of the coaxial cable as a result of the open-circuit induced voltage, V_i (see Fig. 6.3), impressed on the cable external impedance Z_c is:

$$I_s = V_i/Z_c \qquad (7.6)$$

$$= \frac{0.5\ El/\sqrt{2}}{R_s + j\omega L_c - j/\omega C_c} \qquad \text{for } l/\lambda \leqslant 0.5 \qquad (7.7)$$

$$= 0.5\ \omega l C_c E/\sqrt{2} \qquad \text{for } 1/\omega C_c \gg R_c + j\omega Lc \qquad (7.8)$$

$$= \pi l^2 \epsilon E/\sqrt{2} \qquad (7.9)$$

$$\frac{I_s}{E} = 1.96 \times 10^{-5}\ l^2\ f_{MHz} \qquad \text{for } l/\lambda < 0.5 \qquad (7.10)$$

$$= 0.46/f_{MHz} \text{ at } \frac{\lambda}{2} \text{ resonance and all subsequent resonance peaks} \qquad (7.11)$$

where,

R_s = cable shield resistance

L_c = cable external self-inductance

C_c = cable capacitance (Fig. 6.3)

ϵ = capacitance of air = 8.84 pF/m

f = frequency in hertz

f_{MHz} = frequency in MHz

7.8

Equations (7.10) and (7.11) are plotted in Fig. 7.6, which has the dimension of a conductivity in mho-meters. As seen in the figure, the induced cable current increases with frequency at 20 dB/decade until $l = \lambda/2$ is reached. Above $\lambda/2$ the current decreases since the cable now appears as a cascade of small $\lambda/2$ dipoles with opposite polarities. At the worst (an odd number of $\lambda/2$), the current cannot exceed that of one elementary dipole whose electrical length is shrinking at a rate of -20 dB/decade with frequency. Note also that the induced cable current increases with length at 40 dB/decade until $l = \lambda/2$. This is due to the cumulative effect of: (1) increase of cable capacitance with length at 20 dB/decade, plus (2) increase of induced open voltage also proportional to length at 20 dB/decade.

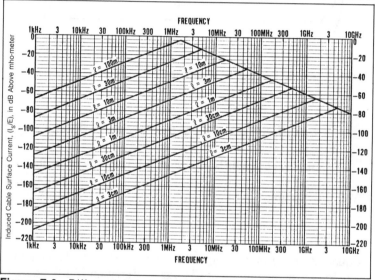

Figure 7.6—Differential-Mode Coupling for Unbalanced Coaxial Lines

7.1.2.2 Transfer Impedance

Figure 7.7 shows that by diffusion the transfer impedance converts the cable surface current, I_s, into an inner longitudinal voltage, V_i, which in turn impresses a differential mode voltage V_o at the victim input terminals.

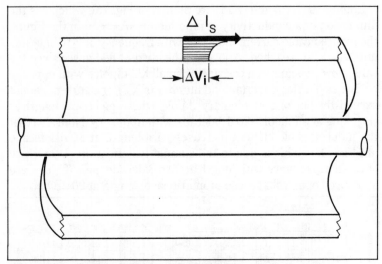

Figure 7.7—Coaxial Transfer Impedance

$$Z_T = \Delta V_i/\Delta I_s \quad \Omega/m \tag{7.12}$$

$$= 2V_o/I_s \text{ (if both ends of the coax are matched)}$$

When Eq. (7.12) is substituted into Eq. (7.1), there results:

$$DMC_{dB} = 20 \log[(I_s/E)(V_o/I_s)] \tag{7.13}$$

$$= 20 \log (V_o/E)$$

Equation (7.14) is, of course, the definition of DMC coupling discussed at the beginning of Chapter 7. Equation (7.13) makes it relatively simple to compute DMC by breaking it down into two parts.

As seen from Eqs. (7.2) and (7.13), the lower the Z_T value, the better the performance since DMC is correspondingly lower. Data for Z_T corresponding to each coaxial cable are best determined by measurement.

Figure 7.8 shows Z_T for several popular coaxial cables. Below about 100 kHz (this is called the **Ohm's Law region**), Z_T is proportional to the surface resistance of the cable. Above about 10 MHz, Z_T is proportional to the mutual inductance of the cable braid. Between these frequencies, the transfer impedance passes

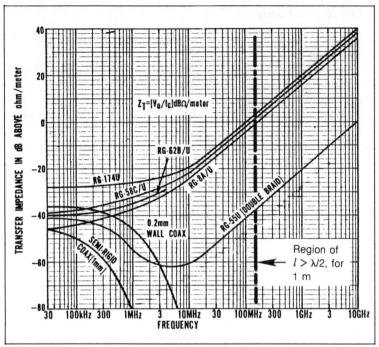

Figure 7.8—Transfer Impedance of Coaxial Cables

through a transition region for single braided cables such as RG-8A/U, RG-58C/U, RG-62B/U and RG-174U. This region, however, shows a negative slope for double-braided shields (e.g., RG-55U) due to skin-depth effects. This effect does not appear for single-braided shields since the convolution or weave of the braid wires results in the induced surface current being the same on both the outside and inside surface of the braid.

When the braid is replaced with a homogeneous shell, tube or wall, the performance of the coaxial cable is entirely different above the Ohm's Law region. For this situation, Fig. 7.8 shows that Z_T is monotonically decreasing with an increase in frequency, since the skin depth is inversely proportional to the square root of frequency. Thus, a thin-wall or semi-rigid coaxial line should be used above about 100 kHz when a superior immunity to ambient electromagnetic fields is desired because of its low Z_T.

7.11

Illustrative Example 7.2

Calculate the differential-mode coupling for 10 m of an RG-8A/U coaxial line at 1 MHz.

From Fig. 7.6, the (I/E) dB coupling for l = 10 m is −48 dB (above 1 mho-meter). Figure 7.8 shows the transfer impedance of RG-8A/U at 1 MHz is −38 dB Ω/m = −18 dBΩ for a 10 m length. Thus, from Eq. (7.2), the differential-mode coupling is −48 dB − 12 dBΩ − 6 dB. This means, for example, that an electric field strength of 10 V/m or 20 dBV/m will produce a DMC voltage at the victim of −66 dBΩ + 20 dBV/m = −46 dBV = 5 mV.

7.1.2.3 Direct Computation of Coupled Voltage (DMC) in Coaxials

When Eqs. (7.10), (7.11) and (7.1) are combined, the following Eq. (7.15) results which can directly relate the differential voltage, V_o, to the incident field E, through the **total** transfer impedance $Z_T \times l$ of the shield:

$$DMC = 1.96 \times 10^{-5} \; l^2 \; f_{MHz} \times (Z_T l/2) \tag{7.15a}$$

$$\approx -100 \text{ dB} + \log (l^2 \times f_{MHz}) + Z_T \text{ dB}\Omega/\text{m} \\ + 20 \log l \tag{7.15b}$$

$$= -100 + 20 \log f + 60 \log l + Z_T \text{ dB}\Omega/\text{m for} \\ l/\lambda < 0.5$$

When the coaxial cable length* exceeds $\lambda/2$, it is no longer correct to multiply $Z_T \Omega$/m by the physical length l of the cable since the current is no longer uniform over the braid but is distributed over a sinusoid. Therefore, l is replaced by $\lambda/2$, giving from Eq. (7.11):

$$DMC = (0.46/f_{MHz}) \times Z_T/2 \times 150/f_{MHz}$$

$$= 30.4 \text{ dB} - 40 \log f_{MHz} + Z_T \text{ dB}\Omega/\text{m} \tag{7.15c}$$

$$\text{for } l \geqslant 0.5 \; \lambda$$

Notice that DMC seems to decrease like f^2. However, remember that Z_T itself still increases with f, giving a net slope of −20 dB/decade for DMC above λ/2. Equations (7.15a) and (7.15c) have been plotted in Fig. 7.9 for several lengths of RG-8A/U. This allows immediate calculation of the voltage at the termination resistance of the coax.*

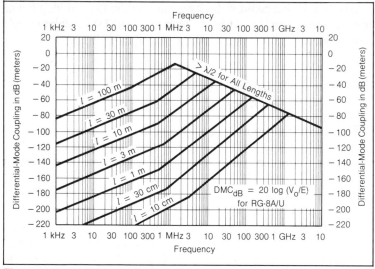

Figure 7.9—DMC Factor (Induced Voltage/Illuminating Field) for Several Lengths of RG8 Coaxial Cable

Illustrative Example 7.3

Calculate the differential-mode voltage directly coupled to 3 m of RG-8A/U coax from a CB transmitter producing locally 3 V/ m at 27 MHz. Figure 7.9 indicates, at 27 MHz, a DM coupling factor of −58 dB for a 3 m length. So the differential voltage at the end of the cable will be:

$$130 \ dB\mu V/m \ - \ 58 \ dB(m) \ = \ 72 \ dB\mu V \ or \ 4 \ mV$$

One must remember that this third path is the pure differential coupling in the cable only, regardless of any possible ground loop. If the coax is connected between two boxes above some conductive ground, there still exist the field-to-cable loop and GLC mechanisms,

---

*If the coax ends are unmatched, calculations become more complex because reflection coefficients come into play. A.A. Smith (see Ref. 1) has given exact solutions and numerical results for many combinations of loads and coax orientation.

as described in Chapter 6, Section 6.4.2. This latter may cause more noise than the pure displacement current of Eq. 7.7. So, why bother with the DM coupling (third path) if the FCM + GLC coupling is worse? Simply because, as often is the case with EMI, they exist in parallel. If one could virtually eliminate the ground loop (using optical isolators or signal transformers etc.), the DM coupling would still exist.

7.1.2.4 Influence of Shield Termination Impedance

The shield transfer impedance is not the only contributor in converting the external EMI into a noise at the victim cable end. The connector contact impedance or pigtail impedance contributes to this noise, as seen in Fig. 7.10. A simple way to evaluate this contribution is to incorporate the shield termination impedance into the expression of Z_T. For braided shield with mediocre optical coverage (high Z_T), the connector or pigtail contribution is negligible since the shield is worse. But for tight braids, triaxial or quadraxial cables, or semirigid cables, the Z_T is very low, so it is important not to degrade it by the termination impedance. In many cases,

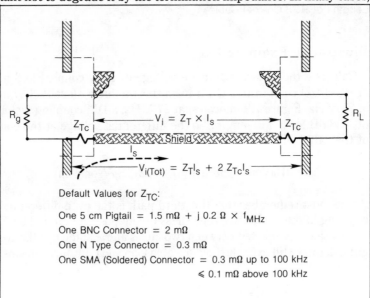

Default Values for Z_{TC}:

One 5 cm Pigtail = 1.5 mΩ + j 0.2 Ω × f_{MHz}

One BNC Connector = 2 mΩ

One N Type Connector = 0.3 mΩ

One SMA (Soldered) Connector = 0.3 mΩ up to 100 kHz

$\leqslant$ 0.1 mΩ above 100 kHz

Figure 7.10—Simple Way of Modeling the Contribution of Shield Termination Impedance to Total Shield Coupling

this is the connector bonding resistance which limits the *in situ* performance of a super-shielded cable. More details on this can be found in Ref. 2, and in Vol. 3, *Electromagnetic Shielding*, of this EMC handbook series.

To provide the designer with a simple way of incorporating the connector Z_T into the prediction values, some default values are suggested in Fig. 7.8 for the most current shield termination hardware.

Illustrative Example 7.4

Ten meters of RG8 coax are exposed to a 1 MHz EMI field. The Z_T of RG8 is −38 dBΩ/m at 1 MHz, therefore the total Z_T for 10 m is −18 dBΩ (0.12 Ω).

1. Find the contribution of the shield terminations if 5 cm (2") pigtails are used at each end. From Fig. 7.8 note, the impedance of 5 cm of small wire at 1 MHz is:

$$Z_{TC} = 1.5 \text{ m}\Omega + j \, 0.3 \, \Omega \approx 0.3 \, \Omega$$

$$2 \times Z_{TC} = 0.6 \, \Omega, \text{ or } -4 \text{ dB}\Omega$$

Therefore, the total Z_T of the cable to be entered into the DMC calculations (Eq. 7.15), or into the GLC calculations as well (Fig. 6.23), is −4 dB Ω since the contributions of the pigtails is much higher than that of the braid alone. The exact value of $Z_{T \, (TOT)}$ would be:

$$Z_{T \, (TOT)} = 0.6 \, \Omega + 0.12 \, \Omega = 0.72 \, \Omega \text{ (or 3 dB}\Omega)$$

2. Find the contribution of the shield terminations if coaxial connectors are used with a $Z_T \leqslant 1$ mΩ from dc to 100 MHz (basically the braid-to-shell and shell-to-receptacle contact resistances):

$$2Z_{TC} = 2 \times 10^{-3} \, \Omega \equiv -54 \text{ dB}\Omega$$

Here the connector impedance does not ruin the shield Z_T, and the total transfer impedance to use is −18 dBΩ.

7.2 Reducing Differential-Mode Coupling

There are several ways to reduce DMC; some involve twisting wires. Most involve some form of shield, tube or conduit.

Differential-mode coupling may be reduced by an application of one or more of the following:

1. For balanced lines:
   a. Use twisted-wire pairs for balanced parallel lines.
   b. Add a single braided shield and ground shield at one end for $l \leqslant \lambda/16$.
   c. Add a second braided shield and ground this shield at the other end, for $l \leqslant \lambda/16$.
   d. Use a low Z_T shield and connect it to the boxes at both ends, for $l > \lambda/16$.
   e. Add a third braided shield and ground it at either end (for $l \leqslant \lambda/16$) or both ends (for $l > \lambda/16$).
   f. Replace braided shield(s) with a solid homogeneous tubular shield or conduit.
2. For unbalanced lines:
   a. Select coaxial cables with lower transfer impedances.
   b. Use a triaxial cable and ground outer braid at one end.
   c. Use semi-rigid coaxial lines.

These nine reduction techniques will be reviewed in the following pages, and examples of each will be given.

7.2.1 Twisted Wire Pairs

Figure 7.11 is a plot of the reduction in DMC coupling offered by twisting a wire pair. The X-axis corresponds to the total number of twists over the length of the wire pair, and the Y-axis is the coupling reduction in dB. (The term **twist** here means one full turn.) The parameter line, $n\lambda$, corresponds to the product of the number of cable twists per meter and the wavelength of the EMI frequency. This parameter accounts for lack of induced voltage cancellations between adjacent twists due to phase differences in the coupling field at each twist element. The user selects the applicable

7.16

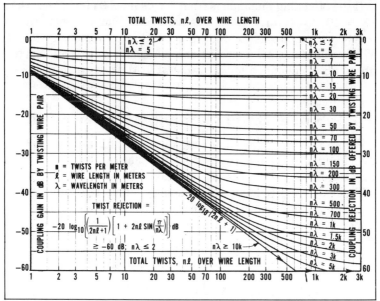

Figure 7.11—DMC Reduction Offered by Twisting Wire Pair

parameter line and the total twists on the X-axis. The DMC coupling reduction is then read on the Y-axis at the intersection of the parameter line and the axis.

Illustrative Example 7.5

For the same ongoing AM broadcast EMI problem, calculate the additional reduction in DMC offered by uniformly twisting the wire pair at 40 twists per meter.

Since the 1 MHz potential interference corresponds to a wavelength of 300 m,* and since the number of twists, n, per meter is 40, the corresponding $n\lambda$ parameter line is 12k. The nl product on the X-axis corresponds to 40 twists per meter × 10 m, for a total number of 400 twists. The intersection of the $n\lambda$ parameter and the nl X-axis yields a reduction in DMC coupling of 56 dB, a very significant improvement.

---

*$\lambda_m = 300/f_{MHz}$

7.17

If the offending radiation is from TV channel 9 at 55 MHz, then nλ = 40 × 5.45 m = 218. This parameter line intersects the nl = 400 on the X-axis to produce a DMC improvement of 36 dB. While still a fair EMI improvement, it is considerably less than the above 56 dB obtained for the twist at 1 MHz.

7.2.2 Single Braided Shield over Wire Pair

Figure 7.12 shows the minimum* shielding effectiveness achieved by adding a braided shield over a wire pair, twisted wire pair or harness, but it does not apply for coaxial lines. It is a plot of the additional DMC reduction in coupling versus the cable length between ground points in decimal fractions of a wavelength (see upper X-axis). Drawing A in the upper left corner is a sketch of the braided shield grounded at either the right or left end. Curve B corresponds to the situation where the cable is grounded at both

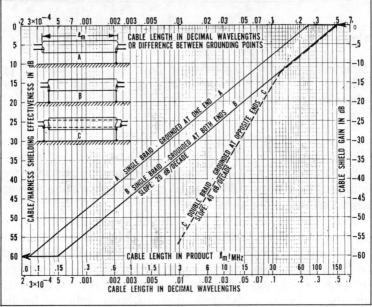

Figure 7.12—DMC Reduction Offered by Braid Shields

---

*The shielding effectiveness is a function of the optical coverage and braid pitch angle. Figure 7.12 is the worst case (least shielding effectiveness) corresponding to relatively loose (open) braids of less than 80 percent. For tighter braids, the least SE is greater than 0 dB, even above λ/2. For super screens, the least SE is greater than 30 dB.

7.18

ends. The corresponding DMC reduction plots are shown in the figure. The minimum improvement decreases with an increase in frequency at the rate of 20 dB/decade and nullifies when the shield resonates at the one-quarter wavelength of EMI frequency.

In the event that the cable should be grounded at more than two points, the upper X-axis then corresponds to length between average ground points in decimal wavelengths. The lower X-axis corresponds to the equivalent product of the cable length between grounding points in meters, times the frequency in megahertz. Note that in the upper right corner of Fig. 7.12 the added minimum shielding effectiveness of a braid-type cable approaches zero when the cable length becomes a significant fraction of a wavelength. Conversely, the figure shows the DMC improvement value truncated at −60 dB to remind the user that the value cannot continue indefinitely because of other higher-order coupling paths or spurious effects.

Illustrative Example 7.6

For the same ongoing EMI problem, calculate the additional reduction in DMC offered by adding a single low-coverage braided shield over the wire pair.

The 1 MHz potentially interfering AM broadcast frequency corresponds to a wavelength of 300 m. Thus, a 10 m cable length corresponds to 0.033 wavelengths. The intersection of this X-axis value with a curve A, corresponding to a single end-grounded shield, indicates that a minimum improvement of approximately 17 dB would be expected from the use of the braided shield.

If the offending radiation were a 100 MHz FM broadcast station, then the 10 m cable length would correspond to 3.3 wavelengths. From the intersection of this X-axis value with curve A, no improvement in DMC reduction is expected from such a thin shield. Measurements indicate that a few dB improvement may typically result, but this is not repeatable under varying conditions.

7.2.3 Double Braided Wire Shield

Figure 7.12 also shows the effect of adding a second braided shield. For this to apply, both shields must be insulated from each other. While the insert in the figure indicates that the inner braided shield is grounded at the left end and the outer braid shield at the right, this particular configuration is not necessary because they can both be grounded at the same end. The only requirement is that both ends of the same shield should not be grounded if one wants to eliminate the ground loop coupling through a mediocre shield (see Section 6.5.3). For these conditions, then, Fig. 7.12 shows that the additional decoupling offered by this double-insulated braided shield corresponds to a slope of 40 dB/decade.

Illustrative Example 7.7

For the same EMI problem, calculate the additional reduction in DMC offered by adding a second braided shield.

The intersection of parameter curve C with the cable length of 0.033 wavelengths yields a minimum reduction of 34 dB. Since 17 dB was already obtained from the use of a single shield, the additional reduction offered by a second braid shield over that of the first is also 17 dB.

7.2.4 Triple Braided Shield

While not shown in Fig. 7.12, the slope corresponding to triple braided insulated shields in which only one end is grounded for each of the three shields yields a shielding versus frequency slope of 60 dB/decade. The net result is a continuation of the preceding two braided shields by adding 20 dB/decade more per shield.

Illustrative Example 7.8

For the same EMI problem, calculate the additional reduction in DMC offered by the third braided shield.

Since this is a continuation of the same technique applied in the preceding two illustrative examples, it is expected that an additional improvement over the second braided shield of 17 dB would result. The net effect, then, is 17 dB improvement per shield: 3×17 dB or 51 dB results.

7.2.5 Solid Shield or Conduit

While not mentioned in the preceding section, one of the principal reasons for the degradation in performance of braided shielding effectiveness with an increase in frequency shown in Fig. 7.12 is due to the lack of homogeneity of the braid. The weave of individual braid wires causes shield current flowing on the outer surface of the braid to also flow on the inner surface. Therefore, there is little net skin-effect isolation offered by the shield braid. The existing isolation comes from reflection loss.

Figure 7.13 shows the reduction in differential mode coupling offered by a solid homogeneous tubular cable shield which, for the best performance, should be bonded to both box cases. The parameter is the wall thickness, and the Y-axis is the absorption loss in dB offered by the tube. Note from studying the figure that large attenuations are now possible at high frequencies for very thin-walled shields since the shield is homogeneous.

The shielding effectiveness is considered as the ratio of the differential voltage induced across the pair if the shield was not there to that when the shield is installed. With a solid tube, this relates to the ratio of the field outside the tube versus the remaining field inside.

Notice that in the case of a solid tube (like, to some extent, with a low Z_T shield) the EMI reduction occurs on the DMC and common mode as well.

Illustrative Example 7.9

For the ongoing EMI problem involving the AM broadcast station at 1 MHz, calculate the additional reduction in DMC offered by adding a 0.5 mm (20 mil) wall thickness tubing made of copper.

Figure 7.13 shows that the intersection of the 0.5 mm wall tubing with the 1 MHz frequency corresponds to about 65 dB of shielding effectiveness. It is seen here that this is far superior to the sum of the three braids and therefore might be considered in lieu of using them. This demonstrates the advantage of a homogeneous shield over leaky ones. For more comprehensive data on the effectiveness of shields, see Ref. 2 or Volume 3 of this handbook series.

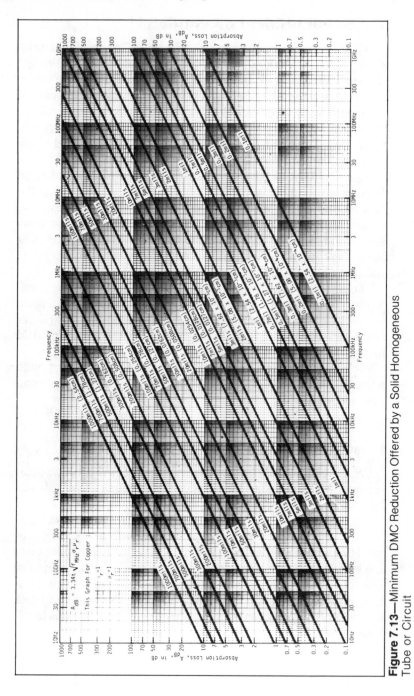

Figure 7.13—Minimum DMC Reduction Offered by a Solid Homogeneous Tube or Circuit

7.3 A Composite Example

It is again timely to summarize much of the preceding material on differential-mode coupling with a composite example using the ongoing EMI problem. As in the composite CMC/GLC problem, a worst case of poor EMC design is deliberately selected and shown in Fig. 7.5. Some of the highlights are:

Signal level: 0.01 mV = 20 dBμV
Victim sensitivity: 0.001 mV = 0 dBμV
Victim bandwidth: 200 kHz
Victim stop-band slope: 20 dB/decade
EMI source: AM broadcast, 1 MHz
EMI field strength: 10 V/m = 140 dBμV/m
A/t ratios: 1,000 cm (default), i.e., 100 pF
All PCB and box cases: grounded
Signal source impedance: 100 Ω
Victim input impedance: 100 Ω
Transmission system: unbalanced
Inside wire separation: 0.5 mm
AWG No.: 26
Cable length: 10 m
Average cable height: 10 cm
All other characteristics: as per Fig. 7.5

The present problem is limited to the third coupling path only of DMC as shown in Fig. 7.1. For convenience, the previous EMI prediction form shown in Fig. 3.12 is repeated in Fig. 7.14 in modified form. Column 1 corresponds to the ambient EMI source of 140 dBμV/m, whereas column 2 is that of the victim sensitivity of 0 dBμV. Column 3 is the difference between the ambient and sensitivity levels (A/N ratio), or 140 dB (above 1 meter).

Next, of columns 4A, 4B, 4C, 4D and 4E in Fig. 3.12, only column 4C is used in Fig. 7.14. This corresponds to the DMC coupling path (the other paths are not applicable in this limited-scope composite example). The DMC path contributed a −86 dB value as previously discussed in Example 7.1 for a 10 m cable with an inside wire separation of 0.5 mm. This value appears in column 4C. Since it is the only coupling path of 4A-4E, −86 dB also appears in column 4.

	①	②	③	(4A)	(4B)	(4C)	(4D)	(4E)	④	⑤	⑥	⑦
OPERATING CONDITIONS	AMB dBμV	N dBμV	A/N dB	GCM GLC	FCM GLC	DMC	C-C	P1·PS PS·V	SUM 4A·4E	AMP REJ	Δ I/N	I/N
OBJECTIVE	▨	▨	▨	▨	▨	▨	▨	▨	▨	▨	▨	-26
START: FIRST RUN	140	0	140	NA	NA	-86	NA	NA	-86	-14	▨	+40

(I/N)dB: ⑦ = ③ + ④ + ⑤

Figure 7.14—Initial EMI Prediction to Determine I/N Ratio

For the amplifier rejection in column 5, Example 4.1 showed that a 1 MHz EMI emission is rejected by 14 dB. This corresponds to the amplifier having a 200 kHz cutoff frequency and a stopband slope of 20 dB/decade. Thus, −14 dB is entered in column 5.

To calculate the resulting I/N ratio of column 7, Eq. (3.17) is used. This is equivalent to adding columns 3, 4 and 5. When this is done:

$$(I/N)_{dB} = (A/N)_{dB} + (CMC/GLC)_{dB} + AR_{dB}$$

$$= 140 \text{ dB} - 86 \text{ dB} - 14 \text{ dB} = 40 \text{ dB} \qquad (7.16)$$

Therefore, 40 dB appears in column 7 of Fig. 7.14. This corresponds to a serious EMI situation, and the amplifier will be jammed and inoperable.

The remaining task is to eliminate the EMI problem by an amount equal to the above-derived $(I/N)_{dB}$, minus the objective $(I/N)_{dB}$. If the original example of −26 dB objective, as shown in Fig. 7.14 is used, 40 dB − (−26 dB) or 66 dB of EMI hardening is required. The technique is to perform one or more iterations of EMI fixes as shown in the lower left-hand region of Fig. 7.1 (see "Add 1-step EMI hardening" and "EMC Sequencing Program" boxes).

While some may prove ineffective, the different EMC fixes that might be attempted are:

1. To increase amplifier rejection:
   a. Increase stopband slope from 20 dB/decade to greater integer multiple values of 20.
   b. Add an EMI filter with one or more stages.

2. To reduce differential-mode coupling:
   a. Twist the wires, (for a balanced line).
   b. Use a single braided shield (for a balanced line).
   c. Use a double braided shield (for a balanced line).
   d. Use a foil wrap shield (for a balanced line).
   e. Use a solid wall tube or conduit.
   f. Use coax with a lower transfer impedance, or a triax (for an unbalanced line).
   g. Use semi-rigid coax (for an unbalanced line).

As discussed later, there is a sequencing procedure for selecting specific fixes. In the meantime a **trial-and-error** approach will be used.

Example 4.1 showed that the −14 dB amplifier rejection entered in column 5 may be increased to −60 dB by increasing the stopband rolloff from 20 dB/decade to 100 dB/decade, making a 46 dB improvement. It was also shown that this was achieved by increasing the interval number of low-pass filter stages from N = 1 to N = 5. Thus, when this is done, Fig. 7.15 shows that the first EMI fix iteration reduces the I/N ratio from 40 dB to −6 dB (Δ improvement in column 6 is 46 dB).

The second iteration shown in Fig. 7.11 involves twisting the wire pair. In Example 7.3, it was shown that 40 twists/meter at 1 MHz reduced the DMC by 56 dB. This 56 dB improvement (column 6, Fig. 7.15) results in an I/N of −62 dB in column 7. At this point, having crossed the −26 dB I/N objective, the problem temporarily ends.

	①	②	③	④A	④B	④C	④D	④E	④	⑤	⑥	⑦
OPERATING CONDITIONS	AMB dBμV	N dBμV	A/N dB	GCM GLC	FCM GLC	DMC	C-C	P1·PS PS·V	SUM 4A·4E	AMP REJ	Δ I/N	I/N
OBJECTIVE												−26
START: FIRST RUN	140	0	140	NA	NA	−86	NA	NA	−86	−14		+40
AMPL SLOPE = 100 dB/D	140	0	140	NA	NA	−86	NA	NA	−86	−60	46	−6
TWIST WIRES 40 TPM	140	0	140	NA	NA	−142	NA	NA	−142	−60	56	−62
AMPL SLOPE = 40 dB/B	140	0	140	NA	NA	−142	NA	NA	−142	−28	−32	−30

(I/N)dB : ⑦ = ③ + ④ + ⑤

Figure 7.15—Three EMI-Fix Iterations to Achieve EMC

In retrospect, it is seen that the EMI fixes have been overdesigned by -26 dB $-$ $(-62$ dB$)$ = 36 dB. Therefore, a relaxation now can be made in the number of rolloff stages in the amplifier design. Column 5 can be increased from -60 dB to $(-60$ dB + 36 dB$)$ = -24 dB. Figure 4.3 shows that a stopband rejection of 24 dB and an f_{EMI}/f_{co} ratio of 5.0 (remember that f_{EMI}/f_{co} = 1 MHz/0.2 MHz = 5) corresponds to N = 1.8 stages. Since only an integer number of stages can exist, N = 2 is selected, which gives 28 dB rejection at 1 MHz. Thus, -28 dB is entered in column 5, and the resultant I/N ratio is now -30. Since this just crosses over the -26 dB I/N objective, no further EMC adjustment is necessary.

7.4 Composite Examples Involving Two Coupling Paths

Section 6.6 presented the second of the five principal coupling paths shown in Fig. 7.16. Section 7.1 described the third principal coupling path shown in the figure. Both sections presented their respective composite examples. Neither example, however, recognized the existence or impact of the other coupling path. The reader should assimilate the information presented in Sections 6.6 and 7.1 before continuing here.

This section shows that design interaction is very pronounced when two coupling paths are involved. It also demonstrates one of

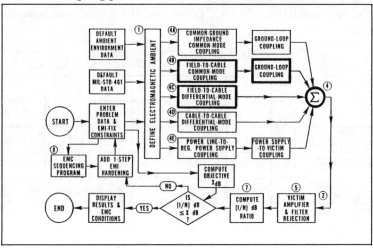

Figure 7.16—EMI Prediction and Analysis Flow Diagram Showing Location of Combined CMC/GLC and DMC Paths

7.26

the most significant aspects of EMC: sometimes EMI fixes appear to work and sometimes they do not. The reason is that only the EMI fix operating on the larger coupling path will produce easily discernable results.

7.4.1 Initial EMI Situation

The ongoing EMI problem involving the 1 MHz AM broadcast station interfering with the 200 kHz low-noise amplifier will be used as summarized in Fig. 7.17. To facilitate discussion, full use will be made of previous illustrative examples. The starting data shown in Fig. 7.17 are as follows:

Signal level: 0.01 mV = 20 dBμV
Victim sensitivity: 0.001 mV = 0 dB/μV
Victim bandwidth: 200 kHz
Victim stop band slope: 20 dB/decade
EMI source: AM broadcast station
EMI field strength: 10 V/m = 140 dBμV/m
A/t ratios: cm (default) i.e. 100 pF
All PCB and box cases: grounded
Signal source impedance: 100 Ω
Victim input impedance: 100 Ω
Transmission system: unbalanced
Box-to-box cable: parallel lines
Inside wire separation: 0.5 mm
AWG No.: 26
Cable length: 10 m
Average cable height: 10 cm

The initial EMI situation (see "START: FIRST RUN") is shown in Fig. 7.18. Column 1 corresponds to the ambient EMI source of 140 dBμV/m, whereas column 2 corresponds to that of the victim sensitivity of 0 dBμV.

Column 3 is the difference between the ambient and sensitivity levels (A/N ratio), or 140 dB (above 1 meter).

Next, of columns 4A, 4B, 4C, 4D and 4E, only two coupling paths are used, viz., columns 4B and 4C (NA = not applicable). As seen in Fig.7.16, these paths correspond to (1) CMC/GLC and (2) DMC. From Illustrative Example 6.1, the CMC is −40 dB at 1 MHz, corresponding to a cable length of 10 m and an average cable height of 10 cm.

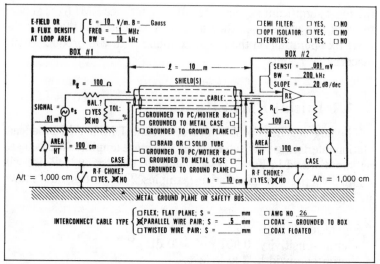

Figure 7.17—Recapitulation of Input Data for Defining the Two-Box Problem

	①	②	③	④A	④B	④C	④D	④E	④	⑤	⑥	⑦
OPERATING CONDITIONS	AMB dBµV	N dBµV	A/N dB	GCM GLC	FCM GLC	DMC	C-C	P1·PS PS·V	SUM 4A·4E	AMP REJ	Δ I/N	I/N
OBJECTIVE												-26
START: FIRST RUN	140	0	140	NA	-47	-86	NA	NA	-47	-14		+79

Figure 7.18—Worksheet for EMI Prediction and Control

From Example 6.5, the GLC is −7 dB at 1 MHz for both PC boards and both cases grounded. The sum of both parts of this coupling path is −47 dB. This is entered in column 4B in Fig. 7.18.

For the differential-mode coupling path in Fig. 7.18, Example 7.1 showed that DMC = −86 dB. This corresponded to a frequency of 1 MHz for a 10 m parallel wire of AWG No. 22 having an inside separation of 0.5 mm. Thus, −86 dB is entered in column 4C in Fig. 7.18.

Column 4 is the sum of the CMC/GLC and DMC paths. To add coherently coupled paths with each expressed in dB, the logarithm of the sum of the antilogarithms is used as explained in Section 3.2. For paths in which the larger or largest is at least 18 dB greater than the next, only the larger or largest need to be selected. For this condition, the error is not more than 1 dB, as shown in Fig. 3.5. To facilitate discussion hereafter, only the larger of the CMC/GLC and DMC coupling paths will be used, regardless of the difference between the two values. Therefore, when adding −47 dB and −86 dB, column 4 shows that the −47 dB CMC/GLC path dominates.

For the amplifier rejection in column 5, Example 4.1 showed that a 1 MHz EMI emission is rejected by 14 dB. This corresponds to the amplifier having a 200 kHz cutoff frequency and a stopband slope of 20 dB/decade. Thus, −14 dB is entered under column 5.

To calculate the resulting I/N ratio of column 7, Eq. (3.17) is used. This is equivalent to adding columns 3, 4 and 5. When this is done:

$$(I/N)_{dB} = (A/N)_{dB} + \text{Larger [CMC/GLC and DMC]}_{dB} + AR_{dB}$$

$$= 140 \text{ dB} - 47 \text{ dB} - 14 \text{ dB} = 79 \text{ dB}$$

Therefore, +79 dB appears in column 7 of Fig. 7.18. This first run gives the starting result previously shown for the CMC/GLC path alone (see Section 6.6) because this path couples so much more EMI than that due to the DMC path (see Section 3.2.2).

7.4.2 Sequencing of EMI Fixes

Now the task remains to eliminate the EMI problem by an amount equal to the above $(I/N)_{dB}$ minus the objective $(I/N)_{dB}$. In Fig. 7.18, under column 7 and across from the objective, it is remembered that −26 dB was computed for a 99 percent probability of no EMI, i.e., for a 99 percent EMC probability. This was illustrated earlier in Example 3.1.Thus, +79 dB $(I/N)_{dB}$ − (−26) dB $(I/N)_{dB}$ objective = 105 dB of required EMI hardening.

In previous sections, a **trial-and-error** approach was used. This is no longer desirable because there are too many options, and the problem is becoming more difficult to manage and control. Instead, an organized approach is needed. The technique used involves an EMC sequencing program as shown in the overall methodology of Fig. 7.19. This program assists in the selection of the proper EMI hardening fix. After this, the program is iterated to calculate the new I/N ratio. It continues until the objective I/N ratio has been achieved. This technique is also used in the EMI prediction software of Ref. 3.

Different versions of sequencing programs exist, depending upon the coupling paths involved. Figure 7.20 shows one such program when the CMC/GLC and DMC paths are both involved. After determining that the objective I/N ratio has not yet been achieved ("N" branch in the figure), the next decision involves determining if the equipment, box or console is in the design stage ("D" branch) or if it is already installed in the field ("F" branch). This is very important since many of the practical EMC options for each are different. This was previously discussed in Section 2.5 regarding the identification of EMC design and retrofit constraints.

If the equipment box or console is in the design stage, one of the first EMC fixes to consider is increasing the stopband rejection of the victim amplifier or logic. Increasing the rolloff in the stopband may be accomplished by increasing N, the number of stages. After this trial, if EMI still exists, it is next necessary to determine which of the two CMC/GLC and DMC paths is the greater. This is important because some fixes provide EMI hardening on one path and not the other, or vice versa.

For the CMC/GLC path, Fig. 7.20 shows the sequence in selecting the EMI fix options. Ordinarily, the uppermost items should be tried first, provided they survive two tests: (1) the fix will give at least a 10 dB improvement, and (2) the user/designer is willing to adopt the particular fix. This puts the user in control. Of course,

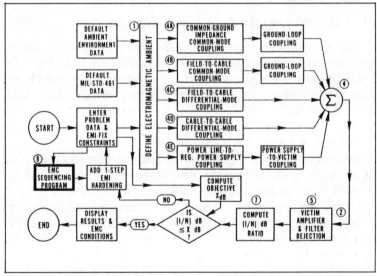

Figure 7.19—EMI Prediction and Analysis Flow Diagram Showing Location of EMC Sequencing Program

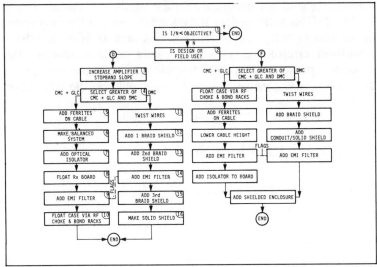

Figure 7.20—One EMC Sequencing Program Corresponding to CMC/GLC and DMC Paths

if he is inexperienced or unsure, the particular fix can be selected on a trial basis.

For the DMC path in Fig. 7.20, the sequencing priority and rationale follow the same methodology as for the CMC/GLC path. In contrasting both the CMC/GLC and DMC paths, it is noted that (with one exception) all fixes are different. This was already dem... .:rated in Sections 6.3 and 6.5 (regarding EMI-control techniques for reducing CMC and GLC) versus Section 7.2, relative to DMC. The one exception is "Add EMI Filter," which works on both paths because, in truth, it is installed at the victim amplifier or logic input port.

If the equipment or console is in the field installation stage (right "F" branch in Fig. 7.20), th₂ first decision involves selecting the greater of the CMC/GLC and DMC paths. This procedure is similar to that of the design stage. In comparing the CMC/GLC paths for both the design and field stages, it is noted that they are not identical since circumstances in a design laboratory necessarily differ from those in the field. For example, it is easier to control cable height in the field (it is unknown in the design stage), whereas one cannot usually change an unbalanced system to a balanced one there. In general, for the field stages, EMI fixes involve external changes to equipments and consoles. Conversely, for the design stage, one concentrates on the internal changes.

Similar arguments apply when comparing the sequencing options of the DMC for both the design and field stages. For the field stage, an additional option for both DMC/GLC and DMC is to **add a shielded enclosure**. This option cuts down or removes the electromagnetic ambient which caused EMI in the first place. Because it is expensive, however, this should be the last option considered.

7.4.3 EMI Problem Solution

The preceding worksheet in Fig. 7.18 has shown that a very significant initial EMI problem exists. The next phase is to perform EMI hardening on a step-by-step basis with the help of the sequencing program in Fig. 7.20. For the present discussion, it is assumed that the item is in the design stage.

The first step suggested in Fig. 7.20 is to increase the amplifier stopband slope. When that fix is applied and the EMI prediction process is iterated one time, the end result is shown in Fig. 7.21. From previous Illustrative Example 4.1, corresponding to a one-stage, 20 dB/decade slope, increase N to a five-stage filter-like performance with a slope of 100 dB/decade. The net improvement is 46 dB (column 6), which reduces I/N from 79 dB to 33 dB (column 7).

Figure 7.21 also shows that the CMC/GLC coupling was −47 dB (column 4B), and the DMC coupling was −86 dB (column 4C). Since CMC/GLC coupling is the larger of the two coupling paths (column 4), the left branch (select greater of CMC + GLC or DMC) in Fig.

	①	②	③	④A	④B	④C	④D	④E	④	⑤	⑥	⑦
OPERATING CONDITIONS	AMB dBµV	N dBµV	A/N dB	GCM GLC	FCM GLC	DMC	C-C	PI·PS PS·V	SUM 4A·4E	AMP REJ	Δ I/N	I/N
OBJECTIVE												−26
START: FIRST RUN	140	0	140	NA	−47	−86	NA	NA	−47	−14		+79
AMPL SLOPE = 100 dB-D	140	0	140	NA	−47	−86	NA	NA	−47	−60	46	+33
(I/N)dB:	⑦ = ③ + ④ + ⑤											

Figure 7.21—First Step in EMI Hardening: Increase Amplifier Stopband Slope

7.20 is followed. This now calls for adding ferrites on the interconnecting cable. It was already shown in Example 6.11 that ferrites would not work at 1 MHz and lower frequencies for the 100 Ω impedance level of the circuit. Thus, that box is bypassed in Fig. 7.20.

The next box in sequence in Fig. 7.20 suggests use of a balanced system. If a 1 percent tolerance is used in a balanced system as previously illustrated for grounded boxes in Example 6.7, Fig. 7.22 shows the new CMC + GLC to be $-40 + (-40) = -80$ dB (column 4B). The net improvement (column 6) is 33 dB. The resultant I/N ratio from this second iteration is shown as 0 dB in column 7 of Fig. 7.22.

	①	②	③	④A	④B	④C	④D	④E	④	⑤	⑥	⑦
OPERATING CONDITIONS	AMB dBµV	N dBµV	A/N dB	GCM GLC	FCM GLC	DMC	C-C	P1·PS PS·V	SUM 4A·4E	AMP REJ	Δ I/N	I/N
OBJECTIVE												-26
START: FIRST RUN	140	0	140	NA	-47	-86	NA	NA	-47	-14		+79
AMPL SLOPE = 100 dB-D	140	0	140	NA	-47	-86	NA	NA	-47	-60	46	+33
BAL GEN/ AMPL = 1%	140	0	140	NA	-80	-86	NA	NA	-80	-60	33	0
(I/N)dB:	⑦ = ③ + ④ + ⑤											

Figure 7.22—Second Step in EMI Hardening: Use Balanced System

Since both CMC/GLC and DMC in Fig. 7.22 are close in amplitude (-80 dB versus -86 dB), it does not matter which path is tried next since it will take both coupling path reductions to result in a noticeable improvement. Thus, the next step in the sequence shown in Fig. 7.20 is to add an optical isolator. Suppose that the designer has decided not to use this fix (remembering that optical isolators are cumbersome to use with low-level analog). The next sequence in Fig. 7.20, then, is to float the board. Thus, the next step will be to float the balanced system at the receiver (Box 2) end. From Fig. 6.22, this results in a GLC of -66 dB (remember -72 dB from the figure +6 dB for one end ungrounded only). Thus, Fig. 7.23 shows CMC/GLC to be -40 dB + $(-66$ dB) = -106 dB in column 4B. Since DMC (column 4C) remains at -86 dB, the combination shown in column 4 is -86 dB.

Because the DMC path is now the larger of the two, Fig. 7.20 indicates that the wires should be twisted. From Illustrative Example 7.3, it was shown that a DMC coupling reduction of 56 dB was achieved for 40 twists per meter (TPM) at 1 MHz. Thus, Fig. 7.24 shows the result of this fourth step in EMI hardening. The DMC has now been reduced from -86 dB to $-86 + (-56) =$ -142 dB (column 4C). Thus, column 4 shows that the larger coupling path is now CMC/GLC = -106 dB. This is a 20 dB improvement over the preceding step in Fig. 7.23. The resulting I/N

Operating Conditions	① AMB dBμV/m	② N dBμV	③ A/N dB	④A GCM GLC	④B FCM GLC	④C DMC	④D C-C	④E PL to PS PS to V	④ SUM 4A to 4E	⑤ AMP REJ	⑥ Δ I/N	⑦ I/N
Objective												-26
Start: First Run	140	0	140	NA	-47	-86	NA	NA	-47	-14		+79
Ampl Slope = 100 dB-D	140	0	140	NA	-47	-86	NA	NA	-47	-60	46	+33
Balance Gen/Ampl = 1%	140	0	140	NA	-80	-86	NA	NA	-80	-60	33	0
Float System at Receiver	140	0	140	NA	-106	-86	NA	NA	-86	-60	6	-6

(I/N) dB: ⑦ = ③ + ④ + ⑤

Figure 7.23—Third Step in EMI Hardening: Float Board at Receiver

Operating Conditions	① AMB dBμV/m	② N dBμV	③ A/N dB	④A GCM GLC	④B FCM GLC	④C DMC	④D C-C	④E PL to PS PS to V	④ SUM 4A to 4E	⑤ AMP REJ	⑥ Δ I/N	⑦ I/N
Objective												-26
Start: First Run	140	0	140	NA	-47	-86	NA	NA	-47	-14		+79
Ampl Slope = 100 dB-D	140	0	140	NA	-47	-86	NA	NA	-47	-60	46	+33
Balance Gen/Ampl = 1%	140	0	140	NA	-80	-86	NA	NA	-80	-60	33	0
Float System at Receiver	140	0	140	NA	-106	-86	NA	NA	-86	-60	0	-6
Twist Wires at 40 TPM	140	0	140	NA	-106	-142	NA	NA	-106	-60	34	-26

(I/N) dB: ⑦ = ③ + ④ + ⑤

Figure 7.24—Fourth Step in EMI Hardening: Use Twisted Wires

ratio is now −26 dB (column 7). Therefore, no further hardening is required.

By way of critique, the preceding two paragraphs illustrate the frustration in classical EMC engineering. Typically, based on his experience, the EMC engineer expected a substantial improvement in I/N reduction by floating the PC board. Here, however, the larger coupling had previously changed from CMC/GLC to DMC to deny the value of the latent improvement. In other words, if the engineer applies an EMI fix to the wrong (more negative) coupling path, no improvement will result.

Could the designer be less ambitious and satisfy himself with an I/N objective of ≈ −10 dB (i.e., less than a 50 percent probability that I exceeds N − 12 dB)? Some relaxation can be achieved in Fig. 7.24. One relaxation is to reduce the 100 dB/decade slope of the victim amplifier to 60 dB/decade (reduce N = 5 to N = 3). The result of this is shown in Fig. 7.25. Two other relaxation options are (1) eliminate the use of a balanced system, or (2) use a lighter twist on the twisted pair.

Returning to Fig. 7.20 for the design stage, it is seen that one may alternate back and forth between the CMC/GLC and DMC paths, depending upon which is the larger of the two. The procedure flows on down, calling up each potential EMI fix in succession. As mentioned previously, there is no guarantee that any one step will

Operating Conditions	① AMB dBμV/m	② N dBμV	③ A/N dB	④A GCM GLC	④B FCM GLC	④C DMC	④D C-C	④E PL to PS PS to V	④ SUM 4A to 4E	⑤ AMP REJ	⑥ Δ I/N	⑦ I/N
Objective												
Start: First Run	140	0	140	NA	−47	−86	NA	NA	−47	−14		+79
Ampl Slope = 100 dB-D	140	0	140	NA	−47	−86	NA	NA	−47	−60	46	+33
Balance Gen/ Ampl = 1%	140	0	140	NA	−80	−86	NA	NA	−80	−60	33	0
Float System at Receiver	140	0	140	NA	−106	−86	NA	NA	−86	−60	6	−6
Twist Wires at 40 TPM	140	0	140	NA	−106	−142	NA	NA	−106	−60	34	−26
Reduce Ampl Slope 60 dB-D	140	0	140	NA	−106	−142	NA	NA	−106	−42	−18	−8

(I/N) dB: ⑦ = ③ + ④ + ⑤

Figure 7.25—Alternate Step in EMI Hardening: Relaxing Amplifier Rejection

work since that must be separately determined in the prediction process. Rather, the sequencing merely suggests which technique might be tried first. If the test items were installed in the field (circle "F" in Fig. 7.20), then the right-hand side of the EMI sequencing program would be applied. The procedure there follows a similar pattern as discussed above.

7.4.4 Three More Illustrative Examples

This section suggests three more Illustrative Examples of EMI problems and solutions using composite coupling paths. The reader should solve them on his own.

1. Identical problem to that of Section 7.4.1 except the frequency is 100 MHz.
2. Similar problem to that of Section 7.4.1 except the interconnecting cable is coaxial line, and the frequency is 100 MHz.
3. Similar problem to that of Section 7.4.1 except the interfering source is a magnetic flux density at 60 Hz.

The step-by-step details of the EMC solution are left up to the reader. However, one set of non-unique solutions to each EMI problem are given in Figs. 7.26 through 7.28, along with some comments.

Figure 7.26 Comments

In Fig. 7.26, 100 MHz, a 10 V/m ambient (shown as 20 dBV/m in column 1) exists with a parallel wire pair. On the first run, the amplifier rejection ($N = 1$) is -54 dB. However, due to the high ratio of f_{EMI}/f_{co} it must be checked that audio rectification does not occur (see Chapter 4, on victim response). For $N = 1$, $f_{EMI}/f_{co} = 100/0.2 = 500$ and $f_{co} = 200$ kHz, the curve in Fig. 4.9 shows that rejection can be as poor as -20 dB. However V_{EMI} at the amplifier input is given by: 20 dBV/m $-$ 28 dB (FCM/GLC) $= -8$ dBv or 400 mV. Equation (4.4) in Chapter 4 shows that this is the range of what causes full audio rectification. Therefore (-20 dB) is only shown as "Ample Rejection."

Second run: Add 2 poles in the rejection circuit of the amplifier, making $N = 3$. Practical limits of components dictate a best default

7.36

Operating Conditions	AMB dBμV (1)	N dBV (2)	A/N dB (3)	GCM GLC (4A)	FCM GLC (4B)	DMC (4C)	C-C (4D)	PL to PS PS to V (4E)	SUM 4A to 4E (4)	AMP REJ (5)	Δ I/N (6)	I/N (7)
Objective												− 26
Start: First Run	20	− 120	140	− 16	− 12	− 62			− 28	− 20		92
Ampl N = 3 Stage	20	− 120	140		− 28	− 62			− 28	− 40	20	72
Balance (1%)	20	− 120	140	− 16	− 56	− 62			− 62	− 40	34	38
Twist at 40 TPM	20	− 120	140		− 72	− 94			− 72	− 40	10	28
EMI Filter, N = 1	20	− 120	140		− 72	− 94			− 72	− 100	60	− 32

(I/N) dB: ⑦ = ③ + ④ + ⑤

Figure 7.26—EMI Prediction and Control from FM Broadcast Station at 100 MHz (The remainder of the problem is the same as Fig. 7.13.)

Operating Conditions	AMB dBμV (1)	N dBV (2)	A/N dB (3)	GCM GLC (4A)	FCM GLC (4B)	DMC (4C)	C-C (4D)	PL to PS PS to V (4E)	SUM 4A to 4E (4)	AMP REJ (5)	Δ I/N (6)	I/N (7)
Objective												− 26
Start: First Run	20	− 120	140	− 16	− 55	− 50			− 50	− 48		42
Change Coax to Triax RG-55	20	− 120	140	− 16	− 93	− 88			− 88	− 54	44	− 2
EMI Filter, N = 1	20	− 120	140		− 93	− 88			− 88	− 54 / − 40	40	− 42

(I/N) dB: ⑦ = ③ + ④ + ⑤

Figure 7.27—EMI Prediction and Control from FM Broadcast Station at 100 MHz (Interconnecting cable is a coaxial cable. The remainder of the problem is the same as Fig. 7.13.)

rejection of −40 dB for N > 3 since audio rectification is still there (see Fig. 4.9).

Third run: Balancing (floating is useless against 100 MHz, though it could be useful for other low-frequency threats). Bring column 4B below 4C. Dominant coupling is now DMC.

Fourth run: DMC is reduced by twisting. I/N is now at + 28 dB.

OPERATING CONDITIONS	① AMB dBG	② N dBV	③ A/N dB	④A GCM GLC	④B FCM GLC	④C DMC	④D C-C	④E PL-PS PS-V	④ SUM 4A-4E	⑤ AMP REJ	⑥ Δ I/N	⑦ I/N
OBJECTIVE												-26
START: FIRST RUN	-14	-120	106		-18 -7	-64			-25	0		81
FLOAT RX BOARD	-14	-120	106		-125	-64			-64	0	39	42
TWIST WIRES AT 40 TPM	-14	-120	106		-125	-120			-120	0	56	-14

(I/N)dB: ⑦=③+④+⑤

Figure 7.28—EMI Prediction and Control from 60 Hz Power Mains Carrying 100 A at a Distance of 1 m (The remainder of the problem is the same as Fig. 7.13)

Fifth run: A good quality EMI filter (nonresonant coaxial capacitors of ferrites for instance) is added, with cutoff frequency sufficiently above 200 kHz, say 1 MHz. Its rejection alone is therefore −40 dB. The EMI voltage at the amplifier's input is now:

$$20 \text{ dBV/m} - 72 \text{ (FCM/GLC)} - 40 \text{ dB (filter)} = -92 \text{ dBV} = 25 \text{ } \mu V$$

This falls below Eq. (4.4) criteria for audio rectification. The full amplifier rejection of at least −60 dB can now be assumed, adding to the −40 dB of filtering. At this point I/N = −32 and the objective is achieved.

Figure 7.27 Comments

First run: The DMC, directly found from curve 7.9 for l = 10 m is −50 dB, higher than FCM + GLC. (At 100 MHz, the 10 m cable is already >λ/2). Amplifier rejection has the same comments as in the previous example.

Second run: Replace RG-8 coax by a double braid (Triax RG55 or RG214) having a better Z_T: −42 dBΩ/m instead of −4. Both

7.38

GLC and DMC are reduced by 38 dB.

Third run: Add good quality EMI filter (with no parasitic resonances at 100 MHz). Same comments as run No. 5 in previous example.

Other option: replace coax by twisted pair and implement same fixes as previous example.

Figure 7.28 Comments

The frequency is 60 Hz with a magnetic ambient of 0.2 gauss (−14 dB gauss). The FCM and DMC curves to use are those for magnetic induction (Figs. 6.12 and 7.4 respectively). Notice there is no amplifier rejection since the EMI is in-band.

7.5 EMI Prediction in the Case of a Broadband Transient (Lightning, EMP, ESD, etc.)

As explained in an introductory part of this book (Chapter 2, Section 2.), the EMI threat may not be at a discrete frequency but, instead, spread over a wide spectrum. In the case of a radiated susceptibility, the ambient would be characterized by its spectral density in volts per meter per hertz (or per megahertz) across the frequency spectrum. To solve this type of problem, an expanded version of the EMI prediction form used so far has been prepared, as shown in Fig. 7.29. The spectrum is divided into frequency "slices" of 1 decade each (line 1.A). The midband amplitude of the field density in dBV/m/Hz is calculated for each slice (Line 1B). Then each amplitude in the middle of a slice is multiplied by the bandwidth of this slice in hertz, resulting in an equivalent field in dBV/m for each particular slice (line 1). The rest of the problem consists of treating each band like the narrowband cases analyzed so far, applying the FCM, GLC, etc. To this effect, the numbering of the columns from the general prediction form has been perpetuated for each prediction step. This should help the reader to familiarize himself with this prediction routine.

#	TOPIC	UNITS	VALUE	10 kHz	100 kHz	1 MHz	10 MHz	100MHz	1 GHz	10 GHz
1	Coverage	Hz		3-30 kHz	30-300 kHz	0.3-3 MHz	3-30 MHz	30-300MHz	0.3-3 GHz	3-30 GHz
1A		dBHz	20 log (Hz)	88	108	128	148	168	188	208
2	EMP	dBV/m/Hz	2A$_T$ + Slope	-32	-32	-35	-52	-80	-120	-160
3	EMP	dBV/m	#2 + dBHz**	56	76	93	96	88	68	48
4	Lightning*	dBA/Hz	2A$_T$ + Slope	-2	-16	-42	-80	-120	-160	-200
5	Lightning*	dB(Z$_o$/m)	60/R							
6	Lightning	dBV/m	4+5+dBHz**							
7	Other	dBV/m								
8	Ambient	dBV/m	3, 6 or 7							
9	CMC	dBV/V/m								
10	GLC	dB								
11	Subtotal	dBV/V/m	9 + 10							
12	DMC	dBV/V/m								
13	Larger	dBV/V/m	11 or 12							
14	Analog/Logic Rejection	dB								
15	Interference	dBV	8+13+14							
16	Sensitivity	dBV	Signal = Noise							
17	I/N Ratio	dB	15 - 16							

$$*H = I/2\pi R; \ E = ZH = 120\pi H = 120\pi I/2pR = 60I/R$$
$$**dBHz = 20 \log (\text{Bandwidth or Coverage, Line #1, in Hz})$$

Figure 7.29—Expanded Version of EMI Prediction Form

Illustrative Example 7.10

A nuclear EMP (NEMP) of 50,000 V/m is illuminating a 10 m long digital link 0.1 m above ground. The characteristics of the EMI are:

Ambient: peak field = 50,000 V/m
Rise time = 10 ns
50 percent pulse width = 250 ns
Victim: TTL digital receiver, unbalanced
Sensitivity = noise margin = 400 mV
Bandwidth = 30 MHz

Figures 7.30 and 7.31 show the steps of the first prediction run. The line 1B corresponds to the spectral density envelope computed by a Fourier transformation of the time domain pulse, as shown in Fig. 7.30. Notice on line 7 the formidable I/N ratio between 1 and 100 MHz. The highest contribution comes from the 3 to

7.40

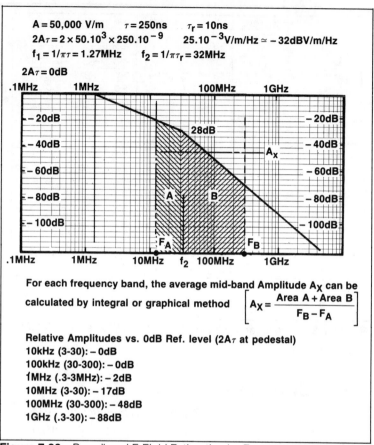

A = 50,000 V/m τ = 250ns τ_r = 10ns

$2A_\tau = 2 \times 50.10^3 \times 250.10^{-9}$ 25.10^{-3}V/m/Hz ≈ – 32dBV/m/Hz

$f_1 = 1/\pi\tau = 1.27$MHz $f_2 = 1/\pi\tau_r = 32$MHz

$2A_\tau = 0$dB

For each frequency band, the average mid-band Amplitude A_X can be calculated by integral or graphical method

$$A_X = \frac{\text{Area A} + \text{Area B}}{F_B - F_A}$$

Relative Amplitudes vs. 0dB Ref. level ($2A_\tau$ at pedestal)
10kHz (3-30): – 0dB
100kHz (30-300): – 0dB
1MHz (.3-3MHz): – 2dB
10MHz (3-30): – 17dB
100MHz (30-300): – 48dB
1GHz (.3-30): – 88dB

Figure 7.30—Broadband E-Field Estimation by Frequency Segments for NEMP Pulse

30 MHz band, where there is not yet victim rejection, while the FCM and GLC have reached their peak. At this point, an I/N ratio of 86 dB means the TTL input actually "sees" 0.4 V x 10 $^{86/20}$ = 8 kV! No optical isolator, filter or signal transformer would survive such transient. Therefore, the efforts should first concentrate in either (1) reducing the cable pickup by shielding or burying the entire area or (2) installing surge suppressor such that the remainder of the pulse does not exceed a 1 kV, a value that conventional decoupling components can withstand.

#	TOPIC	UNITS	VALUE	10kHz	100kHz	1MHz	10MHz	100MHz	1GHz	10GHz
1	COVERAGE	Hz	20 log(Hz)	3-30kHz	30-300kHz	3-3MHz	3-30MHz	30-300MHz	3-3GHz	3-30GHz
1A	COVERAGE	dBHz	20 log(Hz)	88	108	128	148	168	188	208
2	EMP	dBV/m/Hz	2Aᴛ + SLOPE	-32	-32	-34	-50	-80	-120	-160
3	EMP	dBV/m	#2 + dBHz**	56	76	94	98	88	68	48
4	LIGHTNING*	dBA/Hz	2Aᴛ + SLOPE	-2	-16	-42	-80	-120	-160	-200
5	LIGHTNING*	dB(Zₒ/m)	60/R							
6	LIGHTNING	dBV/m	4 + 5 + dBHz**							
7	OTHER	dBV/m								
8	AMBIENT	dBV/m	3, 6 or 7	56	76	94	98	88	68	48
9	CMC	dBV/V/m		-80	-60	-40	-20	-16	-16	-16
10	GLC	dB		-6	-6	-6	0	-20	-30	-40
11	SUBTOTAL	dBV/V/m	9 + 10	-86	-66	-46	-20	-36	-46	-56
12	DMC	dBV/V/m		-126	-106	-86	-66	-62	-62	-62
13	LARGER	dBV/V/m	11 or 12	-86	-66	-46	-20	-36	-46	-56
14	ANALOG/ LOGIC REJECTION	dB		0	0	0	0	-10	-30	-50
15	INTERFERENCE	dBV	8 + 13 + 14	-30	6	48	78	42	-8	-58
16	SENSITIVITY	dBV	SIGNAL = NOISE	-8	-8	-8	-8	-8	-8	-8
17	I/N RATIO	dB	15 - 16	-22	+14	+56	86	+50	0	-50

*H = I/2πR; E = ZH = 120πH = 120πI/2πR = 60I/R

**dBHz = 20 log₁₀ (Bandwidth or coverage, line #1, in Hz)

Figure 7.31—Broadband E-Field EMI Problem Worksheet (NEMP)

7.6 References

1. Smith, A.A., *Coupling of External Electromagnetic Fields to Transmission Lines* (New York: John Wiley and Sons, 1977).
2. White, D.R.J., *Electromagnetic Shielding Materials and Performance* (Gainesville, VA: Interference Control Technologies, Inc., 1980).
3. "Box to Box Radiated Susceptibility," Prediction Software #5220 (Gainesville, Va: Interference Control Technologies, Inc.).

7.7 Bibliography

Acuna, V., "Transfer Impedance Measurement as a Test for EMC," *IEEE EMC Symposium Record* (New York: IEEE), Session 5A, San Antonio, Texas, October 7-9, 1975.

Bates, C.P. and Hawley, G.T., "A Model For Currents and Voltages Induced Within Long Transmission Cables by an Electromagnetic Wave," *IEEE Transactions on EMC,* Volume EMC-13, no. 4, November, 1971.

Bechtold, G.W. and Kozakoff, D.J., "Dipole Mode Response of a Multiconductor Cable above a Ground Place in a Transient Electromagnetic Field," *IEEE Transactions on EMC,* Volume EMC-12, no. 1, February, 1970. K

Bechtold, G.W. and Kozakoff, D.J., "Transmission Line Mode Response of a Multiconductor Cable in a Transient Electromagnetic Field," *IEEE Transactions on EMC,* Volume EMC-12, no. 1, February, 1970.

Bode, T.J., "Workshop on Application of Programmable Calculators to EMC," *IEEE EMC Symposium Record* (New York: IEEE), Session 2B. San Antonio, Texas. October 7-9, 1975.

Casey, K.F., "On the Effective Transfer Impedance of Thin Coaxial Shields (with Editorial Summary)," *IEEE Transactions on EMC,* Volume EMC-18, no. 3, August, 1976.

Dismukes, J.P., et al., "Flexible Braids for Improved Magnetic Shielding of Cables," *IEEE EMC Symposium Record* (New York: IEEE), Session III-A, Atlanta, GA, June 20-22, 1978.

Ditton, V.R., "Coupling to Aerospace Cables at Microwave Frequencies," *IEEE EMC Symposium Record* (New York: IEEE), Session 4B, San Antonio, Texas, October 7-9, 1975.

Hoeft, L.O., "Using Transfer Impedance to Solve EMP Problems," *EMC Technology,* November 1986.

Jarva, W., "Shielding Tests for Cables and Small Enclosures in the 1-to-10 GHz Range," *IEEE Transactions on EMC,* Volume EMC-12, no. 1, February, 1970.

Kalangiun, K.M., "Shield Grounds on Shielded Twisted Pair Single Point Grounded Circuits," *IEEE EMC Symposium Record* (New York: IEEE), Session V-B, Atlanta, GA, June 20-22, 1978.

Landt, K., "Effectiveness of Cable Shielding in Complex Electrical or Electronic Systems by Appropriate Grounding Methods," Second Symposium and Technical Exhibition on EMC, Montreux, Switzerland, June 28-30, 1977.

Lee, K.S.H. and Baum, C.E., "Applications of Model Analysis to Braided Shield Cables," *IEEE Transactions on EMC,* Volume, EMC-17, no. 3, August 1975.

Liao, S.Y., "Light Transmittance and RF Shielding Effectiveness of a Gold Film on a Glass Substrate," *IEEE Transactions on EMC,* Volume EMC-17, no. 4, November 1975.

Martin A., "Introduction to Surface Transfer Impedance" *EMC Technology,* July 1982.

McDowell, C.N. and Berstein, M.J., "Surface Transfer Impedance Measurements on Subminiature Coaxial Cables," *IEEE Transactions on EMC*, Volume EMC-15, no. 4, November 1973.

Merewether, D.E., "Analysis of the Shielding Characteristics of Saturable Ferromagnetic Cable Shields," *IEEE Transactions on EMC*, Volume EMC-12, no. 3, August 1970.

Merewether, D.E., "Design of Shielded Cables Using Saturable Ferromagnetic Materials," *IEEE Transactions on EMC*, Volume EMC-12, no. 3, August 1970.

Osborne, B.W., "The Environmental Compatibility of HF Cablevision Networks," Second Symposium and Technical Exhibition on EMC, Montreux, Switzerland, June 28-30, 1977.

Parker, J.C., Jr., "A Probabilistic Model of Magnetic Induction from Power Distribution Systems," *IEEE EMC Symposium Record* (New York: IEEE), Session IV-B. Atlanta, GA, June 20-22, 1978.

Rashid, A., "A Mathematical Analysis of the EMC of Twisted Wires," *IEEE EMC Symposium Record* (New York: IEEE), Session I-B. Atlanta, GA, June 20-22, 1978.

Saha, J.N., "The Radio Interference Field of an Overhead Transmission Line," *IEEE Transactions on EMC*, Volume EMC-13, no. 4, November 1971.

Schlessinger, L., "Currents Induced by a Plane Wave on an Infinite Wire above a Flat Earth," *IEEE Transactions on EMC*, Volume EMC-17, no. 3, August 1975.

Shiau, Y.; Bridges, J.; and Sellers, G.J., "Wide-Band High Performance, Very Flexible Coaxial Shield," *IEEE EMC Symposium Record* (New York: IEEE), Session III-A. Atlanta, GA. June 20-22, 1978.

Stevens, D., "Analysis of the Shuttle Engine Cable Harness," Second Symposium and Technical Exhibition on EMC, Montreux, Switzerland, June 28-30, 1977.

Still, D.A., "Interaction of Magnetic Fields and Ferromagnetic Shields," *IEEE Transactions on EMC*, Volume EMC-13, no. 2, May 1971.

Tesche, F.M.; Chang, F.K.; and Liu, T.K., "Application of Multiconductor Transmission Line Theory for EMP Analysis: Numerical and Experimental Results," *IEEE EMC Symposium Record* (New York: IEEE), Session IV-A. Atlanta, GA, June 20-22, 1978.

Tesche, F.M. and Liu, T.K., "On the Development of a General Transmission Line Model for EMC and EMP Applications,"

Second Symposium and Technical Exhibition on EMC, Montreux, Switzerland, June 28-30, 1977.

Vance, E.F., "Shielding Effectiveness of Braided-Wire Shields," *IEEE Transactions on EMC*, Volume EMC-17, no. 2, May 1975.

Vance, E.F., *Coupling to Shielded Cables* (New York: John Wiley and Sons, 1978).

Wells, W.C.; Bridges, J.E.; and Pomerantz, M., "Nuclear Electromagnetic Pulse (NEMP) Hardened Cables," *IEEE EMC Symposium Record* (New York: IEEE), Session 4B, San Antonio, TX, October 7-9, 1975.

Whitmer, R.M., "Cable Shielding Performance and CW Response," *IEEE Transactions on EMC*, Volume EMC-15, no. 4, November 1973.

Zach, F.C. and Demattio, R., "Calculation and Measurement of Electromagnetic Influence on Telecommunications Cables in a Subway System by Power Electronic Circuits," Second Symposium and Technical Exhibition on EMC, Montreux, Switzerland, June 28-30, 1977.

Chapter 8
Near Field
Cable-to-Cable Coupling

This chapter describes the fourth of the five principal coupling paths as shown in Fig. 8.1. By capacitive or inductive means, or both, cable-to-cable coupling produces unintentional signals on a victim cable from a nearby source cable carrying either raw power, regulated power, control and signal or even parasitic transients. The undesired coupled signal may appear as both common-mode and differential-mode noise. However, only the latter is computed since

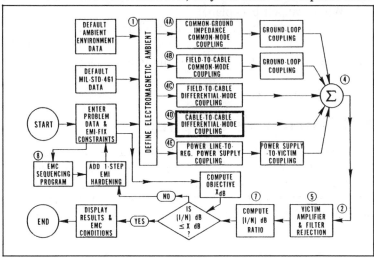

Figure 8.1—EMI Prediction and Analysis Flow Diagram Showing Cable-to-Cable Coupling

it is the differential-mode voltage to which the victim amplifier or logic may be susceptible.

8.1 Cable-to-Cable Coupling Models

The crosstalk coupling mechanism involves both mutual capacitance and inductance between culprit and the victim wire pairs. Sometimes, a ground plane is part of a return circuit path.

Coupling between two wire pairs, between two coaxial lines or between one wire pair and one coaxial line involves both electric and magnetic field coupling. The former is represented by mutual capacitive coupling between the lines, and the latter corresponds to mutual inductive coupling between the EMI source and victim lines. Their representations are made by two single wires above a ground plane with the latter being the return path **for both**. Since it is a poor EMC practice to use a common return path for noisy circuits and susceptible circuits,* this representation may then be modified by the **method of images** to produce the equivalent coupling between wire pairs. Of course, the ground plane may still be used as part of the return circuit path by accident, constraint or otherwise.

There are some cases where an active return is unavoidably shared by the culprit and victim wires, e.g.:

1. Wire-wrapped backplanes
2. Flat cables with a unique return plane
3. Automobiles and some other vehicles (This practice is slowly being abandoned, at least for the most sensitive circuits.)

8.2 Capacitive Coupling

Capacitive coupling predominates when the victim circuit impedance is high relative to 377 Ω. The coupling also increases with frequency and the proximity of the culprit-victim pairs.

Figure 8.2 shows the network involving capacitive coupling between culprit line and victim circuits. The objective is to determine

---

*See Section 5.1 regarding common-ground impedance coupling.

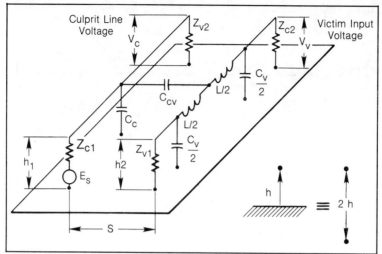

Figure 8.2—Circuit Representation of Capacitive Coupling between Parallel Wires over a Ground Plane, and the Corresponding Geometry for a Wire Pair

how much of the available culprit line voltage, V_c, is coupled into the victim load, Z_v, for varying conditions. The ratio of the victim-to-culprit voltages then becomes the cable-to-cable coupling, CCC:

$$CCC_{dB} = 20 \log (V_v/V_c) \qquad (8.1)$$

The value of CCC_{dB} is often called **crosstalk**. Note that CCC_{dB} is, of course, a negative number because cables cannot exhibit a gain in coupling. However, in technical parlance, the crosstalk is often referred to as XdB, without the minus sign, because everyone knows its significance.

Based on frequently used math models (see Appendix B), the V_v/V_c ratio for capacitive coupling is computed as shown below.

At R_1 end (near end):

$$\frac{V_v}{V_c} = C_{cv}\omega \; \frac{R_1}{R_1 \dfrac{C_v\omega}{2} + 1} \left(\frac{j\dfrac{L\omega}{2} + \dfrac{R_2}{R_2 \dfrac{C_v\omega}{2} + 1}}{jL\omega + \dfrac{R_1}{\dfrac{R_1 C_v\omega + 1}{2}} + \dfrac{R_2}{\dfrac{R_2 C_v\omega + 1}{2}}} \right)$$

$$(8.2a)$$

8.3

At R_2 end (far end):

$$\frac{V_v}{V_c} = C_{cv}\omega \; \frac{R_2}{R_1\frac{C_v\omega}{2}+1} \left(\frac{j\frac{L\omega}{2} + \dfrac{R_1}{R_1\frac{C_v\omega}{2}+1}}{jL\omega+ \dfrac{R_1}{R_1\frac{C_v\omega}{2}+1} + \dfrac{R_2}{R_2\frac{C_v\omega}{2}+1}} \right)$$

(8.2b)

If $R_1 = R_2 = R$, the capacitive coupling at either end is:

$$\frac{V_v}{V_c} = C_{cv}\omega \; \frac{R}{R\frac{C_v\omega}{2}+1} \left(\frac{j\frac{L\omega}{2} + \dfrac{R}{R\frac{C_v\omega}{2}+1}}{jL\omega+ \dfrac{2R}{R C_v\omega+1}} \right)$$

(8.2c)

At low frequencies, if $R_v(C\omega/2) \ll 1$ and $j(L\omega/2) \ll R$, the equation can be simplified as:

$$\frac{V_v}{V_c} = \frac{1}{2} \; C_{cv}\omega \, R$$

(8.3)

where,

$\omega = 2\pi \times$ frequency in hertz

C_{cv} = wire-to-wire coupling capacitance per meter length (see Fig. 8.2)

R_1, R_2 = victim termination resistances (should be replaced by victim impedances if they are inductive or capacitive)

C_v = victim wire capacitance to ground return per meter length

L = victim wire self-inductance

Notice that in this short line model, victim wire capacitance and inductance are broken into two halves.

The C_{cv} term is quite complex and is presented in Appendix B. It is a function of several variables including:

1. Culprit wire radius or AWG number used
2. Culprit wire height above ground plane (or culprit wire pair separation = $2h_1$ by method of images)
3. Culprit wire insulation, especially for closely coupled wire pairs
4. Culprit-to-victim separation distance, s
5. Victim wire radius or AWG number used
6. Victim wire height above ground plane (or victim pair wire separation = $2h_2$ by method of images)
7. Victim wire insulation, especially for closely coupled wire pairs

When Eq. (8.2) is substituted into Eq. (8.1), CCC may be computed for several parameter values and conditions. Table 8.1 shows CCC for capacitive coupling corresponding to two AWG No. 22 wires having a common length of 1 m and an impedance of 100 Ω. The table parameters are the wire height, h (remember the wire height is 2h for a pair rather than h for a single wire above a ground plane), and the wire pair separation distance, s. Both the h and s terms are in millimeters. Although the table is computed for AWG No. 22 (0.6 mm dia.) it can be used for other wire sizes provided that the wire spacing is at least 3 times the wire diameter. More accurate tables for other diameters are given in Appendix B. When $h_1 = h_2$, use an average h $\approx \sqrt{h_1 h_2}$.

In examining Table 8.1, note that for smaller values CCC increases with frequency at 20 dB/decade until the cable approaches an electrical length of $\lambda/10$, whereafter it saturates. While CCC is not significantly affected by small changes in h, it is very substantially affected by wire pair separation. In this respect, note that CCC falls off with increasing separation at -40 dB/decade. Furthermore, CCC is directly affected by both the cable length, l, and victim load impedances, Z_v and Z_{v2} If these impedances are about equal, the correction is:

$$CCC_{dB} = (CCC \text{ in Table } 8.1)_{dB} + 20 \log (Z_v l/100) \leqslant 0 \text{ dB}$$

$$(8.4)$$

For unmatched victim configurations, see Appendix B.

Should the addition of the correction term in Eq. (8.4) make CCC_{dB} greater than zero, then CCC_{dB} is still equal to 0 dB. Crosstalk cannot be positive. This translates into the fact that even if Z_v were infinite, there cannot be a higher voltage across a victim circuit than the source voltage, V_c.

When the frequency is such that the victim/culprit parallel run exceeds 0.1λ, the table still gives an acceptable approximation (envelope), provided (1) no more than $\lambda/4$ is entered in the length correction of Eq. (8.4) and (2) the characteristic impedance of the line Z_0 is used as parameter Z_v instead of the actual terminating resistor.

Consequently, for $l > \lambda/4$, Eq. (8.4) becomes:

$$CCC_{dB} = (CCC \text{ in Table 8.1}) + 20 \log \left(\frac{Z_0}{100} \times \frac{75}{f_{MHz}} \right) \quad (8.4a)$$

Illustrative Example 8.1

Compute the cable-to-cable crosstalk due to capacitive coupling in a harness between two wire pairs having an average separation distance of 3 mm and a 10 m run in a cable tray. The clock rate is 100 kb/s, the rise/fall times are 500 ns, and both cables are operating at a 100 Ω impedance level. Assume the center-to-center distance between the wires of a same pair is 8 mm, giving h = 4 mm.

The second corner frequency, f_c, in the spectrum density of a pulse or pulses corresponding to rise/fall times of 500 ns is:

$$f_c = 1/\pi\tau_r = 637 \text{ kHz} \quad (8.5)$$

For h = 3 to 30 mm and s = 3 mm, Table 8.1 indicates that $(CCC)_{dB} = -57$ dB at 637 kHz. Applying Eq. (8.4) to correct for a 10 m length indicates that the overall CCC is -57 dB + 20 dB + 0 dB = -37 dB. Thus, if the source wire pair is carrying a 3.5 V logic swing, it will be coupled at a level of about 3.5 V = 11 dBV $-$ 37 dB = -26 dBV = 50 mV. This is somewhat below the typical noise immunity level (NIL) of 400 mV. Thus, crosstalk should be no problem.

Table 8.1 - Capacitive Cable-to-Cable Coupling in dB (normalized to 1 meter length and AWG #22 wire)

Culprit = Load = 100 Ohms

Victim: $Z_{v1} = Z_{v2} = 100$ Ohms

Frequency	h=1mm(.5-3)							h=10mm(3-30)							h=100mm(30-300)						
	S=1	S=3	S=10	S=30	S=100	S=300	S=1k	S=1	S=3	S=10	S=30	S=100	S=300	S=1k	S=1	S=3	S=10	S=30	S=100	S=300	S=1k
10Hz	-144	-162	-180	-200	-220	-240	-260	-143	-153	-162	-176	-195	-215	-235	-143	-151	-157	-162	-170	-184	-203
20Hz	-138	-156	-174	-194	-214	-234	-254	-137	-147	-156	-170	-189	-209	-229	-136	-145	-151	-156	-164	-178	-197
30Hz	-135	-152	-171	-191	-211	-231	-251	-133	-144	-153	-167	-185	-205	-225	-133	-142	-147	-153	-161	-174	-193
50Hz	-130	-148	-166	-186	-206	-226	-246	-129	-140	-148	-162	-181	-201	-221	-129	-137	-143	-148	-156	-170	-189
70Hz	-127	-145	-164	-183	-203	-223	-243	-126	-136	-145	-159	-178	-198	-218	-126	-134	-140	-145	-153	-167	-186
100Hz	-124	-142	-160	-180	-200	-220	-240	-123	-133	-142	-156	-175	-195	-215	-123	-131	-137	-142	-150	-164	-183
200Hz	-118	-136	-154	-174	-194	-214	-234	-117	-127	-136	-150	-169	-189	-209	-116	-125	-131	-136	-144	-158	-177
300Hz	-115	-132	-151	-171	-191	-211	-231	-113	-124	-133	-147	-165	-185	-205	-113	-122	-127	-133	-141	-154	-173
500Hz	-110	-128	-147	-166	-186	-206	-226	-109	-119	-128	-142	-161	-181	-201	-109	-117	-123	-128	-136	-150	-169
700Hz	-107	-125	-144	-163	-183	-203	-223	-106	-116	-125	-139	-158	-178	-198	-106	-114	-120	-125	-133	-147	-166
1kHz	-104	-122	-140	-160	-180	-200	-220	-103	-113	-122	-136	-155	-175	-195	-103	-111	-117	-122	-130	-144	-163
2kHz	-98	-116	-134	-154	-174	-194	-214	-97	-107	-116	-130	-149	-169	-189	-96	-105	-111	-116	-124	-138	-157
3kHz	-95	-112	-131	-151	-171	-191	-211	-93	-104	-113	-127	-145	-165	-185	-93	-102	-107	-113	-121	-134	-153
5kHz	-90	-108	-127	-146	-166	-186	-206	-89	-99	-108	-122	-141	-161	-181	-89	-97	-103	-108	-116	-130	-149
7kHz	-87	-105	-124	-143	-163	-183	-203	-86	-96	-105	-119	-138	-158	-178	-86	-94	-100	-105	-113	-127	-146
10kHz	-84	-102	-120	-140	-160	-180	-200	-83	-93	-102	-116	-135	-155	-175	-83	-91	-97	-102	-110	-124	-143
20kHz	-78	-96	-114	-134	-154	-174	-194	-77	-87	-96	-110	-129	-149	-169	-76	-85	-91	-96	-104	-118	-137
30kHz	-75	-93	-111	-131	-151	-171	-191	-73	-84	-93	-107	-125	-145	-165	-73	-82	-87	-93	-101	-114	-133
50kHz	-70	-88	-107	-126	-146	-166	-186	-69	-79	-88	-102	-121	-141	-161	-69	-77	-83	-88	-96	-110	-130
70kHz	-67	-85	-104	-123	-143	-163	-183	-66	-76	-85	-99	-118	-138	-158	-66	-74	-80	-85	-93	-107	-127
100kHz	-64	-82	-100	-120	-140	-160	-180	-63	-73	-82	-96	-115	-135	-155	-63	-71	-77	-82	-90	-104	-124
200kHz	-58	-76	-94	-114	-134	-154	-174	-57	-67	-76	-90	-109	-129	-149	-56	-65	-71	-76	-84	-98	-118
300kHz	-55	-72	-91	-111	-131	-151	-171	-54	-64	-73	-87	-107	-125	-145	-53	-62	-67	-73	-81	-94	-114
500kHz	-50	-68	-87	-106	-126	-146	-166	-49	-57	-68	-82	-101	-121	-141	-49	-57	-63	-68	-76	-90	-110
700kHz	-47	-65	-84	-103	-123	-143	-163	-46	-56	-65	-79	-98	-118	-138	-46	-54	-60	-65	-73	-87	-107
1MHz	-44	-62	-80	-100	-120	-140	-160	-43	-53	-62	-76	-95	-115	-135	-43	-51	-57	-62	-70	-84	-103
2MHz	-38	-56	-74	-94	-114	-134	-154	-38	-47	-56	-70	-89	-109	-129	-37	-45	-51	-56	-64	-78	-97
3MHz	-35	-52	-71	-91	-111	-131	-151	-34	-44	-53	-67	-86	-105	-125	-34	-42	-48	-53	-61	-74	-93
5MHz	-30	-48	-67	-87	-107	-127	-147	-30	-40	-49	-62	-81	-101	-121	-29	-38	-43	-49	-56	-70	-89
7MHz	-28	-45	-64	-84	-104	-124	-144	-28	-37	-46	-60	-78	-98	-118	-25	-35	-38	-44	-51	-67	-86
10MHz	-26	-44	-61	-81	-101	-121	-141	-24	-34	-43	-57	-75	-95	-115	-24	-32	-38	-43	-51	-64	-84
20MHz	-21	-37	-56	-76	-96	-116	-136	-20	-30	-37	-51	-70	-89	-109	-19	-27	-33	-37	-45	-58	-78
30MHz	-19	-35	-50	-73	-93	-113	-133	-17	-28	-34	-48	-67	-86	-106	-17	-24	-30	-34	-41	-55	-74
50MHz	-16	-30	-48	-68	-88	-108	-128	-13	-23	-30	-42	-60	-80	-102	-14	-20	-25	-28	-38	-51	-70
70MHz	-15	-28	-46	-65	-80	-93		-12							-13	-18	-23		-35	-49	-67
100MHz	-14	-28	-46	-66	-86	-106	-126						-78	-98					-33		-46

Note that if the cables were carrying 30 MHz clocks with Schottky logic having $\tau_r = 3$ ns, corresponding to a second corner frequency of 100 MHz, the crosstalk would be –18 dB. Since the 1 m of the table slightly exceeds $\lambda/4$, no more length correction is necessary. The coupled signal would be 11 dBV – 18 dB = –7 dB or 450 mV. This exceeds the logic NIL and EMI would be a serious problem if the wire pairs were untwisted. Practically speaking, twisting would be used, but 30 Mb/s would normally not be sent over a 10 m hard-wire cable run between a computer CPU and its peripherals; it would be retained internal to the CPU cabinet.

8.3 Inductive Coupling

Inductive coupling predominates when the geometric mean of the culprit and victim circuit impedances is low relative to 377 Ω. The coupling also increases with frequency and the proximity of the culprit-victim pairs.

Figure 8.3 shows a similar cable network involving inductive coupling between culprit and victim line circuits. As with capacitive coupling, the objective is to determine how much of the available culprit **line voltage**, V_c, is coupled into the victim load for varying conditions. This ratio of victim-to-culprit voltages then becomes

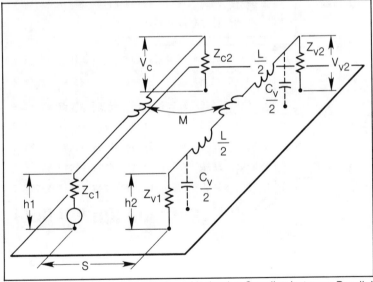

Figure 8.3—Circuit Representation of Inductive Coupling between Parallel Wires over a Ground Plane

the cable-to-cable coupling, CCC. Equation (8.1) also applies, and its negative is often called **crosstalk**.

Based on frequently used math models (see Appendix B), the V_v/V_c ratio for inductive coupling (see Fig. 8.3) is computed as follows.

At R_1 end (near end):

$$\frac{V_v}{V_c} = \frac{\omega M}{Z_{c2}} \left(\frac{\dfrac{R_1}{R_1\dfrac{C_V\omega}{2} + 1}}{j\omega L + \dfrac{R_1}{R_1\dfrac{C_v\omega+1}{2}} + \dfrac{R_2}{R_2\dfrac{C_v\omega+1}{2}}} \right)$$

(8.6a)

At R_2 end (far end):

$$\frac{V_v}{V_c} = \frac{\omega M}{Z_{c2}} \left(\frac{\dfrac{R_2}{R_2\dfrac{C_V\omega}{2} + 1}}{j\omega L + \dfrac{R_1}{R_1\dfrac{C_v\omega+1}{2}} + \dfrac{R_2}{R_2\dfrac{C_v\omega+1}{2}}} \right)$$

(8.6b)

If $R_1 = R_2 = R$ and $RC_v\omega \ll 1$:

$$\frac{V_v}{V_c} = \frac{\omega M}{Z_{c2}} \left(\frac{R}{j\omega L + 2R} \right) \qquad (8.6c)$$

where,

$\omega = 2\pi f \times$ frequency in hertz
Z_{c2} = culprit load impedance in ohms
M = mutual inductance of culprit-victim wires over the coupling length, in henries
C_v = victim wire capacitance to ground
L_v = self-inductance of victim wire in henries

R_1 = victim source resistance in ohms (should be replaced by corresponding impedance if inductive or capacitive)

R_2 = victim load resistance in ohms (should be replaced by corresponding impedance if inductive or capacitive)

Notice that V_c here is the culprit voltage at "point of delivery," i.e., near the culprit load. If the line is long, inductive and Z_c is low, it must be verified that the V_c value entered is correct and not the open source voltage.

Further discussion of the terms is presented in Appendix B. The inductance terms are functions of both the respective height and wire radius or AWG number used. The mutual inductance term, M, is also a function of the wire pair separation, s.

When Eq. (8.6) is substituted into Eq. (8.1), the CCC may be computed for several parameter values and conditions. Table 8.2 shows CCC for inductive coupling corresponding to two AWG No. 22 wire pairs having a common length of 1 m and impedance level of 100 Ω. The table parameters are identical to the previous Table 8.1 and are "h," the wire height above ground (remember the wire height corresponds to 2h for a pair rather than h for a single wire above a ground plane) and the wire pair separation distance, s. Both the h and s terms are in units of millimeters.

In examining Table 8.2, note that several similarities exist for inductive and capacitive coupling (cf. Table 8.1). For lower values of s, CCC increases with frequency at 20 dB/decade until the cable approaches a length of $\lambda/10$ (see 30 MHz region). Therefore, it once again saturates with increasing frequency.

CCC is more sensitive to changes in h for inductive coupling than for capacitive coupling. It is similarly affected by wire pair separation and falls off with increasing s at −40 dB/decade. Similarly, CCC is directly affected by both the cable length, l, and victim load impedance, Z_v. Unlike capacitive coupling, however, inductive coupling is also affected by culprit load impedance, Z_c. The reason is that it involves magnetic coupling which is determined by the current in the culprit circuit. Since the CCC term is a voltage ratio, in converting the culprit line voltage to current, the culprit load impedance must be involved.

For other than high frequencies, Table 8.2 may be adjusted to different length and impedance conditions:

$$CCC_{dB} = (CCC \text{ in Table 8.2})_{dB} + 20 \log \left(\frac{100\, l}{Z_c} \right) \leqslant 0 \text{ dB}$$

$$(8.7)$$

8.10

Table 8.2 - Magnetic Cable-to-Cable in dB (normalized to 1 meter length and AWG #22 wire)

Culprit = Load = 100 Ohms

Victim: $Z_{v1} = Z_{v2} = 100$ Ohms

h=1mm(.5-3)

FREQNCY	S=1	S=3	S=10	S=30	S=100	S=300	S=1k
10Hz	-147	-161	-179	-199	-219	-239	-259
20Hz	-141	-154	-173	-193	-213	-233	-253
30Hz	-137	-151	-170	-189	-209	-229	-249
50Hz	-133	-147	-165	-185	-205	-225	-245
70Hz	-130	-144	-162	-182	-202	-222	-242
100Hz	-127	-141	-159	-179	-199	-219	-239
200Hz	-121	-134	-153	-173	-193	-213	-233
300Hz	-117	-131	-150	-169	-189	-209	-229
500Hz	-113	-127	-145	-165	-185	-205	-225
700Hz	-110	-124	-142	-162	-182	-202	-222
1kHz	-107	-121	-139	-159	-179	-199	-219
2kHz	-101	-114	-133	-153	-173	-193	-213
3kHz	-97	-111	-130	-149	-169	-189	-209
5kHz	-93	-107	-125	-145	-165	-185	-205
7kHz	-90	-104	-122	-142	-162	-182	-202
10kHz	-87	-101	-119	-139	-159	-179	-199
20kHz	-81	-94	-113	-133	-153	-173	-193
30kHz	-77	-91	-110	-130	-149	-169	-189
50kHz	-73	-87	-105	-125	-145	-165	-185
70kHz	-70	-84	-102	-122	-142	-162	-182
100kHz	-67	-81	-99	-119	-139	-159	-179
200kHz	-61	-75	-93	-113	-133	-153	-173
300kHz	-57	-71	-90	-110	-130	-149	-169
500kHz	-53	-67	-85	-105	-125	-145	-165
700kHz	-50	-64	-82	-102	-122	-142	-162
1MHz	-47	-61	-80	-99	-119	-139	-159
2MHz	-41	-55	-75	-93	-113	-133	-153
3MHz	-38	-51	-72	-90	-110	-130	-150
5MHz	-33	-47	-69	-85	-105	-123	-143
7MHz	-30	-44	-67	-83	-102	-119	-139
10MHz	-28	-41	-60	-80	-100	-120	-140
20MHz	-23	-33	-52	-72	-95	-115	-135
30MHz	-20	-30	-49	-69	-89	-109	-132
50MHz	-15	-28	-47	-67	-87	-107	-127
70MHz							-125
100MHz	-13						

h=10mm(3-30)

FREQNCY	S=1	S=3	S=10	S=30	S=100	S=300	S=1k
10Hz	-136	-140	-147	-161	-179	-199	-219
20Hz	-129	-134	-141	-154	-173	-193	-213
30Hz	-126	-130	-137	-147	-170	-189	-209
50Hz	-122	-126	-133	-147	-165	-185	-205
70Hz	-119	-123	-130	-144	-162	-182	-202
100Hz	-116	-120	-127	-141	-159	-179	-199
200Hz	-109	-114	-121	-134	-153	-173	-193
300Hz	-105	-110	-117	-131	-150	-169	-189
500Hz	-102	-106	-113	-127	-145	-165	-185
700Hz	-99	-103	-110	-124	-142	-162	-182
1kHz	-96	-100	-107	-121	-139	-159	-179
2kHz	-89	-94	-101	-114	-133	-153	-173
3kHz	-86	-90	-97	-111	-130	-149	-169
5kHz	-82	-86	-93	-107	-125	-145	-165
7kHz	-79	-83	-90	-104	-122	-142	-162
10kHz	-76	-80	-87	-101	-119	-139	-159
20kHz	-69	-74	-81	-94	-113	-133	-153
30kHz	-66	-70	-77	-91	-110	-130	-149
50kHz	-62	-66	-73	-87	-105	-125	-145
70kHz	-59	-63	-70	-84	-102	-122	-142
100kHz	-56	-60	-67	-81	-99	-119	-139
200kHz	-50	-54	-61	-75	-93	-113	-133
300kHz	-46	-50	-57	-71	-90	-110	-130
500kHz	-42	-46	-53	-67	-85	-105	-125
700kHz	-39	-43	-50	-64	-84	-102	-122
1MHz	-36	-40	-47	-61	-81	-99	-119
2MHz	-30	-34	-41	-55	-75	-93	-113
3MHz	-27	-31	-38	-51	-74	-90	-110
5MHz	-23	-27	-34	-47	-70	-85	-105
7MHz	-20	-24	-31	-44	-66	-84	-102
10MHz	-17	-18	-29	-43	-61	-77	-99
20MHz	-13	-15	-25	-38	-57	-73	-94
30MHz	-11	-12	-24	-36	-53	-71	-92
50MHz	-9	-9	-19	-33	-51	-71	-91
70MHz	-8		-18	-31	-50	-70	-90
100MHz	-7	-11		-32	-50	-70	-90

h=10mm(30-300)

FREQNCY	S=1	S=3	S=10	S=30	S=100	S=300	S=1k
10Hz	-131	-133	-136	-140	-147	-161	-179
20Hz	-125	-127	-129	-134	-141	-154	-173
30Hz	-121	-123	-126	-130	-137	-151	-170
50Hz	-117	-119	-122	-126	-133	-147	-165
70Hz	-114	-116	-119	-123	-130	-144	-162
100Hz	-111	-113	-116	-120	-127	-141	-159
200Hz	-105	-107	-109	-114	-121	-134	-153
300Hz	-101	-103	-105	-110	-117	-131	-150
500Hz	-97	-99	-102	-106	-113	-127	-145
700Hz	-94	-96	-99	-103	-110	-124	-142
1kHz	-91	-93	-96	-100	-107	-121	-139
2kHz	-85	-87	-89	-94	-101	-114	-133
3kHz	-81	-83	-86	-90	-97	-111	-130
5kHz	-77	-79	-82	-86	-93	-107	-125
7kHz	-74	-76	-79	-83	-90	-104	-122
10kHz	-71	-73	-76	-80	-87	-101	-119
20kHz	-65	-67	-69	-74	-81	-94	-113
30kHz	-61	-63	-66	-70	-77	-91	-111
50kHz	-57	-59	-62	-66	-73	-87	-107
70kHz	-54	-56	-59	-63	-70	-86	-104
100kHz	-51	-53	-56	-60	-67	-87	-101
200kHz	-45	-47	-50	-54	-61	-81	-101
300kHz	-41	-43	-46	-50	-57	-77	-97
500kHz	-37	-39	-42	-46	-53	-67	-87
700kHz	-34	-36	-39	-43	-50	-64	-83
1MHz	-31	-33	-36	-40	-47	-61	-80
2MHz	-22	-27	-34	-34	-42	-55	-74
3MHz	-18	-24	-31	-31	-39	-52	-71
5MHz	-16	-20	-23	-25	-30	-48	-67
7MHz	-7	-15	-18	-22	-26	-43	-64
10MHz	-14	-16	-18	-23	-30	-61	-62
20MHz	-10	-12	-15	-19	-26	-40	-58
30MHz	-9	-10	-13	-17	-24	-38	-57
50MHz	-4	-8	-10	-15	-22	-35	-55
70MHz	-5	-7	-10	-14	-21	-35	-54
100MHz	-5		-10		-21	-35	-53

8.11

The same remarks apply for wire diameter and length correction as those made for capacitive coupling.

Illustrative Example 8.2

Use the same Example as 8.1 to compute the cable-to-cable crosstalk due to inductive coupling in a harness between two wire pairs having an average separation distance of 3 mm and a 10 m run in a cable tray. The clock rise time is 500 ns ($1/\pi\tau_r$ = 637 kHz), and both cables are operating at a 100 Ω impedance level.

For h = 10 mm and s = 3 mm, Table 8.2 indicates that $(CCC)_{dB}$ = −44 dB at 637 kHz. Applying Eq. (8.7) to correct for a 10 m length, the overall CCC is −44 dB + 20 dB = −24 dB. Since the circuit impedances are less than 377 Ω, these results show that the magnetic coupling (−24 dB) is somewhat greater than capacitive coupling (−37 dB in Example 8.1).

Illustrative Example 8.3

Calculate the crosstalk between a 60 Hz, 115 Vac power bus, carrying 100 A and a 600 Ω telephone cable. The cable pair separation is 10 cm in adjacent PVC conduits buried over a length of 200 m.

Although the 100 A wiring is obviously not AWG No. 22, the table has been used because the ratio separation/diameter is sufficiently large to neglect the influence of wire curvature.

Table 8.2 indicates that for h = 3 to 30 mm, CCC is about −163 dB. This must now be adjusted for other conditions. The culprit 100 A load at 115 V corresponds to a Z_c of 1.15 Ω. Applying the new conditions to Eq. (8.7) yields:

$$(CCC)_{dB} = -163 \text{ dB} + 20 \log [(100/1.15 \text{ } \Omega) \times 200 \text{ m}]$$

$$= -163 \text{ dB} + 85 \text{ dB} = -78 \text{ dB}$$

The 115 Vac power line is 41 dBV. The coupled differential-mode voltage is:

$$V_v = 41 \text{ dBV} - 78 \text{ dB} = -37 \text{ dBV} = 15 \text{ mV}$$

Thus, there will appear a 15 mV hum voltage on the telephone line. During a hot, summer day when a heavy air conditioning load exists, the power mains current may rise to 200 A, and the coupled hum voltage will also rise. No adjustment has been made in the above example for further reduction due to twists in the telephone cable.

8.4 Composite Cable Coupling

The two preceding sections have treated capacitive and magnetic crosstalk separately as though the other coupling did not exist. In general situations, however, both couplings **do** exist. Since both capacitive and inductive coupling exist simultaneously, the composite takes into account the effect of each contributor, unless one of the two can be neglected. Therefore, it is necessary to solve for each of the two couplings separately, using Eqs. (8.4) and (8.7), then look for their combined effect.

Fig. 8.4 shows that capacitive effect appears **across** the victim line, while magnetic induction appears longitudinally. The direction of the currents is of importance, and it is necessary to know if the coupling is calculated for the victim end which is near the culprit source (near end) or the victim end which is at the opposite side (far end). For the near end, inductive coupling is added to the

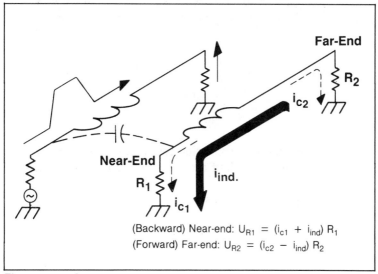

(Backward) Near-end: $U_{R1} = (i_{c1} + i_{ind}) R_1$

(Forward) Far-end: $U_{R2} = (i_{c2} - i_{ind}) R_2$

Figure 8.4—Combined Effect of Inductive and Capacitive Crosstalk

8.13

capacitive. For the far end, inductive coupling is subtracted from the capacitive one. The resulting coupling is then as follows.

Near end:

$$V_{victim} = V_{culprit} \times [\text{capacitive crosstalk coefficient} + \text{inductive crosstalk coefficient}]$$

Far end:

$$V_{victim} = V_{culprit} \times [\text{capacitive crosstalk coefficient} - \text{inductive crosstalk coefficient}]$$

Therefore:

$$\frac{V_{v1}}{V_c} \text{ (near end)} = C_{cv}\omega Z' \left(\frac{j\omega\dfrac{L}{2}+Z''}{j\omega L+Z'+Z''} \right) + \frac{M\omega}{Z_{c2}} \left(\frac{Z'}{j\omega L+Z'+Z''} \right)$$

and

$$\frac{V_{v2}}{V_c} \left(\text{far end, i.e. interchange of } Z' \text{ and } Z'' \right)$$

$$= C_{cv}\omega Z'' \left(\frac{j\omega\dfrac{L}{2} + Z'}{j\omega L+Z'+Z''} \right) - \frac{M\omega}{Z_{c2}} \left(\frac{Z''}{j\omega L+Z'+Z''} \right)$$

$$\text{with } = Z' = \frac{R_1}{R_1 \dfrac{C_v}{2}\,\omega+1} \text{ and } Z'' = \frac{R_2}{R_2 \dfrac{C_v}{2}\,\omega +1}$$

= combination of termination resistance (or eventually impedance) with half the wise self-capacitance to ground

The following simplifications exist:

$$\text{if } R_1 = R_2 = R \text{ and } R\,\frac{C_v\omega}{2} \ll 1$$

$$\frac{V_{v1}}{V_c} \text{ (near end)} = C_{cv}\omega R \left(\frac{j\omega\frac{L}{2}+R}{j\omega L+2R} \right) + \frac{M\omega}{Z_{C2}} \left(\frac{R}{j\omega L+2R} \right)$$

$$\frac{V_{v2}}{V_c} \text{ (far end)} = C_{cv}\omega R \left(\frac{j\omega\frac{L}{2}+R}{j\omega L+2R} \right) - \frac{M\omega}{Z_{C2}} \left(\frac{R}{j\omega L+2R} \right)$$

If, in addition, $\frac{L\omega}{2} \ll R$:

Near End, $\dfrac{V_{v1}}{V_c} = C_{cv}\,\omega\,\dfrac{R}{2} + \dfrac{M\omega}{2Z_{c2}}$

Far End, $\dfrac{V_{v2}}{V_c} = C_{cv}\,\omega\,\dfrac{R}{2} - \dfrac{M\omega}{2Z_{c2}}$

An immediate result is that, if the victim impedances are about the same at both ends, and if the inductive and capacitive couplings differ by less than 20 dB, there will be a noticeable difference between the voltages induced at each end of the victim line. Note that to combine CCC_{ind} and CCC_{cap}, one must **use the actual voltages, and not add or subtract decibels!**

If the two coupling mechanisms differ by more than 20 dB, only the largest of the two will be used, and the resulting error will be less than 5 percent. One can neglect the smallest coupling when it is only 10 dB less than the largest one, in which case the error would be about 30 percent or 2 dB (see Section 3.2, Fig. 3.5, about the error when neglecting one coupling path).

Should the reader need more details about the near end (sometimes termed **backward crosstalk**) and far end (**forward crosstalk**) with digital pulses, Appendix B, Section B.6, provides a complete treatment of this case.

Illustrative Example 8.4

Two logic signal transmission lines have a 40 cm common run between different points on the backplane wiring on a logic card assembly. Both lines use a wire pair and are driven and terminated in 200 Ω. Compute the crosstalk if both lines employ Schottky TTL logic having a 3 V swing with a signal edge rise time of 3 ns.

Using Eq. (8.5), the frequency to use in Tables 8.1 and 8.2 is $1/\pi\tau_r = 1/\pi \times 3 \times 10^{-9} = 106$ MHz. The wire pair separation is not given but will be assumed to be laced together resulting in an s $\approx$ 1 mm. Each pair h value will approximate its insulation thickness (by image method) or h $\approx$ 0.3. All data are summarized on the cable crosstalk form shown in Fig. 8.5. From these conditions, Tables 8.1 and 8.2 yield:

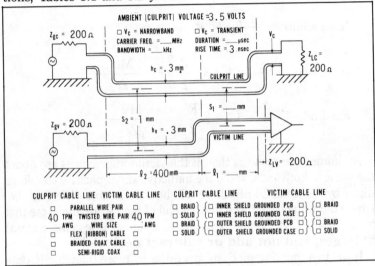

Figure 8.5—Problem Input Data for Example 8.4

Table/Eq.	Coupling	CCC Value	Correction	Total
8.1/8.4	Capacitive	–14 dB	–2 dB	–16 dB
8.2/8.7	Inductive	–13 dB	–14 dB	–27 dB

Capacitive coupling dominates at –16 dB. This corresponds to untwisted wire, parallel run conditions. Thus, crosstalk-induced voltage, V_v is:

$$V_{vdBV} = 20 \log (3 \text{ V}) - 16 \text{ dB}$$

$$= 10 \text{ dBv} - 16 \text{ dB} = -6 \text{ dBV} = 500 \text{ mV}$$

However, for a more accurate prediction, the inductive contributor should be taken into account. The victim line being terminated by the same impedance at both ends, the inductive contribution is:

$$10 \text{ dBV} - 27 \text{ dB} = 17 \text{ dBV} = 150 \text{ mV}$$

Therefore, the near-end crosstalk will be $500 + 150 = 650$ mV. The far-end crosstalk will be $500 - 150 = 350$ mV.

Since V_v is greater than Schottky TTL noise immunity level, EMI may exist.

Let us consider now that all wire pairs are twisted. If they were twisted in the same manner, e.g., clockwise, then the twists would have little to no effect since the mean distance between corresponding wires remains essentially unchanged. To combat this problem in flat ribbon cable, adjacent pairs should be twisted in an opposite direction (e.g., even pairs clockwise and odd pairs counterclockwise).

For $n\lambda = 40 \times 3$ m $= 120$, and $nl = 40 \times 0.4$ m $= 16$, Fig. 7.7 shows the reduction of crosstalk due to twisting is about 25 dB. Since Fig. 7.7 applies for far-field conditions, and since the problem involves the near field, it is not expected that a 50 dB reduction will result when both pairs are twisted. Thus, a worst case of 25 dB improvement is assumed. V_v now becomes:

$$V_{vdBV} = 20 \log (3 \text{ V}) - 16 \text{ dB (crosstalk)} - 25 \text{ dB (twisting)}$$

$$= -31 \text{ dBV} \approx 30 \text{ mV}$$

Since 30 mV is well below the noise immunity of Schottky TTL, no EMI problem exists.

Illustrative Example 8.5

As an extension of the preceding example, suppose that similar twisted wire pairs were used to interconnect the backplanes of two different logic card assemblies located 50 cm apart on the vertical side of a 19 in. cabinet rack housing (see Fig. 8.6). Since the interconnection lines are postulated to be routed along their horizontals on each backplane up to the vertical rails, then run down the rails, a total cable path length of 100 cm is stipulated between assemblies.

Next, assume that the 19 in. cabinet also contains dc motors to activate controlled mechanisms in a mechanical transport process.

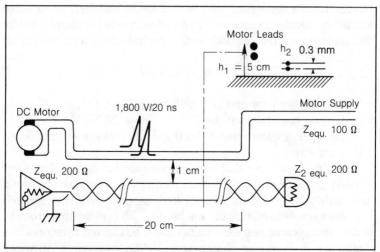

Figure 8.6—Configuration of Crosstalk Example 8.5

Common-mode transients due to brush-commutator sparking on the motor supply lines can achieve amplitudes of 15 times line voltage, or 1,800 V, with rise times as short as 20 ns. Should a region exist in which the motor supply lines come within 1 cm of the logic backplane interconnect loads, but over a common length of only 20 cm, determine if there might exist an EMI problem.

The applicable frequency of Tables 8.1 and 8.2 is $1/\pi\tau_r = 1/\pi$ $\times (20 \times 10^{-9}) = 16$ MHz. The h_1 dimension for the motor wiring is estimated to average 5 cm above the cabinet rails over its length. Since h_2 for the twisted pairs was stated to be 0.3 mm in the preceding example, $h = \sqrt{h_1 h_2}$ or 3.9 nm. Thus, for h = 3 to 30 mm and S = 10 mm (see above) in the tables, there results:

Table/Eq.	Coupling Type	CCC Value	Correction	Total
8.1/8.4	Capacitive	−40 dB	−8 dB	−48 dB
8.2/8.7	Inductive	−27 dB	−14 dB*	−41 dB

Here, inductive coupling is the larger. The coupled differential voltage is 41 dB down from 1,800 V or 65 dBV − 41 dB = 24 dBV

---

*The culprit motor common-mode impedance, at this frequency, is assumed = 100 Ω.

8.18

= 15 V. The 40 twists per meter (TPM) configuration of the backplane leads corresponds to 8 twists over a 20 cm length, the region for which the dc motor supply leads come in proximity. From Fig. 7.7, for nl = 8 and $n\lambda$ = (40 × 18.8) = 750, the decoupling due to twisting is 22 dB. Therefore, the corrected CCC is:

$$24 \text{ dBV} - 22 \text{ dB} = 2 \text{ dBV} = 1.2 \text{ V}$$

This is greater than the 300 mV noise immunity level of Schottky TTL and EMI will likely result. For a more accurate prediction, compute the capacitive contribution:

$$65 \text{ dBV} - 48 \text{ dB} - 22 \text{ dB (twist)} = 5 \text{ dBV or } 0.55 \text{ V}$$

So, near-end noise (on the victim side toward the motor) = 1.2 + 0.55 = 1.75 V. Far-end noise = 1.2 − 0.55 = 0.65 V.

The EMC solution is simple: Reroute the dc motor supply leads away from the backplane wire interconnect cables. Twisting the motor leads will not help since common-mode noise exists in both leads. The EMI reduction goal of 1.2/0.3 = 4 times (or 12 dB) is met. Tables show that increasing the spacing 5 to 30 mm will achieve the objective.

8.5 Bibliography

Cudd, Sali, Benson and Sitch, "Coupling Between Coaxial Cables," *Record of the 1982 International Conference on EMC*, University of Surrey (IERE Pub. no. 56), England.

Mohr, R., "Interference Coupling, Attack it Early," *EDN*, July 1969.

Paul, C.R., "Prediction of Crosstalk in Ribbon Cables," *IEEE EMC Symposium Record* (New York: IEEE), Session 1B, Atlanta, GA, June 20-22, 1978.

Paul, C.R. and Feather, A.E., "Computation of the Transmission Line Inductance and Capacitance Matrices From the Generalized Capacitance Matrix (with Editorial Summary)," *IEEE Transactions on EMC*, Vol. EMC-18, no. 4, November, 1976.

Paul, C.R. and McKnight, J.W., "Prediction of Crosstalk Involving Twisted Pairs of Wires," *IEEE EMC Symposium Record* (New

York: IEEE), Session 1B, Atlanta, GA, June 20-22, 1978.

Rawat, V. and Beal, J.C., "Leaky Cables Treated as Open Waveguides," *Proceedings International Colloquim Leaky-Feeder Communications*, Guildford, Surrey, United Kingdom, April 1974.

Swarts, R.L., "Crosstalk on Cables: A Communications Theoretic Approach," *IEEE Transactions on EMC*, Vol. EMC-14, no. 2, May, 1972.

Chapter 9

Power Mains and Power Supply Coupling

This chapter describes the fifth principal coupling path, which involves coupling from unregulated power mains and dc regulated power supplies, as illustrated in Fig. 9.1. While this is the most severe path of conducted failures, there exist many appropriate EMI hardening techniques.

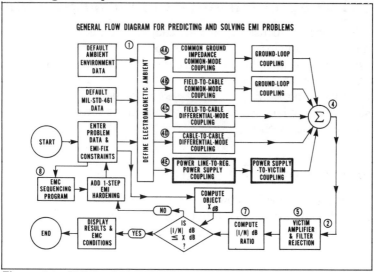

Figure 9.1—EMI Prediction and Analysis Flow Diagram Showing Power Mains and Power Supply Coupling

9.1

The potential EMI may be harmonics of 50, 60 or 400 Hz power, RF communication-electronics pickup signals or broadband energy. Examples of the latter include differential-mode transients due to other users on the line or common-mode transients due to the pickup of radiated signals.

The coupling onto the power mains may be the reverse of the above situation, i.e., coupling from the equipment or system back into the power mains. This emission aspect is covered in Chapter 10.

The first box of the fifth coupling path in Fig. 9.1 deals with the EMI conversion from power mains input to the regulated power supply. It involves any EMI suppressing device such as filters, transformers, Faraday-shielded isolation transformers, motor generators, EMI-hardened MG sets and uninterruptible power supplies (UPSs).

The second box of the fifth coupling path in Fig. 9.1, captioned "Power-Supply-to-Victim Coupling," involves the transmission of surviving EMI through the voltage regulated power supply (linear, switched mode, etc.). Ultimately, the residual voltage will appear at the victim circuit. (Note that the victim may have some intrinsic rejection to power supply noise, which could be accounted for in Box 5.)

9.1 Coupling to and from Power Systems

This section focuses upon EMI coupling between power mains and power supplies or, generally, the power system. Such coupling causes reciprocating interferences between the mains and the equipment power system. A more general discussion of EMI ambients existing on power lines is addressed in Section 2.4.2. The emissions from the power supply regulator itself are covered in Chapter 10, "Emission Control."

9.1.1 Coupling Model

The coupling model shown in Fig. 9.2 depicts common mode (CM) and differential-mode (DM) impedances of both the mains source and the power system and illustrates an associated grounding con-

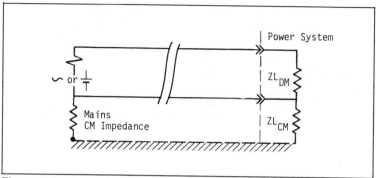

Figure 9.2—General Coupling Model

figuration. Knowledge of actual grounding schemes and associated impedances is important for:

1. Understanding the predominant coupling paths **from the mains to the equipment power system** (susceptibility) or **from the power system to the mains** (emission)
2. Computing CM to DM conversion ratios
3. Selecting adequate filters (susceptibility **and** emissions)
4. Determining system installation requirements

The principal power mains coupling models are depicted in Fig. 9.3, where Z_s = mains source impedance and Z_L = power systems input impedance.

The first question to be asked about the power grounding scheme, source and load impedance is: What is the value of mains impedance? First it must be understood that from dc to a few kilohertz, DM and CM impedances of power mains are roughly equivalent to their dc resistance.* This is sometimes expressed as **short circuit ampacity,** and it is almost always less than 1 Ω. If unknown, default values can be used from dc to a few kilohertz. The following values apply:

1. Large building, high-voltage service entrance, 3 to 10 mΩ
2. Large commercial/industrial room panel (100 kVA), 20 mΩ
3. Branch circuit power outlet, 20 mΩ to 1 Ω

---

*Impedant neutral: In a few countries, neutral is sometimes grounded at the utility power transformer via a 1 kΩ impedance. In this case, dc or low-frequency CM impedance of the source is already high.

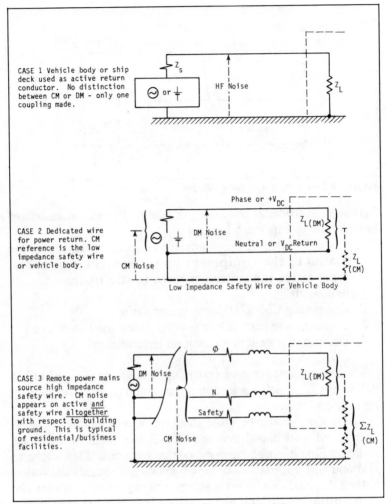

Figure 9.3—Principal Power Mains Coupling Models

These values represent the total mains impedance, i.e., source plus one phase and return wire at the point of observation.

The value of power mains DM or CM impedances above low frequencies depends upon a myriad of variables, some of which are:

1. Frequency of concern
2. Length of the mains distribution network

3. Nature and routing of the mains net (wire size, overhead or buried, type of conduit, etc.)
4. On-line reactive devices (power factor capacitor banks, anti-harmonic chokes, etc.)
5. Fluctuating customer load demands at a given location and time of day

A conservative approach has been considered by several standards organizations (CISPR, CBEMA and FCC). First, one collects appropriate data (referring to Figs. 9.4 and 9.5, Case 2 of Fig. 9.3 applies). Then:

1. For **emission standards**, where the critical aspect is the voltage appearing on ac mains due to equipment emissions, the upper 10 percent of mains impedance statistics is retained. Therefore, the highest risk of interference is covered up to 90 percent of the population. (This means that, even though standard emission tests use a 50 Ω test impedance, the limits have been calculated to protect public ac mains presenting up to 300 Ω impedance above 1 MHz.)
2. For **susceptibility**, the lower 10 percent should be considered to ensure that the worst configuration of susceptibility (i.e., an EMI source with low impedance) is covered in up to 90 percent of product installations.

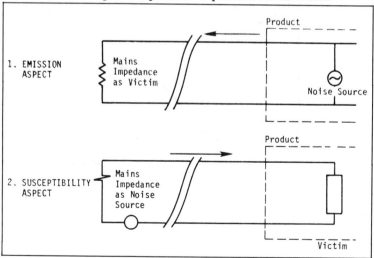

Figure 9.4—General Concept of Emission/Susceptibility in Power Coupling

Another important question which arises is: What is the value of an equipment input impedance? The answer depends upon the front-end circuit of the power system. In the case of input power supply transformers (and assuming that no input filters are involved), the DM input impedance at low frequencies corresponds to the ratio of input voltage over rated input current (see Fig. 9.6).

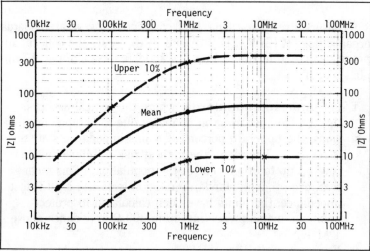

Figure 9.5—Absolute Mains Impedances (CM or DM) of Aggregate U.S. and European Power Networks (min./max./mean)

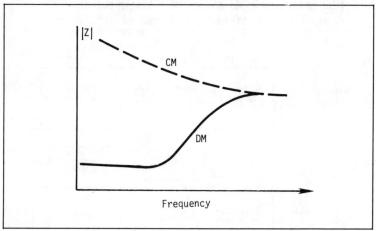

Figure 9.6—Aspect of Power System Input Impedance

9.6

As frequency increases, DM impedance increases linearly due to wiring and transformer input inductance. The CM input impedance is usually high at low frequencies since the power input is floating over the chassis. It decreases linearly when frequency increases, mainly because of capacitance (wiring and PCB to chassis, and chassis to ground).

The best approach for achieving accurate prediction is to measure the actual CM and DM input impedance. If this is impractical, default values as depicted in Fig. 9.7 can be used.

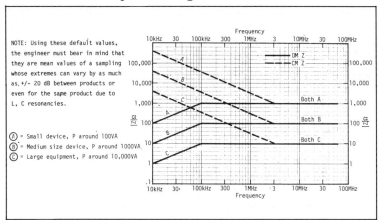

Figure 9.7—Suggested (default) Values of Magnitude of Z_{CM} and Z_{DM} for Current Products

Illustrative Example 9.1

If a line filter with 30 dB attenuation at 3 MHz (CM and DM) is selected for a small terminal consuming 300 Vac, what will be the selection criteria for optimizing the filter?

If **susceptibility** is the main concern:

The filter should be selected for a line impedance of 10 Ω (worst case of Fig. 9.5) and a load impedance of 300 Ω (CM and DM), i.e., between curves A and B of Fig. 9.7.

If **emission** is the main concern:

The filter should be selected for a mains impedance of 50 Ω or 150 Ω* and a machine (source) impedance of 300 Ω.

---

*This depends upon the test impedance (line impedance stabilization network) which will be used for the emission testing.

9.1.2 Coupling of Existing Power Mains Noise and Transients into the Power System

The noise source couples to the power system before reaching the victim circuit as shown in the general flow diagram in Fig. 9.1. The power mains ambient presented in Section 2.4.2 can now be addressed in more detail. If no specification or ambient survey is available, the default time-domain envelope shown in Fig. 9.8a can be used for utility ac mains. If time domain is transposed to frequency domain, a default envelope of spectral amplitudes is as depicted in Fig. 9.8b. The noise of type (1) or (2) corresponds to isolated and infrequently occurring impulses, while CW noise is permanent. In addition to these incidental pulses, there exists a continuous random background noise (6) which must be considered as V/√ MHz when making bandwidth correction. In this case, the

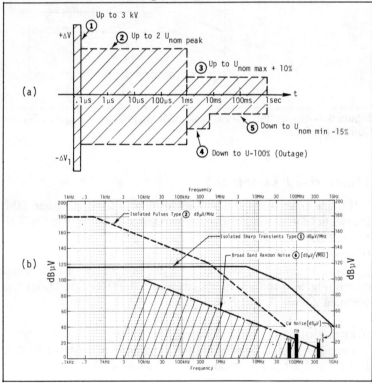

Figure 9.8—Time and Frequency Domain Aspects of Power Line Ambient (continued next page)

9.8

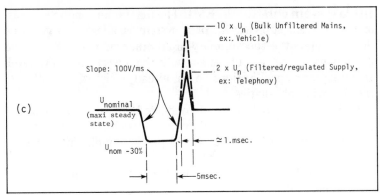

Figure 9.8—(continued)

correction for a victim receiver bandwidth of $B_w \neq 1$ MHz, is:

$$V_{dB} + 10 \log(BW \text{ in MHz}) \qquad (9.1)$$

If the power mains are dc (12 or 24/28 V for vehicles or aeronautics, or 48/60 V for telephony), the existing specifications should be used as power transient data. If not available, the default values of Fig. 9.8c should be used, which are typical for battery-powered mains. To prevent DM and CM noise from affecting the power system, voltage regulators, transient protectors, filters, etc. should be employed, as discussed in Section 9.3.

9.1.3 Coupling from Power System to Power Mains

This aspect of electromagnetic coupling is of special interest. Some specific emission math models are also described in Chapter 10. In contrast to the discussions in previous chapters, the coupling path considered here is in reverse, i.e., equipment noise is reflected on its power input. This results in interference to the external environment which is the concern here. Therefore, the victim has already been identified in terms of:

Intersystem conducted EMI (emission to the external environment): There are several standards ruling on the maximum level allowed on power terminals (CISPR, FCC, MIL-STD-461, etc.).

Intrasystem conducted EMI: The maximum conducted emission that each subpart, X_i, of a system is allowed to generate depends upon the susceptibility of all other subparts, $X_{j \neq i}$, and particularly upon the subsystem with the lowest immunity level. If intrasystem specifications do not already exist, select either of the following alternatives:

1. Specify the same level of conducted emission for each subassembly as that of the whole system. This would result in overdesign but would practically eliminate the need for a main input filter.
2. Establish an intrasystem specification which all subassemblies must meet.

Illustrative Example 9.2

An electric transportation system contains several subparts, and the power input susceptibility for each part is known. They are:

1. An on-board minicomputer (immunity level, N = 0.5 V)
2. Two VHF receivers (N = 0.01 V)
3. Speed sensor amplifiers (N = 10 mV)
4. Voice intercom (N = 30 mV)

By injecting noise amplitudes at several frequencies on the power input, susceptibility patterns as illustrated in Fig. 9.9a were found (see also Section 4.2 regarding in-band/out-of-band victim behavior).

Taking the most susceptible item in each frequency band, the intrasystem EMI budget for power supply conducted emission appears on curve K_1 of Fig. 9.9b. This is a narrowband definition. Since the victims have given bandwidths, if there is a risk that the sources are broadband, a second limit, K_2, can be plotted which corresponds to:

$$K_2 \text{ dB}\mu\text{V/kHz} = \frac{K_1}{\text{bandwidth of the most susceptible item}}$$

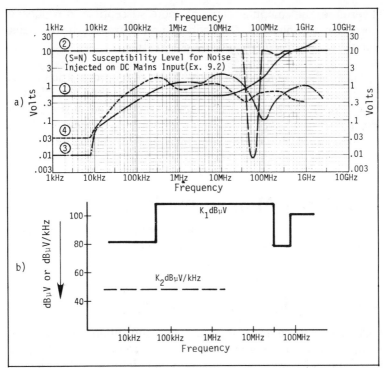

Figure 9.9—Intra-System Power Conducted Noise Allowance of Example 9.2

Illustrative Example 9.3

In the preceding Example 9.2, the computer has a bandwidth of 3 MHz while the voice intercom has a 5 kHz bandwidth. Which one will be the most susceptible below 30 MHz?

For the computer:

N/bandwidth = 0.5 V/(3 × 10⁶) = –136 dBV/Hz = 44 dBµV/kHz

For the intercom:

N/Bandwidth = 0.03 V/(5 × 10³) = –104 dBV/Hz = 76 dBµV/kHz

Therefore, the computer could be more susceptible to wideband noise than the intercom. A broadband limit to protect the computer should be 44 dBμV/kHz (or 104 dBμV/MHz).

This budget seems conservative because no propagation losses have been accounted for between the source and the potential victim through the power wiring. However, power noise is only one among several EMI contributors in each frequency band. To evaluate the risk of several simultaneous EMI contributors in the same frequency, see Section 3.2.

9.2 Power Mains Coupling

Without precautions, the coupling from power mains to system input can be 1/1 since the mains noise nearly always appears as a voltage source (low impedance).

9.2.1 Regulation of Power Mains

Although there are many variations and differences in power mains regulations according to countries or companies involved, the regulation of power mains generally falls into two categories:

A: Steady Limits   U max = U nominal + 10 percent
  (quasi-permanent)   U min = U nominal − 15 percent

B: Incidental Voltage   U min − 10 percent
  Decrease (a few cycles)   ≈ U nom − 25 percent

Category A is due to the fact that power companies try to distribute the nominal voltage to the average distant customers. As a result, customers who are close to the power station have a slight overvoltage at no-load hours, and customers at the far end of the line have a slight undervoltage at full-load hours. In addition, category B occurs during power-up of heavy loads, with a significant inrush current. For instance, power transformers (because of magnetizing currents) and high starting torque motors, exhibit surge currents of 5 to 10 times $I_{nominal}$, which results in larger than normal IR drop in low voltage distribution during a few cycles (up to 0.3 s).

9.3 Reduction of Power Mains Coupling

Once power mains transients are identified, reduction techniques can be applied. One can use passive devices (filters, surge suppressors, isolation transformers) or active devices (line regulators, MG sets, UPSs).

This section addresses Box 4E (Fig. 9.1) of the power line coupling, which is the ratio of:

$$\frac{\text{power mains disturbance amplitude}}{\text{resulting power supply input transient amplitude}}$$

Basically, it is assumed that, without any reduction practice, this coupling would be 1/1, i.e., 0 dB for the worst case.

9.3.1 AC Voltage Regulators

Primarily, ac voltage regulators are designed to suppress long-term ac mains variations, from a few cycles to a quasi-permanent overvoltage or undervoltage (Fig. 9.10). Regulators typically maintain their output voltage to within 1 to 5 percent for an ac input change of +10/−20 percent, and with a response time on the order of one cycle. Therefore, due to this response time, fast voltage changes cannot be regulated in this manner. What simply happens is that, above about 10 times their normal operating frequency, the magnetic transformation ratio vanishes and the differential-mode (line-to-line) noise on the primary is not transferred to the secondary. Also, their rejection to common-mode noise is dependent on the primary-to-secondary parasitic capacitance. Some manufacturers are sensitive to this situation and provide a primary-to-secondary shield to combine the effects of an ac regulator and an isolation transformer (see Section 9.3.4). Therefore, the total isolation of the device is represented by curve A shown in Fig. 9.11.

The CM (or DM) attenuation will be defined as:

$$20 \log \frac{\text{CM (DM) noise on secondary* before insertion of regulator}}{\text{CM (DM) noise on secondary after insertion of regulator}}$$

---

*Sometimes CM attenuation is expressed as the ratio of DM noise appearing on secondary to CM noise. This parameter, which could be called **CM transfer**, must not be confused with the actual CM attenuation.

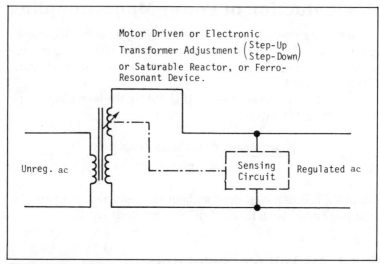

Motor Driven or Electronic
Transformer Adjustment $\left(\begin{array}{l}\text{Step-Up}\\ \text{Step-Down}\end{array}\right)$
or Saturable Reactor, or Ferro-
Resonant Device.

Unreg. ac

Sensing Circuit

Regulated ac

Figure 9.10—AC Regulator Basic Scheme

The shaded area in Fig. 9.11 corresponds to a dV/dt which is too fast to be regulated but which is slow enough to be processed by the usual primary-to-secondary magnetic coupling. For current types of 120 V/60 Hz or 220 V/50 Hz ac regulators, having 3 pF of primary-to-secondary capacitance and 1,000 MΩ of isolation, Table 9.1 can be used to determine default values:

Table 9.1—Default Values for Rejection of Current Types (not Ultra-isolation) AC Regulators

	0 to 60 Hz	60 to 1 kHz	10 kHz	1 MHz	10 MHz	100 MHz
DM Atten.	20 dB	0 dB	40 dB	60 dB	60 dB	20 dB
CM Atten.	180 dB	180 dB	170 dB	90 dB	50 dB	10 dB

The output impedance of an ac regulator is higher than the mains impedance. Typically this output, which becomes the **source impedance for the power system** connected thereto, varies from Z_{out} = full load impedance (i.e., U_{sec}/I_{max} to 10 percent of full load impedance. The importance of this situation is described in Section 9.1.1.

9.14

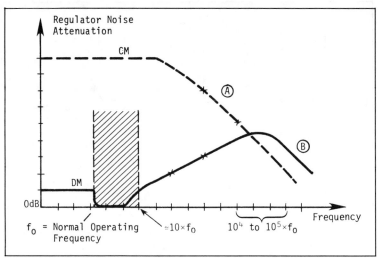

Figure 9.11—CM and DM Attenuation in an AC Mains Regulator

9.3.2 Surge Suppressors

There are two contemporary types of surge suppressors, or transient protection devices. They are the **semiconductor/variable resistor** and the **gas discharge** (spark or crowbar) devices.

The first type behaves electrically like a Zener diode, with an I, (V) curve as shown in Fig. 9.12.

The α term on the curve corresponds to the rise of V/I characteristic beyond breakdown, i.e.:

$$I = KV^{\alpha} \text{ or } \alpha = \frac{\log(I_2/I_1)}{\log(V_1/V_2)} \tag{9.2}$$

The power handling capability is limited by the joule dissipation, i.e., $V_{clamp} \times I_{pulse}$, because a clamp voltage is always present during the pulse current flow. Their response time is very fast, usual-

9.15

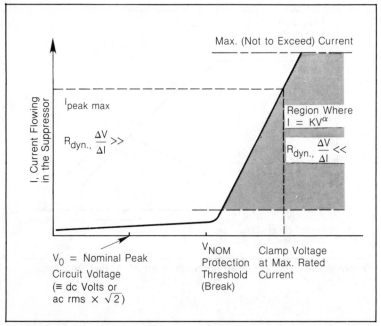

Figure 9.12—Basic Operation of Semiconductor/Variable Resistor Type of Suppressor

ly <100 ns. Therefore, the selection must be done according to the following steps:

1. Determine the maximum steady-state (high-line condition) voltage of power mains in rms, peak ac or dc.
2. Determine maximum temporary voltage the victim can withstand without damage or malfunction.
3. Select the next higher rating (V_{nom}) of an available surge suppressor.
4. Determine the maximum expected pulse current. (Pulse current can be found in environmental statistics or from the surge-withstand specification. These tests are usually made with low-impedance simulators; if the impedance is unknown, a default value of 50 Ω can be assumed.)
5. Find the clamp voltage at maximum expected pulse current. Check that item 5 is *less* than item 2.
6. Check that item 4 does not exceed the current handling capability of the suppressor for the given duration.
7. Compute the actual attenuation using manufacturer's data or the graphical method of Fig. 9.13.

9.16

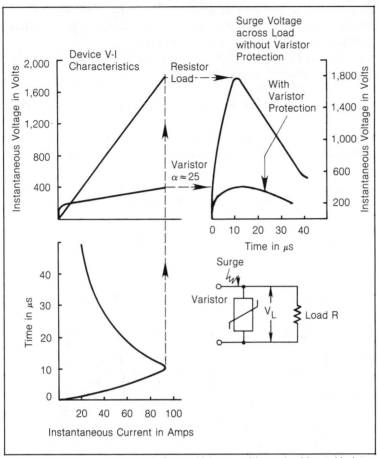

Figure 9.13—Comparison of Surge Voltage with and without Varistor Protection

Illustrative Example 9.4

An 8 × 20 μs surge is expected from lightning induction on a 120 V power line. The open circuit voltage is 2,000 V. Mains and victim impedance represent 20 Ω in this frequency domain. The victim's input components (filters, etc.) cannot withstand more than 400 V.

A metal-oxide suppressor is selected with nominal voltage ≥ (120 + 10 percent) × $\sqrt{2}$ = 185 V. The next available model has a nominal break at 200 V. Since, above its break, a varistor behaves

9.17

as a short (low dynamic resistance), the current is: V/(20 Ω) = 100 A. The clamp voltage is 360 V_{max} (as stated by the manufacturer). This is below our 400 V criterion.

Figure 9.13 gives the shape of the pulse after suppressor insertion. The transient attenuation is then:

$$20 \log(2{,}000 \text{ V}/360 \text{ V}) = 15 \text{ dB} \qquad (9.3)$$

Finally, we must verify that the energy to dissipate across the device, approximately equal to (V × I × half-crest width) does not exceed its energy-handling characteristics.

Figure 9.14 shows another example of semiconductor transient attenuation for a sharp, short-duration transient and its effect in the frequency domain.

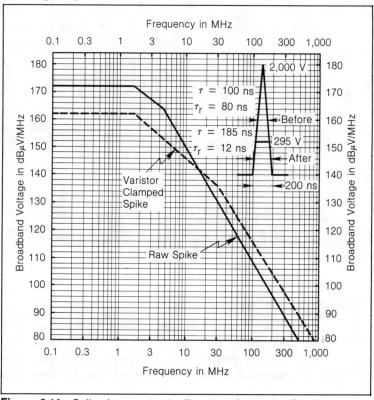

Figure 9.14—Spike Attenuation by Transient Protective Device

The second type of surge suppressor, the **gas-discharge (crowbar) device**, behaves like a neon tube or thyristor device in the breakdown region as shown in Fig. 9.15. After firing, their voltage drop is only a few volts, and their power-handling capability is one order of magnitude greater than that of the semiconductor devices. Conversely, their response time is slower, and the first portion of the sharpest spikes can pass over the gas tube before it reacts. The selection steps are as follows:

1. Determine maximum steady voltage of power mains.
2. Select the next highest rating ($V_{nominal}$) of available gas tube.
3. Determine the peak voltage and rise time of the transient. If unknown use 10 kV/μs.
4. Find the threshold of the gas tube for the slope using manufacturer's curve or default values shown in Fig. 9.16.
5. Be sure that the holdover current will not maintain gap arcing after the surge. If arcing continues, a power input fuse should also be selected to clear this follow-on current.

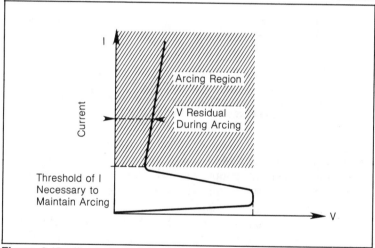

Figure 9.15—Illustration of Gas-Tube Transient Protector

Illustrative Example 9.5

A 350 Vdc gas tube is mounted to protect a 220 Vac line. What protection is offered to a 3 kV/μs lightning-induced surge?

9.19

Since the slope is 3 kV/μs, the curve in Fig. 9.16 shows that the tube will react in ≈ 300 ns, i.e., the first 1 kV front of the pulse will be allowed to pass. Then the tube will glow, and the remaining pulse will be shorted. In this case, the maximum energy content associated with the pulse trailing edge will not enter into the victim (see Fig. 9.17).

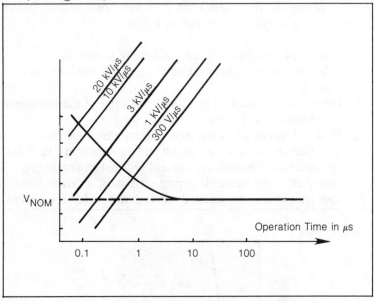

Figure 9.16—Default Values for Gas-Tube Threshold of Operation vs. Pulse Rise Speed (gas tube between 100 to 600 Vdc breakover)

Finally, the question arises as to whether both types of devices should be mounted for DM or CM protection. A differential-mode (line-to-line) transient suppressor will offer no attenuation to common-mode transients, and vice versa. Total protection should include both DM and CM suppressors. In any case, since they will be mounted on a high-energy input, they should be checked for safety compliance, a discussion of which is beyond the scope of this handbook. More details on the lifetime, ratings and secondary effects of surge protectors can be found in Volume 5, *EMI Control in Components,* of this handbook series.

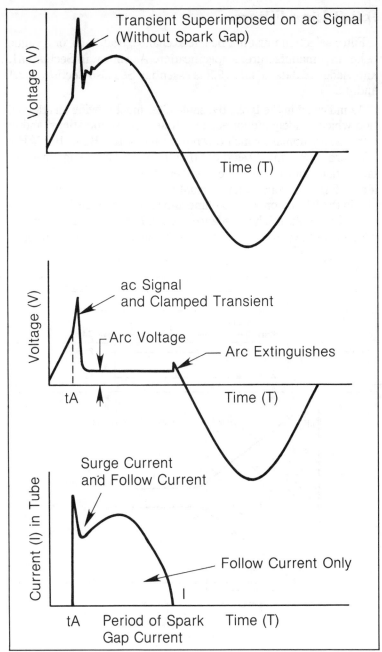

Figure 9.17—Illustrative Example of Gas Tube Attenuation

9.3.3 Line Filters

Filter selection must not be left to chance, traditions, or a vague belief in a manufacturer's specification. As shown in Section 9.1, knowledge of data in Table 9.2 is essential. See also Sections 4.2.1 and 4.2.2).

As indicated in the table, the same filter must provide an attenuation which is adequate for each of these four combinations, and in a frequency domain which can be as vast as 10 kHz to 100 MHz!

Figure 9.18 symbolizes the difficulty for a filter designer to obtain satisfactory results when the real conditions are far from the ideal 50 Ω/50 Ω conditions of usual test arrangements. For example, in the LF region, the machine emission will be difficult to control with a choke (high-impedance circuit). However, the capacitance which could bypass the CM noise is limited by safety regulations

Table 9.2 - Impedance Matrix for Filter Selection

	PRODUCT	FILTER	POWER MAINS
EMISSION	(Power System) Zcm ———————— (Source) Zdm ————————		→ Zcm (Victim) → Zdm
SUSCEPTIBILITY	Zcm ◄———————— (Victim) Zdm ◄————————		Zcm (Source) Zdm

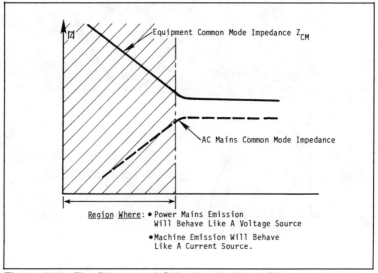

Figure 9.18—The Dilemma of Selecting the Ideal Filter

because of the maximum allowable safety wire 50 Hz leakage. There are two leading criteria possible in selecting a filter. They are the **susceptibility** and **emission** aspects.

9.3.3.1 Susceptibility Criteria for Filter Selection

If the EMI concern is in terms of narrowband suppression, the filter definition is simple. At a given frequency, f_{EMI}:

$$\text{filter attenuation} \geq 20 \log \frac{\text{victim threshold}}{\text{narrowband interference level}}$$

$$(9.4)$$

That is:

$$A_{dB} = N_{dB\mu V} - I_{dB\mu V} \qquad (9.5)$$

The filter cutoff frequency is then found from:

$$A = n \times 20 \log(f_{EMI}/f_{co}) \qquad (9.6)$$

Therefore:

$$f_{co} = \frac{f_{EMI}}{\text{antilog}(A_{dB}/20 \times n)} \qquad (9.7)$$

where,

$$n = \text{number of filter elements}$$

$$f_{EMI} = \text{frequency of concern}$$

Section 4.2 gives detailed graphs on filter rejection.

If the concern is transient (impulse) suppression, when the filter, as is often the case, must protect the equipment from power line spikes (broadband), filter performance can be found using the $f_{co} \times \tau$ universal curve of Fig. 9.19. (The rationale for this figure appears in Section 4.2.)

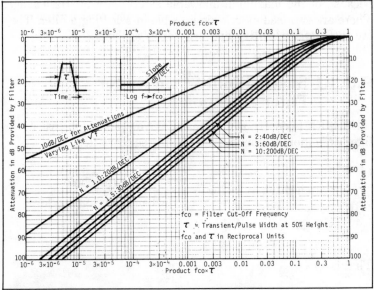

Figure 9.19—Transient and Pulse Attenuation of Filters

Illustrative Example 9.6

What should be the filter characteristics to reduce a 1,500 V, 100 ns transient to 30 V, the estimated safe value to enter the power regulator? The factor 1,500/30 is equivalent to a 34 dB attenuation. For 34 dB with a one-pole filter (n = 1), the curve shows a product $f_{co} \times \tau = 0.002$. In this case:

$$f_{co} = \frac{2 \times 10^{-3}}{100 \times 10^{-9}} = 20 \text{ kHz} \qquad (9.8)$$

In the case of a two-pole (n = 2) filter, the curve shows $f_{co} \times \tau = 0.005$, i.e., $f_{co} = 50$ kHz.

9.3.3.2 Emission Criteria For Filter Selection

Since emissions are generally controlled by specifications which define a maximum amplitude in a given test setup, two approaches are considered. They involve military and civil specifications, respectively. They both have the same objective of conducted emission measurement:

9.24

Military Specifications: Specifications such as MIL-STD-461 (CE03) define the power line emission as the **maximum conducted current** the equipment can generate on its power cord. This is similar to the **short-circuit ampacity** of the noise source and corresponds to situations where the power distribution has a very low impedance. This worst-case impedance is simulated by a 10 μF capacitor of special fabrication to ensure an $X_c < 0.1 \ \Omega$ beyond 150 kHz.

Nonmilitary Specifications: Organizations such as CISPR, VDE and FCC characterize the power line emission RF voltage in a given impedance (LISN 50 Ω or 150 Ω) which is supposed to **represent** the power mains impedance.

Detailed models and examples of conducted emissions and proper filter selection are covered in Chapter 10.

Filter performance problems can be visualized as follows:

1. The manufacturer's performance curve of a filter is merely

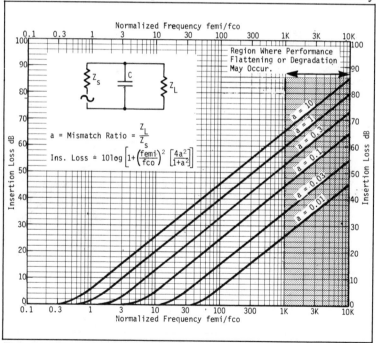

Figure 9.20—Insertion Loss of Bypass Capacitive Filters for Unmatched Source/Load Conditions

the insertion loss of its L,C network in a 50 Ω/50 Ω configuration.

2. Conversely, the user is concerned with equipment performance, not filter performance, and it has been described how the filter will never see 50 Ω in either direction.

Figures 9.21, 9.22, and 9.23 give performances of single-element

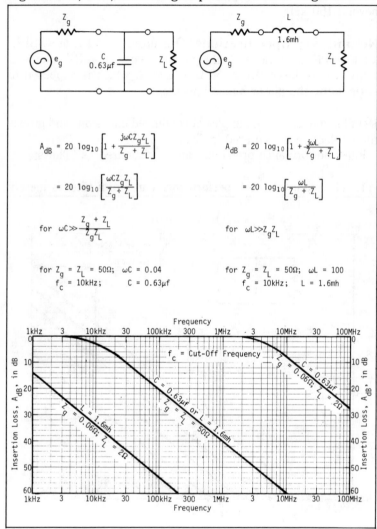

Figure 9.21—Attenuation (Insertion Loss) of a Single-Element Filter in a 50 Ω and in a Low-Impedance Source and Load System

9.26

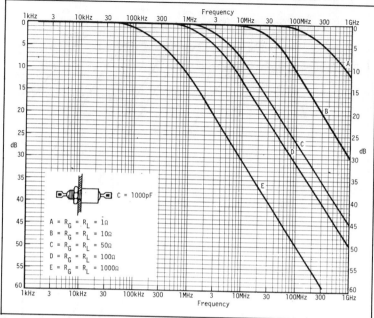

Figure 9.22—Attenuation of Feed-Through Capacitors in Non-ideal Situations (C = 1 nF)

filters in nonstandard source and load arrangements.

An approach for rapidly determining the performances of pi-type lowpass filters follows.

The insertion loss, IL, of a pi-type filter can be expressed (from Ref. 8) as:

$$IL_{dB} = 10 \log (1 + F^2D^2 - 2F^4D + F^6) \qquad (9.13)$$

where,

F = the normalized frequency = f_{EMI}/f_{co}

D = determinant $\left(\dfrac{1}{d^{1/3}} - d^{2/3} \right)$, which itself reflects the damping factor of the filter, i.e., d = L/2 CR^2

The cutoff frequency, f_{co}, can be found, for a pi filter, by:

$$f_{co} = \frac{1}{2\pi} \left(\frac{2}{RLC^2} \right)^{1/3} \qquad (9.14)$$

9.27

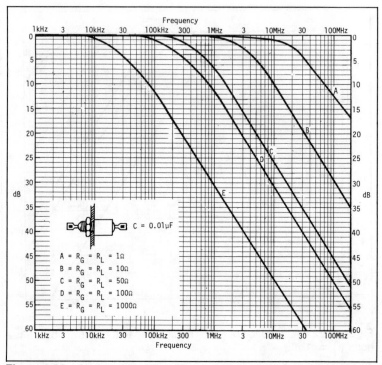

Figure 9.23—Attenuation of Feed-Through Capacitors in Non-ideal Situations (C = 0.01 μF)

To help the engineer, damping factor, d, has been computed for several values of L and C in Table 9.3, assuming standard source/load impedances of 50 Ω. Once the value of d is known, the filter IL curve can be found in Fig. 9.24 and 9.25. Should the circuit impedances differ from 50 Ω, the d value found in Table 9.3 should be corrected as follows before entering the graph. If $R_{(x)} \neq$ 50 Ω, use:

$$K = (50/R_x)^2 \text{ and } d_{(x)} = K d_{(50)}$$

For example, for R = 10 Ω, use:

$$d = d_{(50)} \times (50/10)^2 \qquad (9.15)$$

9.28

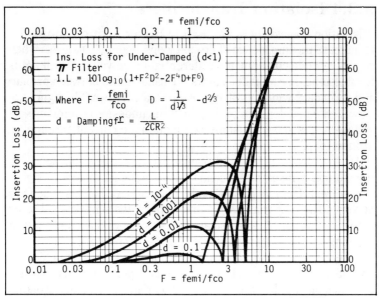

Figure 9.24—Insertion Loss for Under-Damped (d < 1) Pi Filter

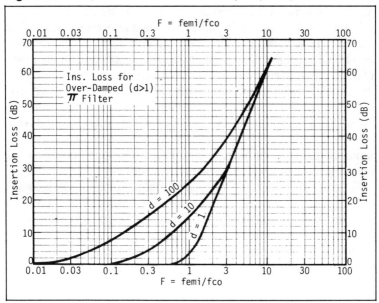

Figure 9.25—Insertion Loss for Over-Damped (d > 1) Pi Filter

9.3.4 Isolation Transformers

Isolation transformers are used to **break ground loops**, i.e., to increase the impedance of ground loops, hopefully to levels where common-mode currents and differential-mode voltages will not be troublesome. Figure 9.26a shows the capacitance between primary and secondary windings of an isolation transformer. The figure also shows an equivalent circuit in which the undesired common-mode voltage, e_n, is shown pushing common-mode current through the ground loop.

At low frequencies, the capacitive reactance between the transformer primary and secondary is so high that there is no significant threat from common-mode current. At high frequencies, however, the potential EMI problem becomes significant. For example, a typical 1 kW isolation transformer has input-output capacitance which produces few decibels reduction to a 1 μs transient from the primary to the secondary. Thus, unshielded (no Faraday shield) isolation transformers may perform well at low frequencies only. Other measures such as Faraday-shielded isolation transformers should be considered for protection against common-mode problems at intermediate and high frequencies.

Figure 9.26b shows a differential-mode (sometimes called **normal-mode**) voltage appearing across the primary of the isolation transformer due to undesired emissions appearing on the power mains. These normal-mode emissions may be expected to couple directly into the secondary at both low frequencies and high frequencies since this is the intentional mode of operation for 50/60/400 Hz power mains. Because the differential mode has relatively little high-frequency attenuation, some special means must be taken to suppress this emission. One such means is the use of a Faraday-shielded isolation transformer.

To combat undesired emissions coupling through isolation transformers, Faraday shields are necessary. Figure 9.27 shows that the primary-to-secondary capacitance has been divided between primary and shield and the shield and secondary. The connection to the shield is brought out externally to the transformer on an insulated standoff terminal to permit the user to connect the shield in some purposeful manner.

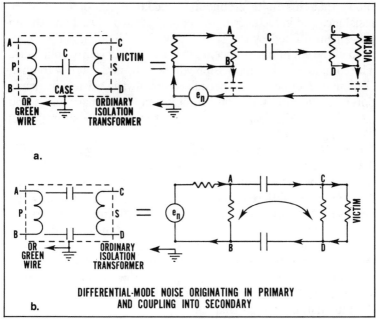

Figure 9.26—Isolation Transformer Showing (a) Common-Mode Noise and (b) Differential-Mode Noise Originating in Primary and Coupling into Secondary

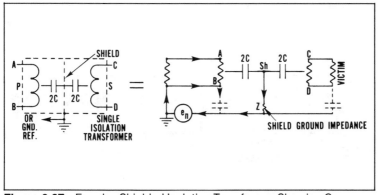

Figure 9.27—Faraday-Shielded Isolation Transformer Showing Common-Mode Noise Originating in Primary and Bypassed before Secondary

The Faraday shield is connected to the reference for the common-mode voltage, i.e., to ground. The schematic drawing on the right

9.31

shows that this finite grounding impedance, Z, comes from the resistance and inductance of the ground strap or bus. Thus, the improvement offered by the shield by voltage-dividing action is the ratio of the shunt impedance, Z, to the series capacitive reactance. The common-mode suppression will be substantial at low frequencies but cannot be infinite because there always exists a dc insulation resistance of 10 or 100 MΩ between the primary and secondary. Then, CM rejection degrades with an increase in frequency like a high-pass filter.

For differential-mode coupling, Fig. 9.28 is the corollary to Fig. 9.27 in which the primary-to-secondary capacitance is divided into two parts by the Faraday shield between the primary and secondary. Since the differential mode appears across the primary, it is necessary to short circuit the primary at high frequencies to suppress the differential-mode coupling. To accomplish this, the shield should be connected to the center tap of the primary. If no center tap exists, then the shield should be connected to the low-voltage side of the transformer. The arrangement shown will be transparent at the 50 /60/400 Hz power mains frequencies but will offer substantial attenuation at high frequencies.

Figure 9.29 shows quantitative values of CM and DM rejection of a typical single-shield isolation transformer (residual primary to

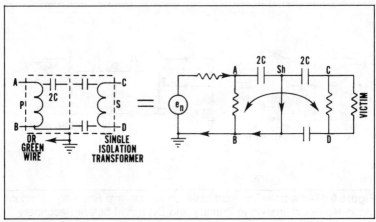

Figure 9.28—Faraday-Shielded Isolation Transformer Showing Differential-Mode Noise Originating in Primary and Bypassed before Secondary

9.32

secondary capacitance ≤ 1 pF). For contrast, an ordinary, unshielded transformer is also shown. The performance of a good Faraday shield can be spoiled if it is grounded via a too-impedant conductor. Performances shown are with a ground bus shorter than 10 cm. Had the ground bus been 1 m long, performances would degrade by about 20 dB.

The preceding four figures indicated that it is necessary to use Faraday shields in isolation transformers to suppress conducted EMI. These shields prevent intermediate and high-frequency common-mode and differential-mode currents from undesirable

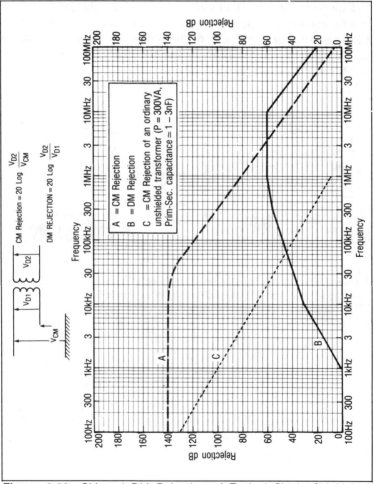

Figure 9.29—CM and DM Rejection of Typical Single Shield Isol-Transformer. For triple shield versions with parasitic capacitance of 10^{-5} Farad, figure is typically 40-60 better above 100 kHz.

9.33

coupling from primary to secondary. It is also observed, however, that no single shield can be optimized to simultaneously suppress both common and differential modes. Since both modes will be present simultaneously, it is necessary to use a **double** Faraday-shielded isolation transformer. This is shown in Fig. 9.30, in which the shield facing the primary is used to suppress differential mode and the shield facing the secondary is used to suppress the common mode, as determined by the respective grounding of both shields in Figs. 9.27 and 9.28.

The equivalent circuit is shown at the right. Here, the differential mode is the push-pull currents, I_d, across the primary. The common-mode currents, I_c, are the push-push, i.e., in-phase across the primary. The remainder of the schematic shows the voltage-dividing action from the primary and secondary to their respective shields and from shield to shield.

Figure 9.31 is a continuation of the preceding figures. It

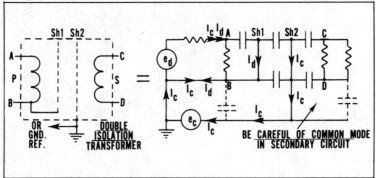

Figure 9.30—Double Faraday-Shielded Isolation Transformer in which Both Common-Mode and Differential-Mode Rejection Is Effected

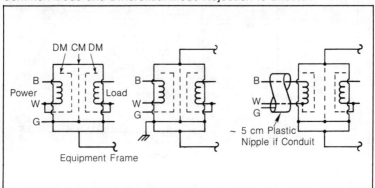

Figure 9.31—Triple Faraday-Shielded Isolation Transformer and its Grounding

represents the performance of a triple-shielded isolation transformer and its grounding under severe conducted electromagnetic ambients on the power bus.

The picture at the left, captioned "good," shows three Faraday shields with the two outer shields used to protect undesired differential-mode emissions on the primary and secondary, respectively. It is assumed here that the load is also generating undesired emissions which are also to be blocked from getting onto the power mains. The center shield, used to block the common-mode emissions, is connected to the transformer frame, which is also connected to the safety wire or ground plane as applicable.

This left illustration is captioned "good" because it successfully blocks the common and differential modes on the black (hot) and white (neutral) wires. However, the undesired common-mode currents flowing on the safety wire are carried, unimpeded, through the transformer to create a potential EMI problem.

The second frame, captioned "better" (by the manufacturer of the transformer), means that the performance is enhanced by breaking the continuity of the polluted safety wire. Thus, the primary shield is returned to the safety wire, whereas the transformer frame develops a new local safety ground. While the safety ground line is now broken, the impedance from the transformer primary to the safety wire return is substantially increased since the circuit from the primary to shield now also contains the resistance and inductance of the safety wire. Since this undesired impedance can become substantial (see Fig. 5.2), the differential-mode suppressing capability is compromised.

The illustration to the right in Fig. 9.31 is captioned "best" because it eliminates the objections in the preceding two frames. The safety wire is broken; that is, it is not continuous between the arriving power mains on the left and the transformer frame on the right. If the power mains cable exists in a conduit, then the conduit also acts like a large safety wire. For this situation, it is also necessary to break the metal conduit, as suggested in the figure, by interposing a threaded plastic nipple section between the frame and the metal conduit. However, this last practice may be in violation of safety codes and should be applied only after a proper evaluation of all safety aspects.

The rest of the "best" figure shows the differential-mode shield returned once again to the primary. This gives a much lower impedance shorting action at high frequencies than that permitted by the center illustration. This avoids the high impedance associated with a long safety wire at high frequencies.

9.4 Power Supply Coupling

The power supply itself, as shown in block 4E of the EMI flow diagram (Fig. 9.1), is involved in processing the conducted noise to the victim circuits. Although the regulator is an active device in reducing voltage fluctuations, it becomes a passive element when EMI noise is faster than its response time, as is often the case. Both aspects of conducted **susceptibility** and **emission** are covered here.

9.4.1 Susceptibility Aspect

A power supply, regarding bulk input voltage fluctuations, can be regarded as a stopband (or high-pass) active filter whose rejection would be:

$$A = \Delta V_{out}/\Delta V_{in} \tag{9.16}$$

$$= \text{dynamic regulation for input voltage changes}$$

On the other hand, this regulation is challenged by the input-output leakage impedance. Above a certain frequency, this impedance decreases sufficiently to allow primary voltage noise to be transferred on the output circuit, regardless of the dynamic regulation.

At the risk of oversimplifying, power supply regulators providing the necessary voltages to the electronic circuit can be categorized as (1) regulators with input-to-output isolation (Fig. 9.32a), or (2) regulators without input-to-output isolation (Fig. 9.32b). Each type is discussed in the following paragraphs.

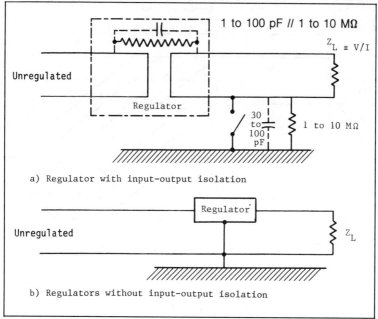

a) Regulator with input-output isolation

b) Regulators without input-output isolation

Figure 9.32—The Two Categories of Power Supplies

9.4.1.1 Regulators with Input-to-Output Isolation

The regulated output is galvanically isolated from the bulk input. The isolation is provided by the 50/60 Hz transformer or by the high-frequency transformer in the case of a switching regulator.

The output can be grounded to the chassis, as is most often the case, or floated if the user has opted for an isolated zero-volt reference, to break possible ground loops. For such a regulator, the response **against differential-mode EMI** (between phase and neutral, or $+V_{bulk}$ and return) is dictated by the dynamic regulation of the power supply for input voltage changes, per Eq. (9.16)

Figure 9.33 shows the rejection against differential mode input fluctuation for regulators having 0.01 percent to 1 percent of line

9.37

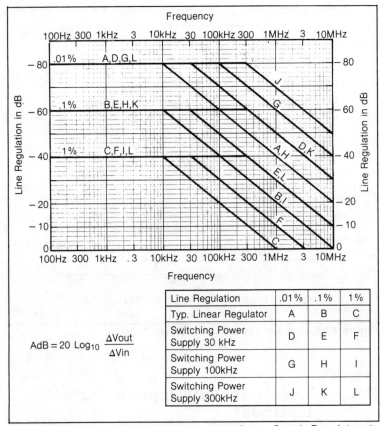

Figure 9.33—Dynamic (Active) Response of Power Supply Regulators to Differential-Mode Input Fluctuations

regulation coefficient. All the curves show a rolloff above a certain frequency. This corresponds to voltage input changes which are beyond the regulator frequency response. This frequency response depends on the design: for a linear regulator, it is generally around 10 to 30 kHz; for a switcher, the regulation bandwidth at best can be taken as the switching frequency itself since the pulse width modulator and the error amplifier cannot react faster than one period. Above this frequency, the rejection falloff depends on the type of dc output filter which is masking the regulator deficiencies. Conservatively, 20 dB/decade has been assumed.

Against common-mode EMI, the rejection of the regulator is dictated by the input-output insulation resistance and leakage capacitance.

$$V_L = V_{cm} \times \frac{Z_L}{(Z_{cp}//R_p + Z_L + Z_{cg})} \qquad (9.17)$$

where,

V_L = resulting voltage across the secondary load

Z_{cp} = impedance of the input/output parasitic capacitance Cp

R_p = input/output insulation resistance (dc)

Z_{cg} = impedance of the zero-volt to ground parasitic capacitance of the secondary ≈ 0 if the secondary reference is grounded to chassis

Figure 9.34 shows the rejection against common-mode input fluctuations for several values of input-to-output isolation, assuming the secondary is grounded to chassis or coupled to it via a stray capacitance of at least 30 pF, which is generally the case when one tries to float the secondary. Note that the curves of Fig. 9.34 are normalized to 1 Ω of load impedance. To adjust to any other load value, add +20 log Z_L Ω to the value found on the curves. Thus:

$$\text{CM rejection} = K_{dB} \text{ (from curves)} + 20 \log Z_L \ \Omega \qquad (9.18)$$

Illustrative Example 9.7

A 5 V, 10 A linear regulator keeps the dc output within 50 mV tolerance for an input varying from 80 to 130 V. What is the rejection for 30 V DM input noise at 300 kHz?

The regulation coefficient is:

$$\Delta V_{out}/\Delta V_{in} = 0.05 \ V/(130 - 80) = 0.1 \text{ percent}$$

Curve B in Fig. 9.33 shows a linear regulator with 0.1 percent

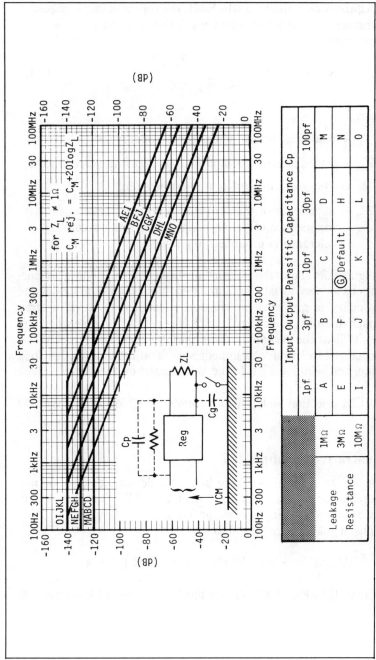

Figure 9.34—CM Rejection of Power Supply Regulator with Input-to-Output Isolation, for 1 Ω of Equivalent Load Impedance (For load impedance = 1 Ω, add 20 log Z_L Ω. If the secondary is floated and has a parasitic capacitance cg< C_p, add a correction = 20 log C_g/C_p.)

9.40

dynamic regulation. At 300 kHz, curve B indicates -30 dB of DM response. So,

$$V_{out} = V_{in} - 30 \text{ dB}$$

$$= 30 \text{ dBV} - 30 \text{ dB} = 0 \text{ dBV or } 1 \text{ V}$$

This is too large a fluctuation for a 5 Vdc bus; therefore, a better input filter has to be provided on the mains side, or a better decoupling filter on the dc output side.

What is the rejection for 300 V CM noise at 300 kHz (could correspond to a 1 μs transient)? For a default value of 3 MΩ and 10 pF, curve G of Fig. 9.34 indicates -94 dB at 300 kHz. Therefore:

$$V_{out} = V_{in} -94 \text{ dB} + 20 \log 0.5 \ \Omega/1$$

$$= 50 \text{ dBV} - 94 - 6 = -50 \text{ dBV or } 3 \text{ mV}$$

9.4.1.2 Regulators without Input-Output Isolation

For this type of regulator, there is no metallic isolation between the input and output sides. In this case, the output section always has the zero-volt grounded to chassis, for obvious safety reasons, and the regulator is a three-terminal device. Therefore, CM and DM noise appear the same way at the input. The result is dictated by the dynamic regulation of the power supply, as per Fig. 9.33.

Illustrative Example 9.8

A power system is made up of an ordinary, unshielded step-down transformer followed by a series regulator. The regulated output voltage remains with 0.1 percent for a 190 to 240 V input range up to 10 kHz. Initially, no filter is provided. The transformer input-output capacitance is 30 pF. The secondary impedances beyond 1 MHz are approximately 10 Ω for either transformer load or regulator loads. The regulator has no galvanic isolation, and it has its zero-volt grounded to a common chassis.

Compute the EMI situation of a 1 kV sharp transient on an ac line ($\tau_r = \tau = 100$ ns), assuming the victim on the load side has a susceptibility, N = 0.4 V.

First, computing the ac mains to power supply (PL-PS in column 4E of Fig. 9.35) gives the CM attenuation for the transformer. At a frequency of $1/\pi\tau_r = 3$ MHz, curve D in Fig. 9.34 shows a CM rejection of -64 dB at 3 MHz. Since the secondary load is approximated by 10 Ω, this first PL-PS rejection is:

$$-64 \text{ dB} + 20 \log 10 \ \Omega = -44 \text{ dB}$$

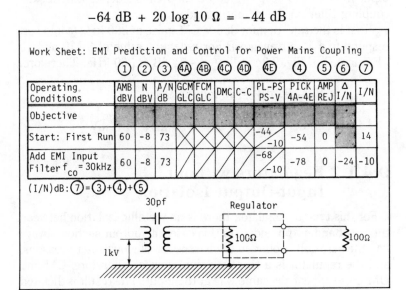

Work Sheet: EMI Prediction and Control for Power Mains Coupling

① ② ③ ④A ④B ④C ④D ④E ④ ⑤ ⑥ ⑦

Operating Conditions	AMB dBV	N dBV	A/N dB	GCM GLC	FCM GLC	DMC	C-C	PL-PS PS-V	PICK 4A-4E	AMP REJ	Δ I/N	I/N
Objective												
Start: First Run	60	-8	73					-44 / -10	-54	0		14
Add EMI Input Filter f_{co} = 30kHz	60	-8	73					-68 / -10	-78	0	-24	-10

(I/N)dB: ⑦=③+④+⑤

30pf

Regulator

1kV   100Ω   100Ω

Figure 9.35—EMI Prediction and Control for Power Mains Coupling

The remaining transient now appears differentially at the input of the linear regulator since it has a zero-volt grounded. The regulator's DM rejection is found on curve B of Fig. 9.33 at 3 MHz: -10 dB. So total rejection is $-44 - 10 = -54$ dB. Since 1 kV is 60 dBV, the victim at the load end will see $60 - 54 = 6$ dBV, or 2 V. This is 14 dB above the noise immunity level.

The prediction chart in Fig. 9.35 shows a remaining interference 14 dB above the sensitivity level, N, of the victim circuit. A first attempt is to use an input filter with a cutoff frequency computed from Fig. 9.19. The attenuation required is $14 + 10$ dB safety margin, or 24 dB. A single-element filter will provide 24 dB for a product $f_{co} \times \tau = 0.008$ (which, in this case, means that $F_{co} = 0.008/0.1 \times 10^{-6}$ s = 80 kHz. The new mains-to-regulator coupling is now $-44 -24 = -68$ dB, and the final I/N is -10 dB.

9.4.2 Noise Generation from the Regulated Side

Fast load changes, especially with digital circuit operation, appear as an ac noise introduction in the power supply output. Whenever they fall in or out of the response speed of the regulator, the noise components can affect EMC in two ways. First, they appear as noise a source for some (victim) loads, Z_n, which are in fact interfered with by the operation of other loads, Z_x, (self-jamming). Although related to the **common impedance coupling** discussed in Section 5.3, the problem here addresses specifically the power supply output characteristics; i.e., the **power supply output impedance** and its **regulation bandwidth.** The resultant output noise can be defined as:

$$V_n = \Delta I \times Z_{(\omega)} \qquad (9.24)$$

where,

ΔI = change in load current

$Z_{(\omega)}$ = power supply output impedance, frequency dependent

The value of ΔI can be, for instance, the sum of all transition currents which can occur simultaneously due to logic state changes in a given time frame.

For relatively slow ΔI occurring during Δt, greater than the minimum time response of the regulator, the output impedance is equivalent to:

$$Z_{outLF} = \Delta V_{out}/\Delta I_{out} \qquad (9.25)$$

Illustrative Example 9.9

A 5 V, 20 A switching regulator has a load regulation of 0.2 percent maximum for a 10 A current change in not less than 300 μs.

$$Z_{\text{outLF}} = \frac{0.2/100 \times 5 \text{ V}}{10 \text{ A}} = 10^{-3} \ \Omega \qquad (9.26)$$

For the fastest current changes, the power supply regulation band is exceeded during the **transient recovery time.** This can be defined as the power supply having an **inductive output impedance.** Figure 9.36 shows the voltage response of a power supply to a spontaneous load change $\Delta I/\Delta t$, while Fig. 9.37 shows a typical Z_{out} in the frequency domain. For example, an 8.5 V, 3 A linear

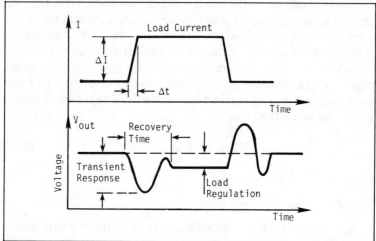

Figure 9.36—Power Regulation in the Time Domain

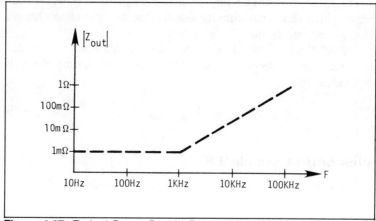

Figure 9.37—Typical Power Supply Output Impedance

9.44

regulator has a transient response of 0.5 V for a 1 A/10 μs current transition. Use $\Delta V = L \, (dI/dt)$:

$$0.5 \text{ V} = L \times \frac{1 \text{ A}}{10 \times 10^{-6}} \qquad (9.27)$$

Therefore, $L = 5 \, \mu\text{H}$. The output impedance at this frequency (i.e., 30 kHz) is:

$$Z_{outHF} = 0.5 \text{ V/1 A} = 0.5 \, \Omega \qquad (9.28)$$

These transients reappear on the primary input. Therefore, the primary side (power line side) exhibits a noise due to circuit operation on its secondary side. In this regard, the power regulator can be considered as a stop-band (high-pass) active filter, or negative resistance, with a transfer function $\Delta V_{in}/\Delta I_{out}$, i.e., a secondary-to-primary rejection:

$$\text{emission rejection} = \frac{\Delta V_{in}}{\Delta I_{out} \times Z_{out}} \qquad (9.29)$$

$$= \frac{\Delta V_{in}}{I_{out} \times Z_{load} \times \% \text{ load regulation}}$$

This is valid up to 1/response time of the regulator where, Z_{out} equals the output impedance of the regulator. This aspect must be considered especially when the power source has a significant output impedance, as in the case of a UPS, power converter, ac voltage regulator, etc.

9.4.3 Summary of Broadband Conducted EMI: Combined Attenuation of Line Filters, Transformers and Regulators

Given the chain of attenuating blocks with various transfer functions which constitute the EMI propagation path across boxes (4E in Fig. 9.1), the following example will show how to synthesize their various performances and weaknesses. Figure 9.38 shows the sequence of building blocks in a typical power supply system, feeding

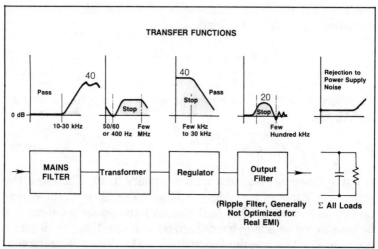

Figure 9.38—Power Supply EMI Propagation Chain (Typical)

an ensemble of loads. Some default values are suggested for their typical best performance, once installed (including the imperfect filter adequacy to source/load impedance, the equivalent series resistance (ESR) of the output filter electrolytic capacitors, etc.). They should be replaced by actual data once the designer determines the characteristics of available components.

In a style similar to the BB radiated example of Chapter 7, Section 7.5, a BB conducted susceptibility prediction form (Fig. 9.39) is used for the following example.

Illustrative Example 9.10

A differential-mode transient appears on the bulk mains input of a power system with the following shape:

Amplitude: 1 kV (measured on actual, normally loaded lines)

Rise time: 100 ns

50 percent pulse width: 10 μs

9.46

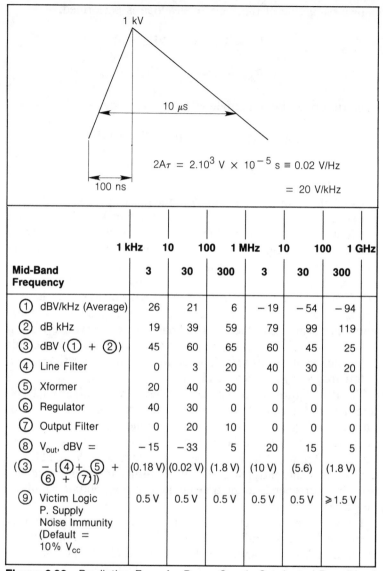

	1 kHz	10	100	1 MHz	10	100	1 GHz
Mid-Band Frequency	3	30	300	3	30	300	
① dBV/kHz (Average)	26	21	6	− 19	− 54	− 94	
② dB kHz	19	39	59	79	99	119	
③ dBV (① + ②)	45	60	65	60	45	25	
④ Line Filter	0	3	20	40	30	20	
⑤ Xformer	20	40	30	0	0	0	
⑥ Regulator	40	30	0	0	0	0	
⑦ Output Filter	0	20	10	0	0	0	
⑧ V_{out}, dBV = (③ − [④ + ⑤ + ⑥ + ⑦])	− 15 (0.18 V)	− 33 (0.02 V)	5 (1.8 V)	20 (10 V)	15 (5.6)	5 (1.8 V)	
⑨ Victim Logic P. Supply Noise Immunity (Default = 10% V_{cc}	0.5 V	0.5 V	0.5 V	0.5 V	0.5 V	⩾1.5 V	

Figure 9.39—Prediction Form for Power Supply Conducted Broadband Susceptibility

A fast evaluation of the Fourier envelope is performed:

$$F_1 = 1/\pi r = 30 \text{ kHz}$$

$$F_2 = 1/\pi \tau_r = 3 \text{ MHz}$$

Spectrum pedestal amplitude:

$$2A\tau = (2 \times 10^3 \times 10 \times 10^{-6}) \text{ V/Hz}$$

$$= 20 \text{ V/kHz}$$

As for the example in Section 7.5, the pulse spectrum is divided in decade slices, and the mid-band spectral density is indicated on the first line. On the second line, the average spectral density, in dBV/kHz, is multiplied by the corresponding bandwidth in kHz (dBkHz, line 2), providing the dBV of line 3.

Then, from line 4 to line 7, the attenuation of each power supply building block is entered using default data of Fig. 9.29 for the transformer, with data from Fig. 9.33 for the regulator. The maximum performance of the line filter has been conservatively taken as 40 dB, deteriorating progressively above 30 MHz. Filter cutoff frequency is about 30 kHz. The power supply output filter has a cutoff frequency of a few kilohertz.

The dBV figure of line 3 is then processed vertically in each column across the cascade of series attenuation, resulting in V_{out} of line 8, in dBV per each band. The corresponding amplitude in volts is indicated in parenthesis. Summing up the voltages contributed by each column results in a worst-case voltage of 19 V (if all terms are adding coherently) or 11.6 V (if all terms are adding randomly). This corresponds to the time domain peak amplitude out of the last filter.

If the victim is a set of typical logic loads, its immunity to power supply noise is generally 10 percent of V_{cc} in band, improving at 20 dB/decade out of band. Line 9 shows a typical TTL power supply immunity of 0.5 V up to 30 MHz. It is clear that:

1. Across the whole spectrum, except in the 1 to 100 kHz region, the immunity threshold is exceeded.
2. The 19 V peak amplitude of the time-domain pulse is probably damaging.

3. The most threatening part is in the 1 to 100 MHz domain.

To reduce the amplitude to an acceptable level in each band, with a sufficient safety factor to ensure that the logic power supply immunity is not upset when integrating over the spectrum, the following is recommended:

1. Use a gas tube or varistor at the input so the 1 kV pulse is reduced to about 400 V.
2. Extend the efficiency of the output filtering above 1 MHz.
3. Improve the efficiency of the input filter in the 3 to 300 MHz region.

9.5 Bibliography

CBEMA/ESC5 Report, "Limits and Methods of Measurement of EMI from Data Processing Equipment," May 1977.

Cowdell, R.B., "Graphic Aids for Feed-Through Capacitor Design," International EMC Symposium, Montreux, Switzerland, May 1975.

General Electric Co., *Transient Suppression Manual* (Schenectady, NY: GE Research and Development, 1978).

Malack, J., "European Line Impedances Survey," *IEEE Transactions on EMC,* February 1976.

Massat, M., *Journees sur la Compatibilite El magnetique,* Lannion, France, Mai 1977.

Report from Working Group 3.4.4, "Guide on Surge Voltages in AC Power Circuits," (New York: IEEE Power Engineering Society, May 1979).

Schlicke, H.M., "Assuredly Effective Filters," *IEEE Transactions on EMC,* August 1976.

Smith, A.A., "Power Line Noise Survey," *IEEE Transactions on EMC,* February 1972.

Taylor, R.E., *RFI Handbook,* (NASA Goddard Space Center, 1971), avail. from National Technical Information Service, Springfield, VA.

Chapter 10

EMI Emission and Control

Up to this final chapter, this handbook has discussed EMI control methodology and procedures only from the view of protecting the receptor or victim from being jammed by the electromagnetic ambient environment. This includes both conducted and radiated susceptibility. There is, however, the reverse problem, viz., how to predict and control conducted and radiated emissions from boxes, interconnected equipments and systems. To address this aspect of EMC, this chapter stresses EMI emissions and their control.

As a side note to the above, the standard priority in EMI control is to first seek out the emission source, then the receptor and finally the coupling path or paths. By eliminating the offending emission source, one or more victims may be protected from EMI. Quite often, however, the emission source is operating legally and cannot be eliminated (e.g., the intentional emission spectrum of a carrier-operated transmitter in contrast to its harmonics). This chapter focuses on the emission sources which are the aim of MIL-STD-461, CISPR, FCC, VDE and other EMC regulations.

10.1 Reciprocity

The **Law of Reciprocity** assures us that most of the components and techniques used to control EMI susceptibility will also control EMI emission. Specifically, it states that **for linear and bi-lateral networks and devices, reverse performance**

will be the same when operated under identical conditions. Therefore, most EMC components and EMI control techniques discussed in this handbook can be expected to give identical EMI emission reduction performance as when used for susceptibility control. For example, the applications of filters, shields, twisting wires and grounding will also work for the control of EMI emission.

The problem developing from reciprocity considerations is twofold:

1. The formatting of useful conducted and radiated emission-level information from equipments and systems is generally expressed differently than that for susceptibility.
2. The law of reciprocity may not apply or is violated for many situations.

Regarding the first consideration, emission levels are expressed in the time and frequency domain, broadband or narrowband in terms of the frequency domain, and in terms of conducted or radiated emissions. This is in contrast to the S/(N + I) criterion used for susceptibility performance assessment in preceding chapters of this handbook. However, the two may be made somewhat parallel if the emission levels are compared with those of MIL-STD-461, CISPR or any of the national levels, such as FCC and VDE. For this situation, the results can be expressed as E/L ratios in which E = emission levels and L = specification limits.

The second consideration evolves when the reciprocity law is not applicable. For example, for filters to give the same insertion loss when operated in reverse (suppress a generated emission rather than a receive signal or noise), either the source or load impedance may have to be identical, or the filter may have to exhibit a mirror image about its network center. A second example involves shields. The interchange of different source and receptor distances to a shield will lead to a different shield effectiveness in the near field. Further, this interchange may affect the linearity, such as for permeable shields, in which saturation may take place.

The above notwithstanding, the law of reciprocity applies to most emission and susceptibility situations.

In the same manner that a methodical **flow diagram** was presented in Section 1.4 for susceptibility prediction, we can establish an emission flow diagram (Fig. 10.1) to itemize all the mechanisms by which a circuit or component can generate interference. In many instances, the Law of Reciprocity will apply, and we will see the five coupling paths of Chapters 4, 6, 7, 8 and 9 being applied in reverse.

The entry of the emission prediction is the **emitting source** which is usually a component or a circuit such as:

Integrated circuits
Switching transistors
Relays, solenoids and motors
High-power amplifiers, drivers, etc.

Since this chapter addresses intrasystem topics, we will not consider radio transmitters, overhead transmission lines and such because these sources are part of the environment over which the designer has little or no control. They have been described in Section 2.4 as pre-existing ambients.

Once the source has been selected, it must be characterized. In the same manner that, in Section 2.3, we characterized the victim response, we need here to identify the **emission signature** of the source in terms of:

1. Amplitude (voltage or current)
2. Output impedance (real and complex)
3. Frequency aspects: single pulse or periodic, pulse width and rise time

Then we see that this internal source can generate EMI via five possible paths through a **mirror mechanism** of what we had seen for susceptibility.

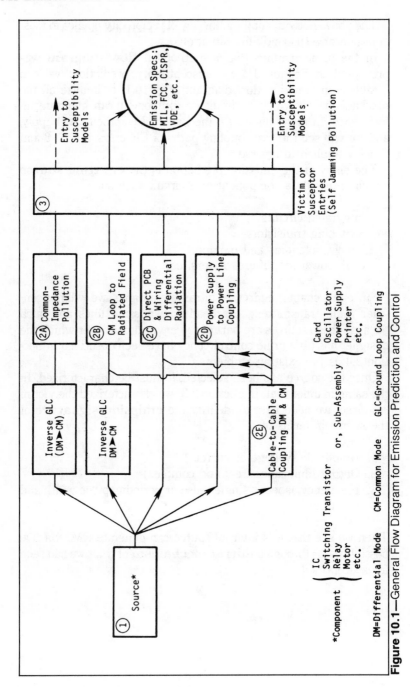

Figure 10.1—General Flow Diagram for Emission Prediction and Control

10.4

10.1.1 Inverse GLC and CM Impedance Pollution

For paths 2A and 2B of Fig. 10.1, it is shown that a DM to CM conversion takes place called **inverse GLC**. This is the mechanism by which an internal source of intentional signal will cause a common-mode current to flow in grounds or other common impedances. Figure 10.2 conceptually shows this mechanism: Some fraction of the intentional signal, instead of returning to the generator via the intended conductor DA, returns by a common-impedance path EF. As a result, a CM voltage will develop along impedance FE (block 2A in Fig. 10.1).

This last part of the mechanism has been described in Chapter 5. This is why the flow diagram of Fig. 10.1 contains a dotted line showing "entry to susceptibility models."

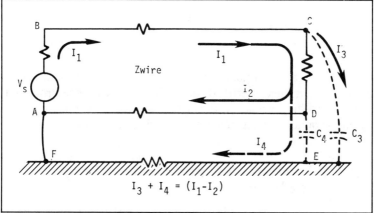

Figure 10.2—Differential-Mode to Common-Mode Conversion

Illustrative Example 10.1

Inside a steel cabinet, a video amplifier is sending 15 MHz digital pulses to a PCB located at 0.30 m. The pulse amplitude is 70 V, corresponding to 40 V on the 15 MHz fundamental voltage. The load impedance is 75 Ω. The parasitic capacitances are:

PCB to ground = 30 pF (C_4 in Fig. 10.2)
High side to ground = 3 pF (C_3 in Fig. 10.2)

The wire inductance (one way) is 0.15 μH, corresponding to 15 Ω at 15 MHz. What is the resulting CM current if the PCB is actually floated?

The current $I_1 \cong 40$ V/ΣZ = 0.5 A

The voltages at points C and D versus ground are:

$$V_{CE} \cong 40 \text{ V} - jL\omega I_1 = 32.5 \text{ V}$$

$$V_{DE} = 0.5 \text{ A} \times jL\omega = 7.5 \text{ V}$$

$$I_3 \cong V_{CE}/X_{C3} = 32.5 \times (3 \times 10^{-12}) \times 2\pi \times 15 \times 10^6$$
$$= 9 \text{ mA}$$

$$I_4 \cong V_{DE}/X_{C4} = 7.5 \text{ V} \times 30 \times 10^{-12} \times 2\pi \times 15 \times 10^6$$
$$= 22 \text{ mA}$$

Therefore, a current of 31 mA at 15 MHz will flow locally in the chassis, i.e., an **unintended** route. Had the PCB been grounded, the ground loop would have caused even more current to return by the ground, causing unacceptable chassis noise.

10.1.2 Inverse GLC and Ground-Loop Radiation

The current returning via ground loops, which may represent 10 or 100 times more area than the intended return circuit, will cause these loops to become EMI **radiators**. Block 2B of Fig. 10.1 shows that the result of the prediction shall be compared to radiated emission limits for compliance assessment. This question of the CM excitation of ground loops, **especially** with external cables, is one of the most overlooked in noise emission problems with modern electronic systems. Section 10.3 will show numerical predictions of the radiated field from external cable loops. The solutions will feature the same fixes as those used against GLC for susceptibility problems (see Section 6.5).

10.1.3 Direct PCB and Wiring Radiation (Differential)

The reciprocal of the concept discussed in Chapter 7, this emission mechanism (2C in Fig. 10.1) is straightforward radiation of PCB traces or wire pairs themselves, independent of any ground loop. The solutions, too, will be similar to the ones shown for field-to-cable, differential-mode coupling:

1. Reduction of pair or trace separation
2. Twisting
3. Shielding
4. Coaxial cables with low transfer impedance

10.1.4 Power Supply to Power Line Coupling

Here, the source is reflecting noise to the power mains through the power supply system. The source of EMI in this case can be the electronic circuits whose high frequency current demand cannot be supplied by the power system without, in turn, interfering with the mains. The EMI source can also be the power regulator itself (switcher, phase control, etc.) which generates high-frequency noise on the power mains. In both cases, these emissions are controlled by military or civilian conducted emission specifications.

10.1.5 Cable-to-Cable Coupling

This last coupling path (2E in the flow diagram of Fig. 10.1) deals with proximity coupling or **crosstalk** between the source leads (culprit) and any nearby wiring. This nearby wiring can be part of a potential victim **inside the same machine**, in which case the diagram suggests a link toward susceptibility models (see Chapter 8). Also, the nearby wiring can be contaminated with no consequence to the internal receiving circuits while causing this wiring to become a secondary, unintentional HF signal **carrier**. Then it will become a **contributor to conducted or radiated EMI**. This is why path 2E shows ramifications to CM loop radiation (2B), differential-mode radiation (2C) and power line coupling (2D).

10.2 Selected Emission Topics

Several selected topics are presented to allow the reader to determine his emission levels from different circuits, components and cables. To provide a number of useful emission levels, the following topics are covered:

1. Field strengths from a straight wire and loop carrying current
2. External field strength from a wire pair or transmission line carrying current
3. Radiated emissions from coaxial cables
4. Conducted emission from a pulse or transient on a cable
5. Radiated emission from a pulse or transient on a cable

10.2.1 Field Strengths from an Ideal Wire and Loop Radiator

Field strengths, at any distance from a current flowing in a straight wire or from current in a loop, are presented below. It is assumed that (1) the emission source has a uniform current in the wire or loop and its dimensions are small compared to the wavelength and the distance from the observation point, and (2) this point is located in **free space**, i.e., it is not close to a metallic surface. Even these restrictions can be accommodated by certain modifications.

The E-field and H-field components from a straight wire source carrying a current (see Fig. 10.3) are:

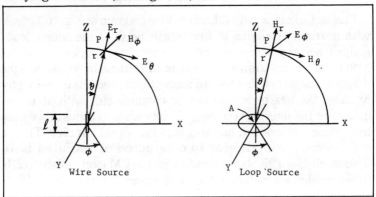

Figure 10.3—Spherical Coordinates Used in Eqs. (10.1) through (10.6)

$$E_\theta = \frac{Il\beta^3}{4\pi\omega\epsilon_0} \left[\frac{-1}{j(\beta r)} + \frac{1}{(\beta r)^2} + \frac{1}{j(\beta r)^3} \right] \sin\theta \ \text{V/m} \quad (10.1)$$

$$E_r = \frac{Il\beta^3}{2\pi\omega\epsilon_0} \left[\frac{1}{(\beta r)^2} + \frac{1}{j(\beta r)^3} \right] \cos\theta \ \text{V/m} \quad\quad (10.2)$$

$$H_\phi = \frac{Il\beta^2}{4\pi} \left[\frac{-1}{j(\beta r)} + \frac{1}{(\beta r)^2} \right] \sin\theta \ \text{A/m} \quad\quad (10.3)$$

where,

I = wire current in amperes

l = wire length in meters

β = electrical length per meter of wavelength = ω/c = $2\pi/\lambda$

ω = radial frequency in radians per second = $2\pi f$

f = frequency in hertz

c = velocity of light = 3×10^8 m/s

ϵ_0 = permittivity of free space = $1/(36\pi \times 10^9)$ f/m

r = distance from source to observation point in meters

θ = angle between zenith wire axis and observation point

ϕ = angle between Y axis and projection of observation point in X-Y plane

The E-field and H-field components from a circular loop carrying a current (see Fig. 10.3) are:

$$H_\theta = \frac{IA\beta^3}{4\pi} \left[\frac{-1}{(\beta r)} + \frac{j}{(\beta r)^2} + \frac{1}{(\beta r)^3} \right] \sin\theta \ \text{A/m} \quad (10.4)$$

$$H_r = \frac{IA\beta^3}{2\pi} \left[\frac{j}{(\beta r)^2} + \frac{1}{(\beta r)^3} \right] \cos\theta \ \text{A/m} \quad\quad (10.5)$$

$$E_\phi = \frac{IA\beta^4}{4\pi\omega\epsilon_o} \left[\frac{-1}{(\beta r)} + \frac{j}{(\beta r)^2} \right] \sin\theta \text{ V/m} \qquad (10.6)$$

where,

A = cross sectional loop area in square meters

Other items are as listed for current-carrying straight wire.

By solving the above equations for the composite electric and magnetic field strengths, Table 10.1 results. The frequency range from 10 Hz to 10 GHz is listed in the left column of the table. The left half of the table corresponds to a short, straight wire of 1 cm length, carrying a current of 1 A. The right half of the table corresponds to a 1 cm sq loop carrying a current of 1 A (a magnetic moment of 1 A × cm^2). Both the left and right halves of the table are further divided into the resulting E-field and H-field strengths. Finally, under each of the indicated field strengths in the table, the distance between source and observation point has been quantized into four decade lengths: R = 1 cm, 10 cm, 1 m and 10 m.

Regarding the electric field from a short, straight wire and for lower frequencies, Table 10.1 indicates that the field strength decreases at a rate of 20 dB/decade of frequency increase and that it decreases with distance increase at a rate of 60 dB/decade, i.e., 1/r^3. Different frequencies in the higher frequency range and different distances yield different results in accordance with the changing propagation terms of Eqs. (10.1) and (10.2).

In contrast to the preceding paragraph, the electric field corresponding to a small circular loop at lower frequencies increases with a frequency increase at a rate of 20 dB/decade. Also, the electrical field strength decreases with a distance increase at the rate of 40 dB/decade, i.e., 1/r^2. However, as in the preceding paragraph, different propagation terms apply at higher frequencies, as indicated in Eq. (10.6).

In contrast to the above, the magnetic field strength is relatively constant over the lower frequency range for both straight wires and circular loops. For the straight wire, the magnetic field strength decreases at the rate of 40 dB/decade of distance increase, whereas for small circular loops it decreases at a rate of 60 dB/decade. When

10.10

Table 10.1—Electric and Magnetic Fields From a Straight 1 cm Wire and 1 cm sq Loop Carrying 1 A, for Ideal Conditions

FRE-QUENCY	L=1 cm; I=1 Ampere — E-Field dBuV/m				H-Field dBuA/m				A=1 cm sq; I=1 Ampere — E-Field dBuV/m				H-Field dBuA/m				FRE-QUENCY
	R=1c	R=10	R=1m	R=10	R=1c	R=10	R=1m	R=10	R=1c	R=10	R=1m	R=10	R=1c	R=10	R=1m	R=10	
10Hz	368	308	248	188	137	97	57	17	15	-25	-65	-105	143	83	23	-37	10Hz
20Hz	362	302	242	182	137	97	57	17	21	-19	-59	-99	143	83	23	-37	20Hz
30Hz	359	299	239	179	137	97	57	17	25	-15	-55	-95	143	83	23	-37	30Hz
50Hz	354	294	234	174	137	97	57	17	29	-11	-51	-91	143	83	23	-37	50Hz
70Hz	351	291	231	171	137	97	57	17	32	-8	-48	-88	143	83	23	-37	70Hz
100Hz	348	288	228	168	137	97	57	17	35	-5	-45	-35	143	83	23	-37	100Hz
200Hz	342	282	222	162	137	97	57	17	41	1	-39	-79	143	83	23	-37	200Hz
300Hz	339	279	219	159	137	97	57	17	45	5	-35	-75	143	83	23	-37	300Hz
500Hz	334	274	214	154	137	97	57	17	49	9	-31	-71	143	83	23	-37	500Hz
700Hz	331	271	211	151	137	97	57	17	52	12	-28	-68	143	83	23	-37	700Hz
1kHz	328	268	208	148	137	97	57	17	55	15	-25	-65	143	83	23	-37	1kHz
2kHz	322	262	202	142	137	97	57	17	61	21	-19	-59	143	83	23	-37	2kHz
3kHz	319	259	199	139	137	97	57	17	65	25	-15	-55	143	83	23	-37	3kHz
5kHz	314	254	194	134	137	97	57	17	69	29	-11	-51	143	83	23	-37	5kHz
7kHz	311	251	191	131	137	97	57	17	72	32	-8	-48	143	83	23	-37	7kHz
10kHz	308	248	188	128	137	97	57	17	75	35	-5	-45	143	83	23	-37	10kHz
20kHz	302	242	182	122	137	97	57	17	81	41	1	-39	143	83	23	-37	20kHz
30kHz	299	239	179	119	137	97	57	17	85	45	5	-35	143	83	23	-37	30kHz
50kHz	294	234	174	114	137	97	57	17	89	49	9	-31	143	83	23	-37	50kHz
70kHz	291	231	171	111	137	97	57	17	92	52	12	-28	143	83	23	-37	70kHz
100kHz	288	228	168	108	137	97	57	17	95	55	15	-25	143	83	23	-37	100kHz
200kHz	282	222	162	102	137	97	57	17	101	61	21	-19	143	83	23	-37	200kHz
300kHz	279	219	159	99	137	97	57	17	105	65	25	-15	143	83	23	-37	300kHz
500kHz	274	214	154	94	137	97	57	17	109	69	29	-11	143	83	23	-37	500kHz
700kHz	271	211	151	91	137	97	57	17	112	72	32	-8	143	83	23	-37	700kHz
1MHz	268	208	148	88	137	97	57	17	115	75	35	-5	143	83	23	-37	1MHz
2MHz	262	202	142	83	137	97	57	18	121	81	41	2	143	83	23	-36	2MHz
3MHz	259	199	139	80	137	97	57	18	125	85	45	6	143	83	23	-36	3MHz
5MHz	254	194	134	77	137	97	57	20	129	89	49	12	143	83	23	-34	5MHz
7MHz	251	191	131	76	137	97	57	22	132	92	52	17	143	83	23	-32	7MHz
10MHz	248	188	128	75	137	97	57	24	135	95	55	22	143	83	23	-30	10MHz
20MHz	242	182	123	81	137	97	58	30	141	101	62	34	143	83	24	-18	20MHz
30MHz	239	179	120	84	137	97	58	33	145	105	66	41	143	83	24	-11	30MHz
50MHz	234	174	117	89	137	97	60	37	149	109	72	49	143	83	26	-2	50MHz
70MHz	231	171	116	92	137	97	62	40	152	112	77	55	143	83	28	4	70MHz
100MHz	228	168	115	95	137	97	64	43	155	115	82	61	143	83	30	10	100MHz
200MHz	222	163	121	101	137	98	70	49	161	122	94	73	143	84	42	22	200MHz
300MHz	219	160	124	105	137	98	73	53	165	126	101	80	143	84	49	29	300MHz
500MHz	214	157	129	109	137	100	77	57	169	132	109	89	143	86	58	38	500MHz
700MHz	211	156	132	112	137	102	80	60	172	137	115	95	143	88	64	44	700MHz
1GHz	208	155	135	115	137	104	83	63	175	142	121	101	143	90	70	50	1GHz
2GHz	203	161	141	121	138	110	89	69	182	154	133	113	144	102	82	62	2GHz
3GHz	200	164	145	125	138	113	93	73	186	161	140	120	144	109	89	69	3GHz
5GHz	197	169	149	129	140	117	97	77	192	169	149	129	146	118	98	78	5GHz
7GHz	196	172	152	132	142	120	100	80	197	175	155	135	148	124	104	84	7GHz
10GHz	195	175	155	135	144	123	103	83	202	181	161	141	150	130	110	90	10GHz

Notes: Radiation Source-to-Victim Distance Quantized into 4 Distances: 1cm, 10cm, 1m & 10m.
For straight wire: E and H = above + 20xLog(LI); L in cm. and I in amperes.
For loop wire: E and H = above + 20xLog(AI); A in sq. cm. and I in amperes.

Dimension of wire or loop must be less than $\lambda/2$. Otherwise replace L or larger dimension of A with $\lambda/2$.

the distance r exceeds $\lambda/2\pi$, however, the significant propagation terms are different in accordance with Eqs. (10.3) through (10.5).

Table 10.1 may be applied to any magnitude of current and length of wire or loop area by scaling the values in the table, provided that the two conditions mentioned in the introductory paragraph are maintained. Thus:

$$E \text{ and } H = \text{Table 10.1 values} + 20 \log (Il) \text{ for wire} \qquad (10.7)$$

$$E \text{ and } H = \text{Table 10.1 values} + 20 \log (AI) \text{ for loop} \qquad (10.8)$$

where,

I = straight or loop wire current in amperes

l = wire length in cm $\leqslant \lambda/2$

A = loop area in cm^2 in which greater dimension $\leqslant \lambda/2$

If l or either dimension in Eqs. (10.7) or (10.8) exceeds $\lambda/2$, then replace l or the dimension with $\lambda/2$.

10.2.2 Field Strengths from Real-Life Circuits

Although perfectly correct in theory, there are several serious restrictions which limit the practical usage of Table 10.1 in its simple form:

1. The distance to the point of observation, r, should be large with respect to the length of the radiating circuit.
2. The electrical length of the circuit should be less than $\lambda/2$, preferably less than $\lambda/10$, so that the assumption of uniform current is met.
3. The single-wire model (electrical excitation) corresponds ideally to a piece of wire floating in the air in which a certain current is forced, a situation seldom seen in practice.
4. The single-wire model assumes that the circuit impedance is infinite in the near field, or at least greater than the reactance of the wire alone. This condition is rarely met except in dipoles or whip antennas.

5. The two preceding constraints seem alleviated if one switches to the loop model. The loop model, indeed, is more workable because it does not carry the premise of a conductor coming from nowhere and going nowhere. But it has a serious constraint anyway: the loop must be an actual short circuit, such as the wave impedance, and hence the E-field is only dictated by the coefficients in Maxwell's equation solutions. If this condition is not met (and it is seldom met except in the case of a few turns in a coil with no other impedance in the loop), the H-field from Table 10.1 will be correct, but the associated E-field will be less than its actual value.

Since, in reality, we deal with neither purely open wires nor with perfect loops, but rather with circuit configurations which are in between, predictions in the near field based on the wire model only would give higher E-field than exists in reality. Predictions based on the ideal loop model would give E-fields lower than reality (optimistic error). Measurements have shown that the latter can be as high as 60 dB or more. Therefore, certain adjustments have to be made.

In the far field, the wave impedance E/H is independent of the circuit source impedance, but in the near field, the wave impedance can never exceed $377 \, \lambda/2\pi r$ (for electric sources), nor can it be less than $377 \times 2\pi r/\lambda$ (for magnetic sources). In between, **the wave impedance is governed by the originating circuit impedance**.

The development of a discrete relation between circuit impedance, Z_c, and wave impedance, Z_w, in the near field is beyond the scope of this handbook. However, the following mathematical relations are suggested for conditions in which the circuit dimensions, $l \ll \lambda$:

$$Z_W \cong \frac{Z_o\lambda}{2\pi r}, \text{ for } Z_c > \frac{Z_o\lambda}{2\pi r} \geqslant Z_o \qquad (10.9)$$

$$\cong Z_c, \text{ for } \frac{Z_o\lambda}{2\pi r} \geqslant Z_c \geqslant Z_o \qquad (10.10)$$

$$\cong Z_o, \text{ for } Z_c = Z_o \text{ or } \frac{\lambda}{2\pi r} \geqslant 1 \qquad (10.11)$$

$$\cong Z_c, \text{ for } Z_o > Z_c \geqslant \frac{Z_o 2\pi r}{\lambda} \qquad (10.12)$$

$$\cong \frac{Z_o 2\pi r}{\lambda}, \text{ for } Z_o > \frac{Z_o 2\pi r}{\lambda} > Z_c \qquad (10.13)$$

Equations (10.9) through (10.13) are plotted in Fig. 10.4 for several values of Z_c including common transmission line impedances of 50, 100, 300 and 600 Ω. To the extent that these conditions exist, the common transmission line impedances, then, permit neither a very high nor very low wave impedance condition to exist when r << $\lambda/2\pi$.

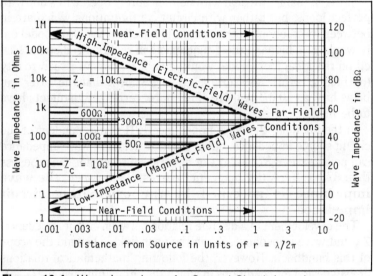

Figure 10.4—Wave Impedance for Several Circuit Impedances

As discussed later, sometimes it is more useful to present Eqs. (10.9) through (10.13) in terms of frequency, f, rather than wavelength.

$$f\lambda_m = C = 1\sqrt{\mu_o \epsilon_o} = 3 \times 10^8 \text{ m/s} \qquad (10.14)$$

or,

$$f_{MHz} = 300/\lambda_m \qquad (10.15)$$

where,

f = frequency in hertz

f_{MHz} = frequency in megahertz

λm = wavelength in meters

C = velocity of light in air

In light of the above, Eqs. (10.9) through (10.13) become:

For a high-impedance circuit in the near field:

$$Z_w = \frac{Z_o \lambda}{2\pi r} = \frac{18,000}{r_m f_{MHz}} \; \Omega \qquad (10.16)$$

For a low-impedance circuit in the near field:

$$Z_w = \frac{Z_o 2 \pi r}{\lambda} = 7.9 \; r_m f_{MHz} \; \Omega \qquad (10.17)$$

For far-field conditions:

$$Z_w = 120\pi = 377 \; \Omega \qquad (10.18)$$

In terms of the more general conditions of any circuit impedance presented in Eqs. (10.9) through (10.13), the generated wave impedance is:

$Z_w \cong 18,000/r_m f_{MHz}$ for $Z_c \geqslant 18,000/r_m f_{MHz}$ $\qquad$ (10.19)

$\cong Z_c$ for $18,000/r_m f_{MHz} \geqslant Z_c \geqslant 7.9 \; r_m f_{MHz}$ $\qquad$ (10.20)

$\cong 7.9 \; r_m \; f_{MHz}$ for $7.9 \; r_m f_{MHz} \geqslant Zc$ $\qquad$ (10.21)

Given these impedance considerations, a more practical model is now achievable, as described below.

In the near field, given that Z = circuit impedance = Zg + Z_L:

If $Z > 7.9 \times r_m \times f_{MHz}$, use modified wire model in which:

$$E_{(w)} = \frac{VA}{4\pi} \left[\frac{1}{r^3} + \frac{j\beta}{r^2} + \frac{\beta^2}{r} \right] \cong \frac{VA}{4\pi r^3} \; \text{in V/m}$$

10.15

where,

V = circuit generator voltage

A = circuit area in m² (the product of circuit length by wire separation)

r = observation distance in meters

Or use:

$$E_{\mu V/m} = \frac{7.9 \times V_{volts} \times A_{cm}^2}{R^3 m} \qquad (10.21a)$$

Alternatively, if $Z < 7.9 \times f_{MHz} \times r_m$, use the ideal loop model as per equation (10.6), i.e.:

$$E_{V/m} \cong \frac{IA\beta^2}{4\pi\omega\epsilon_0 r^2} = \frac{0.63\ IA\ f_{MHz}}{r^2} \qquad (10.21b)$$

where,

I = circuit current

$\beta = \omega/c = 2\pi/\lambda$

If one prefers to enter the circuit generator voltage V:

$$E_{V/m} = \frac{0.63\ VA_m^2\ f_{MHz}}{Zr^2} \qquad (10.21c)$$

where,

Z = circuit impedance

Also:

$$E_{\mu V/m} = \frac{63\ VA_{cm}^2\ f_{MHz}}{Zr^2} \qquad (10.21d)$$

In the far field, regardless of the type of excitation,

$$E_{V/m} \cong \frac{IA\beta^3}{4\pi\omega\epsilon_0 r} = \frac{0.0132\ IA_m^2 f_{MHz}^2}{r} \qquad (10.21e)$$

10.16

(The above equation is derived from Eq. 10.6.)

Referring to the circuit generator voltage, V:

$$E_{V/m} = \frac{0.0132 \; VA_m^2 \; f^2_{MHz}}{Zr} \text{ for } Z \leqslant 377 \; \Omega \text{ and } l \leqslant \lambda/4 \quad (10.21f)$$

A few remarks are in order at this point:

1. We now have a field expression which can be calculated by entering the drive voltage, which is often more easy to identify than the circuit current.
2. Except for very low-impedance loops (less than 7.9 Ω at 1 MHz, less than 7.9 mΩ at 1 kHz), e.g., low-voltage circuits carrying large pulsed currents, it is generally the wire pair model [Eqs. (10.21a) and (10.21e)] which will be used.
3. In the near field, for other than low-impedance loops, the E-field is independent of frequency and depends only on the driving voltage, the circuit area and the distance. Interestingly, the formula applies even down to a dc voltage.
4. In the far field, radiation calculated for a two-wire circuit (see Fig. 10.5) by the "wire model" would be equal to:

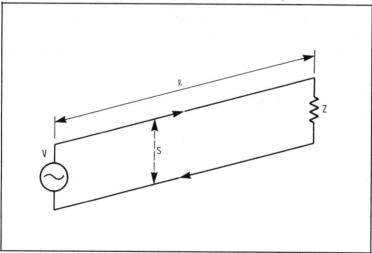

Figure 10.5—Differential Radiation from a Small-Circuit (DM)

$$E_{V/m} = \left(\frac{Il \times 0.2 \, \pi \times f_{MHz}}{r} \right) \times \sin \frac{2\pi s}{\lambda}$$

In the above equation, the first term is the field created by one wire only, and the second term is the cancelling factor due to the opposite field created by the other wire carrying an opposite current.

Since for small values of χ, $\sin \chi \cong \chi$, the expression simplifies to:

$$E_{V/m} = \frac{I \times 0.2 \, \pi \times f}{r} \times \frac{2 \, \pi l \times s}{\lambda}$$

$$= \frac{0.0132 \, V}{Z \times r} \times f^2 \times l \times s$$

This is exactly the same expression as the one found for a radiating loop in the far field: Eq. (10.21f).

5. For $l \geqslant \lambda/4$, the circuit begins to operate like a transmission line or a folded dipole (see Fig. 10.6). The current is no longer uniform and, in the equation, the **length must be clamped** to $\lambda/4$; i.e., the active part of this fortuitous antenna actually "shrinks" when frequency increases. (In addition, the radiation pattern will start to exhibit lobing effects.) Furthermore, if the circuit is not terminated in its matched impedance, there will be standing waves, and the effective circuit impedance will vary according to transmission line theory.

6. In the far field, if the circuit impedance exceeds 377 Ω, the

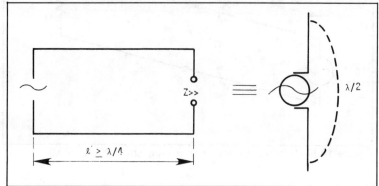

Figure 10.6—Line Equal or Longer than λ/4 Behaving like a Folded λ/2 Dipole

10.18

value of 377 Ω must be entered into Eq. (10.21f). This acknowledges the fact that even an open-ended circuit (Z = ∞) will still radiate due to the displacement current flowing into its self-capacitance.

7. In the far field, the magnitude of the E-field increases like f^2, i.e., 40 dB/decade. Equation (10.21f), for general circuit types, has been plotted in Fig. 10.7 for 1 and 3 m distances, a 1 cm^2 circuit area and normalized to a 1 V excitation.

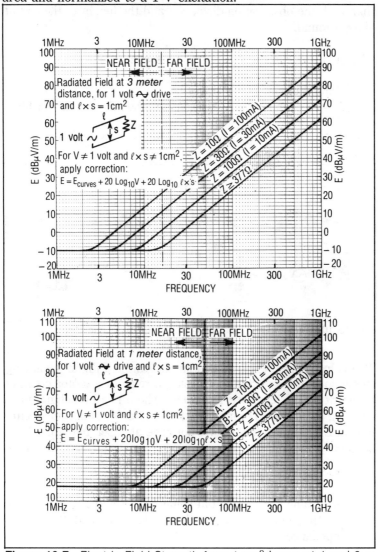

Figure 10.7—Electric Field Strength from 1 cm^2 Loops at 1 and 3 m Distance, for 1 V of Drive Voltage

10.2.3 Application: Differential-Mode Radiation from Simple Circuits

The previous discussion and prediction graphs will allow calculation of the electric and magnetic fields in the simplest configurations—the case of the direct differential-mode radiation, which assumes a small circuit whose largest dimension l is smaller than both the observation distance r and the height of the circuit above ground.

The circuit in question (Fig. 10.8) can consist of:

1. Printed circuit board traces
2. A wire-wrapped or any wired circuit board segment of ribbon cable
3. A discrete wire pair (provided the small length condition is met)

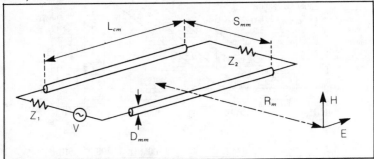

Figure 10.8—Differential-Mode Radiation from Simple Circuit

The culprit signal exciting this circuit can be a digital or analog signal source, a switching transistor, a relay or a motor creating transient spikes, etc. (see Fig. 10.9). There is a branching input entering in Box 2C to remind one that a circuit can become a **carrier** of EMI signals that it does not generate itself but which have been coupled from a nearby circuit by crosstalk (see Chapter 8).

The procedure is then:

1. Determine the differential voltage (or eventually current) at the frequency or frequencies of interest, and the circuit impedance.

10.20

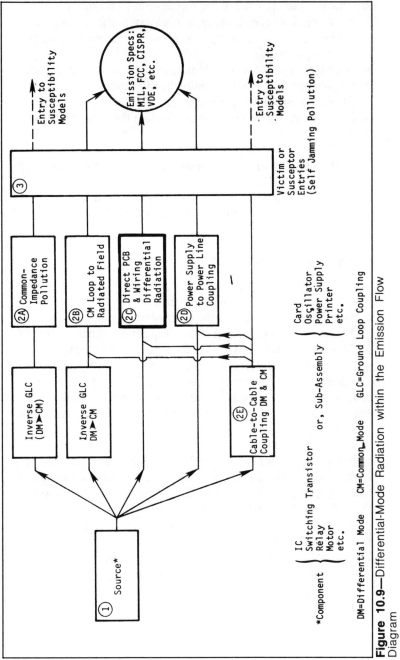

Figure 10.9—Differential-Mode Radiation within the Emission Flow Diagram

2. Check to see if r ≤ λ/6 for the near-field condition.
3. If r ≤ λ/6, determine if the circuit belongs to the low-impedance loop model (Z < 7.9 × f_{MHz} × r_m) or to the wire model (Z > 7.9 × f_{MHz} × r_m).
4. Check to see if l ≤ λ/4. If not, use l_{cm} = 7,500/f_{MHz} (corresponding to l = λ/4) to enter in the model.
5. Check the same for wire separation s.
6. Calculate A = (l × s) cm^2 and calculate the correction 20 log A.
7. Find the field, using:
   a. if voltage is known, E dBμV/m = E_o (from curves) + 20 log A + 20 log V
   b. if current is known, E dBμV/m = E_o (from curves) + 20 log A + 20 log I (or H dBμA/m, or H_o from Table 10.1)

Illustrative Example 10.2

A 5 V, 20 A power supply operates at a switching frequency of 100 kHz. In the secondary loop (formed by the transformer output, the rectifying diodes and the electrolytic capacitor bank), the peak half-wave current is 50 A with a repetition frequency of 100 kHz. The loop dimensions are 3 cm × 10 cm. The impedance of the loop is very low (merely the secondary wiring impedance and the capacitor equivalent series resistance) and estimated to be 0.1 Ω.

What are the E-field and H-field at 1 m at the fundamental frequency of 100 kHz? Compare these to a radiated EMI specification level.

1. For simplification, we will take the peak current as the fundamental amplitude (for a half sine wave, this corresponds to a pessimistic error of about +20 percent). Therefore, the current correction will be 20 log 50 = +34 dB.
2. For 100 kHz, λ/6 is equal to 1/6 × 300 m/0.1 MHz = 500 m. Therefore, 1 m is a near-field situation.
3. Because 0.1 Ω < 7.9 × 0.1 MHz × 1 meter, the loop meets the condition of a low-impedance magnetic radiator and Table 10.1 applies.
4. The area correction is 20 log(3 × 10) cm^2 = +30 dB.

For 100 kHz and r = 1 meter, Table 10.1 gives:

$$E_o = 15 \text{ dB}\mu\text{V/m}$$

$$H_o = 17 \text{ dB}\mu\text{A/m}$$

The actual field computation is shown in Table 10.2.

Table 10.2—Field Computation for Switching Power Supply of Example 10.2

F	Amplitude Correction dB	Area Correction dB	E_odBμV/m	H_odBμA/m	E final	H final
100 kHz	34	30	15		79	
				17		81

Illustrative Example 10.3

A 20 V, 100 MHz RF signal is relayed to several loads via a switch box. The PCB traces in the switch box represent an area of 2.5 × 4 = 10 cm². What is the radiated E-field at 1 m when (1) the circuit is loaded by 75 Ω and (2) the circuit, during "key-up" condition, is open-ended? Compare to the maximum permissible levels of MIL-STD-461B, REO2.

1. The 20 V amplitude corresponds to 26 dBV. When open-ended, one can expect the voltage to double, i.e. 32 dBV.
2. At 100 MHz, $\lambda/6$ is equal to 1/6 × 300/100 = 0.5 m.
3. Therefore, 1 m is already in the far field.
4. The area correction will be 20 log 10 cm² = 20 dB$_{cm2}$
5. For the open condition, where Z = ∞, we will select the curve z > 377 in Fig. 10.7. For 75 Ω we will interpolate between the 100 Ω and 30 Ω curves.
6. At 100 MHz, $\lambda/4$ is 0.75 m. It is unlikely that the longest circuit dimension, in the 10 cm² PCB, will exceed 75 cm. Field computation is shown in Table 10.3.

Table 10.3—Field Computation for RF Circuit of Example 10.3

F	Amplitude Correction dB	Area Correction dB	E_o	H_o	E_{final}	H_{final}	Spec. Limit E	Spec. Limit H
100 kHz (75 Ω)	26	20	44	NA	90	NA	29	NA
100 kHz (open)	32	20	30	NA	82	NA	29	NA

10.23

The specification limit is exceeded by 61 dB when transmitting, and 53 dB when idle. This indicates the amount of reduction which must be accomplished by redesigning the circuit board (going to a microstrip configuration with only 1 mm spacing would provide about 30 dB reduction) and providing a metal shield.

10.2.4 Application: Differential-Mode Radiation from Periodic Non-sinusoidal Signals Having a Narrowband Spectrum

The previous examples dealt with a single-frequency case. When the EMI source is a periodic waveform with a repetition period T, the radiated spectrum can be calculated for each harmonic f_n = n × 1/T by using the simple Fourier envelope of the EMI voltage or current.

However, this assumes that the user is dealing with a narrowband situation; i.e., the repetition frequency f_{EMI} is larger than the victim or measuring instrument bandwidth. The broadband-signal case, where several frequency components are adding up in the bandwidth of concern, will be developed in Section 10.2.5.

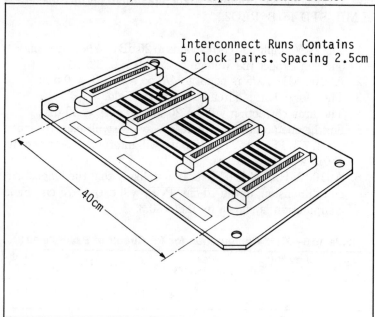

Interconnect Runs Contains
5 Clock Pairs. Spacing 2.5cm

40cm

Figure 10.10—Mother Board of the Radiation Example

10.24

Illustrative Example 10.4: Radiation From a Digital Circuit Board

Estimate the radiated emission from the large card (mother board) shown in Fig. 10.10. The critical (radiating) portion of the circuit consists of:

1. Five clock traces and their returns, carrying 10 MHz clock
2. Voltage swing: 4 V
3. Rise time τ_r: 10 ns
4. Load: 500 Ω (corresponds roughly to a TTL input with 10 pF of capacitance)
5. Trace run: l = 40 cm
6. Pair separations: s = 2.5 cm

Compare the EMI levels to the limits of FCC Part 15 Class B.

For the voltage, the Fourier envelope is constructed using the "template" of Fig. 10.10, where 20 dB/decade and 40 dB/decade slopes have been materialized. The 0 dB reference is given by 2 × amplitude × duty cycle.

A 50 percent duty cycle is assumed; therefore, 2 A × τ/T = 4 V = 12 dBV. Since the curves in Fig. 10.7 are normalized for 1 V, 1 loop and 1 cm², the following dB correction factors must be applied:

1. The actual voltages, in dBV
2. The area of one loop = 20 log l × s cm²
3. The number of synchronous loops = 20 log N

One should remember that when the largest dimension l reaches λ/4, the value entered in the area correction must be clamped to the λ/4 of each harmonic used in the calculation. In this case, 40 cm represents λ/4 for F = 1/4 × 300 MHz/0.4 m = 188 MHz. Therefore, beyond 188 MHz (harmonic no. 18), each step shows a gradually reducing value for the effective area: the efficiency of the antenna decreases, as does the voltage spectrum. As a result, the total radiation profile collapses.

The radiation from the 10 MHz clock is shown in Fig. 10.11. The prediction indicates clearly that the FCC limit is violated by 14 dB; i.e., action has to be taken to reduce the trace's loop. To do this, use a ground plane or shield the equipment housing.

10.25

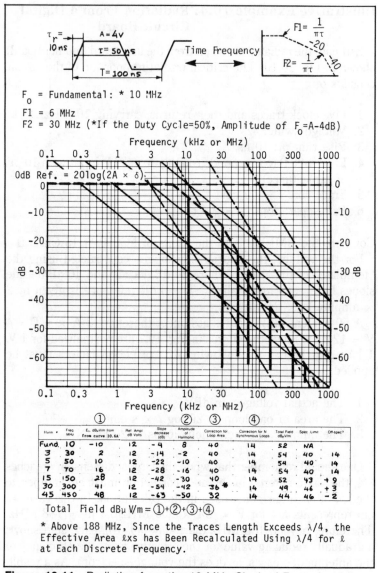

Figure 10.11—Radiation from the 10 MHz Clock of Example 10.4

10.26

For sake of precision, it must be remarked that:

1. The Fourier series gives peak value for each harmonic, while the EMI receiver is scaled in rms, which means a −3 dB difference.
2. The FCC procedure calls for scanning antenna height to search for maximum reading, which means up to +6 dB add-up when the ground-reflected wave arrives in phase with the direct one.

10.2.5 Radiation from Broadband Sources

The previous section developed E-field and H-field emission values from a short wire and small loop excited at single frequencies. This section extends the basic concept to short wires and loops excited by signals whose frequency content occupies a major portion of the frequency spectrum, i.e., broadband signals.

Although the model for narrowband emission propagation has certain technical advantages over more traditional approaches, in the rapidly expanding digital world, an approach involving determination of fields emanating from elements excited by a broadband source is of great value. It is also useful for transients on power mains. Since a broadband source can be expressed as the summation of a number of discrete continuous sine waves via Fourier theory, an approach based on the previous model is suggested.

A typical time-domain digital waveform, such as that shown in Fig. 10.12, can be transferred to the frequency domain and described in terms of the envelope of the maximum values of the Fourier spectrum components:

$$V_{dB\mu V}/MHz = 20 \log (2 \ A\tau) + 240 \qquad (10.22)$$

The plot of the maximum value of the envelope of the Fourier components is shown in Fig. 10.13. The first envelope is the voltage spectral density, while the second is the current density, computed from Ohm's Law as follows:

$$I_{(f)} \ dB\mu A/MHz = V_{(f)} \ dB\mu V/MHz - 20 \log Z_{(f)} \qquad (10.23)$$

where,

$Z_{(f)}$ = circuit impedance at the frequency of interest, in ohms

10.27

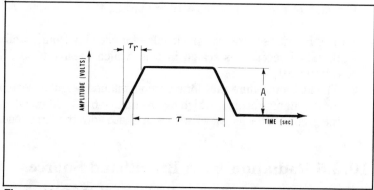

Figure 10.12—Typical Digital Waveform (Broadband Excitation Source)

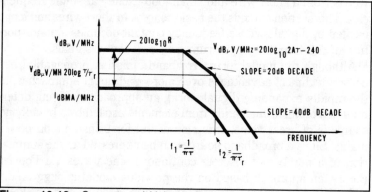

Figure 10.13—Current and Voltage Envelope of Maximum Values of Fourier Spectrum Components

Thus, a value of voltage $V_{(f)}$ or current $I_{(f)}$ spectrum density is obtained which can be used to determine the radiated field's spectrum when the radiating element is excited with this waveform.

In the previous sections, the computed fields were a function of the drive voltage in narrowband terms. Thus, a correction factor is required to also express the field in broadband terms.

At any frequency F_{xMHz} in the spectrum, the broadband voltage in a unity bandwidth of 1 MHz will be equal to:

For $f_x < 1/\pi\tau$:

$$V_{v/MHz} = 2\,V \times \tau$$

10.28

or,

$$\text{dBV/MHz} = 6 + 20 \log A \times \tau$$

where,

V = amplitude of the time domain pulse

τ = the 50% pulse width in μs

For $1/\pi\tau < f_x < 1/\pi\tau_r$:

$$V_{\text{volt/MHz}} = 2 \ V/\pi f_x$$

or,

$$\text{dBV/MHz} = -4 + 20 \log A - 20 \log f_x$$

For $f_x > 1/\pi\tau_r$:

$$V_{\text{volts/MHz}} = 2 \ V/\pi^2\tau_r(f_x)^2$$

or,

$$\text{dBV/MHz} = -14 + 20 \log A - 20 \log \tau_r$$
$$- 40 \log f_x$$

If the results are desired in a bandwidth $B_x \neq 1$ MHz, another correction is necessary equal to $20 \log B_x$ MHz.

To compute the radiated field from small circuits excited by a broadband source, the following steps are necessary:

1. Select frequencies for evaluation.
2. Construct the Fourier spectrum of the pulse, identifying the first and second corner frequencies, f_1 and f_2.
3. Calculate the spectrum density at the pedestal, $2 \times A \times \tau$.
4. For each selected frequency, estimate the approximate circuit impedance, Z.
5. Identify beyond which frequency the $l \geqslant \lambda/4$ condition exists.
6. Extract from Fig. 10.7 (or Table 10.1, in the case of a low-impedance loop) the values of E dBμV/m, and eventually H dBμA/m.
7. Apply the proper area and amplitude corrections.

Illustrative Example 10.5

Consider a train of timing pulses with the following characteristics:

Amplitude: 10 V
Pulse width: 100 ns
Rise time: 10 ns
Repetition period: 10 μs

The pulse train is carried on two parallel wires separated by 3.5 mm over a 0.3 m length. The circuit impedance is 50 Ω. Determine the values of radiated electric field at 1 m, from 100 kHz to 1,000 MHz, and compare them to the limits of MIL-STD-461 REO2.

To simplify computation, an "income tax" form has been used. The repetition period of 10 μs, corresponding to a pulse repetition frequency of 100 kHz, indicates that the signal, in a 1 MHz bandwidth, can be treated as broadband. (Another approach would be to calculate the amplitude of the individual 100 kHz harmonics and to sum them up in a 1 MHz bandwidth, which would produce the same result.)

$$f_1 = 1/\pi\tau = 3.2 \text{ MHz}$$

$$f_2 = 1/\pi\tau_r = 32 \text{ MHz}$$

$$2 \, A\tau = 2 \times 10 \text{ V} \times 0.100 \, \mu\text{s} = 2 \text{ V/MHz}$$

$$= 6 \text{ dBV/MHz}$$

The area correction is:

$$30 \text{ cm} \times 0.35 \text{ cm} \cong 10 \text{ cm}^2 = + 20 \text{ dB cm}$$

The $\lambda/4$ cutoff for 30 cm occurs when:

$$1/4 \times 300/f_{MHz} = 0.30 \text{ m}$$

or,

$$f = 75/0.3 = 225 \text{ MHz}$$

Beyond this frequency, the area of the radiating loop will be changed from $l \times$ s to $\lambda/4 \times$ s. This is accomplished in Table 10.4 by adding

Table 10.4—Computation Form for Radiated EMI of Illustrative Example 10.5

Freq.	Z	① Ref. Value from Table 10 1 or Fig.10.6A E_o	H_o	② 2Aτ Pedestal Amplitude dBV/MHz or dBA/MHz	③ Spectrum decrease, for 20 or 40dB /decade	④ Radiation Area corrections ℓ x S: dB_{cm^2}	⑤ ℓ > λ/4: $dB\frac{\lambda}{4}/\ell$	Final Field Values E dBμV/m/MHz	H dBμA/m/MHz	Specif. RE-02	Δ
100kHz	50Ω	18	NA	6	0	20	NA	44		31	+13
1MHz	50Ω	18	NA	6	0	20	NA	44		26	+18
f_1 = 3MHz	50Ω	18	NA	6	0	20	NA	44		24	+20
10MHz	50Ω	18	NA	6	-10	20	NA	34		22	+12
20MHz	50Ω	20	NA	6	-16	20	NA	30		20	+10
f_2 =30MHz	50Ω	26	NA	6	-20	20	NA	32		21	+11
100MHz	50Ω	46	NA	6	-40	20	NA	32		29	+ 3
300MHz	50Ω	66	NA	6	-60	20	-2	30		37	– 7
1000MHz	50Ω	86	NA	6	-80	20	-12	20		45	-15

E(orH) final = 1 + 2 + 3 + 4 + 5

10.31

a 20 log(λ/4)/l dB correction to the geometric area $l \times s$ beyond 225 MHz.

The calculation steps are shown in the form of Table 10.4, and the graphical results are shown in Fig. 10.14. It is clear that, although the signal would be considered to be a mere 100 kHz, specification limits are exceeded up to $\cong$ 200 MHz. The last column in the form, labeled "Δ", indicates the minimum dB of reduction needed.

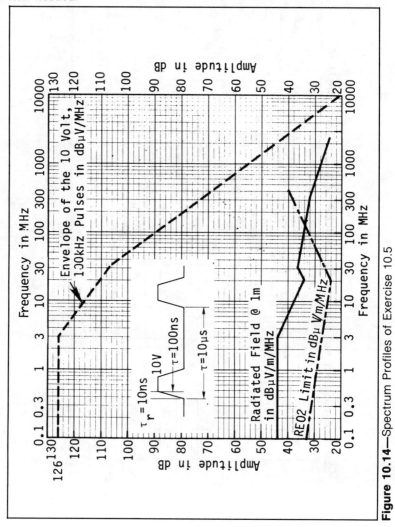

Figure 10.14—Spectrum Profiles of Exercise 10.5

10.32

The methods for reducing DM radiation from a small circuit or wire pair are identical to those explained in Chapter 7 for susceptibility:

1. Reduce the effective area (for instance, by running signal and return on top of each other in PCBs).
2. Twist the wires (for wired circuit).
3. Surround the radiating circuit by a shield.

For method 2, the twisting reduction can be predicted by the same curves as shown in Chapter 7. For method 3, the shielding reduction can also be predicated by the same curves as shown in Chapter 7; i.e., if the shield exceeds $\lambda/4$, resonance problems may nullify the shielding effectiveness unless a shield with very low transfer impedance is used.

10.3 Radiated Emissions from External Cables and Ground Loops

Whenever an equipment has external cables longer than the equipment itself, it is very likely that those cables will become the major contributors to EMI emissions, just as they were for EMI susceptibility. A cable radiates by its differential-mode signal, as discussed in the previous section, but also from the **unwanted** path, i.e., the ground loop (path 2B) in the general flow diagram (see Fig. 10.15), because of the imperfect isolation or symmetry of the desired circuit versus the ground.

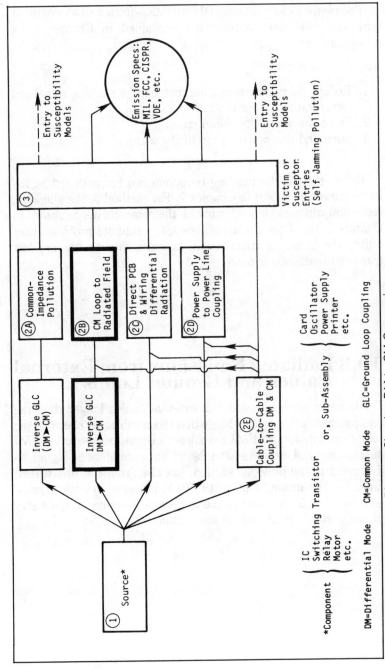

Figure 10.15—General Flow Diagram Showing DM to CM Conversion, Causing Ground Loops to Radiate

10.3.1 Inverse GLC: Ground Loops Excited by Output Signals

When a cable at height, h, from a conductive ground carries a signal, a common voltage is impressed between wires and ground, causing a common-mode current to circulate. This is true when the circuit is **not** perfectly balanced and when, due to either the design or the normal asymmetry of the circuitry, such as a grounded zero-volt reference (ZVR) at one end, a ground loop certainly exists. Even if the load end is not grounded, the ground loop virtually exists due to the circuit to ground parasitic or real capacitance. The simplest case, shown in Fig. 10.16, is where the CM radiation is caused by the asymmetric component of the **intentional signal**.

In this configuration, the common-mode current is:

$$I_{CM} = \frac{V_c}{Z_{CE} + Z_{EF}} + \frac{V_c}{R_L + Z_{DE} + Z_{EF}} \qquad (10.24)$$

or,

$$= V_c \left(\frac{1}{Z_{CE} + Z_{EF}} + \frac{1}{R_L + Z_{DE} + Z_{EF}} \right) \qquad (10.25)$$

where,

Z_{CE} = impedance of the parasitic capacitance from the "hot side" of R_L to the equipment frame

Z_{EF} = machine to ground impedance = short-circuit if the frame is bonded to ground, or impedance of machine-to-ground capacitance if the frame is floated

Z_{DE} = circuit board ZVR-to-frame impedance = short circuit if the ZVR is bonded to the frame, or impedance of the ZVR to frame capacitance if the ZVR is floated

In many cases where the parasitic capacitance of the zero-volt plane to frame is much larger than the parasitic capacitance of the "hot side" of R_L, we can say that $Z_{CE} \gg Z_{DE}$. (This is especially true if the ZVR is grounded.) If $Z_{CE} \gg Z_{DE}$, one can neglect the first term in Eq. (10.24), and the common-mode current simplifies to:

$$I_{CM} \cong \frac{V_c}{R_L + Z_{DE} + Z_{EF}} = \frac{V_s}{Z_w + R_L + Z_{DE} + Z_{EF}}$$

The term $(Z_{DE} + Z_{EF})$ is the floating impedance from ZVR to the common-mode ground, the same term used in Chapter 6 when dealing with susceptibility of ground loops. Therefore:

$$I_{CM} = \frac{Vs}{Z_w + R_L + Z_{float}}$$

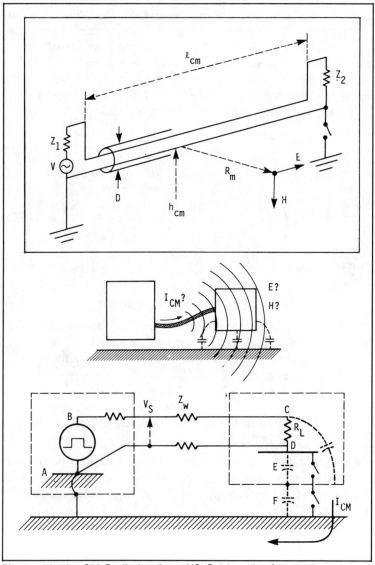

Figure 10.16—CM Radiation from I/O Cables: the Simple Case

The radiation can be computed from Fig. 10.7 using as inputs:

1. The signal source voltage
2. The total circuit-to-ground loop impedance made of the cable impedance plus the floating impedance (if any)
3. The loop area
4. For $l > \lambda/4$, the loop impedance should be replaced by the characteristic impedance of the whole cable above ground (see Table 5.5 in Chapter 5), since the regime becomes a transmission line. The accurate method would require an exact calculation of the actual impedance of the line seen from the source, which is feasible but would exceed the scope of this text. Thus, the loop impedance is averaged by Z_o above $\lambda/4$.

Illustrative Example 10.6

A central processing unit is sending a 3 V, 500 kHz (50 percent duty cycle) clock from Schottky 3 ns logic on external cables. The clock is sent to a peripheral via a wire pair with a total length of 75 cm and a height above ground of 30 cm and terminated in 100 Ω load. The peripheral chassis is grounded via a short wire. Compute the radiated field at 3 m distance for (1) the ZVR grounded to chassis, and (2) the ZVR floated (parasitic capacitance = 10 pF). Compare these to an FCC Part 15J, Class B limit for personal computers from 30 MHz to 1,000 MHz.

To simplify the example, we will run a narrowband estimation. The characteristic parameters are:

Loop area: 75 × 30 cm = 67 dBcm²

First corner frequency, f_1: 320 kHz

Second corner frequency, f_2: $1/\pi\tau_r$ = 100 MHz

Pedestal amplitude (narrowband calculation): 2 A × π/T = 10 dBV

Frequencies where loop dimensions exceed $\lambda/4$:

For l (75 cm) = $F_{(0.75)}$ = 1/4 [300/0.75 m] = 100 MHz

For h (30 cm) = $F_{(0.30)}$ = 1/4 [300/0.3] = 250 MHz

At some selected frequencies, the loop parameters are:

30 MHz = 0.75 m of wire represents about 150 Ω

10 pF (represents about 500 Ω)

Z_L = 100 Ω

100 MHz = loop impedance is replaced by the characteristic impedance of cable above ground $\cong$ 300 Ω

Although floating the PCB provides a slight advantage below 100 MHz, it is clear that beyond this frequency we face exactly the same problem as the ground-loop coupling **susceptibility** aspect (Chapter 6). The parasitic capacitance does not efficiently float the PCB. Figure 10.17 shows that the limit is violated by as much as 8 dB around 100 MHz.

The fixes to apply are basically the same as those for improving GLC isolation above cable resonance:

1. Use ferrite beads over the whole cable (preferably mounted on the signal source side).
2. Use common-mode capacitors on the source end sized to limit the spectrum to what is essential for the signal.

				①	②	③	④		⑤			
				2Aτ/T Pedestal Amplitude	Spectrum decrease	Radiation Area corrections			Final Field Values		Specif.	
		Ref. Value		dBVolt	for 20 or	ℓ x h	ℓ > λ/4		E	H	FCC-15	Δ
Freq.	Z* ohm	E_o	H_o	or dBAmp	40dB/dec	dB cm²	h > λ/4		dBμV/m	dBμA/m	(B)	
500kHz	100	-10	NA	10dBV	-4	67	NA		63	NA	NA	
30MHz	250	6	NA	10	-40	67	NA		43	NA	40	3
100MHz	300	24	NA	10	-50	67	NA		51	NA	43	8
300MHz	300	46	NA	10	-70	67	-13		40	NA	46	-6
1000MHz	300	66	NA	10	-90	67	-33		20	NA	46	-26

*if Z > 377 Ω, clamp value to 377 Ω

Figure 10.17—Illustrative Example 10.6 for PCB, Grounded (E_{final} = 1 + 2 + 3 + 4 + 5)

3. Add a homogeneous shield with low transfer impedance and both ends bonded so that the cable becomes "surrounded" by a ground and any possible CM current returns by this shield instead of the actual CM ground.
4. Replace unbalanced drivers/receivers by true balanced (symmetrical) ones, or use signal transformers (preferably with Faraday shields) on both ends of the link.
5. Use optoisolators or fiber optics.

Illustrative Example 10.7: Combined CM and DM Cable Radiation

For the same 3 V/500 kHz source as in Example 10.6, calculate the DM radiation at 3 m and compare to the CM one. Assuming the wire pair separation is s = 3 mm, the new parameters are:

Loop area: $75 \times 0.3 = 27$ dBcm^2

Loop impedance: 100 Ω (the terminating resistance)

$f_1 = 320$ kHz

$f_2 = 100$ MHz

The results are shown in Table 10.5 and are plotted on Fig. 10.18, against the CM field. It is clear that the CM radiation, about 30 dB above the DM one, is predominant.

Table 10.5—DM Radiation for the Same PCB of Example 10.6

Freq.	Z	Ref.Value E_o	Ref.Value H_o	$2A\tau$	Spectrum decrease	Radiation Area Corrections $\ell{\times}h$ dBcm^2	Radiation Area Corrections $\ell{>}\lambda/4$ dB$\lambda/4/\ell$	Final Field Values $E_{dB\mu V/m}$
500kHz	100			16 dBV	-4	27	NA	
30MHz	100	12		16	-40	27	NA	15
100MHz	100	32		16	-50	27	NA	25
300MHz	100	52		16	-70	27	-10	15
1000MHz	100	72		16	-90	27	-20	5

10.39

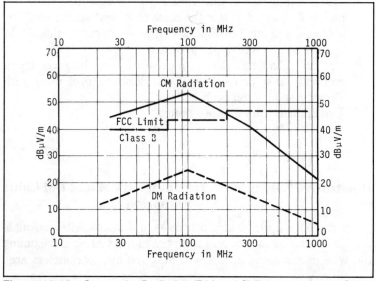

Figure 10.18—Composite Radiation (DM and CM) from an Actual Cable

10.3.2 Inverse GLC: Ground Loops Contaminated by Other Signals

While Section 10.3.1 covered the simple case where the CM current was due only to the leakage of the **intentional signal** through the ground, this section covers the case where the external cable is also carrying high frequency harmonics that are **not part of the intentional signal**, but which have been picked up in the machine by crosstalk, ground pollution, etc. In this case, the external cable becomes the carrier of these by-products and radiates accordingly. This problem of external cable contamination by undesired spurious emissions is one of the major contributors to violation of emission limits like FCC, CISPR, VDE, MIL-STD-461 and TEMPEST.

The first difficulty is to evaluate the amplitude of these undesired components. The pragmatic approach is to measure directly their voltage or current spectrum on the cable itself. This is relatively easy to do but requires at least a representative prototype. How can this be done if the machine does not even exist?

The deterministic approach consists of calculating every possible internal coupling between the inner circuitry and the circuit leads corresponding to the external I/O ports. This is feasible using the coupling prediction explained in Chapters 5 (CM impedance coupling) and 8 (crosstalk). However, this may take considerable time. A simple, crude method is to make the following **by-default** assumption: **Unless one knows otherwise, it is realistic to assume that noise picked up by internal couplings is just below the immunity level of the circuits interfacing the external link in question.**

For instance, with digital TTL logic, assume that the spurious signals picked up will not exceed 3.5 V – 20 dB = 350 mV. This is based on the observation that designers at least tend to make their machines **functionally** operational and that, if this worst-case value were exceeded, the machine would malfunction because of self-jamming.

Figure 10.19 shows conceptually the case of CM radiation by unwanted spurious emissions on the external cable. Then, when the EMI voltages (or currents) have been evaluated by one of the three above-mentioned methods, proceed as in the previous case to calculate the radiated fields, using the loop area and Fourier Spectrum.

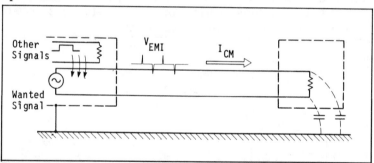

Figure 10.19—CM Radiation From I/O Cables, the Complex Case: Radiation Caused by Unwanted Spurs on I/O Cable

Illustrative Example 10.8

A microprocessor talks to a peripheral via a slow, 20 kHz interface. The cable is 1.5 m long, 0.75 m above ground, terminated into 120 Ω. The microprocessor uses an internal 10 MHz Schottky clock with 3.5 V amplitude. The PCB's zero-volt references are grounded at both ends. For this example, (1) evaluate the worst case amplitude of the 10 MHz residues on the I/O cable, and (2) com-

10.41

pute the CM loop radiated field at 3 m.
The configuration is shown in Fig. 10.20. The input parameters are:

1. Estimated amplitude of 10 MHz coupled spurs: 20 dB below TTL = 350 mV or − 10 dBV
2. Repetition frequency of spurious emissions: 20 MHz (All these internal couplings occur at each transition, i.e., at every rise and fall front.)
3. Pulse width of spurious emissions: equal to clock rise time = 3 ns
4. Pedestal amplitude = $2A\tau/T$ = 2 × 350 mV × 3 ns/50 ns = −27 dBV
5. $f_1 = f_2 = 1/(\pi \times 3 \text{ ns})$ = 100 MHz
6. Loop area (notice that the loop is made of the interconnecting cable **and** the power cord ground wires, assumed to have a vertical drop): 150 cm × 75 cm = 80 dBcm^2
7. For 1.5 m, $\lambda/4$ = 50 MHz
8. For 0.75 m, $\lambda/4$ = 100 MHz
9. Loop impedance = 120 Ω + cable impedance = 120 Ω + j5 Ω × f_{MHz}, to be replaced by characteristic impedance of the cable above ground beyond 50 MHz

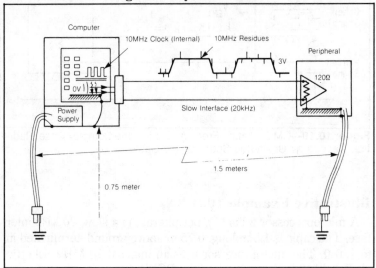

Figure 10.20—Internal Radiation and Crosstalk to External I/O Cable

The calculation table and resulting graph are shown in Fig. 10.21. Note that the radiated EMI is far above the FCC Class B limit shown as reference, and **most of the violation occurs at frequencies which are 1,000 times higher than the frequency of the intentional 20 kHz signal.**

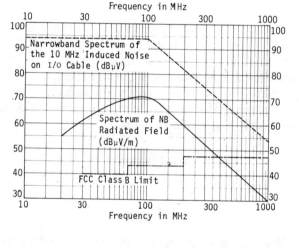

F	Z	Ref. Values		2Aτ	Spectrum decrease	Radiation Area Corrections		Final Field Values	
		E_o	H_o	dBVolts	20 or 40 dB/dec	ℓxh dB_{cm^2}	ℓ>λ/4 h>λ/4	E dBμV/m	H
20	156	2	NA	−27	0	80	0	55	NA
40	233	12	NA	−27	0	80	0	65	NA
100	350	24	NA	−27	0	80	−6	71	NA
300	350	44	NA	−27	−20	80	−26	51	NA
1000	350	64	NA	−27	−40	80	−46	31	NA

Figure 10.21—Calculation Steps and Radiated Field of Example 10.8

10.4 Radiated Emission from Coaxial Cables

When a coaxial cable carries a signal current, that portion of the current circulating on the outer skin of the shield radiates an electromagnetic field (see Fig. 10.22). This field can be related to

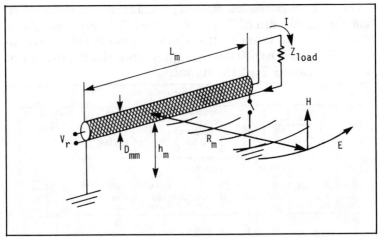

Figure 10.22—Radiation from a Coaxial Cable above Ground

the voltage appearing along the shield due to the transfer impedance of the braid. The better the quality of the braid, the less is this longitudinal shield voltage; i.e., as frequency increases, the signal is confined to the inner surface of the shield due to **skin effect**.

By reciprocity of the transfer impedance concept (see "unbalanced lines" in Chapter 7), the voltage appearing longitudinally along the exterior of the shield is:

$$V_{sh} = I_{signal} \times Z_{t\ \Omega/m} \times l_m \qquad (10.26)$$

$$= \frac{V_{signal}}{Z_{Load}} \times Z_{t\ \Omega/m} \times l_m$$

This voltage drives a current into the loop formed by the shield and the ground.

If the shield is grounded at both ends, it is very likely that in near field the coaxial cable will behave as a magnetic source, since the loop impedance is merely the shield-to-ground-loop impedance, Z_{sg}. This can be taken as:

$$Z_{sg} = R_{sh} + j\omega L_{sh}$$

Eventually, if the shield is grounded via pigtails (a very poor practice), the pigtail's dimensions and impedances must be included in the transfer impedance and loop calculations.

10.44

An approximate default value for a single braid coax, about 5 cm above ground, is:

$$Z_{sg} = [5 \text{ m}\Omega + j4\Omega \times f_{MHz}] \text{ per meter length}$$

Then, to calculate the E-field and H-field from this low-impedance loop, the external shield current can be calculated by:

$$I_{sg} = V_{shield}/Z_{shield}$$

This current is then used as input for Table 10.1.

If the shield is floated from the chassis ground, the coax becomes an electrically driven radiator, and the model of Fig. 10.7 can be used with the shield voltage as an input.

10.5 Magnetic Fields from a Long, Current-Carrying Wire

The preceding section develops field strengths from both wires and loops in which the field distance is large compared to the dimension of the wire or loop. When this restriction does not apply, i.e., the length of the wire is long compared to the orthogonal distance, then the following should be used.

As shown in Section 2.4.4.1 on lightning, the magnetic flux density, B, from a wire carrying a current, I, is

$$B = \mu H = 4\pi \times 10^{-7} \times I/2\pi R = \frac{2 \times I}{R} \times 10^{-7} \text{ Tesla} \quad (10.27)$$

$$= 2 \times 10^{-3} \text{ I/R Gauss}$$

$$= I/2\pi R \text{ A/m} \quad (10.28)$$

Equation (10.27) is tabulated in Table 10.6 to give magnetic flux density and magnetic field strength as a function of distance for a current of 1 A in a single wire (or harness, if common mode).

The flux density from a wire pair carrying a differential-mode current (see Fig. 10.23) is:

$$B = \mu H_1 - \mu H_2 \quad (10.29$$

$$= \frac{\mu I}{2\pi} \left[\frac{1}{R - S/2} - \frac{1}{R + S/2} \right] \tag{10.30}$$

$$= 2 \times 10^{-7}\, I \times \left(\frac{S}{R^2 + S^2} \right) \text{Tesla} \tag{10.31}$$

$$\cong 2 \times 10^{-7} I (S/R^2) \text{ for } R \gg S \tag{10.32}$$

Equation (10.31) is also tabulated in Table 10.6 to give magnetic flux density and magnetic field strength as a function of distance, R, and wire separation, S, for a differential-mode current of 1 A.

Table 10.6—Magnetic Flux Density and Magnetic Field Strength from Long Conductors

MAGNETIC-FLUX DENSITY AND MAGNETIC FIELD STRENGTH FROM A LONG* PARALLEL WIRE PAIR CARRYING 1 AMPERE* OF COMMON OR DIFFERENTIAL-MODE CURRENT

DIST-ANCE*	COMMON MODE		WIRE-TO-WIRE SEPARATION FOR DIFFERENTIAL MODE												
			.3mm		.5mm		.7mm		1mm		2mm		3mm		5mm
	dBpT	dBμA/m	dBpT	dBμA/m	dBpT	dBμA/m	dBpT	dBμA/m	dBpT	dBμA/m	dBpT	dBμA/m	dBpT	dBμA/m	dBpT	dBμA/m
1 cm	146	144	116	114	120	118	123	121	126	124	132	130	136	134	141	139
1.5 cm	143	141	109	107	113	111	116	114	119	117	125	123	129	127	133	131
2 cm	140	138	104	102	108	106	111	109	114	112	120	118	124	122	128	126
3 cm	136	134	96	94	101	99	104	102	107	105	113	111	117	115	121	119
4 cm	134	132	91	89	96	94	99	97	102	100	108	106	112	110	116	114
5 cm	132	130	88	86	92	90	95	93	98	96	104	102	108	106	112	110
7 cm	129	127	82	80	86	84	89	87	92	90	98	96	102	100	106	104
10 cm	126	124	76	74	80	78	83	81	86	84	92	90	96	94	100	98
15 cm	123	121	69	67	76	74	76	74	79	77	85	83	89	87	93	91
20 cm	120	118	64	62	68	66	71	69	74	72	80	78	84	82	88	86
30 cm	116	114	56	54	61	59	64	62	67	65	73	71	76	74	81	79
40 cm	114	112	51	49	56	54	59	57	62	60	68	66	71	69	76	74
50 cm	112	110	48	46	52	50	55	53	58	56	64	62	68	66	72	70
70 cm	109	107	42	40	46	44	49	47	52	50	58	56	62	60	66	64
1 m	106	104	36	34	40	38	43	41	46	44	52	50	56	54	60	58
1.5 m	103	101	29	27	33	31	36	34	39	37	45	43	49	47	53	51
2 m	100	98	24	22	28	26	31	29	34	32	40	38	44	42	48	46
3 m	96	94	16	14	21	19	24	22	27	25	33	31	36	34	41	39
4 m	94	92	11	9	16	14	19	17	22	20	28	26	31	29	36	34
5 m	92	90	8	6	12	10	15	13	18	16	24	22	28	26	32	30
7 m	89	87	2	0	6	4	9	7	12	10	18	16	22	20	26	24
10 m	86	84	-4	-6	0	-2	3	1	6	4	12	10	16	14	20	18
15 m	83	81	-11	-13	-7	-9	-4	-6	-1	-3	5	3	9	7	13	11
20 m	80	78	-16	-18	-12	-14	-9	-11	-6	-8	0	-2	4	2	8	6
30 m	76	74	-24	-26	-19	-21	-16	-18	-13	-15	-7	-9	-4	-6	1	-1
40 m	74	72	-29	-31	-24	-26	-21	-23	-18	-20	-12	-14	-9	-11	-4	-6
50 m	72	70	-32	-34	-28	-30	-25	-27	-22	-24	-16	-18	-12	-14	-8	-10
70 m	69	67	-38	-40	-34	-36	-31	-33	-28	-30	-22	-24	-18	-20	-14	-16
100 m	66	64	-44	-46	-40	-42	-37	-39	-34	-36	-28	-30	-24	-26	-20	-22

Note: Table valid only for wire pair length >> distance or approx > 3 x distance
Magnetic-flux density units are dB above 1 picoTesla = dBpT
Magnetic-field strength units are dB above 1 microampere/meter = dBuA/m
For all currents, I, other than 1 ampere, add 20xlog(I)

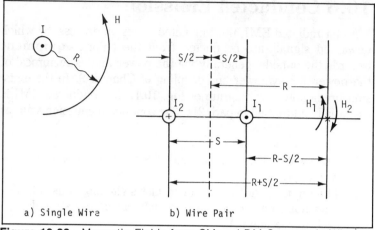

Figure 10.23—Magnetic Fields from CM and DM Currents in Wires

10.5.1 Summary of Radiated Emission Prediction

Use Fig. 10.24 to help select the appropriate prediction method.

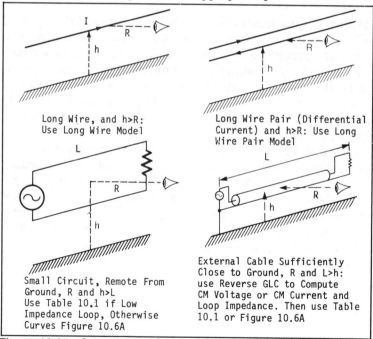

Long Wire, and h>R:
Use Long Wire Model

Long Wire Pair (Differential Current) and h>R: Use Long Wire Pair Model

Small Circuit, Remote From Ground, R and h>L
Use Table 10.1 if Low Impedance Loop, Otherwise Curves Figure 10.6A

External Cable Sufficiently Close to Ground, R and L>h: use Reverse GLC to Compute CM Voltage or CM Current and Loop Impedance. Then use Table 10.1 or Figure 10.6A

Figure 10.24—Selecting the Correct Prediction Method

10.6 Conducted Emission

As for radiated EMI, the conducted emission process, by which unwanted signals are conducted from the culprit **equipment** towards the outside, generally via the power line, is reciprocal of the power supply/power line coupling of Chapter 9. In the emission prediction flow diagram of Fig. 10.1, the conducted EMI is essentially addressed in path 2D. The conducted emission sources can be:

1. The switching transistors and diodes in the power converters/power supplies
2. The digital logic circuits (The fast switching causes transient noise on the dc buses, which can be transferred back to the mains.)

Since emissions are generally covered by specifications which define a maximum amplitude in a given test setup, two approaches are considered. These involve the use of military and nonmilitary specifications as noted below. They both have the same objective of conducted emission measurement.

Military Specifications: Specifications such as MIL-STD-461 (CEO3) define the power line emission as the **maximum conducted current** the equipment can generate on its power cord. This is similar to the **short-circuit ampacity** of the noise source, and corresponds to situations where the power mains have a very low impedance. This worst-case impedance is simulated by a 10 μF capacitor of special fabrication to ensure an Xc < 0.1 Ω beyond 150 kHz.

Figure 10.25 gives the prediction of emission current (CE test) per unit of open voltage of the internal noise source of the product. For example, a noise source in a small airborne equipment grounded to the chassis is assumed to exhibit a 100 kHz harmonic of 90 dBμV, open voltage. What current can be expected in a military conducted emission test, narrowband? From Fig. 10.25, $I_{dB\mu A}$ = 90 − 30 = 60 dBμA. If the specifications require 40 dBμA maximum, a filter with at least 20 dB attenuation at 100 kHz must be provided.

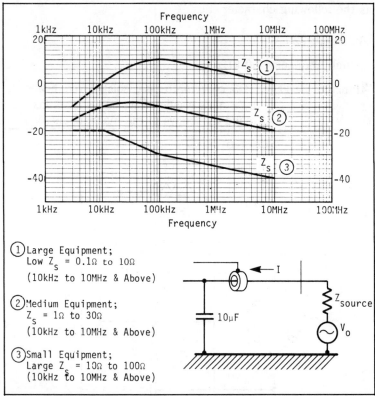

Figure 10.25—Value of Noise Current Per Volt of Noise Source for Several Power System Common-Mode Impedances (Z_{CM})

Civilian Specifications: Civil organizations like CISPR (or VDE) and FCC characterize the power line emission RF voltage in a given impedance (LISN 50 Ω or 150 Ω) which is supposed to **represent** the power mains impedance.

Illustrative Example 10.9

A filter is to be selected for a switching power supply which must meet a certain VDE specification. The power supply (see Fig. 10.26)

10.49

has the following characteristics:

AC input: 220 V

Switch frequency: 50 kHz

Transistor package: TO3, collector-to-case, isolated from heat-sink by a mica washer. The heat-sink is fastened by screws to the machine chassis.

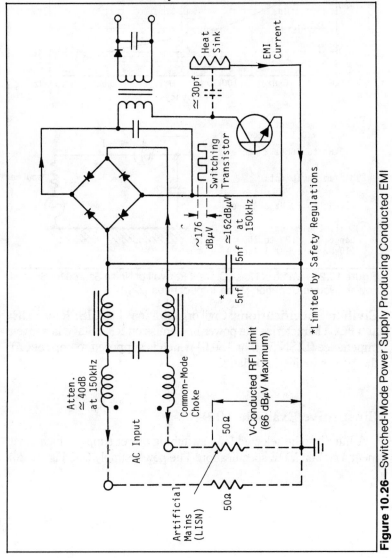

Figure 10.26—Switched-Mode Power Supply Producing Conducted EMI

10.50

The VDE specification restricts the noise on the power line to 66 dBμV above 150 kHz, measured in a 50 Ω impedance, connected line (or neutral) to ground. Does the basic product meet the specification? If not, what filter should be chosen?

The CM current path is shown in Fig. 10.27. The parasitic collector to heat sink capacitance is estimated to be 30 pF. The spectral amplitudes must be computed to assess the 150 kHz case. The bulk dc voltage = $220 \times \sqrt{2} \approx 300$ V. To account for the LdI/dt of the transformer's primary at transistor turn-off, a value of 500 V (174 dBμV) is retained. As a rough estimate, the fundamental 50 kHz spectral line represents:

$$\frac{1}{\pi\tau} \bigg/ \frac{1}{T} = \frac{2\tau}{\pi\tau} = 63 \text{ percent} \qquad (10.33)$$

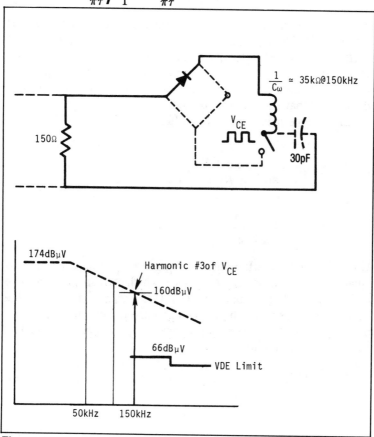

Figure 10.27—Simplified Scheme of CM Current Creating EMI Voltage in a 50 kHz Switcher

10.51

This equals −4 dB of the crest amplitude. Then the spectral envelope decreases by 20 dB/decade. Therefore the 150 kHz harmonic is equal to:

$$174 \text{ dB}\mu\text{V} - 4 \text{ dB} - 20 \log \frac{150 \text{ kHz}}{50 \text{ kHz}} = 160 \text{ dB}\mu\text{V} \quad (10.34)$$

Since the noise is measured in 50 Ω, the amplitude will be given by the dividing network formed by 50 Ω and 30 pF, i.e.:

$$\frac{50}{50 - \dfrac{j}{30 \times 10^{-12} \times 2\pi \times 150 \text{ kHz}}} \approx -57 \text{ dB} \quad (10.35)$$

The 150 kHz harmonic will appear at the test as 160 dBμV − 57 dB = 103 dBμV. Therefore, a filter is needed. Its attenuation should be 103 − 66 (VDE) = 37 dB. This noise, which is of a common-mode nature, will be attenuated by the common-mode components of the input filter. First assume a single common-mode capacitor which must have a value to provide ≅ 40 dB insertion loss at 150 kHz. Since it is a one-order filter:

$$f_{co} = \frac{f_{EMI}}{\text{antilog } 40 \text{ dB}/(20 \times 1)} \quad (10.36)$$

$$f_{co} = \frac{150 \times 10^3}{\text{antilog } 2} \cong 1.5 \text{ kHz}$$

At this frequency (3 dB point), the capacitor must have a reactance equal to the 50 Ω measuring resistance, which corresponds to a value of C = 2 μF. Safety regulations (UL, IEC, etc) forbid such a value because of the excessive 60 Hz ground current and, therefore, they limit the value of line-to-ground capacitors to a maximum 5 nF. The filter must have additional components.

Since the common-mode capacitance of 5 nF has a reactance of 212 Ω at 150 kHz, which barely makes a 3 dB attenuation, an additional inductance is needed.

10.52

The filter inductance to be added can be determined from the voltage limit across 50 Ω:

$$V_{50} \times \frac{V_c \times 50}{j\omega L + 50}$$

with V_C, the voltage across the 5 nF filter capacitor being equal to:

$$V_C = V_{CE} \times \frac{212 \ \Omega}{212 \ \Omega + 35 \ k\Omega}$$

So,

$$V_{50} = \left(\frac{V_{CE} \times 212}{35 \times 10^3} \right) \times \frac{50}{j\omega L + 50}$$

Knowing that $V_{CE} = 160 \ dB\mu V$ or 100 V, and that the objective for V_{50} is 66 $dB\mu V$ or 2 mV, the condition is expressed as:

$$V_{50}/V_{CE} \leqslant \frac{2 \times 10^{-3} \ V}{100 \ V} = 2 \times 10^{-5}$$

$$\text{So, } j\omega L + 50 \geqslant \frac{212 \times 50}{35 \times 10^3 \times 2 \times 10^{-5}}$$

Solving for L,

$$L \geqslant 15 \ mH$$

which is feasible as a common-mode choke for a few ampere power supply.

Another solution would be to reduce the parasitic capacitance from the transistor to ground by using a different heat sink arrangement or a Faraday shield between the collector and the heat sink with the shield bonded to the emitter.

Illustrative Example 10.10

During the switching of digital circuits, due to the large number of fast logic chips being clocked, and the non-null source impedance of the power regulator, the 5 Vdc bus exhibits 100 mV glitches with a 5 MHz repetition rate. Given an input-to-output parasitic capacitance of 30 pF for the power supply, what is the EMI voltage seen by the 50 Ω LISN during an FCC Class B test? The configuration is shown in Fig. 10.28.

Since the duty cycle is 10 percent, the amplitude of the first harmonics will be:

$$2 A \times \tau/T = 20 \text{ mV}$$

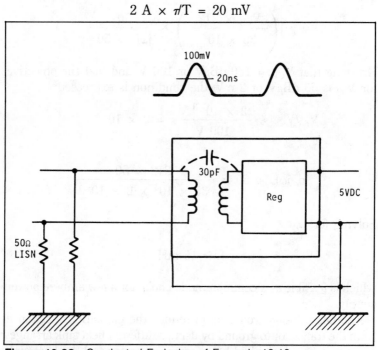

Figure 10.28—Conducted Emission of Example 10.10

The voltage across the 50 Ω measuring impedance will be:

$$V_{(50)} = \frac{50}{X_C + 50} \times V_{noise} \approx 50 \times C\omega \times V_{noise}$$

$$\approx 10^{-2} \times f_{MHz} \times V_{noise}$$

10.54

For instance, at 5 MHz:

$$V_{(50)} = 10^{-2} \times 5 \text{ MHz} \times 20 \text{ mV} = 1 \text{ mV} = 60 \text{ dB}\mu V$$

Since the FCC Class B limit for conducted EMI up to 30 MHz is 48 dBμV, the clock residues exceed the specification by 12 dB at 5 MHz. A filter must be provided with such CM attenuation, or a Faraday Shield must be used in the power supply transformer.

10.7 Bibliography

CISPR Publications 11, 14 and 22 (Geneva: International Electrotechnical Commission).

Di Marzo, A.W., "Graphical Solutions to Harmonic Analysis," *IEEE Transactions on Aerospace and Electronic Systems*, Volume AES 4, No. 5, September 1968.

Jansky and Bailey, "Interference Prediction Study RADC TR-59-224," Volume 1, p. 262, January 1960.

Parker, A.T., *Instruments for the RFI/EMC Engineer*, (Solar Electronics Co., 1977).

U.S. Code of Federal Regulations, Telecommunications, FCC Rules and Regulations, Part 15.

Appendix A

Butterworth and Chebychev Response Functions

Section 4.1, "Victim Receptor Performance," presented the Butterworth low-pass frequency response and that of 0.5 dB, equal-ripple Chebychev. This appendix presents detailed response data for the 1 to 10 and higher stages (or poles) Butterworth function and the corresponding response for 0.1, 0.25, 0.5, and 1 dB equal-ripple Chebychev. For still further details, see Ref. 1.

A.1 Butterworth Response

The Butterworth low-pass transfer function is given by the expression:

$$|t_B(j\omega)|^2 = 1/(1 + \omega^{2n}) \qquad (A.1)$$

Expressing Eq. (A.1) in decibels, the transmission loss, t_{dB}, is:

$$t(\overline{\omega})_{dB} = 10 \log (1 + \overline{\omega}^{2n}) \qquad (A.2)$$

where,

ω = frequency in radians

$\overline{\omega} = f_{EMI}/f_{co}$ = normalized radio frequency

f_{EMI} = frequency of narrowband EMI

f_{co} = cutoff frequency of victim amplifier or logic

A.1

Since the amplitude response is of special interest in the design of low-pass prototype amplifiers and filters, Eq. (A.1) is plotted in Fig. A.1 between $\bar{\omega} = 1$, the normalized 3 dB cutoff frequency, and $\bar{\omega} = 10$, for n = 1 to 10 and n = 12, 15 and 20 stages. Equation (A.1) is also plotted in Fig. A.2 between $\bar{\omega} = 0$ and 1.

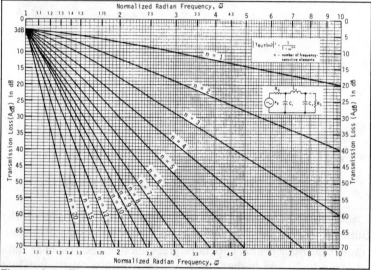

Figure A.1—Transmission Loss of Butterworth Function vs. Frequency for $1.0 \leqslant \bar{\omega} \leqslant 10$

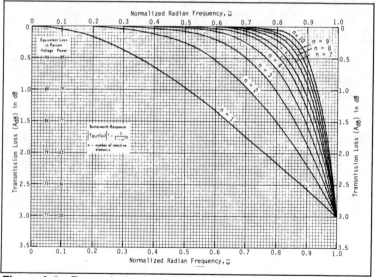

Figure A.2—Transmission Loss of Butterworth Function vs. Frequency for $0 \leqslant \bar{\omega} \leqslant 1.0$, and $A_{dB} \leqslant 3$ dB

A.2

Illustrative Example A.1

Choose the number of stages required for an amplifier having a Butterworth response to give 30 dB of attenuation to interference in the stopband from a Channel 2 television broadcast (54 to 60 MHz) station. The amplifier has a cutoff frequency of 20 MHz. The normalized ratio $\bar{\omega} = f_{EMI}/f_{co}$ is 54/20 = 2.7. From Fig. A.1, 30 dB of attenuation corresponds to η = 3.5 stages. Since only an integer number is possible, η = 4 is selected, which gives 34 dB attenuation at $\bar{\omega}$ = 2.7 or 54 MHz.

Illustrative Example A.2

If necessary, redesign the same amplifier as above on the assumption that not more than 0.5 dB falloff is permitted at 16 MHz in the passband.

The normalized ratio $\bar{\omega} = f_{EMI}/f_{co}$ is 16/20 = 0.8. From Fig. A.2, the intersection of $\bar{\omega}$ = 0.8 and η = 4 corresponds to a transmission loss of about 0.7 dB. To achieve a 0.5 dB transmission loss, Fig. A.2 indicates that η = 5 stages are required. This also corresponds to a transmission loss of 43 dB at $\bar{\omega}$ = 2.7 or 54 MHz. The design engineer will have to determine if an additional stage is worth 0.2 dB advantage in the passband.

A.2 Chebychev Responses

The Chebychev transfer function may be approximated in the stop or rejection band, when $\omega \gg 1$, by the expression:

$$|t_T(j\omega)|^2 = 1/[1 + \epsilon^2 T^2(\omega)] \approx [\epsilon\, T_n(\omega)]^{-2} \qquad (A.3)$$

where,

ϵ = ripple tolerance in the passband, expressed in dB

$$\epsilon_{dB} = -10 \log(1 + \epsilon^2) \qquad (A.4)$$

$T_n(\omega)$ = the Chebychev polynomial of the first kind, as defined below:

$$T_1(\omega) = \omega \qquad (A.5)$$

$$T_2(\omega) = \omega^2 - 1$$

A.3

$$T_3(\omega) = 4\omega^3 - 3\omega$$

$$T_4(\omega) = 8\omega^4 - 8\omega^2 + 1$$

$$T_5(\omega) = 16\omega^5 - 20\omega^3 + 5\omega$$

$$T_6(\omega) = 32\omega^6 - 28\omega^4 + 18\omega^2 - 1$$

$$T_n(\omega) = 2^{n-1}\omega^n - \ldots$$

$$T_{n+1}(\omega) = 2\omega T_n(\omega) - T_{n-1}(\omega)$$

Substituting the $T_n(\omega)$ term in Eq. (A.5) into Eq. (A.3) yields:

$$|t_T(j\omega|^2 \approx [(2\omega)^n \times \epsilon/2]^{-2} \quad \text{for } \omega \gg 1 \qquad (A.6)$$

Expressing Eq. (A.6) in dB, the transmission loss t_{dB}, is:

$$t_{dB} = -20n \log(2\omega) - 20 \log(\epsilon/2) \qquad (A.7)$$

$$= -20n \log \omega - 20 \log \epsilon - 6(n - 1)$$

Since the amplitude response is of special interest in the design of low-pass prototype filters, Eq. (A.3) is plotted in Figs. A.3 to A.6 between $\bar{\omega} = 1$ and $\bar{\omega} = 10$. It is plotted for n = 1 to 10, n = 15 and n = 20, and $\epsilon_{dB} = 0.1, 0.25, 0.5$ and 1.0 dB. Note that the cutoff frequency for the Chebychev response corresponds to the ϵ_{dB} bandwidth and not the 3 dB bandwidth, except when $\epsilon_{dB} = 3$ dB.

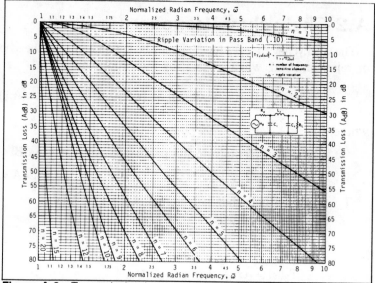

Figure A.3—Transmission Loss of Chebychev Function vs. Frequency ($\epsilon_{dB} = 0.1$ dB Ripple)

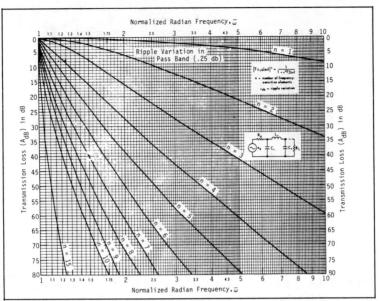

Figure A.4—Transmission Loss of Chebychev Function vs. Frequency (ϵ_{dB} = 0.25 dB Ripple).

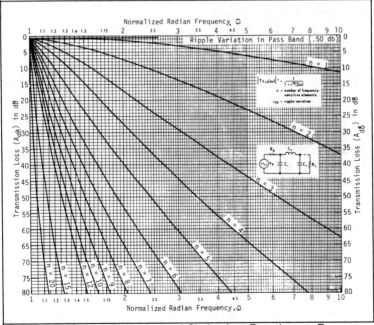

Figure A.5—Transmission Loss of Chebychev Function vs. Frequency (ϵ_{dB} = 0.5 dB Ripple)

A.5

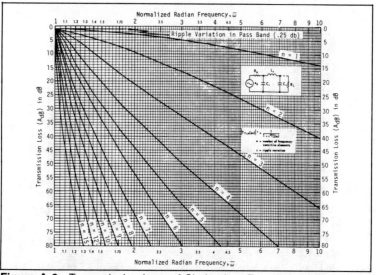

Figure A.6—Transmission Loss of Chebychev Function vs. Frequency (ϵ_{dB} = 1.0 dB Ripple)

Illustrative Example A.3

Using the same example as Illustrative Example A.1, choose the number of stages to give 30 dB attenuation at 54 MHz, provided not more than a 0.5 dB ripple tolerance exists in the passband.

Figure A.5 is used for a 0.5 dB ripple tolerance. For $\bar{\omega}$ = 2.7 and a 30 dB transmission loss, the number of stages required is n = 4, similar to that for a Butterworth response. Since there is no improvement (fewer stages) over that of a Butterworth response, the designer might just as well select a smaller ripple tolerance. Figure A.3, for a 0.1 dB ripple, shows that n = 4 stages will also provide more than 30 dB.

Illustrative Example A.4

Determine the passband ripple response if the problem in Example A.3 requires that the number of stages should be reduced from n = 4 to n = 3.

Figure A.6, corresponding to a 1.0 dB passband ripple response, gives 30 dB attenuation for n = 3 stages and $\bar{\omega}$ = 2.7. This demon-

A.6

strates that for Chebychev functions, greater stopband attenuation can be gained at the expense of greater in-band ripple.

A.3 References

1. White, D.R.J., *Electrical Filters, Synthesis, Design and Applications* (Gainesville, VA: Interference Control Technologies, Inc., 2nd ed., 1980).

Appendix B
Near-Field
Conductor-to-Conductor
Coupling (Crosstalk)

This appendix provides the basic math models associated with **cable-to-cable crosstalk (CCC)** prediction discussed in Chapter 8. Included herein are a number of tables which have been structured to predict capacitive and magnetic cable-to-cable coupling in dB, based upon wire gages, cable lengths, loads and heights above ground relative to corresponding frequencies.

B.1 Introduction

Chapter 8 provided the basic equations for capacitive and inductive crosstalk. However, **mutual capacitance and mutual inductance** corresponding to these couplings, and the details on boundary limitations of the models, have yet to be explained. For frequencies where the wire lengths are short compared to the wavelengths ($l \leqslant \lambda/10$), the models provide satisfactory predictions, which have been confirmed by experiments to be within an error margin of $\pm$ 10 dB. For frequencies where the wire length equals or exceeds $\lambda/4$, a simple prediction model is not achievable since voltage at the victim's termination is very sensitive to reflection conditions. However, even there, the models approximate the **envelope** of the true coupling, so the predicted crosstalk is never less than the actual crosstalk.

B.2 Capacitive Coupling

The exact representation for capacitive coupling is shown in Fig. B.1.

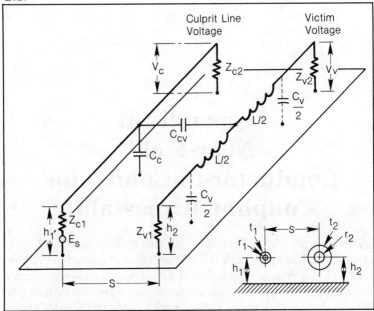

Figure B.1—Circuit Representation of Capacitive Coupling between Parallel Wires over a Ground Plane

B.2.1 Capacitive Crosstalk Equations

Capacitive crosstalk was defined in Section 8.2 and expressed as follows:

$$CCC_{cap} = \frac{V_v}{V_c}$$

$$= C_{cv}\omega \, \frac{R}{(RC_v\omega/2) + 1} \left(\frac{j\dfrac{L\omega}{2} + \dfrac{R}{(RC_V\omega/2) + 1}}{jL\omega + \dfrac{2R}{(RC_v\omega/2) + 1}} \right)$$

(B.1)

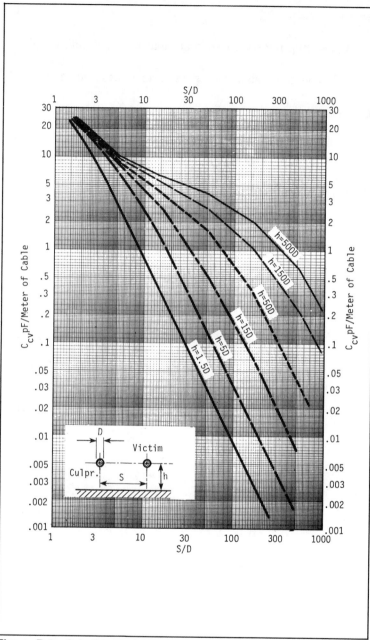

Figure B.2—Culprit-to-Victim Capacitance, C_{cv}, in Function of Spacing and Height above Ground Plane

B.3

where,

C_{cv} = culprit-to-victim mutual capacitance per unit length

R = victim resistance (or impedance) at either end

C_{cv} is a very complex expression:

$$C_{cv} = - \frac{2\pi \, \epsilon_{eff} \, \epsilon_o}{det} \times P_{12} \qquad (B.2)$$

where,

$$P_{12} = \frac{arc\ cosh}{2} \left(\frac{S^2 + \left(r_1^2 - r_2^2 \right)}{2Sr_1} \right)$$

$$+ \frac{arc\ cosh}{2} \left(\frac{S^2 - \left(r_1^2 - r_2^2 \right)}{2Sr_2} \right)$$

$$- \frac{arc\ cosh}{2} \left(\frac{S'^2 + \left(r_1^2 - r_2^2 \right)}{2S'r_1} \right)$$

$$- \frac{arc\ cosh}{2} \left(\frac{S'^2 - \left(r_1^2 - r_2^2 \right)}{2'Sr_2} \right) \qquad (B.3)$$

$$S' = \sqrt{4h_1h_2 + S^2} \qquad (B.4)$$

$$det = arc\ cosh \left(\frac{h_1}{r_1} \right) \times arc\ cosh \left(\frac{h_2}{r_2} \right) - P_{12}^2 \qquad (B.5)$$

$$\epsilon_{eff} = 1 + \frac{\left(\dfrac{t_1 + t_2}{r_1 + r_2} \right)^2 - 1}{0.5 \left(\dfrac{2S + t_1 + t_2}{r_1 + r_2} \right)} \times \left(\epsilon_r - 1 \right) \qquad (B.6)$$

= effective dielectric constant of air and wire insulation combined

ϵ_r = relative dielectric constant of wire insulation
= 2 for Teflon
= 3.5 for PVC, Kapton, Mylar
= 4.5 for Epoxy glass

ϵ_0 = 8.85 pF/meter = absolute dielectric constant of free space

(Note: Arc cosh x is sometimes written = $\cosh^{-1} x$)

C_v = victim wire capacitance to ground =
$(2\pi\epsilon_0/\mathrm{det})$ arc cosh $h_2/r_2 \times l_m$

C_c = culprit wire capacitance to ground =
$(2\pi\epsilon_0/\mathrm{det})$ arc cosh $h_1/r_2 \times l_m$

if h > 3r, this reduces to:

$$\frac{2\pi\epsilon_0}{l_n 2h/r} \times l_m \qquad (B.7)$$

This model has been used to compute the tables of Chapter 8.2 and more detailed tables presented in this Appendix. If the circuits are similar and $r_1 = r_2$, $t_1 = t_2$ and $h_1 = h_2$, then the parameters are simplified as:

$$P_{12} = \text{arc cosh } \frac{S}{2r_1} - \text{arc cosh } \frac{S'}{2r_1}$$

$$\mathrm{det} = \left[\text{arc cosh } \frac{h_1}{r_1} \right]^2 - P_{12}^2$$

$$\epsilon_{\text{eff}} = 1 + \frac{\left(\dfrac{t_1}{r_1}\right)^2 - 1}{1/2\left(\dfrac{S + t_1}{r_1}\right)^2} (\epsilon_r - 1)$$

B.5

If, as in most typical circuits, $r_1 \approx r_2$, $S \geqslant 3r$ and $h \geqslant 1.5\ S$, the terms in arc cosh can be replaced by their logarithmic equivalent and:

$$C_{cv} = 2\pi \times \epsilon_{eff} \times 8.8\ \frac{P}{[l_n(2h/r)]^2 - P^2} \qquad (B.8)$$

where,

$$P = l_n\ \frac{S}{\sqrt{4h^2 + S^2}}$$

For a wire coating dielectric ϵ_r in the 2 to 4 range, ϵ_{eff} can be taken as ≈ 1.25.

B.2.2 Influence of Dimensions

Figure B.2 shows the dependence of C_{cv} on circuit geometry. For a given h, C_{cv} decreases very rapidly when separation S increases (about -40 dB/decade). For a given separation S, C_{cv} increases when h increases up to an asymptotic value where C_{cv} reaches the free-space mutual capacitance. Furthermore, increasing h decreases the victim (or culprit) to ground capacitance, i.e., the limiting effect of this bypass capacitor is less noticeable. However, at the same time, the self-inductance of each wire above ground increases up to its asymptote, i.e., the free-space inductance. This last refinement has not been accounted for. For a given S and h, C_{cv} increase with wire diameter for very close spacings.

When the victim and culprit **are not single wires above ground, but wire pairs** (i.e., the ground plane is not the signal return conductor), the discussion in Chapter 8 suggests the use of the **image method**. This means that two wire pairs (culprit and victim) in Fig. B.3 having a center-to-center separation d = 2 mm will have the same mutual capacitance as two single wires over a ground plane at a distance h = d/2 = 1 mm.*

---

*Actually there is another consideration as the terms C_v and C_c (wire-to-ground capacitances) are also modified when the circuit is made of wire pairs instead of wire and ground.

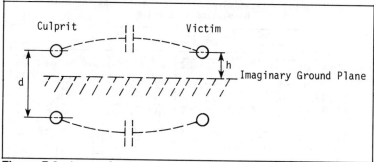

Figure B.3—Image Concept

B.2.3 Influence of Impedances

The tables have been computed for $Z_{v1} = Z_{v2} = 100\ \Omega$. Therefore, different victim impedances, as appearing in the expression of Z_v, will result in a different capacitive crosstalk. If Z_{v1} and Z_{v2} are equal but different from $100\ \Omega$, capacitive crosstalk, CCC_{cap}, is modified by 20 log $(Z_v/100)$. Since capacitive crosstalk is a voltage appearing across the victim wires, when Z_{v1} and Z_{v2} are dissimilar, the correction procedure is:

1. Calculate the equivalent resistance of victim circuit:

$$Z_v = \frac{Z_{v1} \times Z_{v2}}{Z_{v1} + Z_{v2}}$$

2. Find the capacitive crosstalk by:

$$CCC_{table} + 6\ dB + 20\ \log \left(\frac{Z_v}{100} \times l_m \right)$$

3. If Z_{v1} and Z_{v2} are very dissimilar (differ by a factor of 3 or more), take the lesser of the two for Z_v.

Tables B1 and B5 contain more detailed predictions for h = 1, 3, 10 and 30 mm, in terms of AWG Nos. 30, 22 and 14. The thicker the wire gage (all other dimensions being equal), the higher the term C_{cv} and, accordingly, the crosstalk.

Near-Field Conductor-to-Conductor Coupling (Crosstalk)

Table B.1 - Capacitive Cable-to-Cable Coupling in dB
Normalized to 1 meter

Culprit: AWG# = 22 . Cable Length = 1 meters. Load: 100 Ohms.
Victim: AWG# = 22 . Cable Length = 1 meters. Load: Z_{v1} = Z_{v2} = 100 Ohms.

FREQNCY	h=1mm(.5-2)							h=3mm(2-5)						
	S=1	S=3	S=10	S=30	S=100	S=300	S=1k	S=1	S=3	S=10	S=30	S=100	S=300	S=1k
10Hz	-144	-162	-180	-200	-220	-240	-260	-144	-156	-171	-190	-210	-230	-250
20Hz	-138	-156	-174	-194	-214	-234	-254	-138	-150	-165	-184	-204	-224	-244
30Hz	-135	-152	-171	-191	-211	-231	-251	-134	-147	-161	-180	-200	-220	-240
50Hz	-130	-148	-166	-186	-206	-226	-246	-130	-142	-157	-176	-196	-216	-236
70Hz	-127	-145	-164	-183	-203	-223	-243	-127	-139	-154	-173	-193	-213	-233
100Hz	-124	-142	-160	-180	-200	-220	-240	-124	-136	-151	-170	-190	-210	-230
200Hz	-118	-136	-154	-174	-194	-214	-234	-118	-130	-145	-164	-184	-204	-224
300Hz	-115	-132	-151	-171	-191	-211	-231	-114	-127	-141	-160	-180	-200	-220
500Hz	-110	-128	-147	-166	-186	-206	-226	-110	-122	-137	-156	-176	-196	-216
700Hz	-107	-125	-144	-163	-183	-203	-223	-107	-119	-134	-153	-173	-193	-213
1kHz	-104	-122	-140	-160	-180	-200	-220	-104	-116	-131	-150	-170	-190	-210
2kHz	-98	-116	-134	-154	-174	-194	-214	-98	-110	-125	-144	-164	-184	-204
3kHz	-95	-112	-131	-151	-171	-191	-211	-94	-107	-121	-140	-160	-180	-200
5kHz	-90	-108	-127	-146	-166	-186	-206	-90	-102	-117	-136	-156	-176	-196
7kHz	-87	-105	-124	-143	-163	-183	-203	-87	-99	-114	-133	-153	-173	-193
10kHz	-84	-102	-120	-140	-160	-180	-200	-84	-96	-111	-130	-150	-170	-190
20kHz	-78	-96	-114	-134	-154	-174	-194	-78	-90	-105	-124	-144	-164	-184
30kHz	-75	-92	-111	-131	-151	-171	-191	-74	-87	-101	-120	-140	-160	-180
50kHz	-70	-88	-107	-126	-146	-166	-186	-70	-82	-97	-116	-136	-156	-176
70kHz	-67	-85	-104	-123	-143	-163	-183	-67	-79	-94	-113	-133	-153	-173
100kHz	-64	-82	-100	-120	-140	-160	-180	-64	-76	-91	-110	-130	-150	-170
200kHz	-58	-76	-94	-114	-134	-154	-174	-58	-70	-85	-104	-124	-144	-164
300kHz	-55	-72	-91	-111	-131	-151	-171	-54	-67	-81	-100	-120	-140	-160
500kHz	-50	-68	-87	-106	-126	-146	-166	-50	-62	-77	-96	-116	-136	-156
700kHz	-47	-65	-84	-104	-124	-144	-164	-47	-60	-74	-93	-113	-133	-153
1MHz	-44	-62	-81	-101	-121	-141	-161	-44	-56	-71	-90	-110	-130	-150
2MHz	-39	-56	-75	-95	-115	-135	-155	-38	-51	-65	-84	-104	-124	-144
3MHz	-35	-53	-71	-91	-111	-131	-151	-35	-47	-62	-81	-100	-120	-140
5MHz	-31	-48	-67	-87	-107	-127	-147	-31	-43	-58	-76	-96	-116	-136
7MHz	-29	-46	-65	-85	-105	-125	-145	-28	-40	-55	-74	-93	-113	-133
10MHz	-27	-43	-62	-82	-102	-122	-142	-26	-38	-52	-71	-91	-111	-131
20MHz	-23	-38	-57	-77	-97	-117	-137	-22	-33	-47	-66	-86	-106	-126
30MHz	-21	-36	-55	-75	-95	-115	-135	-19	-30	-44	-63	-83	-103	-123
50MHz	-19	-34	-52	-72	-92	-112	-132	-17	-27	-41	-60	-80	-100	-120
70MHz	-18	-32	-51	-71	-91	-111	-131	-16	-26	-39	-58	-78	-98	-118
100MHz	-17	-31	-50	-70	-90	-110	-130	-15	-24	-38	-57	-77	-97	-117

B.8

Table B.2 - Capacitive Cable-to-Cable Coupling in dB
Normalized to 1 Meter

Culprit: AWG# = 22 . Cable Length = 1 meters. Load: 100 Ohms.
Victim: AWG# = 22 . Cable Length = 1 meters. Load: $Z_{v1} = Z_{v2}$ = 100 Ohms.

FREQNCY	h=10mm(5-20)							h=30mm(20-50)						
	S=1	S=3	S=10	S=30	S=100	S=300	S=1k	S=1	S=3	S=10	S=30	S=100	S=300	S=1k
10Hz	-143	-153	-162	-176	-195	-215	-235	-143	-152	-159	-167	-181	-200	-220
20Hz	-137	-147	-156	-170	-189	-209	-229	-137	-146	-153	-161	-175	-194	-214
30Hz	-133	-144	-153	-167	-185	-205	-225	-133	-143	-149	-158	-172	-190	-210
50Hz	-129	-139	-148	-162	-181	-201	-221	-129	-138	-145	-153	-167	-186	-206
70Hz	-126	-136	-145	-159	-178	-198	-218	-126	-135	-142	-150	-164	-183	-203
100Hz	-123	-133	-142	-156	-175	-195	-215	-123	-132	-139	-147	-161	-180	-200
200Hz	-117	-127	-136	-150	-169	-189	-209	-117	-126	-133	-141	-155	-174	-194
300Hz	-113	-124	-133	-147	-165	-185	-205	-113	-123	-129	-138	-152	-170	-190
500Hz	-109	-119	-128	-142	-161	-201.	-198	-109	-118	-125	-133	-147	-166	-186
700Hz	-106	-116	-125	-139	-158	-178	-198	-106	-115	-122	-130	-144	-163	-183
1kHz	-103	-113	-122	-136	-155	-175	-195	-103	-112	-119	-127	-141	-160	-180
2kHz	-97	-107	-116	-130	-149	-169	-189	-97	-106	-113	-121	-135	-154	-174
3kHz	-93	-104	-113	-127	-145	-165	-185	-93	-103	-109	-118	-132	-150	-170
5kHz	-89	-99	-108	-122	-141	-161	-181	-89	-98	-105	-113	-127	-146	-166
7kHz	-86	-96	-105	-119	-138	-158	-178	-86	-95	-102	-110	-124	-143	-163
10kHz	-83	-93	-102	-116	-135	-155	-175	-83	-92	-99	-107	-121	-140	-160
20kHz	-77	-87	-96	-110	-129	-149	-169	-77	-86	-93	-101	-115	-134	-154
30kHz	-73	-84	-93	-107	-125	-145	-165	-73	-83	-89	-98	-112	-130	-150
50kHz	-69	-79	-88	-102	-121	-141	-161	-69	-78	-85	-93	-107	-126	-146
70kHz	-66	-76	-85	-99	-118	-138	-158	-66	-75	-82	-90	-104	-123	-143
100kHz	-63	-73	-82	-96	-115	-135	-155	-63	-72	-79	-87	-101	-120	-140
200kHz	-57	-67	-76	-90	-109	-129	-149	-57	-66	-73	-81	-95	-114	-134
300kHz	-54	-64	-73	-87	-105	-125	-145	-53	-63	-69	-78	-92	-110	-130
500kHz	-49	-59	-68	-82	-101	-121	-141	-49	-58	-65	-73	-87	-106	-126
700kHz	-46	-56	-65	-79	-98	-118	-138	-46	-55	-62	-70	-84	-103	-123
1MHz	-43	-53	-62	-76	-95	-115	-135	-43	-52	-59	-67	-81	-100	-120
2MHz	-37	-48	-56	-70	-89	-109	-129	-37	-46	-53	-61	-75	-94	-114
3MHz	-34	-44	-53	-67	-86	-105	-125	-34	-43	-49	-58	-72	-91	-110
5MHz	-30	-40	-49	-63	-81	-101	-121	-30	-39	-45	-53	-67	-86	-106
7MHz	-28	-37	-46	-60	-79	-98	-118	-27	-36	-42	-51	-65	-83	-103
10MHz	-25	-34	-43	-57	-76	-95	-115	-25	-33	-39	-48	-62	-81	-100
20MHz	-21	-29	-38	-52	-70	-90	-110	-20	-28	-34	-42	-56	-75	-95
30MHz	-19	-27	-35	-49	-67	-87	-107	-18	-25	-31	-39	-53	-72	-92
50MHz	-17	-24	-32	-45	-64	-84	-104	-16	-22	-28	-36	-50	-68	-88
70MHz	-15	-22	-30	-43	-62	-82	-102	-15	-21	-26	-34	-48	-66	-86
100MHz	-15	-21	-28	-42	-60	-80	-100	-14	-19	-24	-32	-46	-64	-84

Table B.3 - Capacitive Cable-to-Cable Coupling in dB
Normalized to 1 Meter

Culprit: AWG# = 30 . Cable Length = 1 meters. Load: 100 Ohms.
Victim: AWG# = 30 . Cable Length = 1 meters. Load: $Z_{v1} = Z_{v2}$ = 100 Ohms.

FREQNCY	h=1mm(.5-2)							h=3mm(2-5)						
	S=1	S=3	S=10	S=30	S=100	S=300	S=1k	S=1	S=3	S=10	S=30	S=100	S=300	S=1k
10Hz	-155	-169	-188	-208	-228	-248	-268	-152	-162	-176	-195	-214	-234	-254
20Hz	-149	-163	-182	-202	-222	-242	-262	-146	-156	-170	-189	-208	-228	-248
30Hz	-145	-160	-178	-198	-218	-238	-258	-143	-152	-166	-185	-205	-225	-245
50Hz	-141	-155	-174	-194	-214	-234	-254	-138	-148	-162	-181	-201	-221	-241
70Hz	-138	-152	-171	-191	-211	-231	-251	-135	-145	-159	-178	-198	-218	-238
100Hz	-135	-149	-168	-188	-208	-228	-248	-132	-142	-156	-175	-194	-214	-234
200Hz	-129	-143	-162	-182	-202	-222	-242	-126	-136	-150	-169	-188	-208	-228
300Hz	-125	-140	-158	-178	-198	-218	-238	-123	-132	-146	-165	-185	-205	-225
500Hz	-121	-135	-154	-174	-194	-214	-234	-118	-128	-142	-161	-181	-201	-221
700Hz	-118	-132	-151	-171	-191	-211	-231	-115	-125	-139	-158	-178	-198	-218
1kHz	-115	-129	-148	-168	-188	-208	-228	-112	-122	-136	-155	-174	-194	-214
2kHz	-109	-123	-142	-162	-182	-202	-222	-106	-116	-130	-149	-168	-188	-208
3kHz	-105	-120	-138	-158	-178	-198	-218	-103	-112	-126	-145	-165	-185	-205
5kHz	-101	-115	-134	-154	-174	-194	-214	-98	-108	-122	-141	-161	-181	-201
7kHz	-98	-112	-131	-151	-171	-191	-211	-95	-105	-119	-138	-158	-178	-198
10kHz	-95	-109	-128	-148	-168	-188	-208	-92	-102	-116	-135	-154	-174	-194
20kHz	-89	-103	-122	-142	-162	-182	-202	-86	-96	-110	-129	-148	-168	-188
30kHz	-85	-100	-118	-138	-158	-178	-198	-83	-92	-106	-125	-145	-165	-185
50kHz	-81	-95	-114	-134	-154	-174	-194	-78	-88	-102	-121	-141	-161	-181
70kHz	-78	-92	-111	-131	-151	-171	-191	-75	-85	-99	-118	-138	-158	-178
100kHz	-75	-89	-108	-128	-148	-168	-188	-72	-82	-96	-115	-135	-154	-174
200kHz	-69	-83	-102	-122	-142	-162	-182	-66	-76	-90	-109	-128	-148	-168
300kHz	-65	-80	-98	-118	-138	-158	-178	-63	-72	-86	-105	-125	-145	-165
500kHz	-61	-75	-94	-114	-134	-154	-174	-58	-68	-82	-101	-121	-141	-161
700kHz	-58	-72	-91	-111	-131	-151	-171	-55	-65	-79	-98	-118	-138	-158
1MHz	-55	-69	-88	-108	-128	-148	-168	-52	-62	-76	-95	-115	-135	-155
2MHz	-49	-63	-82	-102	-122	-142	-162	-46	-56	-70	-89	-109	-129	-149
3MHz	-45	-60	-79	-99	-118	-138	-158	-43	-52	-67	-85	-105	-125	-145
5MHz	-41	-56	-74	-94	-114	-134	-154	-39	-48	-62	-81	-101	-121	-141
7MHz	-39	-53	-72	-92	-112	-132	-152	-36	-45	-59	-78	-98	-118	-138
10MHz	-36	-50	-69	-89	-109	-129	-149	-33	-42	-57	-75	-95	-115	-135
20MHz	-31	-45	-64	-84	-104	-124	-144	-28	-37	-51	-70	-90	-110	-130
30MHz	-28	-42	-61	-81	-101	-121	-141	-26	-34	-48	-67	-87	-107	-127
50MHz	-26	-40	-58	-78	-98	-118	-138	-23	-31	-45	-64	-84	-104	-124
70MHz	-24	-38	-57	-76	-96	-116	-136	-21	-29	-43	-62	-82	-102	-122
100MHz	-23	-36	-55	-75	-95	-115	-135	-20	-28	-42	-60	-80	-100	-120

Table B.4 - Capacitive Cable-to-Cable Coupling in dB
Normalized to 1 Meter

Culprit: AWG# = 30 . Cable Length ≈ 1 meters. Load: 100 Ohms.
Victim: AWG# = 30 . Cable Length = 1 meters. Load: $Z_{v1} = Z_{v2}$ = 100 Ohms.

FREQNCY	========= h=10mm(5.20) =========							========= h=30mm(20-50) =========						
	S=1	S=3	S=10	S=30	S=100	S=300	S=1k	S=1	S=3	S=10	S=30	S=100	S=300	S=1k
10Hz	-151	-158	-166	-180	-198	-218	-238	-150	-156	-162	-170	-184	-203	-223
20Hz	-145	-152	-160	-174	-192	-212	-232	-144	-150	-156	-164	-178	-197	-217
30Hz	-141	-148	-156	-170	-189	-209	-229	-141	-147	-152	-160	-174	-193	-213
50Hz	-137	-144	-152	-166	-184	-204	-224	-136	-142	-148	-156	-170	-189	-209
70Hz	-134	-141	-149	-163	-182	-201	-221	-133	-139	-145	-153	-167	-186	-206
100Hz	-131	-138	-146	-160	-178	-198	-213	-130	-136	-142	-150	-164	-183	-203
200Hz	-125	-132	-140	-154	-172	-192	-212	-124	-130	-136	-144	-158	-177	-197
300Hz	-121	-128	-136	-150	-169	-189	-209	-121	-127	-132	-140	-154	-173	-193
500Hz	-117	-124	-132	-146	-164	-184	-204	-116	-122	-128	-136	-150	-169	-189
700Hz	-114	-121	-129	-143	-162	-181	-201	-113	-119	-125	-133	-147	-166	-186
1kHz	-111	-118	-126	-140	-158	-178	-198	-110	-116	-122	-130	-144	-163	-183
2kHz	-105	-112	-120	-134	-152	-172	-192	-104	-110	-116	-124	-138	-157	-177
3kHz	-101	-108	-116	-130	-149	-169	-189	-101	-107	-112	-120	-134	-153	-173
5kHz	-97	-104	-112	-126	-144	-164	-184	-96	-102	-108	-116	-130	-149	-169
7kHz	-94	-101	-109	-123	-142	-161	-181	-93	-99	-105	-113	-127	-146	-166
10kHz	-91	-98	-106	-120	-138	-158	-178	-90	-96	-102	-110	-124	-143	-163
20kHz	-85	-92	-100	-114	-132	-152	-172	-84	-90	-96	-104	-118	-137	-157
30kHz	-81	-88	-96	-110	-129	-149	-169	-81	-87	-92	-100	-114	-133	-153
50kHz	-77	-84	-92	-106	-124	-144	-164	-76	-82	-88	-96	-110	-129	-149
70kHz	-74	-81	-89	-103	-122	-141	-161	-73	-79	-85	-93	-107	-126	-146
100kHz	-71	-78	-86	-100	-118	-138	-158	-70	-76	-82	-90	-104	-123	-143
200kHz	-65	-72	-80	-94	-112	-132	-152	-64	-70	-76	-84	-98	-117	-137
300kHz	-61	-68	-76	-90	-109	-129	-149	-61	-67	-72	-80	-94	-113	-133
500kHz	-57	-64	-72	-86	-105	-124	-144	-56	-62	-68	-76	-90	-109	-129
700kHz	-54	-61	-69	-83	-102	-121	-141	-53	-59	-65	-73	-87	-106	-126
1MHz	-51	-58	-66	-80	-99	-118	-138	-50	-56	-62	-70	-84	-103	-123
2MHz	-45	-52	-60	-74	-93	-112	-132	-44	-50	-56	-64	-78	-97	-117
3MHz	-42	-48	-57	-70	-89	-109	-129	-41	-47	-52	-61	-75	-93	-113
5MHz	-37	-44	-52	-66	-85	-105	-125	-37	-42	-48	-56	-70	-89	-109
7MHz	-35	-41	-50	-63	-82	-102	-122	-34	-40	-45	-53	-67	-86	-106
10MHz	-32	-38	-47	-60	-79	-99	-119	-31	-37	-42	-50	-64	-83	-103
20MHz	-27	-33	-41	-55	-74	-93	-113	-26	-32	-37	-45	-59	-78	-98
30MHz	-24	-30	-38	-52	-71	-90	-110	-24	-29	-34	-42	-56	-75	-94
50MHz	-21	-27	-35	-48	-67	-87	-107	-21	-25	-30	-38	-52	-71	-91
70MHz	-20	-25	-33	-46	-65	-85	-105	-19	-23	-28	-36	-50	-69	-89
100MHz	-18	-23	-31	-44	-63	-83	-103	-18	-22	-26	-34	-48	-67	-87

Near-Field Conductor-to-Conductor Coupling (Crosstalk)

Table B.5 - Capacitive Cable-to-Cable Coupling in dB
Normalized to 1 Meter

Culprit: AWG# = 14 . Cable Length = 1 meters. Load: 100 Ohms.
Victim: AWG# = 14 . Cable Length = 1 meters. Load: Z_{v1} = Z_{v2} = 100 Ohms.

FREQNCY	h=10mm(5-20)							h=30mm(20-50)						
	S=1	S=3	S=10	S=30	S=100	S=300	S=1k	S=1	S=3	S=10	S=30	S=100	S=300	S=1k
10Hz	-131	-146	-158	-172	-191	-210	-230	-131	-145	-155	-164	-178	-197	-216
20Hz	-125	-140	-151	-166	-184	-204	-224	-125	-139	-148	-158	-172	-191	-210
30Hz	-121	-136	-148	-162	-181	-201	-221	-121	-136	-145	-154	-168	-187	-207
50Hz	-117	-132	-144	-158	-177	-196	-216	-117	-131	-141	-150	-164	-183	-202
70Hz	-114	-129	-141	-155	-174	-193	-213	-114	-128	-138	-147	-161	-180	-200
100Hz	-111	-126	-138	-152	-171	-190	-210	-111	-125	-135	-144	-158	-177	-196
200Hz	-105	-120	-131	-146	-164	-184	-204	-105	-119	-128	-138	-152	-171	-190
300Hz	-101	-116	-128	-142	-161	-181	-201	-101	-116	-125	-134	-148	-167	-187
500Hz	-97	-112	-124	-138	-157	-176	-196	-97	-111	-121	-130	-144	-163	-182
700Hz	-94	-109	-121	-135	-154	-173	-193	-94	-108	-118	-127	-141	-160	-180
1kHz	-91	-106	-118	-132	-151	-170	-190	-91	-105	-115	-124	-138	-157	-176
2kHz	-85	-100	-111	-126	-144	-164	-184	-85	-99	-108	-118	-132	-151	-170
3kHz	-81	-96	-108	-122	-141	-161	-181	-81	-96	-105	-114	-128	-147	-167
5kHz	-77	-92	-104	-118	-137	-156	-176	-77	-91	-101	-110	-124	-143	-162
7kHz	-74	-89	-101	-115	-134	-153	-173	-74	-88	-98	-107	-121	-140	-160
10kHz	-71	-86	-98	-112	-131	-150	-170	-71	-85	-95	-104	-118	-137	-156
20kHz	-65	-80	-91	-106	-124	-144	-164	-65	-79	-89	-98	-112	-131	-150
30kHz	-61	-76	-88	-102	-121	-141	-161	-61	-76	-85	-94	-108	-127	-147
50kHz	-57	-72	-84	-98	-117	-136	-156	-57	-71	-81	-90	-104	-123	-142
70kHz	-54	-69	-81	-95	-114	-133	-153	-54	-68	-78	-87	-101	-120	-140
100kHz	-51	-66	-78	-92	-111	-130	-150	-51	-65	-75	-84	-98	-117	-136
200kHz	-45	-60	-72	-86	-105	-124	-144	-45	-59	-69	-78	-92	-111	-130
300kHz	-41	-56	-68	-82	-101	-121	-141	-41	-56	-65	-74	-88	-107	-127
500kHz	-37	-52	-64	-78	-97	-116	-136	-37	-51	-61	-70	-84	-103	-122
700kHz	-34	-49	-61	-75	-94	-114	-134	-34	-48	-58	-67	-81	-100	-120
1MHz	-31	-46	-58	-72	-91	-110	-130	-31	-45	-55	-64	-78	-97	-116
2MHz	-26	-40	-52	-66	-85	-105	-125	-26	-40	-49	-58	-72	-91	-111
3MHz	-23	-37	-48	-63	-81	-101	-121	-23	-36	-45	-54	-68	-87	-107
5MHz	-20	-33	-44	-58	-77	-97	-117	-20	-32	-41	-50	-64	-83	-103
7MHz	-18	-30	-41	-56	-74	-94	-114	-18	-30	-38	-47	-61	-80	-100
10MHz	-16	-28	-39	-53	-71	-91	-111	-16	-27	-36	-44	-58	-77	-97
20MHz	-14	-23	-34	-48	-66	-86	-106	-14	-22	-30	-39	-53	-72	-92
30MHz	-13	-21	-31	-45	-63	-83	-103	-13	-20	-28	-36	-50	-69	-89
50MHz	-12	-18	-28	-42	-60	-80	-100	-12	-18	-25	-33	-47	-66	-85
70MHz	-11	-17	-26	-40	-59	-78	-98	-11	-16	-23	-31	-45	-64	-83
100MHz	-11	-16	-25	-38	-57	-77	-97	-11	-15	-21	-29	-43	-62	-82

B.12

B.3 Inductive Coupling

The exact representation for inductive coupling is shown in Fig. B.4. In Section 8.3 [Eq. (8.6)], the inductive coupling was defined as:

$$CCC_{ind} = \frac{V_v}{V_c} = \left(\frac{Z_{v2}}{Z_{v1} + Z_{v2} + j\omega L_v l} \right) \frac{\omega M l}{Z_{c2}} \qquad (B.9)$$

where,

> M = mutual inductance between culprit and victim in henries per meter
>
> Z_{c2} = culprit load impedance in ohms
>
> L_v = self-inductance of victim wire in henries per meter

$$= \frac{\mu_o}{2\pi} \, l_n \left(\frac{2h_2}{r_2} - 1 \right) \qquad (B.10)$$

Z_{v1}, Z_{v2} = victim source and load impedances in ohms
l = cable length in meters

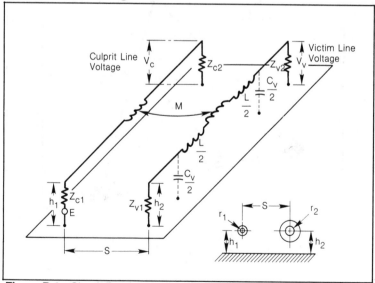

Figure B.4—Circuit Representation of Inductive Coupling between Parallel Wires over a Ground Plane

The term M is complex. For a unit length, it is:

$$= \frac{\mu_o}{2\pi} l_n \left[\frac{\left(h_1 + h_2 \right)^2 + S^2}{\left(h_1 - h_2 \right)^2 + S^2} \right] \tag{B.11}$$

where,

μ_o = permeability of free space, $4\pi \times 10^{-7}$ H/m

Therefore, if $h_1 = h_2 = h$, M in air becomes:

$$M = 2 \times 10^{-7} l_n \left(\frac{4h^2}{S^2} + 1 \right) \text{ H/m}$$

$$\approx 0.4 \, l_n \left(\frac{2h}{S} \right) \mu\text{H/m} \quad \text{if } \frac{h}{S} > 3$$

Since the mutual inductance has a dependence on geometry as mutual capacitance, the effect of dimensions on crosstalk is similar to capacitive coupling (see Fig. B.5). However, the inductive coupling

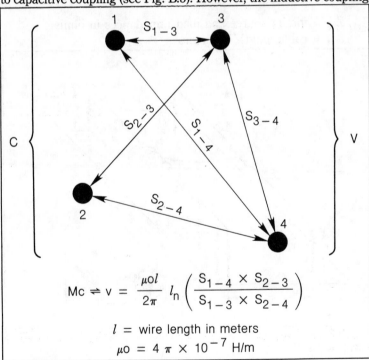

$$Mc \rightleftharpoons v = \frac{\mu_o l}{2\pi} l_n \left(\frac{S_{1-4} \times S_{2-3}}{S_{1-3} \times S_{2-4}} \right)$$

l = wire length in meters

$\mu_o = 4\pi \times 10^{-7}$ H/m

Figure B.5—Expression of Mutual Inductance for Any Random Arrangement of Culprit and Victim Pairs

increases more rapidly with an increase in height. Figures B.6 and B.7 show the geometric variations for M and L_v.

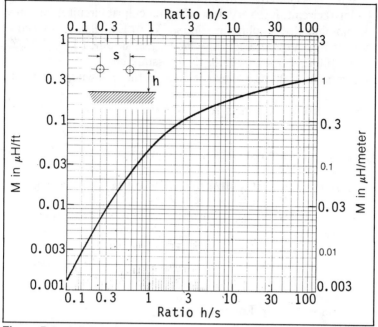

Figure B.6—Influence of Circuit Geometry on Culprit-to-Victim Mutual Inductance, M

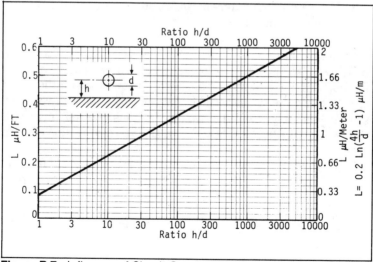

Figure B.7—Influence of Circuit Geometry on Self-Inductance of Single Wire above Ground [term L_v in Eq. (8.6)]

B.3.1 Influence of Impedances

Since the inductive crosstalk is due to current in the primary (culprit) circuit, it is very dependent on culprit circuit impedance. To simplify the coupling prediction, V_c in Eq. (B.9) is defined as culprit **line voltage**, and the model has assumed $I_{culp} = V_c/Z_{c2} = V_c/100 \ \Omega$. If $Z_{c2} \neq 100 \ \Omega$, the crosstalk has to be corrected by the ratio of $100 \ \Omega/Z_c$, which is done in the following equation:

$$CCC_{ind}dB = CCC \text{ in table } + 20 \log \left(\frac{100}{Z_c} \times l \right) \qquad (B.12)$$

IF Z_{c1} and Z_{c2} are not equal, the following approach is suggested:

1. **If the culprit voltage is really the line voltage**, the culprit load impedance, Z_{c2} is used in Eq. (B.12)
2. **If only the culprit source voltage V_{co} is known**, compute the line voltage as follows:

$$V_c = V_{co} \frac{Z_{c2}}{Z_{c1} + Z_{c2}} \qquad (B.13)$$

and use Z_{c2} in Eq. (B.12).

3. **If the culprit current is known**, a value of $Z_c = V_c/I_c$ should be forced.

Although having less influence, the secondary (victim) impedances also should be accounted for, since the inductive coupling appears like a longitudinal source, **in series** with the victim circuit. Since the tables assume that the series induced voltage is shared equally between the two terminations, the coupling coefficient of Eq. (B.12) should be given an additional correction equal to:

$$6 \text{ dB } + 20 \log \frac{Z_{v2}}{Z_{v1} + Z_{v2} + jLv\omega} \text{ for load end } Z_{v2} \text{ (far end)} \qquad (B.14)$$

$$6 \text{ dB } + 20 \log \frac{Z_{v1}}{Z_{v1} + Z_2 + jLv\omega} \text{ for near end } Z_{vl} \qquad (B.15)$$

B.16

So the total correction, when all Z_c and Z_v are unequal and $\neq$ 100 Ω, becomes, for victim end Z_{v2}:

$$CCC_{ind} \; dB = CCC_{table} + 20 \log \left(\frac{100}{Z_c} \times l \right) \qquad (B.16)$$

$$+ \; 20 \log \left(\frac{Z_{v2}}{Z_{v1} + Z_{v2} + jL_v\omega} \right) + 6 \; dB$$

If victim impedances are sufficiently large compared to wiring inductance, the term $L_v\omega$ can be neglected. For instance, at 1 MHz, 1 m of wire represents about 6 Ω, which can be negligible versus 100 Ω, but certainly not if victim impedance makes only a few ohms.

When frequency is such that the victim/culprit parallel run exceeds 0.1 λ, the table still gives acceptable approximations (envelope) provided (1) no more than $l = \lambda/4$ is entered in the length correction, and (2) the characteristic impedance of culprit line is used as parameter Z_c, instead of actual terminating impedance.

Tables B.6 to B.10 give more detailed predictions for h = 1, 3, 10 and 30 mm, for other than AWG No. 22 wire sizes.

Illustrative Example B.1

Compute inductive crosstalk between a 115 V/400 Hz line carrying 10 A and a remote sensing circuit which has a driver output impedance of 150 Ω and a receiver input impedance of 10 kΩ, with a sensitivity of 1 mV. The averaged pair h is 10 mm, and the separation is 1 cm on a 30 m parallel run in the same tray.

By the image method, enter 5 mm as the value of h. Using Table B.10 (a conservative approach, to consider the power cable gage only), it is found that CCC_{ind} = –115 dB. Since Z_{c1} (AC mains source impedance) is very low, 115 V is the line voltage and Z_c = 115 V/10 A = 11.5 Ω.

$$CCC_{ind} = -115 \; dB + 20 \log \left(\frac{100 \; \Omega}{11.5 \; \Omega} \times 30 \; m \right)$$

$$+ \; 20 \log \left(\frac{10 \; k\Omega}{10 \; k\Omega + 115 \; \Omega} \right) + 6 \; dB = -60 \; dB$$

Because 115 Vac corresponds to 41 dBV_{rms}, V_v = 41 – 60 dBV = –19 $dBV_{rms} \equiv$ 0.11 V, far above the circuit susceptibility.

Near-Field Conductor-to-Conductor Coupling (Crosstalk)

Table B.6 - Magnetic Cable-to-Cable Coupling in dB
Normalized to 1 Meter Length

Culprit: AWG# = 22 . Cable Length = 1 meters. Load: 100 Ohms.
Victim: AWG# = 22 . Cable Length = 1 meters. Load: $Z_{v1} = Z_{v2}$ = 100 Ohms.

FREQNCY	============= h=1mm(.5-2) =============							============= h=3mm(2-5) =============						
	S=1	S=3	S=10	S=30	S=100	S=300	S=1k	S=1	S=3	S=10	S=30	S=100	S=300	S=1k
10Hz	-147	-161	-179	-199	-219	-239	-259	-140	-147	-161	-180	-200	-220	-240
20Hz	-141	-154	-173	-193	-213	-233	-253	-134	-141	-155	-174	-194	-214	-234
30Hz	-137	-151	-170	-189	-209	-229	-249	-130	-138	-152	-171	-190	-210	-230
50Hz	-133	-147	-165	-185	-205	-225	-245	-126	-133	-147	-166	-186	-206	-226
70Hz	-130	-144	-162	-182	-202	-222	-242	-123	-130	-144	-163	-183	-203	-223
100Hz	-127	-141	-159	-179	-199	-219	-239	-120	-127	-141	-160	-180	-200	-220
200Hz	-121	-134	-153	-173	-193	-213	-233	-114	-121	-135	-154	-174	-194	-214
300Hz	-117	-131	-150	-169	-189	-209	-229	-110	-118	-132	-151	-170	-190	-210
500Hz	-113	-127	-145	-165	-185	-205	-225	-106	-113	-127	-146	-166	-186	-206
700Hz	-110	-124	-142	-162	-182	-202	-222	-103	-110	-124	-143	-163	-183	-203
1kHz	-107	-121	-139	-159	-179	-199	-219	-100	-107	-121	-140	-160	-180	-200
2kHz	-101	-114	-133	-153	-173	-193	-213	-94	-101	-115	-134	-154	-174	-194
3kHz	-97	-111	-130	-149	-169	-189	-209	-90	-98	-112	-131	-150	-170	-190
5kHz	-93	-107	-125	-145	-165	-185	-205	-86	-93	-107	-126	-146	-166	-186
7kHz	-90	-104	-122	-142	-162	-182	-202	-83	-90	-104	-123	-143	-163	-183
10kHz	-87	-101	-119	-139	-159	-179	-199	-80	-87	-101	-120	-140	-160	-180
20kHz	-81	-94	-113	-133	-153	-173	-193	-74	-81	-95	-114	-134	-154	-174
30kHz	-77	-91	-110	-129	-149	-169	-189	-70	-78	-92	-111	-130	-150	-170
50kHz	-73	-87	-105	-125	-145	-165	-185	-66	-73	-87	-106	-126	-146	-166
70kHz	-70	-84	-102	-122	-142	-162	-182	-63.	-70	-84	-103	-123	-143	-163
100kHz	-67	-81	-99	-119	-139	-159	-179	-60	-67	-81	-100	-120	-140	-160
200kHz	-61	-75	-93	-113	-133	-153	-173	-54	-61	-75	-94	-114	-134	-154
300kHz	-57	-71	-90	-110	-130	-150	-170	-50	-58	-72	-91	-110	-130	-150
500kHz	-53	-67	-85	-105	-125	-145	-165	-46	-53	-67	-86	-106	-126	-146
700kHz	-50	-64	-82	-102	-122	-142	-162	-43	-51	-65	-83	-103	-123	-143
1MHz	-47	-61	-79	-99	-119	-139	-159	-40	-48	-61	-80	-100	-120	-140
2MHz	-41	-55	-73	-93	-113	-133	-153	-34	-42	-56	-74	-94	-114	-134
3MHz	-38	-51	-70	-90	-110	-130	-150	-31	-38	-52	-71	-91	-111	-131
5MHz	-33	-47	-66	-85	-105	-125	-145	-27	-34	-48	-67	-87	-107	-127
7MHz	-31	-44	-63	-83	-103	-123	-143	-24	-32	-45	-64	-84	-104	-124
10MHz	-28	-41	-60	-80	-100	-120	-140	-21	-29	-43	-62	-81	-101	-121
20MHz	-23	-36	-55	-75	-95	-115	-135	-17	-24	-38	-57	-77	-97	-117
30MHz	-20	-33	-52	-72	-92	-112	-132	-14	-22	-36	-54	-74	-94	-114
50MHz	-17	-30	-49	-69	-89	-109	-129	-12	-19	-33	-52	-72	-92	-112
70MHz	-15	-28	-47	-67	-87	-107	-127	-10	-18	-31	-50	-70	-90	-110
100MHz	-13	-27	-45	-65	-85	-105	-125	-9	-16	-30	-49	-69	-89	-109

Table B.7 - Magnetic Cable-To-Cable Coupling In dB

Culprit: AWG# = 22 . Cable Length = 1 meters. Load: 100 Ohms.
Victim: AWG# = 22 . Cable Length = 1 meters. Load: Z_{v1} = Z_{v2} = 100 Ohms.

FREQNCY	========= h=10mm(5-20) =========							========= h=30mm(20-50) =========						
	S=1	S=3	S=10	S=30	S=100	S=300	S=1k	S=1	S=3	S=10	S=30	S=100	S=300	S=1k
10Hz	-136	-140	-147	-161	-179	-199	-219	-133	-136	-140	-147	-161	-180	-200
20Hz	-129	-134	-141	-154	-173	-193	-213	-127	-130	-134	-141	-155	-174	-194
30Hz	-126	-130	-137	-151	-170	-189	-209	-123	-126	-130	-138	-152	-171	-190
50Hz	-122	-126	-133	-147	-165	-185	-205	-119	-122	-126	-133	-147	-166	-186
70Hz	-119	-123	-130	-144	-162	-182	-202	-116	-119	-123	-130	-144	-163	-183
100Hz	-116	-120	-127	-141	-159	-179	-199	-113	-116	-120	-127	-141	-160	-180
200Hz	-109	-114	-121	-134	-153	-173	-193	-107	-110	-114	-121	-135	-154	-174
300Hz	-106	-110	-117	-131	-150	-169	-189	-103	-106	-110	-118	-132	-151	-170
500Hz	-102	-106	-113	-127	-145	-165	-185	-99	-102	-106	-113	-127	-146	-166
700Hz	-99	-103	-110	-124	-142	-162	-182	-96	-99	-103	-110	-124	-143	-163
1kHz	-96	-100	-107	-121	-139	-159	-179	-93	-96	-100	-107	-121	-140	-160
2kHz	-89	-94	-101	-114	-133	-153	-173	-87	-90	-94	-101	-115	-134	-154
3kHz	-86	-90	-97	-111	-130	-149	-169	-83	-86	-90	-98	-112	-131	-150
5kHz	-82	-86	-93	-107	-125	-145	-165	-79	-82	-86	-93	-107	-126	-146
7kHz	-79	-83	-90	-104	-122	-142	-162	-76	-79	-83	-90	-104	-123	-143
10kHz	-76	-80	-87	-101	-119	-139	-159	-73	-76	-80	-87	-101	-120	-140
20kHz	-69	-74	-81	-95	-113	-133	-153	-67	-70	-74	-81	-95	-114	-134
30kHz	-66	-70	-77	-91	-110	-129	-149	-63	-66	-70	-78	-92	-111	-130
50kHz	-62	-66	-73	-87	-105	-125	-145	-59	-62	-66	-73	-87	-106	-126
70kHz	-59	-63	-70	-84	-102	-122	-142	-56	-59	-63	-71	-84	-103	-123
100kHz	-56	-60	-67	-81	-99	-119	-139	-53	-56	-60	-67	-81	-100	-120
200kHz	-50	-54	-61	-75	-93	-113	-133	-47	-50	-54	-61	-75	-94	-114
300kHz	-46	-50	-57	-71	-90	-110	-130	-43	-46	-50	-58	-72	-91	-110
500kHz	-42	-46	-53	-67	-85	-105	-125	-39	-42	-46	-54	-67	-86	-106
700kHz	-39	-43	-50	-64	-82	-102	-122	-36	-39	-43	-51	-65	-83	-103
1MHz	-36	-40	-47	-61	-79	-99	-119	-33	-36	-40	-48	-62	-80	-100
2MHz	-30	-34	-41	-55	-74	-93	-113	-27	-30	-34	-42	-56	-75	-94
3MHz	-27	-31	-38	-52	-70	-90	-110	-24	-27	-31	-39	-53	-71	-91
5MHz	-23	-27	-34	-48	-66	-86	-106	-20	-23	-27	-35	-49	-67	-87
7MHz	-20	-24	-31	-45	-64	-84	-104	-18	-21	-25	-32	-46	-65	-85
10MHz	-17	-22	-29	-43	-61	-81	-101	-15	-18	-22	-30	-44	-63	-82
20MHz	-13	-17	-25	-38	-57	-77	-97	-11	-14	-18	-26	-40	-58	-78
30MHz	-11	-15	-22	-36	-55	-74	-94	-9	-12	-16	-24	-38	-56	-76
50MHz	-9	-13	-20	-34	-52	-72	-92	-7	-10	-14	-22	-36	-55	-74
70MHz	-8	-12	-19	-33	-51	-71	-91	-6	-9	-13	-21	-35	-54	-73
100MHz	-7	-11	-18	-32	-50	-70	-90	-5	-8	-13	-20	-34	-53	-73

Table B.8 - Magnetic Cable-To-Cable Coupling In dB

Culprit: AWG# = 30 . Cable Length = 1 meters. Load: 100 Ohms.
Victim: AWG# = 30 . Cable Length = 1 meters. Load: $Z_{v1} = Z_{v2}$ = 100 Ohms.

FREQNCY	h=1mm(.5-2)							h=3mm(2-5)						
	S=1	S=3	S=10	S=30	S=100	S=300	S=1k	S=1	S=3	S=10	S=30	S=100	S=300	S=1k
10Hz	-147	-161	-179	-199	-219	-239	-259	-140	-147	-161	-180	-200	-220	-240
20Hz	-141	-154	-173	-193	-213	-233	-253	-134	-141	-155	-174	-194	-214	-234
30Hz	-137	-151	-170	-189	-209	-229	-249	-130	-138	-152	-171	-190	-210	-230
50Hz	-133	-147	-165	-185	-205	-225	-245	-126	-133	-147	-166	-186	-206	-226
70Hz	-130	-144	-162	-182	-202	-222	-242	-123	-130	-144	-163	-183	-203	-223
100Hz	-127	-141	-159	-179	-199	-219	-239	-120	-127	-141	-160	-180	-200	-220
200Hz	-121	-134	-153	-173	-193	-213	-233	-114	-121	-135	-154	-174	-194	-214
300Hz	-117	-131	-150	-169	-189	-209	-229	-110	-118	-132	-151	-170	-190	-210
500Hz	-113	-127	-145	-165	-185	-205	-225	-106	-113	-127	-146	-166	-186	-206
700Hz	-110	-124	-142	-162	-182	-202	-222	-103	-110	-124	-143	-163	-183	-203
1kHz	-107	-121	-139	-159	-179	-199	-219	-100	-107	-121	-140	-160	-180	-200
2kHz	-101	-114	-133	-153	-173	-193	-213	-94	-101	-115	-134	-154	-174	-194
3kHz	-97	-111	-130	-149	-169	-189	-209	-90	-98	-112	-131	-150	-170	-190
5kHz	-93	-107	-125	-145	-165	-185	-205	-86	-93	-107	-126	-146	-166	-186
7kHz	-90	-104	-122	-142	-162	-182	-202	-83	-90	-104	-123	-143	-163	-183
10kHz	-87	-101	-119	-139	-159	-179	-199	-80	-87	-101	-120	-140	-160	-180
20kHz	-81	-95	-113	-133	-153	-173	-193	-74	-81	-95	-114	-134	-154	-174
30kHz	-77	-91	-110	-129	-149	-169	-189	-70	-78	-92	-111	-130	-150	-170
50kHz	-73	-87	-105	-125	-145	-165	-185	-66	-73	-87	-106	-126	-146	-166
70kHz	-70	-84	-102	-122	-142	-162	-182	-63	-70	-84	-103	-123	-143	-163
100kHz	-67	-81	-99	-119	-139	-159	-179	-60	-67	-81	-100	-120	-140	-160
200kHz	-61	-75	-93	-113	-133	-153	-173	-54	-61	-75	-94	-114	-134	-154
300kHz	-57	-71	-90	-110	-130	-150	-170	-50	-58	-72	-91	-110	-130	-150
500kHz	-53	-67	-85	-105	-125	-145	-165	-46	-54	-67	-86	-106	-126	-146
700kHz	-50	-64	-82	-102	-122	-142	-162	-43	-51	-65	-83	-103	-123	-143
1MHz	-47	-61	-79	-99	-119	-139	-159	-40	-48	-62	-80	-100	-120	-140
2MHz	-41	-55	-73	-93	-113	-133	-153	-34	-42	-56	-74	-94	-114	-134
3MHz	-38	-51	-70	-90	-110	-130	-150	-31	-38	-52	-71	-91	-111	-131
5MHz	-34	-47	-66	-86	-106	-126	-146	-27	-34	-48	-67	-87	-107	-127
7MHz	-31	-45	-63	-83	-103	-123	-143	-24	-32	-46	-65	-84	-104	-124
10MHz	-28	-42	-61	-80	-100	-120	-140	-22	-29	-43	-62	-82	-102	-122
20MHz	-23	-37	-56	-76	-96	-116	-136	-17	-25	-39	-57	-77	-97	-117
30MHz	-21	-35	-53	-73	-93	-113	-133	-15	-23	-36	-55	-75	-95	-115
50MHz	-18	-32	-51	-70	-90	-110	-130	-13	-20	-34	-53	-73	-93	-113
70MHz	-17	-30	-49	-69	-89	-109	-129	-12	-19	-33	-52	-72	-92	-112
100MHz	-16	-29	-48	-68	-88	-108	-128	-11	-18	-32	-51	-71	-91	-111

Table B.9 - Magnetic Cable-To-Cable Coupling In dB

Culprit: AWG# = 30 . Cable Length = 1 meters. Load: 100 Ohms.
Victim: AWG# = 30 . Cable Length = 1 meters. Load: $Z_{v1} = Z_{v2}$ = 100 Ohms.

FREQNCY	h=10mm(5-20)							h=30mm(20-50)						
	S=1	S=3	S=10	S=30	S=100	S=300	S=1k	S=1	S=3	S=10	S=30	S=100	S=300	S=1k
10Hz	-136	-140	-147	-161	-179	-199	-219	-133	-136	-140	-147	-161	-180	-200
20Hz	-129	-134	-141	-154	-173	-193	-213	-127	-130	-134	-141	-155	-174	-194
30Hz	-126	-130	-137	-151	-170	-189	-209	-123	-126	-130	-138	-152	-171	-190
50Hz	-122	-126	-133	-147	-165	-185	-205	-119	-122	-126	-133	-147	-166	-186
70Hz	-119	-123	-130	-144	-162	-182	-202	-116	-119	-123	-130	-144	-163	-183
100Hz	-116	-120	-127	-141	-159	-179	-199	-113	-116	-120	-127	-141	-160	-180
200Hz	-109	-114	-121	-134	-153	-173	-193	-107	-110	-114	-121	-135	-154	-174
300Hz	-106	-110	-117	-131	-150	-169	-189	-103	-106	-110	-118	-132	-151	-170
500Hz	-102	-106	-113	-127	-145	-165	-185	-99	-102	-106	-113	-127	-146	-166
700Hz	-99	-103	-110	-124	-142	-162	-182	-96	-99	-103	-110	-124	-143	-163
1kHz	-96	-100	-107	-121	-139	-159	-179	-93	-96	-100	-107	-121	-140	-160
2kHz	-89	-94	-101	-114	-133	-153	-173	-87	-90	-94	-101	-115	-134	-154
3kHz	-86	-90	-97	-111	-130	-149	-169	-83	-86	-90	-98	-112	-131	-150
5kHz	-82	-86	-93	-107	-125	-145	-165	-79	-82	-86	-93	-107	-126	-146
7kHz	-79	-83	-90	-104	-122	-142	-162	-76	-79	-83	-90	-104	-123	-143
10kHz	-76	-80	-87	-101	-119	-139	-159	-73	-76	-80	-87	-101	-120	-140
20kHz	-69	-74	-81	-95	-113	-133	-153	-67	-70	-74	-81	-95	-114	-134
30kHz	-66	-70	-77	-91	-110	-129	-149	-63	-66	-70	-78	-92	-111	-130
50kHz	-62	-66	-73	-87	-105	-125	-145	-59	-62	-66	-73	-87	-106	-126
70kHz	-59	-63	-70	-84	-102	-122	-142	-56	-59	-63	-71	-84	-103	-123
100kHz	-56	-60	-67	-81	-99	-119	-139	-53	-56	-60	-67	-81	-100	-120
200kHz	-50	-54	-61	-75	-93	-113	-133	-47	-50	-54	-61	-75	-94	-114
300kHz	-46	-50	-57	-71	-90	-110	-130	-43	-46	-50	-58	-72	-91	-111
500kHz	-42	-46	-53	-67	-85	-105	-125	-39	-42	-46	-54	-67	-86	-106
700kHz	-39	-43	-50	-64	-82	-102	-122	-36	-39	-43	-51	-65	-83	-103
1MHz	-36	-40	-47	-61	-79	-99	-119	-33	-36	-40	-48	-62	-80	-100
2MHz	-30	-34	-41	-55	-74	-94	-114	-27	-30	-35	-42	-56	-75	-95
3MHz	-27	-31	-38	-52	-70	-90	-110	-24	-27	-31	-39	-53	-71	-91
5MHz	-23	-27	-34	-48	-66	-86	-106	-20	-23	-27	-35	-49	-68	-88
7MHz	-20	-25	-32	-45	-64	-84	-104	-18	-21	-25	-33	-46	-65	-85
10MHz	-18	-22	-29	-43	-62	-81	-101	-16	-18	-23	-30	-44	-63	-83
20MHz	-14	-18	-25	-39	-57	-77	-97	-12	-15	-19	-26	-40	-59	-79
30MHz	-12	-16	-23	-37	-55	-75	-95	-10	-13	-17	-25	-38	-57	-77
50MHz	-10	-14	-21	-35	-53	-73	-93	-8	-11	-15	-23	-37	-55	-75
70MHz	-9	-13	-20	-34	-52	-72	-92	-7	-10	-14	-22	-36	-55	-74
100MHz	-8	-12	-19	-33	-52	-71	-91	-7	-9	-14	-21	-35	-54	-74

B.21

Table B.10 - Magnetic Cable-To-Cable Coupling In dB

Culprit: AWG# = 14 . Cable Length = 1 meters. Load: 100 Ohms.
Victim: AWG# = 14 . Cable Length = 1 meters. Load: $Z_{v1} = Z_{v2}$ = 100 Ohms.

FREQNCY	h=10mm(5-20)							h=30mm(20-50)						
	S=1	S=3	S=10	S=30	S=100	S=300	S=1k	S=1	S=3	S=10	S=30	S=100	S=300	S=1k
10Hz	-137	-140	-147	-161	-179	-199	-219	-134	-136	-140	-147	-161	-180	-200
20Hz	-131	-134	-141	-154	-173	-193	-213	-128	-130	-134	-141	-155	-174	-194
30Hz	-128	-130	-137	-151	-170	-189	-209	-124	-126	-130	-138	-152	-171	-190
50Hz	-123	-126	-133	-147	-165	-185	-205	-120	-122	-126	-133	-147	-166	-186
70Hz	-120	-123	-130	-144	-162	-182	-202	-117	-119	-123	-130	-144	-163	-183
100Hz	-117	-120	-127	-141	-159	-179	-199	-114	-116	-120	-127	-141	-160	-180
200Hz	-111	-114	-121	-134	-153	-173	-193	-108	-110	-114	-121	-135	-154	-174
300Hz	-108	-110	-117	-131	-150	-169	-189	-104	-106	-110	-118	-132	-151	-170
500Hz	-103	-106	-113	-127	-145	-165	-185	-100	-102	-106	-113	-127	-146	-166
700Hz	-100	-103	-110	-124	-142	-162	-182	-97	-99	-103	-110	-124	-143	-163
1kHz	-97	-100	-107	-121	-139	-159	-179	-94	-96	-100	-107	-121	-140	-160
2kHz	-91	-94	-101	-114	-133	-153	-173	-88	-90	-94	-101	-115	-134	-154
3kHz	-88	-90	-97	-111	-130	-149	-169	-84	-86	-90	-98	-112	-131	-150
5kHz	-83	-86	-93	-107	-125	-145	-165	-80	-82	-86	-93	-107	-126	-146
7kHz	-80	-83	-90	-104	-122	-142	-162	-77	-79	-83	-90	-104	-123	-143
10kHz	-77	-80	-87	-101	-119	-139	-159	-74	-76	-80	-87	-101	-120	-140
20kHz	-71	-74	-81	-95	-113	-133	-153	-68	-70	-74	-81	-95	-114	-134
30kHz	-68	-70	-77	-91	-110	-129	-149	-64	-66	-70	-78	-92	-111	-130
50kHz	-63	-66	-73	-87	-105	-125	-145	-60	-62	-66	-73	-87	-106	-126
70kHz	-60	-63	-70	-84	-102	-122	-142	-57	-59	-63	-70	-84	-103	-123
100kHz	-57	-60	-67	-81	-99	-119	-139	-54	-56	-60	-67	-81	-100	-120
200kHz	-51	-54	-61	-75	-93	-113	-133	-48	-50	-54	-61	-75	-94	-114
300kHz	-48	-50	-57	-71	-90	-110	-130	-45	-46	-50	-58	-72	-91	-110
500kHz	-43	-46	-53	-67	-85	-105	-125	-40	-42	-46	-54	-67	-86	-106
700kHz	-40	-43	-50	-64	-82	-102	-122	-37	-39	-43	-51	-65	-83	-103
1MHz	-37	-40	-47	-61	-79	-99	-119	-34	-36	-40	-48	-62	-80	-100
2MHz	-32	-34	-41	-55	-74	-93	-113	-28	-30	-34	-42	-56	-75	-94
3MHz	-28	-31	-38	-51	-70	-90	-110	-25	-27	-31	-39	-52	-71	-91
5MHz	-24	-27	-34	-47	-66	-86	-106	-21	-23	-27	-35	-48	-67	-87
7MHz	-21	-24	-31	-45	-63	-83	-103	-19	-20	-25	-32	-46	-65	-85
10MHz	-19	-21	-28	-42	-61	-81	-101	-16	-18	-22	-29	-43	-62	-82
20MHz	-14	-17	-24	-37	-56	-76	-96	-12	-13	-18	-25	-39	-58	-78
30MHz	-12	-14	-21	-35	-54	-74	-94	-10	-11	-16	-23	-37	-56	-76
50MHz	-9	-12	-19	-33	-51	-71	-91	-7	-9	-13	-21	-35	-54	-73
70MHz	-8	-10	-18	-31	-50	-70	-90	-6	-8	-12	-20	-34	-52	-72
100MHz	-7	-9	-16	-30	-49	-69	-89	-5	-7	-11	-19	-33	-51	-71

B.4 Accommodations of CCC$_c$ and CCC$_i$ for Other than Single Wires or Parallel Pairs

As long as the culprit-to-victim distance, as well as cable length, remain small compared to the wavelength of the culprit signal, the quasistatic assumption used in establishing the equations for CCC capacitive (CCC$_c$) and CCC inductive (CCC$_i$) is valid since the victim is in the **induction field** region of the culprit, and the lines are electrically short. Therefore, the capacitive and magnetic contributions can be dealt with separately. It is further assumed that the situation is that of a "weak" coupling, i.e., the fraction of the current derived from the culprit is relatively small and does not affect the culprit line voltage. With the above assumptions, the following cases will be examined:

> Twisted wire pairs
> Flat cables
> Influence of shielding
> Crosstalk for common-mode configurations

B.4.1 Influence of Twisting

a. For a small wire pair separation, s, relative to the distance, h, to a nearby ground plane (i.e., s << h), if **only one of the pair is twisted**, the twisting reduction of Fig. 7.7 (Chapter 7) can be applied to inductive and capacitive crosstalk. This is due to the fact that the isolation from a common ground plane creates a balanced condition for the wire pair(s).

b. For other configurations where s = h or s > h, if **one pair is twisted**, the twisting reduction of Fig. 7.7 is applicable to magnetic coupling but has practically no effect on near-field capacitive coupling.

This is visualized in Fig. B.8, showing a balanced line with unbalanced source and load. The line is exposed to the capacitive coupling from a nearby culprit wire. If there are n

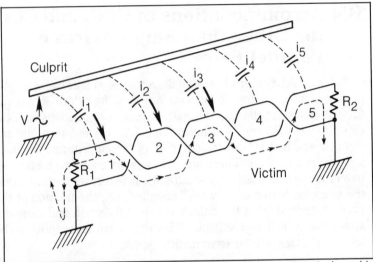

Figure B.8—Effect of Twisting on Capacitive Coupling. Only i_1, i_3 and i_5 are contributing to the total current in R_1 and R_2.

small loops, for each loop the coupling capacitance is equal to $C_{cv} \times l/n$. When the number of small loops is even, the currents caused by each loop pickup are of opposite sign in each consecutive loop, and their cancellation across the termination resistances R_{v1} R_{v2} is perfect (i.e., twisting reduction is quasi-infinite). But if n is odd, it is easily demonstrated that (n + 1)/2 loops contribute to current injection in the victim's far end termination, R_{V2}, while the remaining (n – 1)/2 loops have no effect. For instance, in Fig. B.8, three of the five loops are creating capacitive crosstalk. The ratio of the voltage after twisting to the voltage before twisting tends towards 0.5 when n increases, i.e., the improvement for capacitive crosstalk cannot exceed 6 dB. In general, since it is not possible to depend on an exactly even number of twists, the odd case will be conservatively assumed.

c. If both wire pairs are twisted, the coupling reduction may vary from near zero to more than one pair twisting reduction. Zero reduction occurs for both twisted pairs convolving in the same direction [either clockwise (CW) or counterclockwise (CCW)] such that each small loop rotates in company of its "mating" loop on the other pair.

If the pairs are twisted in opposite directions (one CW, the other CCW), the twisting reduction is that of one pair twisting augmented by the effect of constantly swapping the proximal wire segments between the hot and return sides, which causes cross polarization at each half turn. For flat ribbon cables, adjacent pairs could be twisted in opposite directions or twisted with slightly different pitches.

d. If the victim's source and load are **balanced**, the twisting is effective against both capacitive **and** magnetic coupling.

B.4.2 Flat Cables

Flat cables are especially prone to crosstalk since, in essence, conductors are run parallel with very close and regular spacing. The capacitive crosstalk is further increased by the wires being embedded in a dielectric whose ϵ_r is >1. Although the conductors arrangement in flat cables lends itself very well to the use of the crosstalk model and tables of Chapter 8, the identification of "s" and "h" in certain configurations may not be obvious. Figure B.9 shows the most frequent types of arrangements. In the case captioned in A, the flat cable is the type with an internal ground plane for common signal return. The parameters s and h are directly used for entering Tables 8.1 and 8.2. However, since the coupling occurs entirely within a dielectric like PVC, teflon, polyethylene, etc., the value found for CCC$_c$ must be increased by 20 log ϵ_r.

In case B, all signal wires share in common a single ground wire (a poor configuration, which should be avoided). The heights, h_1 and h_2 can be very large if the culprit and victim wires are far from the ground wire, resulting in greater crosstalk.

In case C, the alternate signal-ground-signal arrangement provides a minimum of crosstalk since the grounded wire acts as a Faraday shield between the potential culprit and victim, typically causing a 14 to 16 dB reduction in crosstalk compared to the situation in A. This is due to the residual coupling capacitance being only one fifth of that with the ordinary signal-signal arrangement. However, this is assuming that the intermediate shield conductor is exactly at ground potential over its entire length. Since this is no longer true at HF, a small noise is coupled through the shield, which adds up to the crosstalk from the residual capacitance C_2 of configuration C.

This shield contribution can be calculated in two steps: first, the culprit wire induces a small noise in the shield wire, whose im-

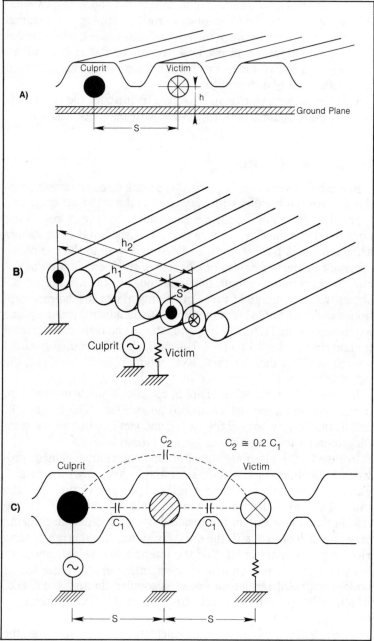

Figure B.9—Crosstalk with Various Flat Cable Arrangements (continued next page)

B.26

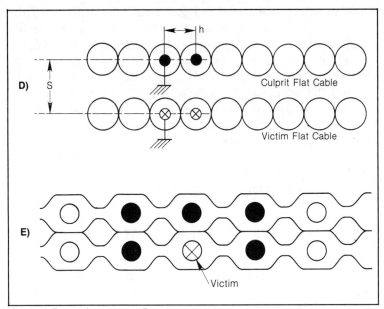

Figure B.9—(continued)

pedance as an intermediary victim can be taken as R + jωL. Then, the noise coupled in this grounded wire acts as a crosstalk source toward the actual victim circuit.

In D, the figure shows a stack of several flat cables, with the wires of one layer causing crosstalk with the ones of the next layers. Ground wires are not very efficient in this case, and the solution is to use a ground plane between each layer, i.e., use flat cables with an internal or overall conductive foil.

Finally, in E, Fig. B.9 shows the contribution of more than one culprit wire. If n wires carrying synchronous signals surround the victim at identical distances, the total crosstalk is n times (i.e., aggravated by 20 log n) the value computed for one culprit-victim set.

B.4.3 Influence of Shielding

If one of the wire pair is shielded and the shield is single-end grounded, the shielding attenuation depicted in Fig. 7.8 (Chapter 7) can be applied to capacitive crosstalk, but it has practically no effect on near-field inductive coupling unless the braided shield is permeable. If the preceding shield is grounded at both ends, the coupling reduction depicted in Fig. 7.8 still applies for capacitive crosstalk. There is a danger, however, that common-mode coupling could now degrade performance as explained in Section 6.5.3. If the culprit wire pair is a coaxial line, and its braided jacket (return circuit) is grounded at both ends, the crosstalk can be computed by using the jacket voltage as the actual coax driving voltage. The crosstalk is computed from the tables by using the jacket height, h, above a ground plane and its separation distance, s, from the other wire pair. By reciprocity, the role of the coax and wire pair may be interchanged to give the same crosstalk. If both lines are coaxial and grounded at both ends, then each has the height, h, for computing crosstalk. This is developed in Section B.5.

B.4.4 Crosstalk for Common-Mode Situations

Crosstalk can also be computed from a wire pair carrying common-mode current rather than from the traditional normal-mode (differential-mode) voltage. If the common-mode (CM) impedance can be measured or estimated, the CM voltage is computed relative to the wire pairs' nearby ground plane height, h. The crosstalk is then calculated in the same manner as in Chapter 6 to convert the victim pair CM voltage into a DM voltage (GLC).

If a balanced pair is laid over a ground plane, it can be considered as a single culprit conductor carrying the common-mode current. Then the common-mode voltage induced by crosstalk on the victim pair, considered also as a single wire, can be computed.

Illustrative Example B.2

Following the previous example of a 115 V power line parallel to a sensing circuit wiring on a 30 m run, assume a sharp common-mode line transient of 1 kV with a rise time of 50 ns. Since the second corner frequency $1/\pi\tau_r \approx 6.4$ MHz, this corresponds to $\lambda/4$ = 12 m. Therefore, correction l is 12 m at maximum. The culprit impedance is now the common-mode impedance of the power line which at this frequency (beyond $l = \lambda/4$) is actually the characteristic impedance of the circuit formed by the line and the ground. As a default value, this can be taken as 50 Ω for medium size power wiring running close to ground (Section 9.1.1). Since the signal wire is a smaller gage, a characteristic impedance to ground of 200 Ω will be assumed (Section 5, Table 5.5). Here the full height, h =

B.28

10 mm, is entered in the table, with the same separation s = 1 cm.

From Table B.2 at 6.4 MHz:

$$CCC_{cap} = -41 \text{ dB} + 20 \log \left(\frac{200 \ \Omega}{100 \ \Omega} \times 12 \text{ m} \right) = -13 \text{ dB}$$

$$(B.17)$$

From Table B.10, at 6.4 MHz:

$$CCC_{ind} = -31 \text{ dB} + 20 \log \left(\frac{100 \ \Omega}{50 \ \Omega} \times 12 \text{ m} \right) = -3.5 \text{ dB}$$

$$(B.18)$$

The inductive coupling is the largest, but at this point the capacitive coupling, only 9 dB below, starts to make some contribution on some points of the line where both contributors add constructively.

Since 1 kV = 60 dBV, the induced CM voltage on the sensing line will be 56.5 dBV, i.e., 600 V. First, this CM voltage might upset the breakdown input-to-ground isolation of the receiver. Then, the final action is to apply the GLC ratio (developed in Section 6) to find what the actual DM voltage is appearing on the receiver input.

B.5 Crosstalk between Coaxial Cables

Based on the crosstalk model and the transfer impedance of coaxial cables, the following model can be made. The model involves 3 steps:

1. Find V_{sh1}, the culprit shield outer voltage. No matter how the shield is grounded, an outer shield voltage develops which is equal to:

$$V_{sh1} = I_{culprit} \times Z_T = \frac{V_{culprit}}{R_{load}} \times Z_T, \text{ per meter length} \quad (B.19)$$

This **open voltage** will become the source voltage for the circuit (1) when it couples into victim coax (see Fig. B.10).

B.29

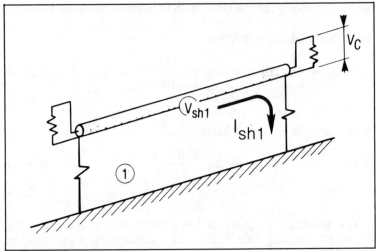

Figure B.10—First Step of Coaxial Cable Crosstalk Mechanism

2. Then, circuit 1 is coupling into circuit 2 (which is the victim shield-to-ground circuit) by mutual capacitance and inductance. This will create a longitudinal voltage on shield 2 (see Fig. B.11).

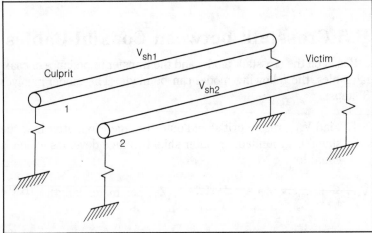

Figure B.11—Second Step of Coaxial Cable Crosstalk Mechanism

3. This voltage on shield 2 creates a current in the shield-to-ground loop (or shield end-to-end capacitance if floated), which then induces, by Z_t of victim, a voltage inside coaxial cable 2, i.e., the victim EMI voltage. This step is similar to ground-loop coupling in the case of a coax. The complete model for coaxial-to-coaxial cable crosstalk is shown in Fig. B.12.

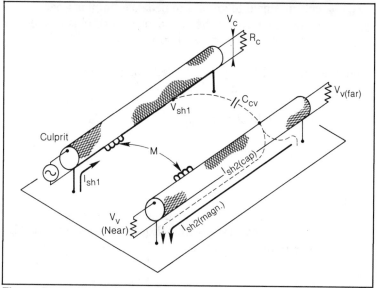

Figure B.12—Complete Model for Coaxial-to-Coaxial Cable Crosstalk

B.5.1 Inductive Contributor to the Coaxial Cable

Inside shield no. 1, the internal culprit current is:

$$I_c = V_c/R_c \tag{B.20}$$

Therefore,

$$V_{sh1} = (V_c/R_c) \times Z_{T1} \times l \tag{B.21}$$

The outer current driven by V_{sh1} into the shield-to-ground loop no. 1 is:

$$I_{sh1} = \frac{V_{sh1}}{Z_{sh1} \times l} \tag{B.22}$$

where,

V_c = culprit load voltage at culprit coax end
R_c = culprit load
Z_{T1} = culprit coaxial shield transfer impedance in ohms per meter
l = culprit cable length in meters
Z_{sh1} = culprit shield-to-ground impedance, in ohms per meter, comprising the shield resistance plus connectors or pigtails and the loop inductance

Then, the voltage magnetically induced along shield no. 2 (victim) by I_{sh1}, through their mutual inductance is:

$$V_{sh2} = I_{sh1} \times M\omega l = [V_{sh1}/(Z_{sh1} \times l)] \times M\omega l$$

$$= (V_c/R_c) \times (Z_{T1}l/Z_{sh1}l) \times M\omega l \qquad \text{(B.23)}$$

where,

M = shield-to-shield mutual inductance, in henries per meter, which can be derived from Eq. (B.11) as if the shields were round conductors
$\omega = 2\pi f$

The victim's shield voltage, V_{sh2}, pushes a current, I_{sh2}, into the loop formed by shield no. 2 and ground:

$$I_{sh2} = V_{sh2}/(Z_{sh2} \times l)$$

Finally, this current through transfer impedance Z_{T2} induces an EMI voltage, V_v, at each end of the victim's coax (impedance matching being assumed):

$$V_v = 1/2 \, I_{sh2} \times Z_{T2} \times l \qquad \text{(B.24)}$$

$$= 1/2 \, (V_{sh2}/Z_{sh2}l) \times Z_{T2}l \qquad \text{(B.25)}$$

where,

Z_{sh2} = victim's shield-to-ground impedance per meter length
Z_{T2} = victim's shield transfer impedance in ohms per meter

Replacing V_{sh2} by its value from Eq. (B.23), the inductive crosstalk expression is:

$$\frac{V_v}{V_c} = \frac{1}{2} \left(\frac{Z_{T1}\, Z_{T2}}{Z_{sh1}\, Z_{sh2}} \right) \frac{M\omega l}{R_c} \qquad \text{*(B.26)}$$

If $Z_{T1} = Z_{T2} = l$ and $Z_{sh1} = Z_{sh2} = Z_{sh}$, then:

$$\frac{V_v}{V_c} = \frac{1}{2} \left(\frac{Z_T}{Z_{sh}} \right)^2 \frac{M\omega l}{R_c} \qquad \text{(B.27)}$$

$$= \left(\frac{Z_T}{Z_{sh}} \right)^2 \frac{\pi M f l}{R_c}$$

for, l in meters, f in megahertz and M in microhenries per meter

If the computation is desired in the time domain instead of the frequency domain, the equation becomes:

$$\frac{V_v}{V_c} = \frac{1}{2} \left(\frac{Z_T}{Z_{sh}} \right)^2 \frac{M l}{t_r R_c} \qquad \text{(B.28)}$$

where,

t_r = culprit signal rise or fall time in microseconds (for M in microhenries)

As already mentioned in Chapters 6 and 7, when the cable length exceeds $\lambda_{EMI}/2$, it becomes unjustified to multiply the shield linear transfer impedance, Z_T, in ohms per meter by the physical length, l. This latter is replaced by $\lambda/2$. All the same, Z_{sh} is replaced by Z_o, the characteristic impedance of the shield above ground. Finally, the multiplier of the mutual coupling itself is no longer l but $\lambda/2$. In this case, Eq. (B.28) becomes:

$$\frac{V_v}{V_c} \text{ at } f_x = \frac{1}{2} \left(\frac{Z_{T(fx)}}{Z_o} \right)^2 \times \frac{\lambda^3}{8} \times \frac{M\pi f_x}{R_c} \qquad \text{(B.29)}$$

$$\frac{V_v}{V_c} \text{ dB} = 134 + 40 \log (Z_{T(fx)}/Z_o) + 20 \log M - 20 \log R_c - 40 \log f_x$$

$$\text{(B.30)}$$

---

*Notice that the length terms l have disappeared from the brackets because both Z_T and Z_{sh} are generally proportional to l. This may not be true when length exceeds $\lambda/2$.

where,

$Z_{T(fx)}$ = transfer impedance of the shield at frequency f_x
f_x = frequency in megahertz of the culprit signal
M = mutual inductance in microhenries per meter

B.5.2 Capacitive Contributor

The approach is rather similar to that of the inductive contributor, except that the victim shield voltage is due to the capacitive divider between C_{cv}, the shield-to-shield capacitance and the victim's shield-to-ground impedance. Since this latter is rather low (unless one end is floated), the capacitive contributor in the coaxial crosstalk is generally negligible.

$$V_{sh1} = (V_c/R_c) \times Z_{T1} \times l$$

In each half-length of victim's shield no. 2, the current driven from shield no. 1 by capacitive coupling is:

$$1/2\ I_{sh2} = V_{sh1} \times 1/2\ C_{cv}\omega l = \left(\frac{V_c Z_{T1} l}{R_c} \right) \times 1/2\ C_{cv}\omega l$$

At either end of the victim's coax, the voltage across victim's load is:

$$V_v = \frac{I_{sh2}}{2} \times Z_{T2} \times l/2 = \frac{1}{4} \times \frac{V_c}{R_c} \times (Z_{T1}\ Z_{T2}\ l^2)\ \text{etc.}$$

In the above equation, the $Z_{T2} \times l/2$ represents transfer impedance over half the length. From this equation, the capacitive crosstalk term is:

$$\frac{V_v}{V_c} = \frac{C_{cv}\omega l}{4\ R_c} \times (Z_{T1}\ Z_{T2}\ l^2)$$

where,

V_c = culprit voltage at the load end
R_c = culprit load
Z_{T1}, Z_{T2} = culprit and victim shield transfer impedances in Ω/m

C_{cv} = shield-to-shield mutual capacitance, in farads per meter, which can be derived from Eq. (B.2) or Fig. B.2, as if the shields were round conductors

If $Z_{T1} = Z_{T2} = Z_T$, then:

$$\frac{V_v}{V_c} = 0.25 \; (C_{cv}\omega l/R_c) \times (Z_T l)^2 \qquad \text{(B.31)}$$

As mentioned previously for the inductive contributor, when the cable length exceeds $\lambda_{EMI}/2$, the length multipliers must be limited to $\lambda_{EMI}/2$. Equation (B.31) becomes, at frequency f_x:

$$\frac{V_v}{V_c} \; dB = 134 + 40 \log Z_{T(fx)} + 20 \log C_{cv} \qquad \text{(B.32)}$$
$$- 20 \log R_c - 40 \log f_{MHz}$$

for C_{cv} in picofarads

B.5.3 Total Crosstalk between Two Coaxial Cables

When merging both magnetic and capacitive contributors, the curves of Figs. B.13 and B.14 result. It is found that:

1. Both couplings vary like $(Z_t)^2$.
2. Inductive crosstalk always predominates until the cable length approaches $\lambda/4$, where the capacitive effect becomes significant, adding to the magnetic one at the near end of the victim cable.
3. Isolation between two coaxial cables is always excellent—better than 80 dB—and should not cause problems in normal situations. However, when one of the coaxial cables carries high power levels, and the other one receives very low levels, a problem may arise. The worst-case conditions, i.e., near-end crosstalk, have been assumed (see Chapter 8, Section 8.4, for a definition of near-end versus far-end).
4. Below the low cutoff frequency of the coaxial cables (i.e. 3 to 4 kHz), the shields become inefficient in suppressing magnetic crosstalk (while still efficient as electrostatic shields). The return currents for both circuits are returning via the ground plane instead of the shields, and the crosstalk is approximately the same as if the two center conductors were unshielded.

B.35

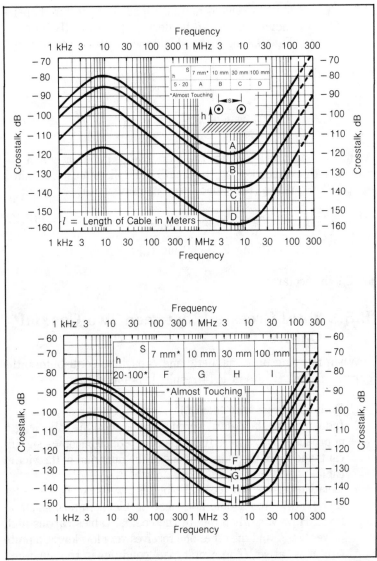

Figure B.13—Crosstalk between 50 or 75 Ω Coaxial Cables, Type RG 58 or RG 62 (outside Diameter 7 mm) for 1 m of Parallel Run. Correction for any length: Xtalk = Xtalk from curve + 20 log l, for l in meters. The dotted lines above 150 MHz are to remind of the λ/2 clamp for a 1 m length.

B.36

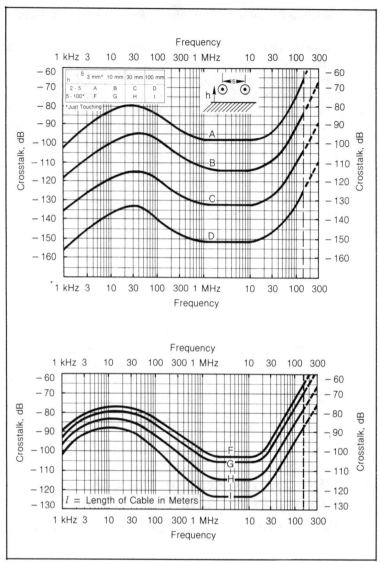

Figure B.14—Crosstalk between 50 or 75 Ω Coaxial Cables, Type RG 174 or RG 178 (outside Diameter 2 mm) per meter of Parallel Run. Correction for any length: Xtalk = Xtalk from graph + 20 log l, for l in meters. The dotted lines above 150 MHz are to remind of λ/2 clamp for a 1 m length.

B.37

The procedure for using the graphs of Figs. B.13 and B.14 is:

1. Locate the cable separation and height and select the proper curve.
2. Check that the cable length in meters is $\leq 150/f_{MHz}$.
3. Find the crosstalk from the curve and correct by 20 log l.
4. If the cable is electrically long, calculate the dimension $\lambda/2$ to be used for length correction. Correct the crosstalk found in curves in Figs. B.13 and B.14 by 20 log $\lambda/2$, i.e., 20 log $150/f_{MHz}$.

The graphs have been established for culprit loads of 50 to 75 Ω, and typical transfer impedances, Z_T, of the referenced cables. If different culprit load resistances or shield types are used, the correction is:

$$\text{Correction} = 40 \log (Z_{Tnew}/Z_{Tref}) + 20 \log (50 \ \Omega/R_c)$$

where,

Z_{Tnew} = transfer impedance of the new cable in ohms per meter, at the frequency of concern in Ω/m

Z_{Tref} = transfer impedance in Ω/m, at the same frequency, of the coax used for the curves in Figs. B.13 and B.14. This Z_T can be found in the curves of Fig. 7.8 of Chapter 7 (coaxial DMC).

$$\text{or,} = 2(Z_{Tnew} - Z_{Tref}) + 20 \log (50/R_c)$$

if Z_{Tnew} and Z_{Tref} are already expressed in dBΩ/m.

B.5.4 Illustrative Examples of Coaxial-to-Coaxial Crosstalk Calculations

1. Assume two cables with the following conditions:

Common length: 3 m
Separation: 10 mm
Height: 50 mm
Culprit and victim cables: RG 62
Culprit Signal: 30 V, 25 MHz (CW)

From Fig. B.10, curve G, the crosstalk is −124 dB for 1 m. A 3 m length corresponds to $\lambda/2$ for f = 150/3 = 50 MHz. Therefore, the cables are not electrically long at 25 MHz. The length correction is 20 log 3 m = +10 dB. Vvictim = 20 log 30 V − 124 + 10 = −84 dBV, or +36 dBμV.

2. With the same layout, calculate crosstalk for a 10 V culprit signal at 200 MHz.

At 200 MHz, is 150/200 = 0.75 m. Therefore, the cable is electrically long. The crosstalk is found at 200 MHz from curve G in Fig. B.10, and corrected for 0.75 m. Curve G, at 200 MHz, indicates −82 dB. V_{victim} = 20 log 10 V − 82 dB + 20 log 0.75 m = −64.5 dBV, or 55 dBμV.

3. Recalculate crosstalk for condition 2 if the cables are replaced by a double braid RG 55-U.

From Fig. 7.8, Chapter 7, the Z_T of RG 55-U at 200 MHz is −35 dBΩ/m, while Z_{Tref} for RG 62 is about +2 dBΩ/m. The improvement is 2[−35 − (+2)]= −74 dB. The new coupled voltage is 55 dBμV − 74 dB = −19 dBμV.

B.6 Crosstalk between Printed Circuit Traces

Crosstalk between traces is one serious concern in printed circuits at the backplane or daughter card level, as well as at the microcircuit level (integrated circuits, hybrid modules). The need for high integration causes thin printed lines to be run closer and closer. At the same time they carry digital signals with faster and faster transition times.

The general models of Chapter 8 and Sections B.2 through B.3 of this Appendix can be transposed to printed circuits provided that the mutual capacitances are recalculated for the rectangular cross section of the printed traces, and that the ϵ_r of the phenolic paper, epoxy glass or ceramic substrate is accounted for. This, plus the fact that victim trace usually terminates into a load greater than 100 Ω, causes the crosstalk in printed circuits to be mostly capacitive.

Two cases need to be considered:

1. Trace lengths shorter than λ/4 (electrically short line) where the lumped element approach is acceptable

2. Trace lengths equal or greater than $\lambda/4$, where a transmission line approach is necessary

Both cases will be described in the following text.

B.6.1 Electrically Short Lines

In this case, the methodology given in Chapter 8 can be used in a straightforward manner. However, a crosstalk coefficient normalized to 1 m length would be impractical to use for PCB traces; their parallel runs are generally much shorter. Therefore, a new table (see Fig. B.15) has been prepared, giving the capacitive crosstalk (the one which generally dominates) per centimeter length. Also, to make quick estimations easier, the right-hand entries of the table are expressed in terms of rise (or fall) times. The procedure to apply in using the table is the following:

1. Select the geometry corresponding to the culprit-victim cross section.
2. Define culprit critical frequency or rise time.
3. Find the corresponding crosstalk per unit length (cm).
4. Apply length correction = $20 \log l_{cm}$ (do not use above $l > 1/4$ of culprit wavelength).
5. Apply impedance correction if $Z_{victim} \neq 100$ by computing: Correction = $20 \log (Z_{victim}/100)$

Illustrative Example B.3: Two Traces with a 15 cm Parallel Run

Trace width W = 20 mils (0.5 mm)

Trace separation S = 20 mils (0.5 mm)

No ground plane

Culprit = Schottky logic, 4 V swing, 3 ns rise time

Victim = Schottky logic, noise margin typical 1 V, worst case

0.4 V (input low)

Victim impedances = one gate low output impedance (about 50 Ω) on driving side, parallel with one gate low input impedance (about 1,000 Ω) on load side so total victim impedance = 46 Ω

W/S (Ccv pF/cm) Freq	W/h = 5 (Cvg = 2 pF/cm) Zo ≅ 34 Ω				W/h = 3 (Cvg = 1 pF/cm) Zo ≅				W/h = 1 (Cvg = 0.35 pF/cm) Zo ≅				W/h = 0.3 or no gnd return below traces (Cvg < 0.1 pF/cm) Zo ≥ 120 Ω				Culprit Pulse Rise Time
	0.1 (0.02)	0.3 (0.04)	1 (0.08)	3 (0.16)	0.1 (0.03)	0.3 (0.06)	1 (0.1)	3 (0.2)	0.1 (0.05)	0.3 (0.10)	1 (0.20)	3 (0.28)	0.1 (0.08)	0.3 (0.12)	1 (0.30)	3 (0.40)	
1 kHz	−158	−152	−146	−140	−154	−148	−144	−138	−150	−144	−138	−136	−146	−142	−134	−132	10 µs
3 kHz	−148	−142	−136	−130	−144	−138	−134	−128	−140	−134	−128	−126	−136	−132	−126	−122	3 µs
10 kHz	−138	−132	−126	−120	−134	−128	−124	−118	−130	−124	−118	−116	−126	−122	−114	−112	1 µs
30 kHz	−128	−122	−116	−110	−124	−118	−114	−108	−120	−114	−108	−106	−116	−112	−104	−102	300 ns
100 kHz	−118	−112	−106	−100	−114	−108	−104	−98	−110	−104	−98	−96	−106	−102	−94	−92	100 ns
300 kHz	−108	−102	−96	−90	−104	−98	−94	−88	−100	−94	−88	−86	−96	−92	−84	−82	30 ns
1 MHz	−98	−92	−86	−80	−94	−88	−84	−78	−90	−84	−78	−76	−86	−82	−74	−72	10 ns
3 MHz	−88	−82	−76	−70	−84	−78	−74	−68	−80	−74	−68	−66	−76	−72	−64	−62	3 ns
10 MHz	−78	−72	−66	−60	−74	−68	−64	−58	−70	−64	−58	−56	−66	−62	−54	−52	1 ns
30 MHz	−68	−62	−56	−50	−64	−58	−54	−48	−60	−54	−48	−46	−56	−52	−44	−42	0.3 ns
100 MHz	−58	−52	−46	−40	−54	−48	−44	−38	−50	−44	−38	−36	−46	−42	−34	−32	0.1 ns
300 MHz	−55	−46	−39	−33	−51	−43	−36	−30	−44	−36	−30	−28	−38	−32	−24	−22	0.03 ns
1 GHz	−53	−43	−33	−27	−50	−40	−30	−24	−42	−29	−22	−18	−32	−24	−16	−12	
3 GHz	−52	−42	−32	−26	−49	−39	−29	−23	−40	−27	−19	−15	−31	−21	−13	−9	
10 GHz	−51	−41	−31	−25	−48	−38	−28	−22	−38	−26	−18	−14	−30	−20	−12	−8	

NOTES:

• Epoxy glass is assumed ($\epsilon_r \cong 4$).

• Xtalk given as 20 log ($V_{victim}/V_{culprit}$) per cm of parallel run. For other lengths, add 20 log (lcm).

• For $Z_{victim} \neq 100\ \Omega$ (10 to 300 Ω), add 20 log ($Z_{victim}/100$).

• Clamp to 0 dB. Xtalk cannot be positive.

• Example of some typical values: W = 20 mils (0.5 mm) S = 30 mils (0.75 mm) for single layer. h = 30-40 mils (0.7 to 1mm). For multilayer h = 5 mils (0.12 mm).

• In regions above 1 GHz, where Xtalk approaches 0 dB, lesser actual voltages may appear due to strong "loading" of the culprit by the victim.

$$xtalk_{dB} = 20 \log \frac{Z_V}{Z_V + \frac{1}{jC_{cv}\omega}} =$$

$$20 \log \frac{RC_{cv}\omega}{\sqrt{[R\omega(C_{cv}+C_{vg})]^2 + 1}}$$

Figure B.15—Capacitive Crosstalk between PCB Traces for $Z_V \approx 100\ \Omega$

Crosstalk = -38 dB (table value) + 20 log l_{cm} (length correction) + 20 log 46/100 impedance correction)

Crosstalk = -38 dB + 24 dB +(-7 dB) = -21 dB = 9 percent

V_{victim} 4 V × 0.09 = 360 mV

This is slightly less than the worst-case signal line noise margin, so no problem normally can be expected. However, if several adjacent culprit lines or fan-out of several devices are running close to the victim trace, capacitive crosstalk may build up enough to upset the threshold of the receiving gate. We should also consider this value too high compared to an I/N budget of -10 or -20 dB.

B.6.2 Electrically Long Lines

With fast digital pulses, it is common for the transition time, τ_r, to be shorter than the propagation delay of the line. In this case, a pulse rise front will be completely formed at the generator side of the line before the load side has even seen it. This condition for a line to be electrically long expresses as:

$$\tau_r \leqslant T_{pd} \tag{B.33}$$

where,

T_{pd} = propagation delay

= l/v

l = line length

v = wave velocity = 30 cm/ns in air

= $30/\sqrt{\epsilon_r}$ cm/ns in a dielectric

= 15 cm/ns in epoxy glass ($\epsilon_r \approx 4$)

In such conditions, the voltage and current are no longer uniform along the line and the simple C_{cv}, M_{cv} crosstalk equivalent circuit used previously must be replaced by a distributed-element approach; i.e., ultimately, by transmission line theory. A complete treatment of the crosstalk between coupled transmission lines can be found in Refs. 1 through 3. Only the essential aspects will be mentioned here, and the final simplified equations will be provided for design and prediction. The lumped-element approached used in Chapter 8 as a basic crosstalk model can still help to explain the transmission line crosstalk, provided that only a short fraction of the line is considered at a time. As already explained in Section 8.4, the victim line sees the capacitive and magnetic crosstalk currents adding toward the near end (backward crosstalk) while they subtract toward the far end (forward crosstalk). In a given time increment, the culprit voltage and current transitions are only seen by one segment of the victim wire. This segment has a length equal to the length occupied by the culprit transition, called the "wavefront length," l_T. The crosstalk terms for this segment are:

In the forward direction: $X_F = (X_c - X_i)l_T$

In the backward direction: $X_B = (X_c + X_i)\, l_T$

where,

X_c and X_i = capacitive and inductive crosstalk coefficients per unit length

Looking at the forward crosstalk first, as the culprit signal progresses by one l_T increment, it couples another pulse, V_{v2}, into the victim's line, identical to the former pulse, V_{v1}. However, in the same amount of time, V_{v1} has moved forward by a distance l_T, such that V_{v1} and V_{v2} add in amplitude. Therefore, when the culprit wave front has completed its trip over the line length l, the addition of the travelling pulses, V_{v1}, $V_{v2} \ldots V_{vn}$ on the victim's wire has reached a total value of:

$$V_{v(F)} = \Delta V_c(X_c - X_i)l_T \times l/l_T$$

first increment   number of wavefront lengths

$$= \Delta V_c \left(\frac{C_{cv}Z_{02}}{\Delta t} - \frac{M_{cv}}{Z_{01}\Delta t} \right) l \qquad \text{(B.34)}$$

where,

ΔV_c = culprit voltage

Δt = culprit voltage rise time

Z_{01}, Z_{02} = characteristic impedance of culprit and victim line, respectively

B.43

M_{cv}, C_{cv} = mutual capacitance and mutual inductance,
per unit length

If $Z_{o1} = Z_{o2} = Z_o$, and if the lines terminate into a load equal to Z_o, some of the terms can be regrouped, thus defining a crosstalk constant for a given geometry as:

$$K_F = 0.5[C_{cv} \times Z_o - (M_{cv}/Z_o)]$$

such that:

$$V_{v(F)} = K_F \, \ell \, \Delta V_c / \Delta t$$

K_F is therefore expressed as seconds per meter or, more conveniently, nanoseconds per meter. The above results can be summarized as follows:

The amplitude of the forward coupled voltage increases with the coupled length ℓ and the rate of change of the culprit signal. Its width equals the rise (or fall) time of this culprit signal. Since it is the difference of the capacitive and magnetic contributors, its amplitude is often negligible. If $X_i > X_c$, the forward crosstalk has the opposite polarity.

Looking now at the backward crosstalk, we see that as the culprit front progresses, the coupled pulse regresses. In a given time increment, the pulse coupled to the victim wire is the sum of the capacitive and inductive influence. At each consecutive time increment, the induced pulses are stacking one after the other, as seen in Fig. B.16. Considering, here again, that only one wavefront length l_T can be coupled at a time, the total backward victim voltage, if the lines are terminated into their characteristic impedance, is:

$$V_{v(B)} = 0.5\Delta V_c \left(\frac{C_{cv}Z_{o2}}{\Delta t} + \frac{M}{Z_{o1}\Delta t} \right) l_T \qquad (B.35)$$

As previously observed, if we define a backward crosstalk constant, K_B, if $Z_{o1} = Z_{o2} = Z_o$ and considering that:

$$l_T = V\Delta t = \frac{3 \times 10^8 \text{ m/s}}{\sqrt{\epsilon_r}} \times \Delta t$$

B.44

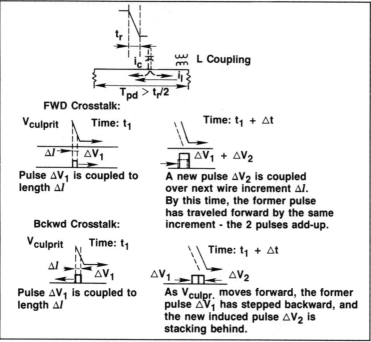

Figure B.16—Crosstalk with Electrically Long Lines

Eq. (B.35) is rewritten as:

$$V_{v(B)} = \Delta V_c K_B$$

where,

$$K_B = 0.5 \left(C_{cv} Z_o + \frac{M_{cv}}{Z_o} \right) \frac{3 \times 10^8}{\sqrt{\epsilon_r}}$$

Notice that while K_F was in nanoseconds per meter, K_B is dimensionless.

The above results summarize as follows:

The amplitude of the backward coupled voltage is proportional to the culprit voltage and the velocity in the line, but independent of the line length. The pulse polarity is the same as the culprit one, and its duration is equal to twice the propagation delay of the coupled length. Both this amplitude and duration are a more serious concern than for the forward crosstalk. Both K_F and K_B are shown, for printed circuits boards, in Fig. B.17.

B.45

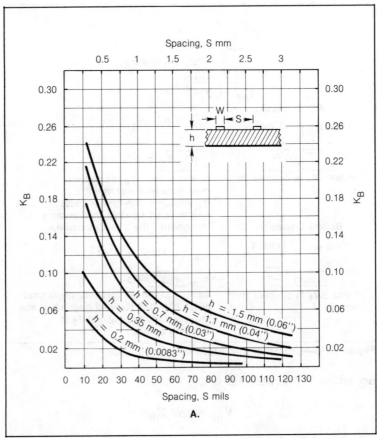

Figure B.17—Back (KB) and Forward (KF) Crosstalk Coefficients versus Typical PCB Trace Spacing. Each line is assumed terminated in its characteristic impedance. Relative dielectric constant is assumed to be $\epsilon_r \approx 4$. The curves are applicable for widths from 0.22 to 0.7 mm. (continued next page)

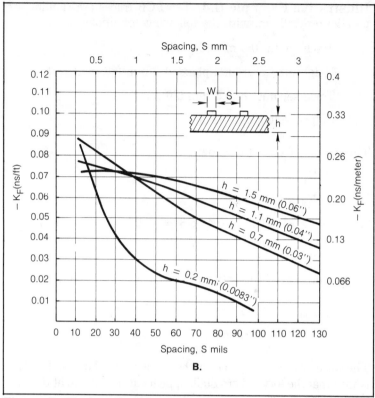

Figure B.17—(continued)

Illustrative Example B.4: Two PCB traces are running parallel over 40 cm, with the following conditions:

Trace width: 0.5 mm (20 mil)

Height above ground plane: 1.5 mm (60 mil.)

Trace separation: 0.5 mm (20 mil.)

Culprit voltage: 3 V/1 ns

The curves of Fig. B.17 show:

$$K_B = 0.2$$

$$K_F = -0.23 \text{ ns/m}$$

$$V_{v(F)} = -0.23 \times 0.4 \times 3 = -0.27 \text{ V, duration 1 ns}$$

$$V_{v(B)} = 0.2 \times 3 \text{ V} = 0.6 \text{ V}$$

The duration of this latter pulse, for a line in epoxy glass, is:

$$2 \times T_{pd} = (2 \times 3.3 \text{ ns/m}) \times \sqrt{\epsilon_r} \times 0.4 \text{ m}$$

$$= 2 \times 2.6 \text{ ns}$$

The waveforms and sequence of these pulses are shown in Fig. B.18. Notice that the forward crosstalk appears at the far end at the same time as the culprit voltage (delay = T_{pd}). .

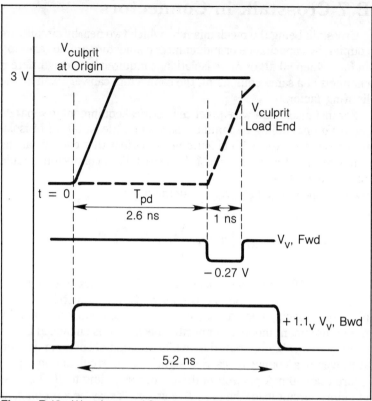

Figure B.18—Waveform and Sequence of Forward and Backward Pulses for the 40 cm PCB Traces Example

B.7 Crosstalk in Connectors

Crosstalk being the mechanism by which two nearby circuits are coupled by capacitance or inductance, connectors are not exempt. In fact, when 60 dB or more isolation is required between different channels of a same equipment, the connectors can very well be the limiting factor.

For instance, it is a wise practice in critical equipment to separate the different cabling by families, based on at least 30 dB of isolation between classes. To be sure not to defeat that concept at the connector level by more than 1 dB, crosstalk in connectors should stay below 50 dB.

Crosstalk in decibels, X_{dB}, is defined as:

$$X_{dB} = 20 \log \frac{V_{\text{noise on victim pin}}}{V_{\text{noise on culprit pin}}}$$

Figure B.19 shows the capacitive crosstalk versus frequency (or rise time) in a typical "Sub D" connector. Crosstalk increases when pin-to-pin spacing decreases. The capacitive crosstalk is generally the predominant mode in connectors because it is enhanced by the ϵ_r of the insulating material, while magnetic coupling is not. However if a connector carries significant current in some pins (more than 30 mA per volt of drive, corresponding to 30 Ω or less of culprit circuit load) the inductive crosstalk may be a problem as well. In the latter case, it is sometimes expressed as a coupling impedance or transfer impedance, relating to the culprit pin current:

$$Z_{\text{crosstalk}} = \frac{V_{\text{noise on victim pin}}}{I_{\text{noise in culprit pin}}}$$

This inductive coupling is shown in Fig. B.20.

If the victim pin is surrounded by more than one "culprit pin," the crosstalk aggravates by:

20 log N (for coherent culprit signals)

10 log N (for non-coherent culprit signals)

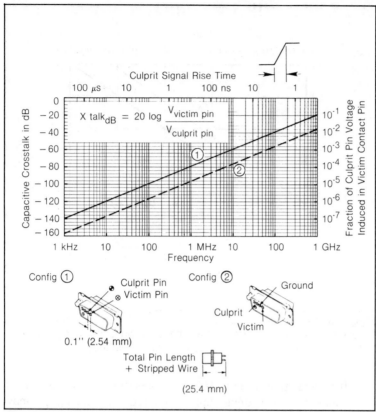

Figure B.19—Capacitive Crosstalk in Standard Signal Interface Connectors

where,

> N = number of adjacent pins within the same distance of the victim pin

To reduce crosstalk in connectors:

a. Use careful segregation of culprit and victim pins avoiding, for instance, some pin assignments where large power contacts could be next to small signal ones.
Example: In the same connector, contacts carrying 10 W (or 40 dBm) will be used along with contacts going to analog circuits with a sensitivity of 1 mV across 1 kΩ (or −60 dBm).

B.51

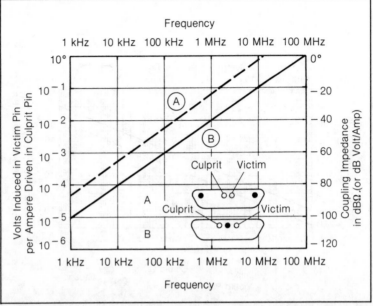

Figure B.20—Pin-to-Pin Inductive Coupling in Type D Connectors as a Function of Culprit Pin Current. The voltage shown is the voltage at either end of the victim circuit if they have similar resistance.

It is clear that at least 100 dB of isolation is needed in that connector which, depending on the frequency of concern, may not be easy to achieve.

   b. Insert ground pins between culprit and victim contacts. Figures B.19 and B.20 show the influence of ground pin distribution over the crosstalk in a connector.

B.8 References

1. Catt, Ivor, "Crosstalk in Digital Systems," *IEEE Transactions on Computers,* December 1967.
2. DeFalco, John, "Reflection and Crosstalk in Logic Circuits," *IEEE Spectrum,* July 1970.
3. Metzger, G. and Vabre, J.P., *Transmission Lines with Pulse Excitation* (Academic Press, 1969).

Appendix C

Additional GLC Reduction Using Ground Inductors and Cabinet Bond

This appendix provides the derivation of subject heading used in ground-loop coupling (GLC) reduction discussed in Chapter 5.

Figure C.1 shows the **before** and **after** situations for the resulting GLC improvement. For this to apply, the following conditions must be satisfied:

1. An inductor must be used in either or both cabinet grounding paths to the safety ground plane.
2. The cabinets must be bonded by a wire or strap and routed parallel and close to the interconnecting cable.
3. If the safety ground is not a metallic plane, but is a safety wire such as an AWG No. 12, the scheme either will not work or will perform poorly.
4. It is assumed that, prior to the fix, the two boxes were directly grounded to common plane. Under these conditions, the GLC improvement is the ratio of V_{AB} with choke and bond to V_{AB} without choke and bond, i.e, merely V_{AB}/V_i.

The equivalent circuit of Fig. C.1 is shown in Fig. C.2. The im-

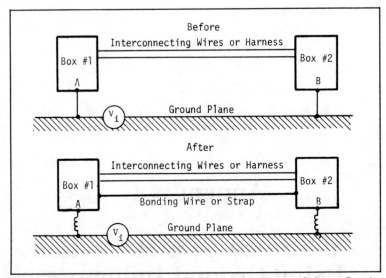

Figure C.1—Improvement in GLC Using Inductor and Cabinet Bond

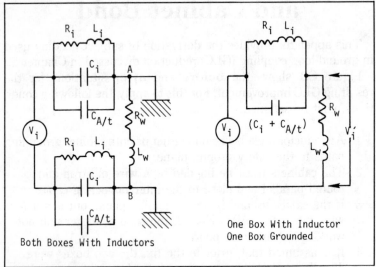

Figure C.2—Equivalent Circuit of Fig. C.1

provement in GLC, GLC_i, by the use of this scheme is:

$$LC_{idB} = 20 \log \left[1 + \frac{2(R_i + pL_i)}{[pC(R_i + pL_i) + 1](R_w + pL_w)} \right]$$

(C.1)

C.2

where,

R_w = wire or strap resistance of cabinet bond

L_w = wire or strap inductance of cabinet bond

R_i = resistance of inductor

L_i = inductance of inductor

C = winding capacitance of inductor + the A/t capacitance

$pC = j\omega C = j2\pi fC$

For dc and extremely low frequencies in which $R_i \gg \omega L_i$, $R_w \gg \omega Lw$, and $RiC\omega \ll 1$, Eq. (C.1) becomes:

$$GLC_{idB} = 20 \log(1 + 2R_i/R_w) \qquad (C.2)$$

For the mid-frequency range in which $R_i \ll \omega L_i$, $R_w \ll \omega L_w$ and $\omega^2 LC \ll 1$, Eq. (C.1) becomes:

$$GLC_{idB} = 20 \log(1 + 2L_i/L_w) \qquad (C.3)$$

Finally, for very high frequencies in which $\omega^2 L_i C \gg 1$, Eq. (C.1) becomes:

$$GLC_i = 20 \log(1 - 2/\omega^2 L_i C) \approx 0 \text{ dB} \qquad (C.4)$$

Equation (C.1) is plotted in Fig. C.3 for a typical 100 μH inductor made of AWG No. 18 wire (minimum NEC requirement) wrapped on a ferrite rod or toroid. The circuit values for this are: R_i = 0.3 Ω, L_i = 100 μH, $C_i \approx$ 100 pF. For 1 m of AWG No. 2, R_w = 510 $\mu\Omega$/m and $L_w \approx$ 1 μH/m. As seen from both Fig. C.3 and the above equations for A/t $\leqslant$ 1,000:

At dc: GLC_{idB} = 61 dB

At mid frequencies: GLC_{idB} = 44 dB

At VHF/UHF: GLC_{idB} = 0 dB

To correct the improvement read from Fig. C.3 for any length of interconnecting cable between Box 1 and Box 2, GLC_i becomes:

$$GLC_{idB} = GLC_{dB} \text{ (Fig. C.3)} - 20 \log l \qquad (C.5)$$

$\geqslant$ 0 dB for any length

C.3

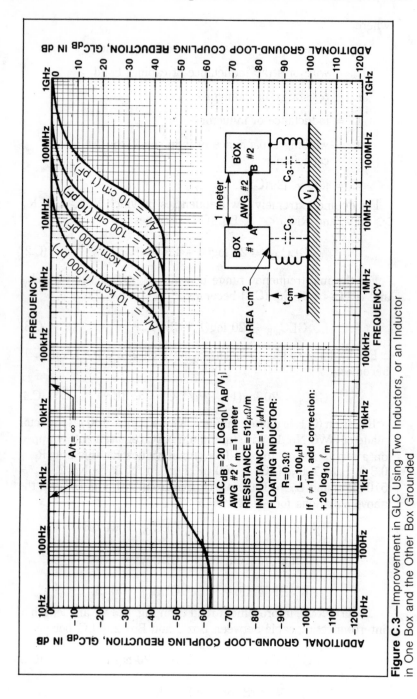

Figure C.3—Improvement in GLC Using Two Inductors, or an Inductor in One Box and the Other Box Grounded

Appendix D

Ground-Loop Coupling

This appendix presents the basic math models associated with ground-loop coupling (GLC). It also presents a number of GLC design illustrations for both balanced and unbalanced drivers and receivers.

D.1 Basic GLC Math Model Derivation, below Resonance

From dc to the first resonance of the cable above ground, the GLC can be approached as a lumped-element network, assuming that cable self-inductance and capacitance can be represented by a simple LC circuit.

Figure D.1 shows a simplified diagram of the GLC situation. The variables and nomenclature are as follows:

R_{g1} = signal or driver source impedance (high side)

R_{g2} = signal or driver source impedance (low side)

   $\approx R_{g1}$ ($\pm$ X percent) for balanced driver

   = 0 for unbalanced driver

R_{L1} = load or receiver input impedance (high side)

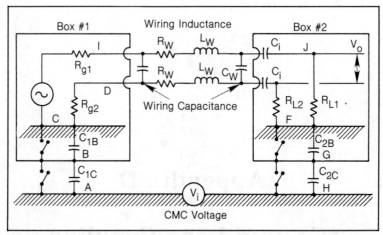

Figure D.1—Ground-Loop Coupling Variables

R_{L2} = load or receiver input impedance (low side)

$\approx R_{L1}$ ($\pm$ X percent) for balanced receiver

= 0 for unbalanced receiver

$$R_w = \frac{\rho l}{A} \tag{D.1}$$

where,

ρ = resistivity of wire in ohm-meters

= 1.72×10^{-8} for copper

l = wire length in meters

A = wire cross-sectional area in m^2

= $10^{-6} \times$ cross-sectional area in mm^2

thus,

$$R_w = 2.19 \times 10^{-2} \times l/d^2 \quad \text{for d in millimeters} \tag{D.2}$$

C_w = one half of the total wire-to-wire capacitance since, under the lumped element assumption, one can consider them as concentrated at cable ends

D.2

$$= \frac{\pi \epsilon_0}{2} \cosh^{-1}(s/d) \text{ F/m} \qquad (D.3)$$

$\approx 0.5 \ \pi \epsilon_0 / l_n(2s/d)$ for $s \geq 2d$ (less than 2 percent error)

$$= 13.9 / l_n(2s/d) \quad \text{pF/m} \qquad (D.4)$$

Notice that C_w, typically in the 30 to 100 pF/m range, has generally no shunting effect until few megahertz or more, unless both terminating resistances are high (> 1 kΩ).

L_w = common-mode inductance of the single wire above ground.

This self-inductance is larger than the differential self-inductance of the isolated wire pair. It also combines with the common-mode mutual inductance, M_c, between the loops formed by each of wires 1 and 2 and their return planes. It can be demonstrated that the **total** common-mode inductance of the two wires above ground is equal to $(L_{wo} + M_c)/2$.

L_{wo} depends on the ratio of the wire height above ground to the wire diameter, while M_c depends on the wires height and their spacing. M_c also depends on the wire pair arrangement versus the ground plane, i.e., side by side or one atop the other.

L_w therefore consists of:

1. L_{wo} = self inductance of an isolated wire above ground

   $= 0.2 \ l_n(4h/d - 1) \ \mu\text{H/m}$ for $h <$ total cable length

2. M_c = common-mode mutual inductance between the two wires versus ground

   $= 0.1 \ l_n[(4h^2 + s^2)/(s^2)]$

   $\approx 0.2 \ l_n(2h/s) \quad \mu\text{H/m}$, for $h/s \geq 2$

The definitions of s, d and h are as shown in Fig. D.2. Since the

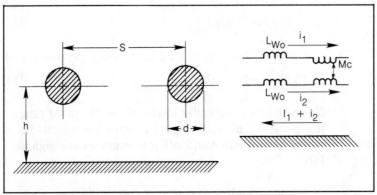

Figure D.2—Defining S/d and h Dimensions

separation s is always > d, h/d is always > h/s, and L_{wo} is always > M_c. For instance, with a typical pair where s = 2d:

When h/d = 3,

$$M = 0.22 \ \mu H/m$$

$$L = 0.48 \ \mu H/m$$

so, $M = 0.45 \ L$

When h/d = 100,

$$M = 0.92 \ \mu H/m$$

$$L = 1.2 \ \mu H/m$$

so, $M = 0.76 \ L$

Therefore, we can retain a typical ratio of M = 0.5 L, and

$$L_w = L_{wo} + M_c = (1 + 0.5) \times 0.2 \ l_n(4h/d - 1) \qquad (D.5)$$

$$= 0.3 \ l_n(4h/d - 1) \ \mu H/m \text{ for one wire}$$
above ground

The PCB, mother board or backplane wiring-to-case capacitance, C_{1B} and C_{2B} in Fig. D.1, and the metal case to ground plane capacitance, C_{1C} and C_{2C}, are calculated by the parallel-plate capacitance relations:

$$C = \epsilon A/t \text{ farads} \tag{D.6}$$

$$= 0.0884 \ A/t \tag{D.7}$$

where,

A = equivalent area of plate capacitance in cm^2

t = equivalent height or separation in centimeters

If only one end is floated, C_{1B}, C_{2B}, C_{1C} or C_{2C} is defined by Eq. (D.6) or (D.7). If both ends are floated, then the capacitances are added in series to yield the total capacitance, C_T:

$$C_T = \frac{C_{1B}C_{2B}}{C_{1B} + C_{2B}} = 0.0884 \ \frac{A_{1B}A_{2B}}{A_{1B}t_{2B} + A_{2B}t_{1B}} \tag{D.8}$$

If $C_{1B} = C_{2B}$, then,

$$C_T = \frac{C_{1B}}{2}$$

Finally, the series capacitors C_1, shown on the victim's side, represent the residual capacitance of the optical isolator or signal isolation transformer which may have been provided for ground loop elimination. Obviously, if there are no such devices, the calculation will replace both C_i by a short.

D.2 The Ground-Loop Coupling below Resonance

From Fig. D.1, GLC is:

$$GLC_{dB} = 20 \ \log(V_o/V_i) \tag{D.9}$$

Figure D.1 is redrawn as shown in Fig. D.3 with the values of R_w, L, C, and C_T having been developed in the previous Secion D.1. The value of (V_o/V_i) is:

$$\overline{ZZ}/(Z + 1/j\omega C_T) \tag{D.10}$$

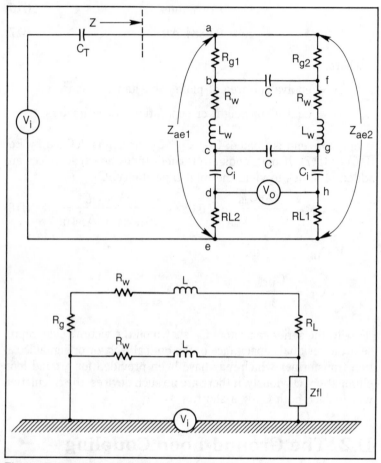

Figure D.3—Equivalent Circuits

where,
$$Z = \frac{Z_{ael} \, Z_{ae2}}{Z_{ael} + Z_{ae2}}$$

$$Z_{ael} = Z_{ab} + Z_{bc} + Z_{cd} + Z_{de} \qquad (D.11)$$

$$Z_{ae2} = Z_{af} + Z_{fg} + Z_{gh} + Z_{he} \qquad (D.12)$$

$$\overline{Z} = \left| \frac{Z_{de}}{Z_{ae1}} - \frac{Z_{he}}{Z_{ae2}} \right| \text{ for general balanced case}$$

$$\overline{Z} = \frac{Z_{he}}{Z_{ae2}} \text{ for unbalanced source and load} \qquad (D.13)$$

$$Z_{ab} = \cfrac{1}{\cfrac{1}{R_{g2}} + \cfrac{1}{R_{g1} + \cfrac{1}{j\omega C + \cfrac{1}{2R_W + 2j\omega L + \cfrac{1}{j\omega C + \cfrac{1}{R_{L1} + R_{L2} + \cfrac{2}{j\omega C_i}}}}}}}$$

with Z_{af} similar to Z_{ab} except interchange $R_{g2} \rightleftharpoons R_{g1}$
$$R_{L2} \rightleftharpoons R_{L2}$$

$$Z_{bc} = \cfrac{1}{\cfrac{1}{R_w + j\omega L} + \cfrac{1}{R_w + \cfrac{1}{\cfrac{1}{R_{g1} + R_{g2}} + j\omega C} + \cfrac{1}{j\omega C + \cfrac{1}{R_{L1} + R_{L2} + \cfrac{2}{j\omega C_i}}} + j\omega L}}$$

Z_{fg}: Interchange $R_{g2} \rightleftharpoons R_{g1}$
$$R_{L2} \rightleftharpoons R_{L1}$$

D.7

$$Z_{cd} = \cfrac{1}{j\omega C_i + \cfrac{1}{R_{L1} + R_{L2} + \cfrac{1}{j\omega C_i} + \cfrac{1}{j\omega C + \cfrac{1}{2R_W + 2j\omega L + \cfrac{1}{j\omega C + \cfrac{1}{R_{g1} + R_{g2}}}}}}}$$

Z_{gh}: Interchange $R_{g2} \rightleftharpoons R_{g1}$
$\qquad\qquad\quad R_{L2} \rightleftharpoons R_{L1}$

$$Z_{de} = \cfrac{1}{\cfrac{1}{R_{L2}} + \cfrac{1}{R_{L1} + \cfrac{2}{j\omega C_i} + \cfrac{1}{j\omega C + \cfrac{1}{2R_W + 2j\omega L + \cfrac{1}{j\omega C + \cfrac{1}{R_{g1} + R_{g2}}}}}}}$$

Z_{he}: Interchange $R_{g2} \rightleftharpoons R_{g1}$
$\qquad\qquad\quad R_{L2} \rightleftharpoons R_{L1}$

D.3 Simplified Model for Very Low Frequencies

At certain frequencies, the following approximations can be made:

$$L_w \omega \ll R_g + R_L$$
$$L_w \omega > R_w$$
$$Z_{fl} > R_g + R_L$$

When this is the case, GLC, for the unbalanced link shown in Fig. D.3, can be simplified (Fig. D.3A) as:

$$GLC = \frac{R_L}{R_g + R_L + j\omega L_w} \times \frac{L_w\omega + R_w}{Z_{fl}} \qquad (D.14)$$

where,

Z_{fl} = impedance of the total floating capacitance C_T

On the other hand, at extremely low frequencies (ELF) and down to dc, the GLC value is limited by the insulation resistance between the PCB, insulation wires, etc., and the chassis or ground, which cannot be infinite. Although values of 1,000 MΩ or more are technically achievable, it is more realistic to assume that, due to humidity, dust and so forth, practical insulation resistances R_{iso} are in the range of 10^7 to 10^8 Ω, which gives the lower (or dc) asymptote of GLC. This is equal to:

$$20 \log(R_L/(R_g + R_L) \times R_w/(L \times R_{iso})$$

For AWG No. 22, $R_g = R_L$, and $R_{iso} = 10^8$ Ω. This results in:

$$GLC \ min = -192 \ dB \ for \ 1 \ m \ wire$$
$$= -172 \ dB \ for \ 10 \ m \ wire$$
$$= -152 \ dB \ for \ 100 \ m \ wire$$

D.4 GLC at Resonance

For the floated configuration (one end or both), the circuit formed by the return wire above ground and the floating capacitance(s) can be regarded, at and near resonance, as an RLC resonant circuit whose complex impedance equals:

$$Z_{loop} = \sqrt{R_w^2 + [L_w\omega - (1/C_T\omega)]^{\pm}} \qquad (D.15)$$

When $L\omega = 1/C\omega$, this circuit oscillates with a more or less pronounced Q factor, depending on the value of R_w. The lesser the wire resistance, the sharper the resonance. However, although Q factors of 3 to 10 have been measured in some cases (which would cause the GLC to become positive), the peaking is somewhat limited by the fact that at these typical frequencies (generally few megahertz or more) the wire has entered its skin effect region where its ac resistance is higher than the dc value, according to the formula:

$$R_{ac} = R_{dc} \frac{r}{2\delta} \qquad (D.16)$$

where,

r = wire radius

δ = skin depth at a given frequency

$= 0.06/\sqrt{f_{MHz}\, \mu_r \sigma_r}$ in millimeters $\qquad (D.17)$

For instance, given a 0.6 mm wire dia. (AWG No. 22), its skin depth region will begin around 4 MHz. Above this frequency, the ac resistance of a 0.6 mm dia. wire can be found from Eq. (D.16), resulting in:

$$R_{ac} = 0.125 \sqrt{f_{MHz}} \;\; \Omega/m \text{ for copper}$$

In addition, the contact resistance of connectors, terminal boards, etc. at cable ends and transitions contributes to the increase of the purely resistive term. Finally, the ground plane itself, whatever it consists of metal or earth, has a non-null RF resistance which "spoils" the Q of the whole loop. All this practically results in a curve shape as shown in Figs. D.4 to D.10, where the GLC values approach 0 dB for the floated case.

A few remarks are in order:

1. Each different value of C (or A/t) parameter creates a different resonant frequency, the larger C corresponding to the lowest resonance.
2. For a given value of C at each end, the resonance shifts down by $\sqrt{2}$ if only one PCB (or box) is floated.
3. At resonance, the floated GLC is slightly worse than the all-grounded GLC. This explains the frequent frustrations and contradictions reported in EMI-fix cases where similar equipments, depending upon their cable lengths,

were improved at one location by floating the zero-volt reference, and at an other one by grounding the same reference. Consequently, all the GLC curves shown at the end of this Appendix have been "defaulted" to 0 dB in the region of resonant frequencies.

D.5 GLC above Resonance

Above the first resonance, the lumped-element approach described so far does not stand (see Ref.1). Simply speaking, a wire pair cannot be considered any longer as an "L" or "Pi" filter, and a distributed element approach becomes necessary. This ultimately leads to a transmission line model, which is necessary when one deals with an electrically long line. Since the line formed by the return wire(s) above ground can be either terminated in a short (grounded end) or left open ended (floating), we have a common-mode transmission line which is totally mismatched.

For the all-grounded case, since the loop impedance (starting from dc) begins as a short, the first resonance corresponds to a maximum of the loop impedance, i.e., a lesser GLC. As frequency increases, the cable length encounters successive resonances and anti-resonances over each multiple integer of $\lambda/4$, causing the GLC (all grounded) to run through successive peaks and nulls.

For the floated case, the loop CM impedance starts from dc with an infinite impedance, continuously decreasing as frequency increases, down to a value bounded by the resistance of the return wire (when $L\omega = 1/C\omega$). From then on, the floated case GLC will also run through successive peaks and nulls, corresponding to I_{max} and V_{min} of an open-ended transmission line. The peaks and nulls of the floated GLC generally exhibit a $\lambda/4$ shift compared to the peaks and nulls of the all grounded GLC, since they are in opposite phase.

Therefore to simplify the graphical presentation, a worst-case envelope is assumed, aligned on the tops of the peaks. This envelope would remain horizontal forever if the line were ideal (lossless and matched at both ends). Hopefully, because of the copper losses (ac resistance increasing as $\sqrt{f}$), the dielectric losses and the mismatch losses across every connector plus source and load interfaces, the envelope of the peaks exhibits a rolloff $1/\sqrt{f}$ (10 dB per decade). The effect of this attenuation is barely noticeable for lengths less than 1 m up to 10 GHz, but is quite significant for 30 or 100 m cable lengths.

D.6 The Case of Broadband EMI

The envelope approach, in the case of broadband (BB) EMI (i.e. the Fourier harmonics being very closely packed over a wide spectrum, or a single transient EMI where the Fourier series is replaced by the Fourier integral) could cause some pessimistic results. This is due to the fact that, successively, the actual Fourier spectrum has been replaced by its worst-case envelope, then the field-to-cable, common-mode coupling (FCM) has also been replaced above $\lambda/2$ by the envelope of its peaks and so has been the GLC above resonance. The result of this triple envelope summation can create a cascaded overestimate which can be evaluated by actually integrating the three functions and comparing the result to the **envelope results**. The total error in this case is 0.42, i.e. a correction of 7.5 dB should be applied to the GLC curves above resonance, **in the case of BB EMI** source. This shows as a dotted line captioned **BB** on the GLC curves.

D.7 Hybrid Links (Unbalanced and Balanced)

Situations may occur where, either imposed by component availability or inherited from some former design, a hybrid link exists, i.e. the source is unbalanced (grounded transducer for instance) while the receiving amplifier is balanced. This hybrid situation generally results in a GLC which is (1) as poor as the **grounded unbalanced** case when both ends are grounded, and (2) about 6 to 12 dB worse than the **floated unbalanced** case when one or both ends floats. The only advantage of the hybrid arrangement is a reduction of resonance peaks due to the damping introduced by R/2 in the lower branch of the balanced end.

In case the designer needs to predict GLC with a hybrid link, the simplified equations below resonance are:

Both ends grounded:

$$\text{GLC} = \frac{R_L L_w \omega (1 + x) - R_L R_g}{[R_g + jL_w\omega + R_w + R_L(1 + x)](R_L + jL_w\omega + R_w)} \quad (\text{D}.18)$$

Floated:

$$GLC = C_T\omega \ \frac{R_L L_w \omega (1 + x) - R_L R_g}{R_L(1 + x) + j2L_w\omega + R_g} \tag{D.19}$$

where,

R_L, L_w, R_w and C_T are the same terms as in the general GLC equation of Fig. D.1. Note that X is the percent of tolerance of the balanced end. As long as X < 10 percent, it has little effect on the GLC of hybrid system, due to the unbalance forced by the source.

D.8 Simplified GLC Math Models and Summary of Various GLC Slopes (Unbalanced Case)

The following equations allow to us draw the envelope of the GLC coefficient across its different regimes. As already mentioned, at and above resonance the model is leveled on the peaks, i.e. a worst-case envelope. All equations are valid approximations for wire diameters from 0.25 to 1 mm (AWG No. 30 to No. 18).

1. Lower Asymptote (down to DC), Floated case

This is the minimum value the GLC could ever take:

$$GLC = 20 \log \frac{R_L}{R_g + R_L} \times \frac{R_w}{2\,R_{iso}} \tag{D.20}$$

$$\cong -192 \text{ dB} + 20 \log l$$

where,

R_{iso} = dc insulation resistance of the wires, transformer secondary windings, PCB etc., versus chassis or installation ground

l = cable length

2. Low frequency (from Lower asymptote up to First Resonance), Floated Case

$$\text{GLC} = 20 \log \frac{R_L}{R_g + R_L} \times \frac{R_w + jL_w\omega}{\sqrt{R_w^2 + \left(L_w\omega - \dfrac{1}{C_T\omega}\right)^2}} \quad \text{(D.21)}$$

$$= -104 + 20 \log \frac{R_L}{R_g + R_L} + 20 \log (0.05 + j6 \ \Omega \times$$

$$f_{MHz}) + 20 \log l + 20 \log C_{T(pF)} + 20 \log f_{MHz}$$

$$\cong \ - 90 \ \text{dB} + 20 \log \frac{R_L}{R_g + R_L} + 20 \log C_{T(pF)} +$$

$$20 \log l + 40 \log f_{MHz}$$

for $L_w\omega > R_w$ i.e. generally above 1.5 kHz

Notice that in the two latter equations, C is expressed in pF for convenience.

3. Low Frequency, Grounded Both Ends (DC to First Resonance)

$$\text{GLC} = 20 \log \frac{R_L}{R_g + R_L + j6 \ \Omega \times f_{MHz}} \quad \text{(D.22)}$$

4. At $f_{res} = \dfrac{1}{2\pi\sqrt{L_w C_T}}$, for All Configurations

$$\text{GLC} \approx 0 \ \text{dB} \quad \text{(D.23)}$$

5. At any Frequency $f_x > f_{res}$ for All Configurations

$$\text{GLC}_{(max)} \cong 0 \ \text{dB} - 10 \log (f_x/f_{res}) \quad \text{(D.24)}$$

It must be remembered that C_T is the total floating capacitance such that if 100 pF of parasitic capacitance exists at each end, a fully floated configuration corresponds to C_T = 50 pF.

D.9 GLC Design Graphs

This section presents many design graphs of GLC which meet most design needs. A few typical ones have already appeared in Chapter 6 as Figs. 6.16 through 6.18. The GLC graphs are quantized into the following sets:

Unbalanced Circuits

For all wire sizes	use AWG No. 22
For $l \leqslant 0.17$ m	use l = 0.1 m
0.17 m < $l \leqslant 0.55$ m	use l = 0.3 m
0.55 m < $l \leqslant 1.7$ m	use l = 1 m
1.7 m < $l \leqslant 5.5$ m	use l = 3 m
5.5 m < $l \leqslant 17$ m	use l = 10 m
17 m < $l \leqslant 55$ m	use l = 30 m
l > 55 m	use l = 100 m

Balanced Circuits

For any AWG No.	use AWG No. 22
For any R_g and R_L	use 100 Ω
For tolerance $\leqslant 3\%$	use 1%
tolerance > 3%	use 10%
For $l \leqslant 0.3$ m	use l = 0.1 m
0.3 m < $l \leqslant 3$ m	use l = 1 m
3 m < $l \leqslant 30$ m	use l = 10 m
l > 30 m	use l = 100 m

To make this quantization more functionally useful, it has been rearranged into Table D.1 for unbalanced and balanced circuits. The interconnecting cable length is divided into half decade steps from 10 cm to 100 m. The number appearing in the table box corresponds to the applicable figure number to use. Thus, for example, for a 100 Ω unbalanced circuit source and load network of AWG No. 24 and 3 m length, Fig. D.7 would be used.

D.15

Table D.1—Criteria for Selection of Applicable GLC Figure Number

Unbalanced Circuits		
	$R_g = R_L$ Any Value $> 10\ \Omega$	$R_L > 3\ R_g$
$l \leqslant 0.17$ m	D.4	Add
0.17 m $< l \leqslant 0.55$ m	D.5	+ 6 dB
0.55 m $< l \leqslant 1.7$ m	D.6	to the
1.7 m $< l \leqslant 5.5$ m	D.7	corresponding
5.5 m $< l \leqslant 17$ m	D.8	GLC
17 m $< l \leqslant 55$ m	D.9	curve
$l > 55$ m	D10	
Balanced Circuits		
AWG #	Any	
R_g and R_L	Any	
Tolerance	$\leqslant$ 3%	> 3%
$l \leqslant 0.3$ m	D.32	D.36
$0.3 < l \leqslant 3$ m	D.33	D.37
3 m $< l \leqslant 30$ m	D.34	D.38
$l > 30$ m	D.35	D.39

For balanced circuits, Table D.1 also shows the criteria for selecting the applicable GLC figure number. Here the main heading involves the tolerance in the components (usually resistance) between the upper and lower legs (R_{g1} versus R_{g2} and R_{L1} versus R_{L2}. Estimates have been made regarding the average quantization error of Table D.1. It is estimated to be about 8 dB. It can be reduced by suitable interpolation between the quanta boards.

D.16

D.10 Sensitivity of GLC Curves to Circuit Geometry and Termination Resistances (Unbalanced Case)

The GLC curves presented in Chapter 6 and in this Appendix have been established for typical h/d ratios in the 100 range, corresponding, for instance, to a 0.6 mm dia. wire located 50 to 100 mm above ground.

Influence of Wire Diameter

The influence of wire diameter on GLC is rather weak. For instance, with a height of 50 mm, going from a 1 mm dia. (AWG No. 18) to a 0.25 mm dia. (AWG NO. 30) wire would change the L_w term from 1.6 μH/m to 2 μH/m, i.e. a shift of less than 3 dB in the GLC curves.

Influence of Cable Height, h, Above Ground

This influence could be more of a concern since the range of possible heights is rather expansive. However, since in Eq. (D.5), L_w is governed by the natural logarithm of h/d, changing h from 0.1 m to 1 m, for instance, with a 0.6 mm dia. wire would change L_w from 1.8 μH/m to 2.5 μH/m, i.e. a 2.8 dB aggravation of the GLC.

Influence of Termination Resistances

The influence of the source and load resistances can be seen in the first term of Eq. (D.14):

$$\frac{R_L}{R_g + R_L + j\omega L_w}$$

Since in virtually any application the load resistance is presumed to be equal or higher than the generator resistance, the first term (provided that $R_L > j\omega L_w$, which is generally the case) can vary from 0.5 for $R_g = R_L$ to 1 for $R_L = \infty$.

The GLC curves presented have been established for $R_g = R = 100 \, \Omega$. For all cases where R_g and R_L are different from 100 Ω but are still of the same value, no change is necessary. For all cases where $R_L > 3 \, R_g$, a +6 dB factor should be added to the GLC curves.

In summary, due to the less than ±3 dB variance introduced by typical range of heights and wire diameter, no specific GLC curves have been developed for different wire sizes and heights. For very high load resistances, like an $R_g = 10 \, \Omega$ and $R_L = 1,000 \, \Omega$ arrangement, a maximum of +6 dB should be added to the curves.

D.17

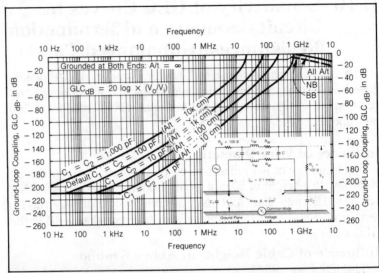

Figure D.4—GLC for Unbalanced Circuits Having a Source and Load Impedance of 100 Ω and AWG No. 22 Cable Length of 0.1 m

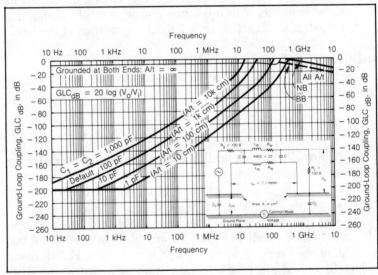

Figure D.5—GLC for Unbalanced Circuits Having a Source and Load Impedance of 100 Ω and AWG No. 22 Cable Length of 0.3 m

D.18

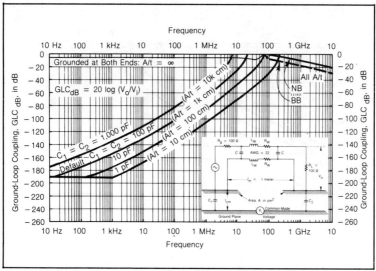

Figure D.6—GLC for Unbalanced Circuits Having a Source and Load Impedance of 100 Ω and AWG No. 22 Cable Length of 1 m

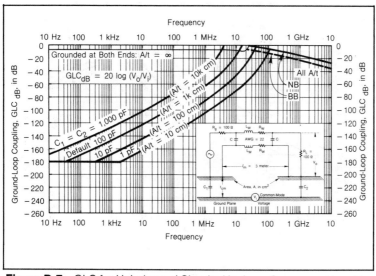

Figure D.7—GLC for Unbalanced Circuits Having a Source and Load Impedance of 100 Ω and AWG No. 22 Cable Length of 3 m

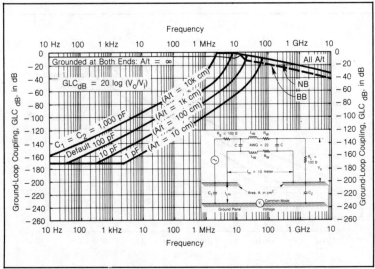

Figure D.8—GLC for Unbalanced Circuits Having a Source and Load Impedance of 100 Ω and AWG No. 22 Cable Length of 10 m

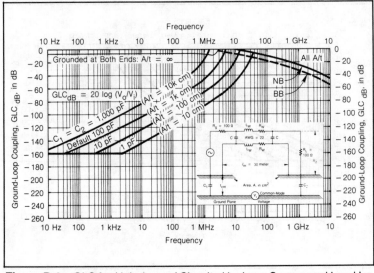

Figure D.9—GLC for Unbalanced Circuits Having a Source and Load Impedance of 100 Ω and AWG No. 22 Cable Length of 30 m

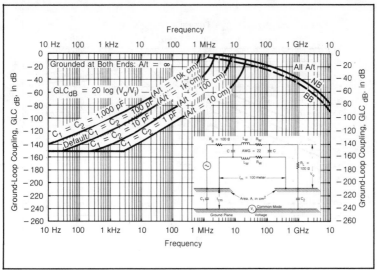

Figure D.10—GLC for Unbalanced Circuits Having a Source and Load Impedance of 100 Ω and AWG No. 22 Cable Length of 0.1 m

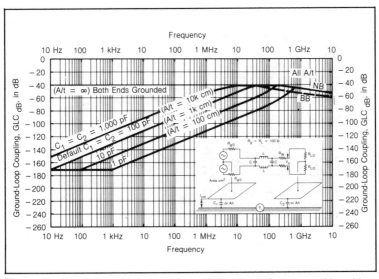

Figure D.11—GLC for Balanced Circuits Having a Source and Load Impedance of 100 Ω, 1 Percent Tolerance, and AWG No. 22 Cable Length of 0.1 m

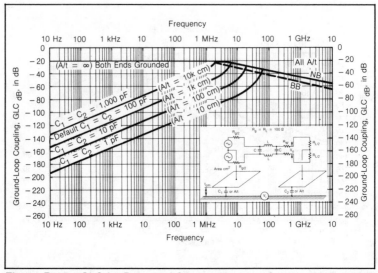

Figure D.12—GLC for Balanced Circuits Having a Source and Load Impedance of 100 Ω 1 Percent Tolerance, and AWG No. 22 Cable Length of 1 m

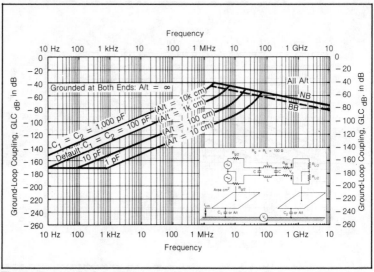

Figure D.13—GLC for Balanced Circuits Having a Source and Load Impedance of 100 Ω, 1 Percent Tolerance, and AWG No. 22 Cable Length of 10 m

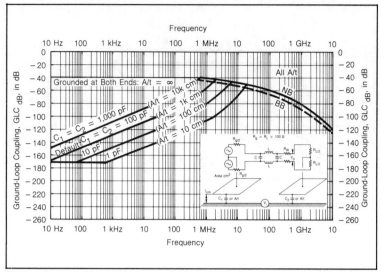

Figure D.14—GLC for Balanced Circuits Having a Source and Load Impedance of 100 Ω, 1 Percent Tolerance, and AWG No. 22 Cable Length of 100 m

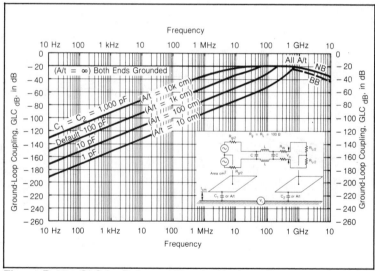

Figure D.15—GLC for Balanced Circuits Having a Source and Load Impedance of 100 Ω, 10 Percent Tolerance, and AWG No. 22 Cable Length of 0.1 m

D.23

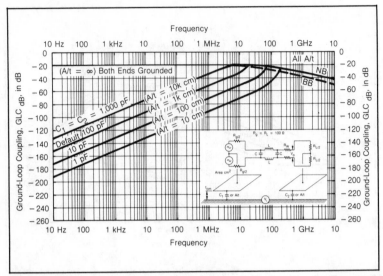

Figure D.16—GLC for Balanced Circuits Having a Source and Load Impedance of 100 Ω, 10 Percent Tolerance, and AWG No. 22 Cable Length of 1 m

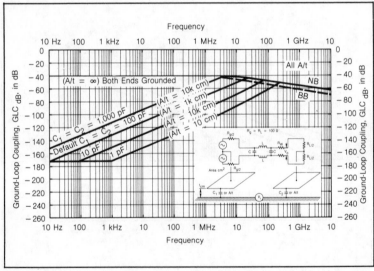

Figure D.17—GLC for Balanced Circuits Having a Source and Load Impedance of 100 Ω, 10 Percent Tolerance, and AWG No. 22 Cable Length of 1 m

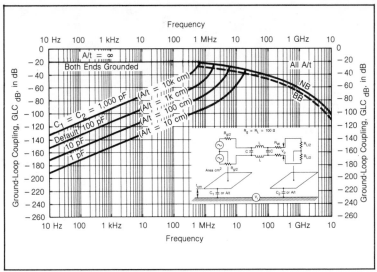

Figure D.18—GLC for Balanced Circuits Having a Source and Load Impedance of 100 Ω, 10 Percent Tolerance, and AWG No. 22 Cable Length of 100 m

D.11 References

1. Paul, Clayton R., "Frequency Response of Multiconductor Transmission Lines Illuminated by an Electromagnetic Field," *IEEE EMC Symposium Record* (New York: IEEE), Session 3A, San Antonio, TX, October 7-9, 1975, and pub. *IEEE Transactions on EMC*, Vol. EMC 18, no. 4, November 1976.

Figure 18—... ... ... the front corner, and roof ... ... for full foliage, and at ... ... 22.2 dB at ... of foliage.

DTI References

1. Tam, Clavin T. DU square, "Analysis of RCS scattering... Exploitation based illumination... at distances..." *IEEE EICSP-RCS...*, New York... ... ... SA Symposium..., October 9 1978 and 1980... U... ... SA... ..., W..., EM... ... ... March 4 1966.

Appendix E
Field Strength and
Power Density Conversions

Electromagnetic ambients are usually expressed in terms of electric field strengths or magnetic flux densities. Occasionally, they are expressed in units of power density. The relations are developed herein together with conversion tables.

E.1 Power Density and Electric Field Relations

The power density, P_D, is the radiated power flux flow or power per unit cross-sectional area at a receiving or victim site. As stated in Section 2.4.5 on radiated ambients from licensed transmitters:

$$P_D = E \times H = E^2/Z \qquad (E.1)$$

where,
  E = electric field strength in volts per meter
  H = magnetic field strength in amps per meter
  Z = wave impedance, E/H
     = 120 π = 377 Ω for far fields

The wave impedance may be much greater or smaller than

377 Ω in the near field. The near-to-far-field interference distance R_f, is defined as:

$$R_f \approx \lambda/2\pi, \text{ for } D < \lambda/2 \tag{E.2}$$

$$R_f \approx D^2/2\lambda, \text{ for } D > \lambda/2 \tag{E.3}$$

where,

$\quad$ D = maximum dimension of the radiation element or system
$\quad \lambda$ = wavelength in meters = c/f = $300/f_{MHz}$ $\qquad$ (E.4)
$\quad$ c = velocity of light = 3×10^8 m/s
$\quad$ f = frequency in hertz
f_{MHz} = frequency in megahertz

Equation (E.1) may be expressed in decibels for different units, i.e.:

$$P_D \text{ dBW/m}^2 = 20 \log E_{v/m} - 10 \log Z \tag{E.5}$$

$$= E_{dBV/m} - 25.8 \text{ dB}\Omega \text{ for far-field conditions} \tag{E.6}$$

$$= E_{dB\mu V/m} - 146 \text{ dB} \tag{E.7}$$

or,

$$P_D \text{ dBm/m}^2 = P_D \text{ dBW/m}^2 + 30 \text{ dB} \tag{E.8}$$

$$\approx E_{dB\mu V/m} - 116 \text{ dB} \tag{E.9}$$

The above equations are computed and listed in Tables E.1 and E.2. Also listed are equivalent magnetic terms, discussed below. Table E.1 lists electric field strength as the independent variable in the left column from 280 dBμV/m to −60 dBμV/m.

Table E.1—Electric-field Strength-to-Magnetic Fields-to-Power Densities

dBμV/m	V/m	dBμA/m	A/m	dBpT	pT & nT	nT & T	Gauss	Tesla	dBW/m²	dBm/m²	mW/cm²
280	10^8	228.5	2.65×10^5	230.5	3.33×10^{11}	3.33×10^8	3.33×10^3	.333	134.3	164.3	2.67×10^{12}
260	10^7	208.5	2.65×10^4	210.5	3.33×10^{10}	3.33×10^7	333	.033	114.3	144.3	2.67×10^{10}
240	10^6	188.5	2.65×10^3	190.5	3.33×10^9	3.33×10^6	33.3	.003	94.3	124.3	2.67×10^8
220	10^5	168.5	265	170.5	3.33×10^8	3.33×10^5	3.33	3.33×10^{-4}	74.3	104.3	2.67×10^6
200	10^4	148.5	26.5	150.5	3.33×10^7	3.33×10^4	.333	3.33×10^{-5}	54.3	84.3	2.67×10^4
180	10^3	128.5	2.65	130.5	3.33×10^6	3.33×10^3	.0333	3.33×10^{-6}	34.3	64.3	267
160	100	108.5	.265	110.5	3.33×10^5	333	3.33×10^{-1}	3.33×10^{-7}	14.3	44.3	2.67
140	10	88.5	.0265	90.5	3.33×10^4	33.3	3.33×10^{-4}	3.33×10^{-8}	-5.7	24.3	.0267
120	1	68.5	2.65×10^{-3}	70.5	3.33×10^3	3.33	3.33×10^{-5}	3.33×10^{-9}	-25.7	4.3	2.67×10^{-4}
100	.10	48.5	2.65×10^{-4}	50.5	333	.333	3.33×10^{-6}	3.33×10^{-10}	-45.7	-15.7	2.67×10^{-6}
80	.01	28.5	2.65×10^{-5}	30.5	33.3	.0333	3.33×10^{-7}	3.33×10^{-11}	-65.7	-35.7	2.67×10^{-8}
60	10^{-3}	8.5	2.65×10^{-6}	10.5	3.33	3.33×10^{-3}	3.33×10^{-8}	3.33×10^{-12}	-85.7	-55.7	2.67×10^{-10}
40	10^{-4}	-11.5	2.65×10^{-7}	-9.5	.333	3.33×10^{-5}	3.33×10^{-9}	3.33×10^{-13}	-105.7	-75.7	2.67×10^{-12}
20	10^{-5}	-31.5	2.65×10^{-8}	-29.5	.0333	3.33×10^{-5}	3.33×10^{-10}	3.33×10^{-14}	-125.7	-95.7	2.67×10^{-14}
19	8.91×10^{-6}	-32.5	2.36×10^{-8}	-30.5	.0297	2.97×10^{-5}	2.97×10^{-10}	2.97×10^{-14}	-126.7	-96.7	2.12×10^{-14}
18	7.94×10^{-6}	-33.5	2.10×10^{-8}	-31.5	.0265	2.65×10^{-5}	2.65×10^{-10}	2.65×10^{-14}	-127.7	-97.7	1.68×10^{-14}
17	7.08×10^{-6}	-34.5	1.87×10^{-8}	-32.5	.0236	2.36×10^{-5}	2.36×10^{-10}	2.36×10^{-14}	-128.7	-98.7	1.34×10^{-14}
16	6.31×10^{-6}	-35.5	1.67×10^{-8}	-33.5	.0210	2.10×10^{-5}	2.10×10^{-10}	2.10×10^{-14}	-129.7	-99.7	1.06×10^{-14}
15	5.62×10^{-6}	-36.5	1.49×10^{-8}	-34.5	.0187	1.87×10^{-5}	1.87×10^{-10}	1.87×10^{-14}	-130.7	-100.7	8.43×10^{-15}
14	5.01×10^{-6}	-37.5	1.33×10^{-8}	-35.5	.0167	1.67×10^{-5}	1.67×10^{-10}	1.67×10^{-14}	-131.7	-101.7	6.70×10^{-15}
13	4.47×10^{-6}	-38.5	1.18×10^{-8}	-36.5	.0149	1.49×10^{-5}	1.49×10^{-10}	1.49×10^{-14}	-132.7	-102.7	5.32×10^{-15}
12	3.98×10^{-6}	-39.5	1.05×10^{-8}	-37.5	.0133	1.33×10^{-5}	1.33×10^{-10}	1.33×10^{-14}	-133.7	-103.7	4.23×10^{-15}
11	3.55×10^{-6}	-40.5	9.40×10^{-9}	-38.5	.0118	1.18×10^{-5}	1.18×10^{-10}	1.18×10^{-14}	-134.7	-104.7	3.36×10^{-15}
10	3.16×10^{-6}	-41.5	8.38×10^{-9}	-39.5	.0105	1.05×10^{-5}	1.05×10^{-10}	1.05×10^{-14}	-135.7	-105.7	2.12×10^{-15}
9	2.82×10^{-6}	-42.5	7.46×10^{-9}	-40.5	9.40×10^{-3}	9.40×10^{-6}	9.40×10^{-11}	9.40×10^{-15}	-136.7	-106.7	2.12×10^{-15}
8	2.51×10^{-6}	-43.5	6.65×10^{-9}	-41.5	8.38×10^{-3}	8.38×10^{-6}	8.38×10^{-11}	8.18×10^{-15}	-137.7	-107.7	1.68×10^{-15}
7	2.24×10^{-6}	-44.5	5.93×10^{-9}	-42.5	7.46×10^{-3}	7.46×10^{-6}	7.46×10^{-11}	7.46×10^{-15}	-138.7	-108.7	1.34×10^{-15}
6	2.00×10^{-6}	-45.5	5.28×10^{-9}	-43.5	6.65×10^{-3}	6.65×10^{-6}	6.65×10^{-11}	6.65×10^{-15}	-139.7	-109.7	1.06×10^{-15}
5	1.78×10^{-6}	-46.5	4.71×10^{-9}	-44.5	5.93×10^{-3}	5.93×10^{-6}	5.93×10^{-11}	5.93×10^{-15}	-140.7	-110.7	8.43×10^{-16}
4	1.58×10^{-6}	-47.5	4.20×10^{-9}	-45.5	5.28×10^{-3}	5.28×10^{-6}	5.28×10^{-11}	5.28×10^{-15}	-141.7	-111.7	6.70×10^{-16}
3	1.41×10^{-6}	-48.5	3.74×10^{-9}	-46.5	4.71×10^{-3}	4.71×10^{-6}	4.71×10^{-11}	4.71×10^{-15}	-142.7	-112.7	5.32×10^{-16}
2	1.26×10^{-6}	-49.5	3.33×10^{-9}	-47.5	4.20×10^{-3}	4.20×10^{-6}	4.20×10^{-11}	4.20×10^{-15}	-143.7	-113.7	4.23×10^{-16}
1	1.12×10^{-6}	-50.5	2.97×10^{-9}	-48.5	3.74×10^{-3}	3.74×10^{-6}	3.74×10^{-11}	3.74×10^{-15}	-144.7	-114.7	3.36×10^{-16}
0	10^{-6}	-51.5	2.65×10^{-9}	-49.5	3.33×10^{-3}	3.33×10^{-6}	3.33×10^{-11}	3.33×10^{-15}	-145.7	-115.7	2.67×10^{-16}
-20	10^{-7}	-71.5	2.65×10^{-10}	-69.5	3.33×10^{-4}	3.33×10^{-7}	3.33×10^{-12}	3.33×10^{-16}	-165.7	-135.7	2.67×10^{-18}
-40	10^{-8}	-91.5	2.65×10^{-11}	-89.5	3.33×10^{-5}	3.33×10^{-8}	3.33×10^{-13}	3.33×10^{-17}	-185.7	-155.7	2.67×10^{-20}
-60	10^{-9}	-111.5	2.65×10^{-12}	-109.5	3.33×10^{-6}	3.33×10^{-9}	3.33×10^{-14}	3.33×10^{-18}	-205.7	-175.7	2.67×10^{-22}

Table E.2—Magnetic Flux Density-to-Field Strength-to-Power Densities

dBpT	pT/m²	nT/T	Gauss	Tesla	dBµA/m	A/m	dBµV/m	V/m	dBW/m²	dBm/m²	mW/cm²
240	10^{12}	10^9	10^4	1	238	8×10^5	289.5	3×10^8	143.8	173.8	2.4×10^{13}
220	10^{11}	10^8	10^3	.1	218	8×10^4	269.5	3×10^7	123.8	153.8	2.4×10^{11}
200	10^{10}	10^7	10^2	.01	198	8×10^3	249.5	3×10^6	103.8	133.8	2.4×10^9
180	10^9	10^6	10	.001	178	796	229.5	3×10^5	83.8	113.8	2.4×10^7
160	10^8	10^5	1	10^{-4}	158	80	209.5	3×10^4	63.8	93.8	2.4×10^5
140	10^7	10^4	.1	10^{-5}	138	8	189.5	3×10^3	43.8	73.8	2.4×10^3
120	10^6	10^3	.01	10^{-6}	118	.8	169.5	300	23.8	53.8	23.9
100	10^5	10^2	.001	10^{-7}	98	.08	149.5	30	3.8	33.8	.24
80	10^4	10	10^{-4}	10^{-8}	78	.008	129.5	3	-16.2	13.8	.0024
60	10^3	1	10^{-5}	10^{-9}	58	8×10^{-4}	109.5	.3	-36.2	-6.2	2.39×10^{-5}
40	100	.1	10^{-6}	10^{-10}	38	8×10^{-5}	89.5	.03	-56.2	-26.2	2.39×10^{-7}
20	10.000	.01	10^{-7}	10^{-11}	18	7.96×10^{-6}	69.5	.003	-76.2	-46.2	2.39×10^{-9}
19	8.913	8.91×10^{-3}	8.91×10^{-8}	8.91×10^{-12}	17	7.09×10^{-6}	68.5	2.67×10^{-3}	-77.2	-47.2	1.90×10^{-9}
18	7.943	7.94×10^{-3}	7.94×10^{-8}	7.94×10^{-12}	16	6.32×10^{-6}	67.5	2.38×10^{-3}	-78.2	-48.2	1.51×10^{-9}
17	7.079	7.08×10^{-3}	7.08×10^{-8}	7.08×10^{-12}	15	5.63×10^{-6}	66.5	2.12×10^{-3}	-79.2	-49.2	1.20×10^{-9}
16	6.310	6.31×10^{-3}	6.31×10^{-8}	6.31×10^{-12}	14	5.02×10^{-6}	65.5	1.89×10^{-3}	-80.2	-50.2	9.50×10^{-10}
15	5.623	5.62×10^{-3}	5.62×10^{-8}	5.62×10^{-12}	13	4.47×10^{-6}	64.5	1.69×10^{-3}	-81.2	-51.2	7.55×10^{-10}
14	5.012	5.01×10^{-3}	5.01×10^{-8}	5.01×10^{-12}	12	3.99×10^{-6}	63.5	1.50×10^{-3}	-82.2	-52.2	6.00×10^{-10}
13	4.467	4.47×10^{-3}	4.47×10^{-8}	4.47×10^{-12}	11	3.55×10^{-6}	62.5	1.34×10^{-3}	-83.2	-53.2	4.76×10^{-10}
12	3.981	3.98×10^{-3}	3.98×10^{-8}	3.98×10^{-12}	10	3.17×10^{-6}	61.5	1.19×10^{-3}	-84.2	-54.2	3.78×10^{-10}
11	3.548	3.55×10^{-3}	3.55×10^{-8}	3.55×10^{-12}	9	2.82×10^{-6}	60.5	1.06×10^{-3}	-85.2	-55.2	3.01×10^{-10}
10	3.162	3.16×10^{-3}	3.16×10^{-8}	3.16×10^{-12}	8	2.52×10^{-6}	59.5	9.49×10^{-4}	-86.2	-56.2	2.39×10^{-10}
9	2.818	2.82×10^{-3}	2.82×10^{-8}	2.82×10^{-12}	7	2.24×10^{-6}	58.5	8.46×10^{-4}	-87.2	-57.2 *	1.90×10^{-10}
8	2.512	2.51×10^{-3}	2.51×10^{-8}	2.51×10^{-12}	6	2.00×10^{-6}	57.5	7.54×10^{-4}	-88.2	-58.2	1.51×10^{-10}
7	2.239	2.24×10^{-3}	2.24×10^{-8}	2.24×10^{-12}	5	1.78×10^{-6}	56.5	6.72×10^{-4}	-89.2	-59.2	1.20×10^{-10}
6	1.995	2.00×10^{-3}	2.00×10^{-8}	2.00×10^{-12}	4	1.59×10^{-6}	55.5	5.99×10^{-4}	-90.2	-60.2	9.50×10^{-11}
5	1.778	1.78×10^{-3}	1.78×10^{-8}	1.78×10^{-12}	3	1.42×10^{-6}	54.5	5.33×10^{-4}	-91.2	-61.2	7.55×10^{-11}
4	1.585	1.58×10^{-3}	1.58×10^{-8}	1.58×10^{-12}	2	1.26×10^{-6}	53.5	4.75×10^{-4}	-92.2	-62.2	6.00×10^{-11}
3	1.413	1.41×10^{-3}	1.41×10^{-8}	1.41×10^{-12}	1	1.12×10^{-6}	52.5	4.24×10^{-4}	-93.2	-63.2	4.76×10^{-11}
2	1.259	1.26×10^{-3}	1.26×10^{-8}	1.26×10^{-12}	0	1.00×10^{-6}	51.5	3.78×10^{-4}	-94.2	-64.2	3.78×10^{-11}
1	1.122	1.12×10^{-3}	1.12×10^{-8}	1.12×10^{-12}	-1	8.93×10^{-7}	50.5	3.37×10^{-4}	-95.2	-65.2	3.01×10^{-11}
0	1.000	10^{-3}	10^{-8}	10^{-12}	-2	7.96×10^{-7}	49.5	3.00×10^{-4}	-96.2	-66.2	2.39×10^{-11}
-20	.1	10^{-4}	10^{-9}	10^{-13}	-22	8×10^{-8}	29.5	3×10^{-5}	-116.2	-86.2	2.4×10^{-13}
-40	.01	10^{-5}	10^{-10}	10^{-14}	-42	8×10^{-9}	9.5	3×10^{-6}	-136.2	-106.2	2.4×10^{-15}
-60	.001	10^{-6}	10^{-11}	10^{-15}	-62	8×10^{-10}	-10.5	3×10^{-7}	-156.2	-126.2	2.4×10^{-17}

E.2 Magnetic and Electric Field Relations

Equation (E.10) shows the relation between the magnetic field strength and electric field strength:

$$H = E/Z \tag{E.10}$$

$$H_{A/m} = E_{V/m}/377 \ \Omega \text{ for far-field conditions} \tag{E.11}$$

or,

$$H_{dBA/m} = E_{dBV/m} - 51.5 \text{ dB}\Omega \tag{E.12}$$

$$H_{dB\mu A/m} \approx E_{dB\mu V/m} - 52 \text{ dB}\Omega \tag{E.13}$$

The magnetic flux density, B, is related to the magnetic field strength:

$$B = \mu H \text{ (tesla) for H in A/m} \tag{E.14}$$

where,

$$\mu = \text{permeability of air}$$

$$= 4\pi \times 10^{-7} \text{ henries per meter}$$

thus,

$$B_{dBT} = H_{dBA/m} - 118 \text{ dB} \tag{E.15}$$

$$B_{dB\mu T} = H_{dB\mu A/m} + 2 \text{ dB} \tag{E.16}$$

Often, the reference for B is given in units of gauss (G), instead of Tesla (T):

$$B_G = 10^4 \ B_T \tag{E.17}$$

In the EMC disciplines, the magnetic flux density is often expressed in units of dB picotesla (dBpT):

$$B_{dbpT} = B_{dBT} + 240 \text{ dB} \qquad (E.18)$$

Thus, combining Eqs. (E.15) and (E.18) yields:

$$B_{dBpT} = H_{dBA/m} + 122 \text{ dB} \qquad (E.19)$$

Occasionally, B is expressed in units of gamma (or nanotesla):

$$B_\Gamma = 10^{-9} \text{ T} \qquad (E.20)$$

$$B_{dB\Gamma} = B_{dBpT} - 60 \text{ dB} \qquad (E.21)$$

$$= H_{dBA/m} + 62 \text{ dB} \qquad (E.22)$$

Finally, combining Eqs. (E.10) and (E.14), yields:

$$B = \mu E/Z \qquad (E.23)$$

$$= E/C \quad \text{for far fields} \qquad (E.24)$$

or,

$$B_T = E_{dBV/m} - 169.5 \text{ dB} \qquad (E.25)$$

$$B_G \approx E_{dBV/m} - 90 \text{ dB}^* \qquad (E.26)$$

$$= E_{dB\mu V/m} - 210 \text{ dB} \qquad (E.27)$$

The above relations are used in computing the magnetic field terms appearing in Tables E.1 and E.2. They are also used in computing the values of B in the left-hand listings of Table E.2 for B ranging from 10^4 G (1 T) to 10^{-4} G.

---

*This relation may be used to relate Figs. 6.9 and 6.12 for CMC and Figs. 7.3 and 7.4 for DMC.

Appendix F
Impedance of a
Metal Ground Plane

Section 5.2 develops the impedance of a metal ground plane. However, for low frequencies, the approximation results in an error of 2 (3 dB) too high in resistance. Thus, the following development is precise and constitutes the basis for which Table 5.1 is developed.

$$Z_B = R_1 + j\omega L_i = (1 + j) R_s (\cosh \tau t / \sinh \tau t) \tag{F.1}$$

$$\tau = (1 + j) \sqrt{\pi f \mu \sigma} = \frac{1 + j}{\delta} \tag{F.2}$$

where,

$$j = \sqrt{-1}$$

$$\delta = 1/\sqrt{\pi f \mu \sigma}$$

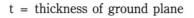

t = thickness of ground plane

L_i = internal inductance of metal plane

$$Z = (1 + j) \sqrt{\frac{\pi f \mu}{\sigma}} \left\{ \frac{\cosh [(1 + j) \sqrt{\pi f \mu \sigma}\ t]}{\sinh [(1 + j) \sqrt{\pi f \mu \sigma}\ t]} \right\} = R_i + j\omega L_i$$

$$\tag{F.3}$$

The terms for R_i and ωL_i need to be extracted. After some (fairly extensive) manipulation:

$$R_i = \left(\frac{1}{\sigma\delta}\right)\left(\frac{\sinh \dfrac{2t}{\delta} + \sin \dfrac{2t}{\delta}}{\cosh \dfrac{2t}{\delta} - \cos \dfrac{2t}{\delta}}\right) \qquad (F.4)$$

$$\omega L_i = \left(\frac{1}{\sigma\delta}\right)\left(\frac{\sinh \dfrac{2t}{\delta} - \sin \dfrac{2t}{\delta}}{\cosh \dfrac{2t}{\delta} - \cos \dfrac{2t}{\delta}}\right) \qquad (F.5)$$

Appendix G
Extension to Simple Emanation Prediction Models

The technique for predicting radiated emanations via the use of short wire and small loop models, described previously, is subject to restriction of geometry excitation and surroundings. These restrictions can be removed with a more complex computational procedure. The following extensions to the basic emanations prediction model of the previous section include:

1. Prediction of emanations for any relationship of length of radiating element to observation point
2. Prediction of emanations from source elements experiencing nonuniform current excitation
3. Prediction of emanations from elements in the presence of conducting surfaces.
4. Prediction of emanations from source elements having multiple exciting currents, such as multiconductor cables
5. Prediction of emanations from nonlinearly arrayed sources such as interconnecting cables

The extensions apply to all radiating loops and linear elements, and the developments described apply equally in both cases. The developments are typically presented in terms of either a loop or an element, and the practical examples are in terms of cables which are almost universally felt to be the most likely radiating element.

G.1 Discussion of Restrictions for Simple Models

As described in Section 10.2.1, assumptions are made that restrict the applicability of the simple model based on an exact solution to Maxwell's equations for emanations from either the short, straight wire or small loop. The comment is made that these restrictions can be accommodated, and methods for this accommodation are the topics of this section.

Two assumptions or restrictions were made. First, there is uniform excitation of the radiating element, and its dimensions are small compared to the distance from the observation point. Second, the observation point is located in free space, i.e., is not close to metallic surfaces.

The first assumption provides for a simplified development of the solution, because no exciting signal phase data is carried forward. The second assumption forces the far-field condition, whereby all components of the arriving wave are in phase at the observation point. Thus, both assumptions and the attendant restrictions involve carrying forward the exciting signal phase in the computations.

If the exciting signal phase information is carried forward, the attendant limitations of the simple model may be removed. For example, one of the predominant uses of the more sophisticated techniques is to predict emanations from a cable arrayed for test prior to the construction of either the equipment to be tested (or the interconnecting cable) for conditions that conflict with the restrictions of application of the simple approach.

The second assumption is simplifying in that the incidence of an electromagnetic wave upon metallic surfaces can produce reflected waves that can add destructively or constructively. Constructive reflected waves could provide a maximum of double the expected values without the presence of reflecting surfaces. Destructive reflected waves could cause interference which would result in values of at least one-hundredth of those values expected.

In practice it is difficult, if not impossible, to separate effects from one another. However, for the purpose of this discussion, and in the context of assumptions, effects can be segregated, described and modeled separately. Actually, most practical problems will require incorporation of most, if not all, of these computational procedures.

G.2 Prediction of Emanations for Conductors for *l*/d ≥ 0.1

The prediction of emanations values from either linear elements or loops in violation of the criteria (the observation point is larger than the length of the radiating element by a factor of ten, for example), can be accomplished by revising the prediction procedure. The need for revision is evident by the necessity for determining design requirements prior to the construction of such electronic equipment.

One of the most analyzed problems is the prediction of emanations arising from a cable arrayed for test in accordance with the requirements of MIL-STD-462, Method REO2. Figure G.1 shows a sketch of the physical arrangement required for testing. A 41" vertical rod antenna is placed 1 m from the equipment under test (EUT). The EUT is installed on a copper covered test bench, 10 cm from its front edge. Also, a 2 m cable (power or signal) is arrayed along the front of the bench for testing. A plan view of this is shown in Fig. G.2. Figure G.3 extracts the pertinent information computation, i.e., a length of cable 2 m long and 1 m from the observation point.

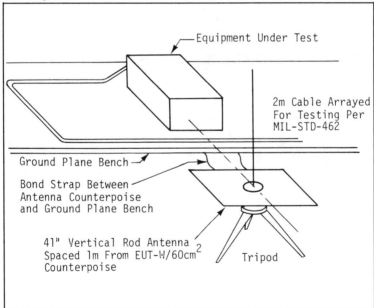

Figure G.1—Typical Test Setup for MIL-STD-462, Method REO2

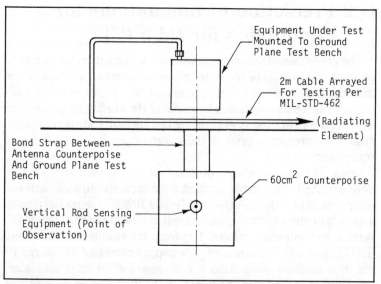

Figure G.2—Typical Test Setup for MIL-STD-462, Plan View

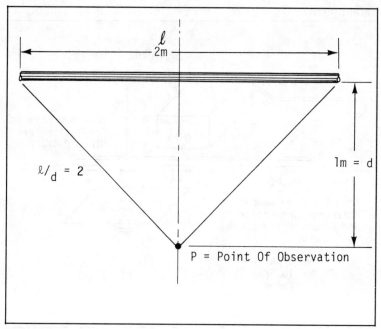

Figure G.3—Diagram Showing Critical Data for Input to Prediction Process (Neglecting Images)

This, of course, is not a complete situation. Figure G.4 shows a cross-sectional view of the test array where several images of the emanating element and cable exist due to the presence of a metallic wall. Before the effects of these various images (see Section G.3) can be evaluated, a discussion of the basic prediction procedure is essential.

Figure G.3 shows that the ratio of length of the cable, l, to the distance from the cable to the observation point, d, is:

$$l/d = 2/1 = 2$$

This is not in compliance with the requirement d $\gg$ l and be essentially limited at d = 10/l or d/l = 0.1, indicating that the exact solution to Maxwell's equations described in Section 10.2.1 is no longer valid. In fact, if one of the typical near-field/far-field interface criteria, r = $\lambda/2\pi$, is chosen and set to the distance of 1 m, this corresponds to a near-field/far-field interface of 47 MHz. This means that different sections of the total length of the cable have differing effects and therefore contribute different fractions to the total field observed at the observation point. Generally, the approach to be taken is to divide the emanating element into a number of segments. Then each segment can be evaluated individually in terms of its electromagnetic field contribution providing amplitude

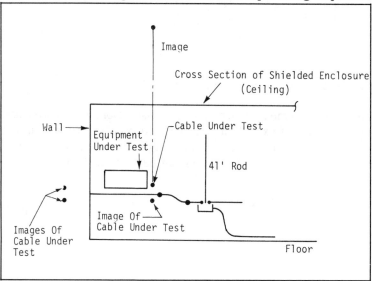

Figure G.4—Typical Test Setup for MIL-STD-462, Method REO2 Cross Section

and phase information at the observation point. After this is done, the total EM field, at the observation point, can be developed by performing a vector summation of the field from each segment.

An example of how this process can be accomplished is shown in Fig. G.5. Here, the radiating element has been arbitrarily broken into 10 segments. From the center of each segment, a radial length, r_i, to the observation point has been established, forming an angle, θ_i. The individual evaluation of each segment is necessary to determine the phase of the arriving E-field at the observation point. The evaluation of each segment is as shown in Fig. G.6, which shows segment 1 at distance r_i and at an angle θ_i from the

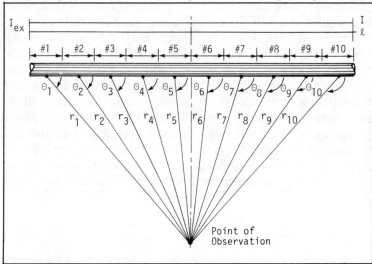

Figure G.5—Segmentation of Emanating Element

emanating element which, for this discussion, is experiencing uniform current excitation. If a perpendicular is struck from the element to the observation point, a right triangle is formed, and the length of r_i for all segments can be computed from:

$$r_i = \left\{ d^2 + \left[\frac{l}{2} - (2q - 1)\left(\frac{l/n}{2} \right) \right]^2 \right\}^{1/2} \tag{G.1}$$

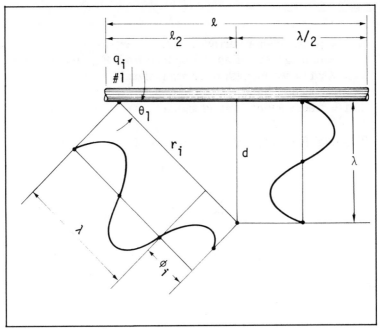

Figure G.6—Evaluation of the Single Segment

where,

r_i = distance from the center of the i segment
d = distance from the center of the emanating element
l = length of the emanating element
q = element number, from left to right
n = total number of elements composing l

Actually, r_i is the distance of evaluation for the field contribution for each segment. As also shown in Fig. G.6, the range of r_i, in terms of wavelengths from the emanating element, can be significant. The magnitude of E_i at r_i can be determined by interpolation from Table 10.1. The phase for the uniform excitation case can be obtained from:

$$\phi_i = \frac{r_i}{\lambda}\ (360) - \text{integer}\left(\frac{r_i}{\lambda}\right) \qquad \text{(G.2)}$$

G.7

where,

ϕ_i = phase of signal arriving at the observation point
r_i = propagation distance (obtained from Eq. 10.29)
λ = c/f = wavelength of exciting signal
c = speed of light $\approx 3 \times 10$ m/s
f = frequency of exciting signal

The total field intensity at the observation point is then:

$$\bar{E}_T \angle \phi_T = \bar{E} = \sum_{q=1}^{n} \vec{E}_i = \sum_{q=1}^{n} E_i \angle \phi_i$$

The number of segments, n, for division may be determined from Walter's expression for minimum distance for a valid result for a source of length, l, divided into n segments:

$$d = \frac{2l^2}{\lambda n^2} \tag{G.3}$$

where all variables are as previously designated. Rearranging the terms gives:

$$n = \sqrt{\frac{2l^2}{\lambda d}} \tag{G.4}$$

The value of n varies with l/d and frequency. Arbitrarily choosing l/d = 2 (the cable setup for Method RE02 testing), the number of segments for computation versus frequency of excitation is shown in Fig. G.7.

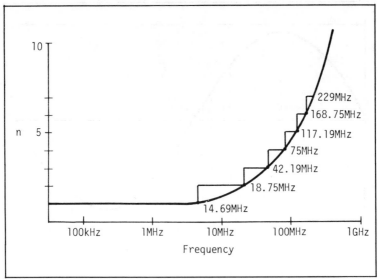

Figure G.7—Number of Required Segments versus Frequency for l/d = 2

G.2.1 Prediction of Emanations from Conductors Experiencing Non-uniform Excitation

From a pragmatic point of view, the greatest percentage of emissions will arise from conductors which are experiencing non-uniform excitation as shown in Fig. G.8. As shown in this figure, if the length of the element is short i.e., $l ≤ \lambda/10$ with respect to the wavelength, a uniform excitation may be assumed. As the radiating element becomes a more and more significant fraction of a wavelength, then the assumption of uniform excitation will not hold. Where, for example, $l = \lambda/2$, then a full change in value can be from +I at l = 0 to −I at $l = \lambda/2$.

A simple approximation is possible for incorporating the effects of non-uniform excitation, which can also be employed for l/d ratios

G.9

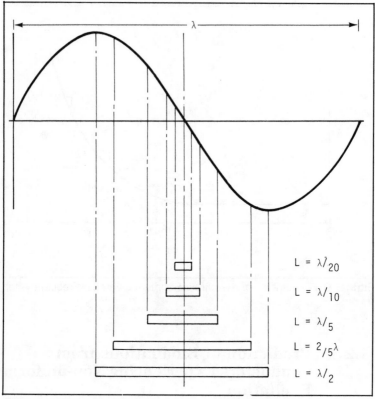

Figure G.8—Example of Non-uniform Excitation as a Function of Emanating Element Length

greater than 0.1 and can be extended to any excitation with any phase distribution.

An example of non-uniform amplitude and phase excitation is shown in Fig. G.9. The linearly varying amplitude and phase relationships of the exciting current are shown in the top plots of the figure. The element to be evaluated is shown below divided into four segments, the necessary approximations of current amplitude (assumed over the given segment) and phase (also assumed linear over the same segment division). Thus, segment 1 is excited by I_1 at phase ψ_1, segment 2 is excited by I_2 at ψ_2, etc. For this case, each segment is evaluated individually for its drive current,

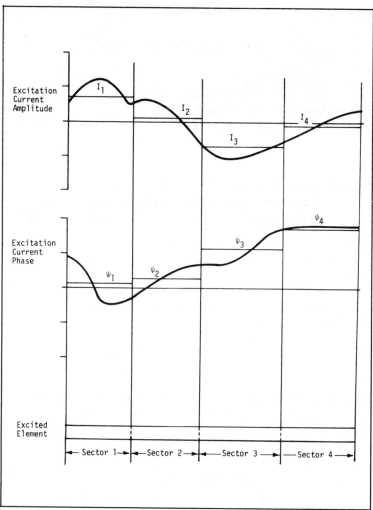

Figure G.9—Non-uniform Current and Phase Excitation of Emanating Element

amplitude and phase for a given observation point and, as previously shown, the contribution of all elements are vectorially summed at the observation point. The phase of the exciting source is carried forward. Thus:

$$\vec{E} = |\vec{E}| < \alpha = \sum_{q=1}^{n} E_i (\phi_i + \psi_i) \qquad (G.5)$$

where,

$\vec{E}$ = electric field vector at the observation point
$|\vec{E}|$ = magnitude of E
α = total phase angle
E_i = Table 10.1 value for segment due to I_i
ϕ_i = phase shift due to distance r_i
ψ_i = phase of I_i in segment I

G.2.2 Prediction of Emanations from Conductors with Both Uniform and Non-uniform Excitation and $l/d \geqslant 0.1$

As an example of computation, consider an emanating element of length 4 m and a observation point 2 m from and centered on the emanating element. The element is excited at 75.0 MHz by $I \sin(\omega t + \phi)$, where ϕ is $\pi/2$ for the first $\lambda/2$ and $-\pi/2$ for the second $\lambda/2$. This excitation is shown in Fig. G.10. Assume $I_{max} = 10$ mA. The number of segments for subdivision is given by:

$$n = \left(\frac{2l^2}{\lambda d} \right)^{1/2} = \left(\frac{2(4)^2}{4.2} \right) = 4 \qquad (G.6)$$

Alternately, the number of segments for subdivision can be found by entering Fig. G.7 at 75 MHz and again finding n = 4. The distances from the center of each segment to the observation point is given by:

$$r_i = \left\{ d^2 + \left[l/2 - (2q - 1) \left(\frac{l/n}{2} \right) \right]^2 \right\}^{1/2} \qquad (G.7)$$

$$r_1 = \left\{ (2)^2 + \left[4/2 - \left(2(1) - 1 \right) \left(\frac{4/4}{2} \right) \right]^2 \right\}^{1/2} = 2.5 \qquad (G.8)$$

$$r_2 = \left\{ (2)^2 + \left[4/2 - \left(2(2) - 1 \right) \left(\frac{4/4}{2} \right) \right]^2 \right\}^{1/2} = 2.06 \qquad (G.9)$$

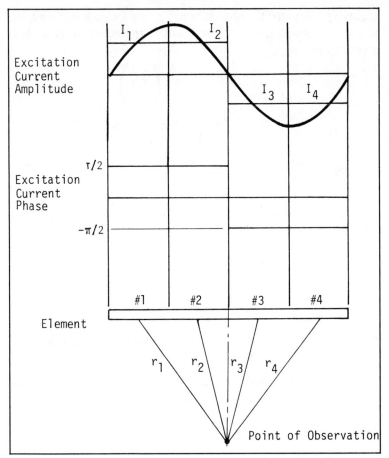

Figure G.10—Emanating Element with Non-uniform Excitation and
$l/d = 2$

$$r_3 = \left\{ (2)^2 + \left[4/2 - \left(2(3) - 1 \right) \left(\frac{4/4}{2} \right) \right]^2 \right\}^{1/2} = 2.06$$

$$(G.10)$$

$$r_4 = \left\{ (2)^2 + \left[4/2 - \left(2(4) - 1 \right) \left(\frac{4/4}{2} \right) \right]^2 \right\}^{1/2} = 2.5$$

$$(G.11)$$

Having computed the observation distance for each segment, the phase retardation from each segment to the observation point is given by:

$$\phi_i = \frac{r_i}{\lambda} \, (360°) - \text{int.} \left(r_i/\lambda \right) \tag{G.12}$$

$$\phi_1 = \phi_4 = \frac{2.5}{4} \, (360°) - \text{int.} \left(2.5/4 \right) = 0.63 \, (360°) = 226.8°$$

$$\phi_2 = \phi_3 = \frac{2.06}{4} \, (360°) - \text{int.} \left(2.5/4 \right) = 0.52 \, (360°) = 185.4°$$

From Table 10.1, for a frequency of excitation of 75 MHz, E can be found by interpolation:

E_1 @ 2.5 m = 108 dBμV/m = 251 mV/m (for 1 A and 1 cm = 251 × 100 cm × 0.01, for our case)

E_2 @ 2.06 m = 112 dBμV/m = 398 mV/m (for 1 A and 1 cm = 398 × 100 × 0.01, for our case)

E_3 @ 2.06 m = 112 dBμV/m = 398 mV/m (for 1 A and 1 cm = 398 × 100 × 0.01, for our case)

E_4 @ 2.5 m = 108 dBμV/m = 251 mV/m (for 1 A and 1 cm = 251 × 100 cm × 0.01, for our case)

All that remains is to vector sum the four components:

$$\bar{E} = E_1 \,\underline{/\psi_1 + \phi_1} \; + E_2 \,\underline{/\psi_2 + \phi_2} \; + E_3 \,\underline{/\psi_3 + \phi_3} \; + E_4 \,\underline{/\psi_4 + \phi_4}$$

$$= 251 \text{ mV/m} \,\underline{/180° + 226°} \; + 398° \,\underline{/180° + 185°} \; + 398$$

$$\underline{/-180 + 185°} \; + 251 \,\underline{/-180° + 226°}$$

$$= 251 \text{ mV/m} \,\underline{/46°} \; + 398 \,\underline{/5°} \; + 398 \,\underline{/5°} \; + 251 \,\underline{/46°}$$

$$= 1140 + j430 = 1.218 \text{ v/m} \,\underline{/20°} \; = 121 \text{ dBμV/m} \,\underline{/20°}$$

G.3 Prediction of Emanations from Sources in the Near Vicinity of a Metallic Surface

As discussed in Section G.2 and shown in Fig. G.4, one of the more typical applications of predictive procedures (such as those described in this chapter) is in the prediction of emanations from a cable arrayed from Method REO2 testing for design control applications. This prediction can be accomplished by constructing an image, or images, an equal distance behind the metallic surface and evaluating the total field from both of these sources. This is made much more complex since, for each image considered, an identical amount of computation must be accomplished. Then the emanating fields from the original source and each image must be vectorially summed, often in three dimensions, with the set of images formed by the metallic surface. A simple, coplanar example is shown in Fig. G.11.

Of more interest is the situation previously discussed, shown in Fig. G.4, of the MIL-STD-462 Method REO2 arrangement in a shielded enclosure. For this condition, no less than four images are shown, each of which must be evaluated separately from its location to the observation point, and a vector sum is formed from the results of the original emanating element and the four images.

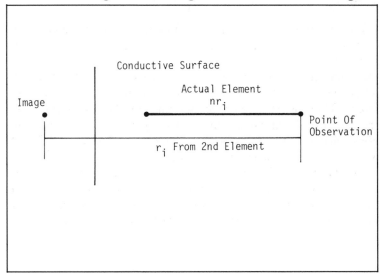

Figure G.11—Coplanar Example

G.4 Radiation Pattern Effects from Emanating Elements

In all previous discussions, the observation point has been symmetrical with respect to the two ends of the emanating source. If the system under evaluation is considered under artificially imposed conditions, symmetry of the evaluating model may be forced. In other cases, this may not be possible. In general, a pattern factor may need to be considered, particularly when the element excitation is not uniform, and the maxima of the emanations may not be perpendicular to the emanating element. For example, a complete solution for a short dipole is:

$$E_\theta = \frac{j60\,[I_o]}{r} \left[\frac{\cos\,(\beta L\,\cos\,\theta)/2 - \cos\,(\beta L/2)}{\sin\,\theta} \right] \quad (G.13)$$

$$H_\phi = \frac{j[I_o]}{2\pi r} \left[\frac{\cos\,(\beta L\,\cos\,\theta)/2 - \cos\,(\beta L/2)}{\sin\,\theta} \right] \quad (G.14)$$

where,

$$[I_o] = I_o\,e^{i\omega}\,(t \times r/c)$$

The shape of the far field is given by the factor in the brackets. The factors preceding the brackets in G.13 and G.14 give the instantaneous magnitude of the fields as functions of the antenna current and the distance, r. To obtain the rms value of the field, we let $[I_o]$ equal the rms current at the location of the current maximum. There is no factor involving phase in G.13 or G.14, since the center of the antenna is taken as the phase center. Hence, any phase change of the fields as a function of ϴ will be a jump of 180° when the pattern factor changes sign.

As examples of the far-field patterns of linear, center-fed antennas, three antennas of different lengths will be considered. Since the amplitude factor is independent of the length, only the relative field patterns as given by the pattern factor will be compared.

Case 1: 1/2 Wavelength Antenna

When L = $\lambda/2$, the pattern factor becomes:

$$E = \frac{\cos\left[(\pi/2)\cos\theta\right]}{\sin\theta} \qquad \text{(G.15)}$$

This pattern is shown in Fig. G.12, part a. It is only slightly more directional than the pattern of an infinitesimal or short dipole, which is given by sin ⊖. The beamwidth between half-power points of the 1/2 wavelength antenna is 78°, as compared to 98° for the short dipole.

Case 2: Full-Wave Antenna

When L = λ, the pattern factor becomes:

$$E = \frac{\cos(\pi\cos\theta) + 1}{\sin\theta} \qquad \text{(G.16)}$$

This pattern is shown in Fig. G.12, part b.

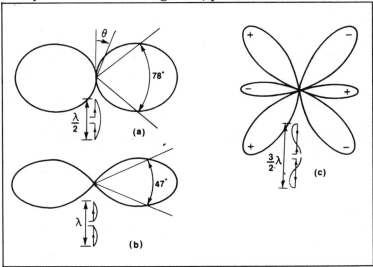

Figure G.12—Far-Field Patterns of 1/2 Wavelength, Full Wavelength and 3/2 Wavelength Antennas. The antennas are center-fed, and the current distribution is assumed to be sinusoidal.

G.17

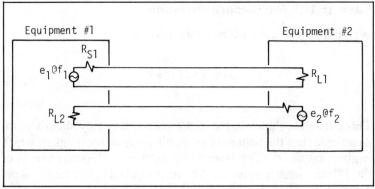

Figure G.13—Two Equipments Exchanging Signals through a Single Cable

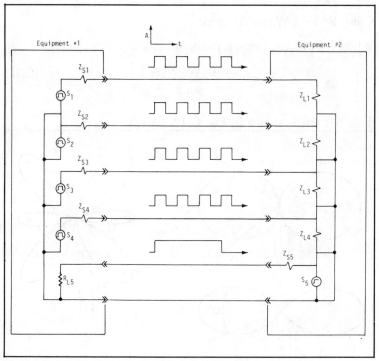

Figure G.14—Multiconductor Digital Cable

Case 3: 3/2 Wavelength Antenna

When L = 3λ/2, the pattern factor is:

$$E = \frac{\cos\,[(3\pi/2)\,\cos\,\theta]}{\sin\,\theta} \tag{G.17}$$

The pattern for this case is presented in Fig. G.12, part c. With the mid point of the antenna as phase center, the phase shifts 180° at each null, with the relative phase of the lobes being indicated by the + and – signs.

In all three cases (a, b and c), the space pattern is a figure of revolution of the pattern shown around the axis of the antenna. Thus, this may be needed to carry forward the more accurate result.

G.5 Other Applications of Emanation Prediction Models

Moving into the more pragmatic areas, one can consider the application of these several techniques to more realistic situations, i.e., cable emanations for cables containing multiple conductors and cables arrayed for test or in an operational environment in an irregular manner.

G.5.1 Extension of Cable Emanation Predictions to Multiconductor Cables

The developments of the preceding sections, presenting methodology for prediction of cable emanations levels, have been based on the simplest interconnecting cable model: two parallel wires; a signal and return. The model was selected because of its extreme simplicity and because of the ease in developing the conceptual approach. Unfortunately, this model has very little meaning in terms of real cables whose complexity far exceeds the simple model. This section presents an approach for extending the basic methodology developed from the previous sections to multiconductor cables.

The propagation phenomenon for signals exciting a single conductor has been well described. If the cable is composed of multiple conductors, and if these multiple conductors are in close proximity (i.e., if d + d' ≈ d, i.e. d' << d, where d is the distance to the observation point), then d' is the total diameter of the multiconductor cable. Then the prediction of emanations may be reduced to a single step for propagation analysis, and the multiconductor cable prediction becomes a problem in determining appropriate excitation currents as an input to the emanation prediction process.

Figure G.13 shows two equipments interconnected through a single cable. As shown, equipment one is transmitting signal e_1 at frequency f_1 to Equipment 2. In the same manner, Equipment 2 is transmitting signal e_2 at frequency f_2 to Equipment 1. It is obvious that for this condition, each signal can be evaluated by the procedures of Section 10.2 or 10.3, and the electromagnetic field from each signal can be evaluated by the procedures of Section 10.2 or 10.3, and the electromagnetic field from each signal can be "summed" in the frequency domain to give what might be termed a **composite frequency specrum**. Conversely, the summing can be performed prior to prediction of emanating fields, forming a **composite excitation spectrum**, which can then be subjected to the emanation prediction process. This second approach is taken as the simplest process for more complex interconnecting cables.

A digital interconnection cable is shown in Fig. G.14. It has four parallel data channels from Equipment 1 which transfer data when an enable signal is set in Equipment 2. An amplitude versus time representation of the four data channels and the enabling signal is shown above each individual conductor in the cable. The cable, as configured, shows five signal lines with one ground—a typical construction for logic interconnect cables. We desire to determine a composite spectrum for the excitations to the cable which, in turn, can be used to compute the radiated emission spectrum.

Each individual spectrum of logic current drive can be computed as described in Section 10.2.4. However, a simplification can be made. Remember, for a loop, the actual emanations are a function of $I \times l$. For the cable shown, l is constant for all six conductors, and if a standard logic family is assumed, all of the currents will be equal and in phase. Thus, we can replace the current diode in each individual wire by an equivalent conductor with four times the current. This is shown quantitatively in Fig. G.15. This concept can be extended to any combination of exciting signals.

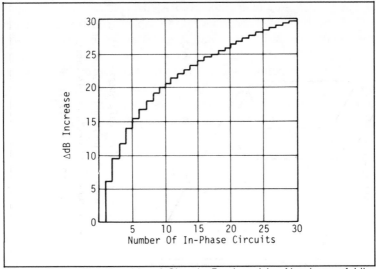

Figure G.15—Relationship of Signals Produced by Numbers of Like In-Phase Circuits

G.5.2 Prediction of Emanations from Irregularly Arrayed Cables

Development of expected values of emanations from irregularly arrayed cables is a complex operation, but it can be accomplished by subdividing an individual cable into sectors, each of which is considered independently. As an illustration of this approach, Fig. G.16 shows a home entertainment system as a seen from the rear. Four interconnecting cables are employed:

1. Receiver to left speaker
2. Receiver to right speaker
3. Receiver to turntable
4. Receiver to FM antenna

Let us determine the emanations from Cable 1, the receiver to the left speaker. The intentional signal of interest will be 50 W maximum driven into an 8 Ω speaker.

$$I = \sqrt{\frac{P}{R}} = \sqrt{\frac{50}{8}} = 2.50 \text{ A} \qquad (G.18)$$

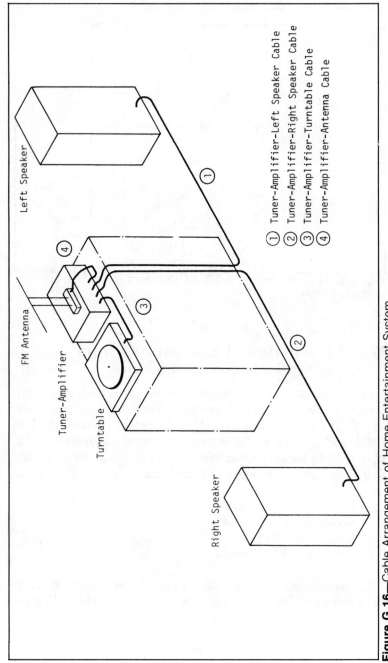

1. Tuner–Amplifier–Left Speaker Cable
2. Tuner–Amplifier–Right Speaker Cable
3. Tuner–Amplifier–Turntable Cable
4. Tuner–Amplifier–Antenna Cable

Left Speaker

FM Antenna

Tuner–Amplifier

Turntable

Right Speaker

Figure G.16—Cable Arrangement of Home Entertainment System

For purposes of computation, we will assume that the equivalent peak power may be approximated by a 20 kHz sine wave, where 20 kHz is the maximum frequency capability of the output amplifier.

To make this problem more interesting, we will further assume that the FM tuner local oscillator +27 dBm into 50 Ω (108 to 118 MHz) and its second harmonic at +20 dBm (216 to 236 MHz) are inadequately suppressed and also appear on the receiver-to-left-speaker interconnecting cable. The excitation spectrum is shown in Fig. G.17. We will assume a vertical height of 1 m for the receiver-to-floor portion of the cable, 3 m length for the floor run from below the tuner amplifier and 1/10 m from the floor up to the speaker input terminals. The two short sections immediately adjacent to the speaker and tuner amplifier will be ignored. This array of cable is shown in isometric view in Fig. G.18, and as a front and top view.

Let us determine the emanations at an arbitrarily chosen point P, as shown centered on the horizontal portion of the cable 1.5 m from the cable and 1 m high from the floor.

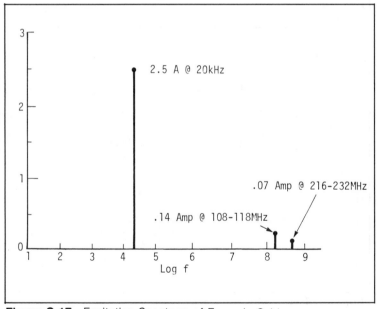

Figure G.17—Excitation Spectrum of Example Cable

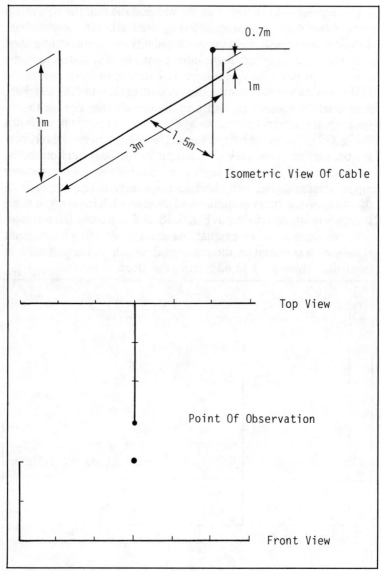

0.7m

1m

1m

3m   1.5m

Isometric View Of Cable

Top View

Point Of Observation

Front View

Figure G.18—Isometric View of Cable Array

The approach to be taken is to consider each of the three sections of the cable independently and determine the field value at the point of excitation from each segment on an amplitude versus frequency basis. We then vector sum the amplitude versus frequency spectrum from each segment to determine the total amplitude versus frequency spectrum at the observation point. Further, all computations need to be carried forward in three dimensions to assure validity.

Certain preliminary evaluations must be made on each section of the cable to determine which of the several prediction models discussed should be employed for developing the emanating field values as a function of frequency. These checks have to do with the assumptions and restrictions applied to each model. Once the appropriate emanations models are established, the prediction process can proceed in a straightforward manner.

Assume a vertical height of 1 m for the tuner/amplifier to floor portion of the cable, 3 m length for the floor run from below the tuner amplifier and 1/10 m from the floor up to the speaker input terminals. The two short sections immediately adjacent to the speaker and tuner amplifier will be ignored. This array of cable is shown in isometric view in Fig. G.18.

Determinations of emanations at an arbitrarily chosen point P, as shown centered on the horizontal portion of the cable 1.5 m from the cable and 1 m high from the floor, are accomplished by successive application of the radiated emissions prediction model for each of the three cable segments, for each exciting frequency, to determine the net E-field at the observation point. When the field contribution for each signal at each frequency is found, they are again vectorially summed to provide the value of E_T as a function of frequency.

Appendix H

Field Reinforcement in the Vicinity of a Finite Metallic Structure

The calculations and graphic aids used so far have generally assumed that the cables are located at some height above a quasi-infinite ground plane and that the incident E-fields and H-fields are uniform around the cable. Some actual situations may impose different conditions.

One frequently encountered circumstance is that of long, metallic objects such as aircraft, missiles, helicopters, ships, metal towers or masts, etc. When illuminated by a uniform field, if the length of the structure corresponds to $\lambda/2$, the object behaves as a resonant dipole with a maximum current in the middle and opposite voltage maxima on the ends. Due to the rather low losses in the metallic dipole, these voltages and currents in turn create a strong E-field reradiation around the tips, and a strong H-field reradiation around the middle (see Fig. E.1).

Although this passive dipole cannot "create energy," the near-field E or H terms close to the reradiating structure can be locally higher than the original incident field. In such a case, a victim cable or circuit installed in those areas may be exposed to a locally stronger field by the reradiation of its supporting ground, which is no longer than an infinite plane. For instance, Fig. E.2 shows the local values in multiples of $E_{incident}$ for a thin structure with a length-to-width ratio of 8:10.

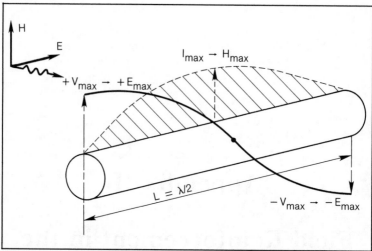

Figure H.1—E-Field and H-Field Reradiated by an Undamped Dipole at Resonance

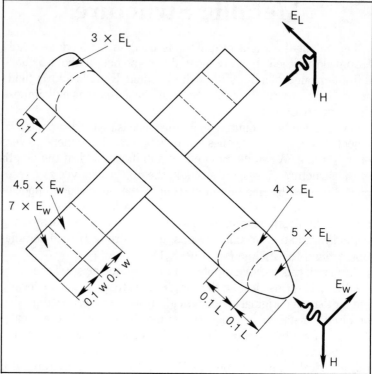

Figure H.2—Average Values of the Field Reinforcement at the Tips of a Thin Structure (Form Factor $\approx$ 10) with Length, L, and Wing Span, W

Illustrative Example H.1

In a missile, a 1 m cable harness is located in the nose. The missile has a metallic main beam with 6 m length which provides shielding for the cable inside. The rest of the body is nonconductive panels. The $\lambda/2$ resonance of a thin, 6 m dipole is:

$$f_o = 150 \text{ MHz}/l = 150/6 = 25 \text{ MHz}$$

Due to the fatness (or **form factor**) of the beam, its actual resonance will be at 0.8 to 0.9 f_o, or 20 to 22 MHz. Therefore, if the missile is exposed to an EMI field at a frequency in the 20 to 25 MHz range, or *any odd multiple*, with a polarization parallel to the beam, the first L/10 portion of the cable (0.6 m) in the nose will be immersed in an average field equal to five times the incident field. The remaining 0.4 m portion will be in a four times stronger field. Therefore, the whole harness may be considered as exposed to an average field equal to 4.6 times the initial incident field. This value should become the new ambient for calculating the various field-to-cable couplings (FCM, DMC, etc.).

The problem would be similar if the structure were excited by a broadband field such as an EMP, provided that the pulse rise time corresponds to a spectrum second corner frequency high enough to excite the structure's first resonance.

Other Books Published by ICT

1. Carstensen, Russell V., *EMI Control in Boats and Ships*, 1979.
2. Denny, Hugh W., *Grounding for Control of EMI*, 1983.
3. Duff, Dr. William G., *A Handbook on Mobile Communications*, 1980.
4. Duff, Dr. William G. and White, Donald R.J., Volume 5, *Electromagnetic Interference Prediction & Analysis Techniques*, 1972.
5. Feher, Dr. Kamilo, *Digital Modulation Techniques in an Interference Environment*, 1977.
6. Gabrielson, Bruce C., *The Aerospace Engineer's Handbook of Lightning Protection*, 1987.
7. Gard, Michael F., *Electromagnetic Interference Control in Medical Electronics*, 1979.
8. Georgopoulos, Dr. Chris J., *Fiber Optics and Optical Isolators*, 1982.
9. Georgopoulos, Dr. Chris J., *Interference Control in Cable and Device Interfaces*, 1987.
10. Ghose, Rabindra N., *EMP Environment and System Hardness Design*, 1983.
11. Hart, William C. and Malone, Edgar W., *Lightning and Lightning Protection*, 1979.
12. Herman, John R., *Electromagnetic Ambients and Man-Made Noise*, 1979.
13. Hill, James S. and White, Donald R.J., Volume 6, *Electromagnetic Interference Specifications, Standards & Regulations*, 1975.
14. Jansky, Donald M., *Spectrum Management Techniques*, 1977.
15. Mardiguian, Michel, *Interference Control in Computers and Microprocessor-Based Equipment*, 1984.
16. Mardiguian, Michel, *Electrostatic Discharge—Understand, Simulate and Fix ESD Problems*, 1985.
17. Mardiguian, Michel, *How to Control Electrical Noise*, 1983.
18. Smith, Albert A., *Coupling of External Electromagnetic Fields to Transmission Lines*, 1986.
19. White, Donald R.J., *A Handbook on Electromagnetic Shielding Materials and Performance*, 1980.
20. White, Donald R.J., *Electrical Filters—Synthesis, Design & Applications*, 1980.
21. White, Donald R.J., *EMI Control in the Design of Printed Circuit Boards and Backplanes*, 1982. (Also available in French.)
22. White, Donald R.J. and Mardiguian, Michel, *EMI Control Methodology & Procedures*, 1985.
23. White, Donald R.J., Volume 1, *Electrical Noise and EMI Specifications*, 1971.
24. White, Donald R.J., Volume 2, *Electromagnetic Interference Test Methods and Procedures*, 1980.
25. White, Donald, R.J., Volume 3, *Electromagnetic Interference Control Methods & Techniques*, 1973.
26. White, Donald R.J., Volume 4, *Electromagnetic Interference Test Instrumentation Systems*, 1980.
27. Duff, William G., and White, Donald R.J., Volume 5, *Prediction and Analysis Techniques*, 1970.
28. White, Donald R.J., Volume 6, *EMI Specifications, Standards and Regulations*, 1973.
29. White, Donald R.J., *Shielding Design Methodology and Procedures*, 1986.
30. *EMC Technology 1982 Anthology*
31. *EMC EXPO Records 1986, 1987, 1988*

All of the books listed above are available for purchase from Interference Control Technologies, Inc., Don White Consultants, Subsidiary, State Route 625, P.O. Box D, Gainesville, Virginia 22065 USA. Telephone: (703) 347-0030; Telex: 89-9165 DWCI GAIV.

Index

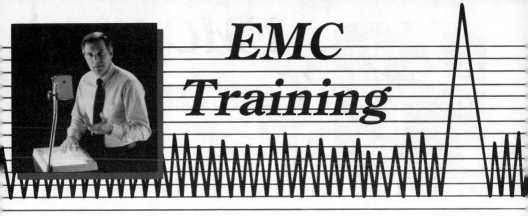

EMC Training

Interference Control Technologies, Inc. (ICT) is the premier EMI/EMC and TEMPEST training organization in the world. Founded in 1970 as Don White Consultants, Inc., ICT has educated over 45,000 degreed electronic engineers, technicians, scientists and managers from over 49 countries, representing over 1300 organizations.

All ICT seminars are designed to provide the latest pragmatic insight and methodology to *real-world* interference control and noise suppression issues. Our goal is to equip each student not only with the appropriate theory but with field-tested, proven solutions.

ICT achieves this objective in two ways. First, by providing an instructor who is both a seasoned communicator and a practicing expert in his field. Collectively our staff brings over 600 years of international work experience from diverse industrial, commercial, military and regulatory backgrounds.

Secondly, ICT updates its extensive student handout materials regularly to ensure clarity and relevancy. All students receive a notebook with a copy of every transparency presented, as well as, hardbound handbooks, computer software, an *EMC Technology* magazine subscription and other related materials.

Seminars can be taught in one of seven different languages and are regularly scheduled throughout the Unites States, Europe, the Middle and Far East, South America and Austrailia.

ICT also offers any one of its more than 25 standard seminars as is, or we can tailor any class to meet the clients specific need. These seminars can then be taught at the client's facility and at a time most conducive to the client's schedule.

Course Titles Inclide:

Grounding & Shielding
Practical EMI Fixes
EMC Design & Measurement
Intro to EMI/RFI/EMC
TEMPEST: Design & Measurement
TEMPEST: Facilities Design
Plus 15 other EMI control courses!

for more information ...

**Interference Control
Technologies
PO Box D
Gainesville, Va 22065
703-347-0030**

ICT−

EMC Testing

THE MEASURE OF SUCCESS

Electro Service Corporation has assembled a staff of the *Right People*. People with the *need-to-know* to get your product to the marketplace quickly.

Years of work and millions of dollars in development money can go to waste when regulatory delays occur, often because of a simple problem: not knowing the correct regulations and procedures to obtain approvals in the shortest time. ESC can prevent those regulatory delays because we understand the system, inside and out, and guide you through the maze to compliance acceptance.

FULL SERVICE CAPABILITY

ESC will ensure your product gets the careful consideration it deserves. We specilaize in obtaining product approvals from these regulatory agencies:

Canadian Standards Association
Electrical Testing Labs
Canadian Dept. of Communicatons
Dept. of Health & Human Services
FederalCommunictions Commission
TUV Rheinland USA
Underwriters Laboratories
Verband Deutscher Elektrotechniker

MEETING YOUR TESTING NEEDS

ESC uses sophisticated testing equipment and procedures, RF screen rooms, test sites, and ground planes to provde RFI/EMI test capabilities from 10 kHz to 60 GHz. ESC can meet your testing needs if you manufacture or market any of the following similar devices:

* Business/Industrial Equipment
* Computers/Computer Peripherials
* Home Appliances
* Industrial Radio Systems
* Multi-Band Receivers
* Office Equipment
* Public Broadcast Receivers
* Radio-Controlled Devices
* Satellite Receivers
* Security Systems
* Telephones/ Auto Dialers
* Transformers
* Transmitters/ Receivers
* Video Games

for more information ...

**Electro Service
Corporation
2 Davis Drive
Belmont, CA 94002
415-592-5111**

-ICT-

EMC Books

HANDBOOKS

ICT provides over 30 technical handbooks on EMI/EMC and related disciplines. Written by practicing experts in their field each book is designed to go beyond the tutorial by providing the reader with practical applications, illustrative examples as well as tested and proven methodologies. Each book is packed with illustrations, graphs, tables and math models, and is writen in a clear, consise format to assure the reader understanding and immediate use of the material.

GENERAL TITLES AND APPLICATIONS

Electromagnetic Shielding
Electrical Filters
ESD - Understand, Simulate and Fix
EMC Pocket Primer
EMP Environment and System
  Hardness Design
EXPO Symposium Records
How to Contol Electrical Noise
Grounding for the Control of EMI
Lightning and Lightning Protection

SPECIFIC TITLES AND APPLICATIONS

Aerospace Engineers Handbook of Lightning Protection, Coupling of External Electromagnetic Fields to Transmition Lines, EMI Control in Computers and Microprocessor-Based Equipment, EMI Control in the Design of PCBs and Backplanes, Fiber Optics and Optical Isolators.

THE MUST EMI/EMC LIBRARY

(1) EMI Control Methodology and Procedures *and* (2) Shielding Design Methodology and Procedures.

THE EMC SOURCE
(A 12-Volume EMI/EMC Series)

Vol 1 Fundamentals of EMC
Vol 2 Grounding and Bonding
Vol 3 Electromagnetic Shielding
Vol 4 Filters & Power Conditioning
Vol 5 EMC in Components & Devices
Vol 6 EMI Test Methods/Procedures
Vol 7 EMC in Telecommunications
Vol 8 EMI Control Methodology
Vol 9 USA Commercial Standards
Vol 10 Int'l Commercial Standards
Vol 11 USA MIL-STDs Part 1
Vol 12 USA MIL-STDs Part 2

ICT

EMC Magazine

EMC TECHNOLOGY MAGAZINE

EMC Technology magazine meets the need for up-to-date information and addresses critical noise suppression issues facing the design engineer and his management. Each issue is developed around a central theme covering either new design technology or applications, product and component development, or test and measurement procedures, techniques and equipment.

Each article is written with a pragmatic slant not only to define the problem but also eliminate it. The *must* objective is that each article not only inform but instruct.

Each issue contains a number of supporting *Departments* giving the reader the latest news on *Meetings and Conferences, People, Places and Events, Products and Service, and Standards and Regulations.*

Many issues also include *Hands-on Reports* and product evaluations. Rounding out each issue are thought provoking editorials and *Letters to the Editor*, Special Products, brochure and catalog listings, and an advertising matrix and index created for easy cross referencing of product and service advertisements.

In addition to the six bi-montly issues

EMC Technology also provides two special issues each year. Its annual *Buyers Guide and Sales Directory* provides the reader with alphabetical listings of vendors complete with product description, sales contact, locations and telephone numbers, and a listing of vendors by Product or Service provided. The second special issue is set aside for unique topics requiring in-depth coverage and emphasis.

EMC EXPO

EMC EXPO is an annual international symposium designed solely for the issues of EMI/EMC, Electrical Noise suppression and other relative disciplines. Over 50 papers are presented in 20 technical workshops.

Exhibitors provide hands-on demonstrations as well as free information and literature.

---

for more information ...

**Interference Control
Technologies
PO Box D
Gainesville, Va 22065
703-347-0030**

—ICT—

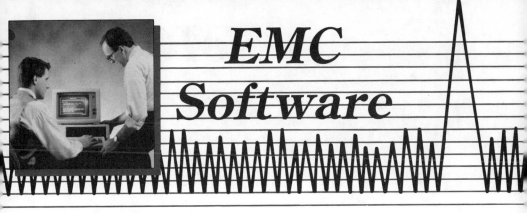

EMC Software

CAE SOFTWARE

These programs will predict and eliminate interference problems during product conceptualization rather than at the more costly prototype or retofit stages. Tedious calculations now take only minutes displaying with accuracy effects of design criteria supplied by the user.

PROGRAM 5220:
TWO BOX RADIATED EMI SUSCEPTABILITY CONTROL

This program will enable the user to detect and measure radiation susceptability levels from interconnected equipment, ground loops and radiation to/from cables, and common and differential mode sources.

The user is provided with comparative data predicting interference levels with both analog and logic victum sensitivities. Prompters will provide various fix options to help achieve maximim cost savings.

PROGRAM 5300:
BOX RADIATED EMISSION AND CONTROL

This program will enable you to detect and measure applicable radiated emission levels from, printed curcuits, backplanes, chips, and internal cabling.

A composite of radiation levels emanating from the input design are compared against specification limits. Prompters will provide various fix options to help achieve the most economical solution.

PROGRAM 5500:
EMC DESIGN OF BOXES, CASES, CABINETS AND ENCLOSURES

This program enables the user to design shielding housings against specified or synthesized shielding requirements. Selection criteria include type of material used (metals or composites), surface impedance and thickness. Aperature designs are defined and tested, with failures indicated and fix options provided.

All design criteria are combined and overall shielding performance is determined.

ICT-